OXFORD EARLY CHRISTIAN TEXTS

General Editor
HENRY CHADWICK

———

CYRIL OF ALEXANDRIA
SELECT LETTERS

CYRIL OF ALEXANDRIA

SELECT LETTERS

EDITED AND TRANSLATED BY
LIONEL R. WICKHAM

OXFORD
AT THE CLARENDON PRESS
1983

Oxford University Press, Walton Street, Oxford OX2 6DP
London Glasgow New York Toronto
Delhi Bombay Calcutta Madras Karachi
Kuala Lumpur Singapore Hong Kong Tokyo
Nairobi Dar es Salaam Cape Town
Melbourne Auckland

and associates in
Beirut Berlin Ibadan Mexico City Nicosia

Oxford is a trade mark of Oxford University Press

Published in the United States by
Oxford University Press, New York

British Library Cataloguing in Publication Data
Cyril, of Alexandria
 Select letters.—(*Oxford early Christian texts*)
 1. Jesus Christ
 I. Title   *II. Wickham, Lionel R.*
 232   *BT200*
 ISBN 0–19–826810–6

Library of Congress Cataloging in Publication Data
Cyril, Saint, Bishop of Alexandria, ca. 370–444.
 Cyril of Alexandria, select letters.
 (Oxford early Christian Texts)
 Bibliography: p.
 Includes index.
 1. Cyril, Saint, Bishop of Alexandria, ca.
 370–444. 2. Theology—Early church, ca. 30–600.
 I. Wickham, Lionel R. II. Title. III. Series.
 BR65.C952E5 1983 230'.14'0924 82–14554
 ISBN 0–19–826810–6

Printed in Great Britain
at the University Press, Oxford
by Eric Buckley,
Printer to the University

PREFACE

THERE are many whom I want to thank for help in the preparation of this work. I have mentioned some of them in the
book but others I must also name here. First there are the great
libraries of Basle, Berlin, Florence, Leiden, London, Munich,
Oxford, Paris and Venice and their distinguished servants who
have traced manuscripts and answered queries. Along with these I
must thank also Dr. Walter Hayes, of the Pontifical Institute of
Medieval Studies in Toronto, and the Institut de Recherche et
d'Histoire des Textes of Paris, who have helped in the same
manner. I have a special debt of gratitude to the general editor of
the series, Professor Henry Chadwick, without whose encouragement and counsel 20 years ago I should never have ventured
upon patristic scholarship. To my former University of South-
ampton I am under obligation for its support of this publication
in difficult times. I am in heavy debt to my old friend and former
colleague, Dr. F. J. Williams, who took time off from Callimachus
to read the proofs of another Alexandrine. If this work has any
merit, Cyril ought to be grateful, as I certainly am, to my wife,
Helen, who contributed the encouragement without which it
would never have seen the light of day. My son Henry helped
with the indexes; filial duty could scarcely go further. I thank
them all and trust that they will have helped to make the 'seal
of the fathers' more widely understood, for that was my aim in
undertaking this book.

LIONEL RALPH WICKHAM

Honley, 1982

CONTENTS

ABBREVIATIONS

Loofs   F. Loofs, *Nestoriana* (Halle, 1905).

Pusey 1, 2, 3 P. Pusey, *Sancti Patris Nostri Cyrilli Archiepiscopi Alexandrini in D. Joannis Evangelium. Accedunt Fragmenta Varia necnon Tractatus ad Tiberium Diaconum duo* (3 vols.; Oxford, 1872).

ACO   *Acta Conciliorum Oecumenicorum*, ed. E. Schwartz (Berlin and Leipzig, 1924–).

CCSL   *Corpus Christianorum Series Latina* (Turnholt, 1953–).

DHGE   *Dictionnaire d'Histoire et de Géographie Ecclésiastiques* (Paris, 1912–).

DTC   *Dictionnaire de Théologie Catholique* (Paris, 1903–).

JTS   *Journal of Theological Studies*, New Series (Oxford, 1950–).

LSJ   *A Greek–English Lexicon*, compiled by H. G. Liddell and R. Scott, revised H. S. Jones (Oxford, 1940).

NTS   *New Testament Studies* (Cambridge, 1954–).

PG   *Patrologiae Cursus completus Series Graeca*, ed. J. P. Migne (Paris, 1857–).

PGL   *A Patristic Greek Lexicon*, ed. G. W. H. Lampe (Oxford, 1961).

PL   *Patrologiae Cursus completus Series Latina*, ed. J. P. Migne (Paris, 1841–).

PLS   eiusdem *Supplementum* (1958–).

PO   *Patrologia orientalis* (Paris, 1907–).

RAC   *Reallexikon für Antike und Christentum* (Stuttgart, 1950–).

RB   *Revue Biblique* (Paris, 1915–).

REA   *Revue des études anciennes* (Bordeaux, 1899–).

RHE   *Revue d'histoire ecclésiastique* (Louvain, 1900–).

RSR   *Recherches de science religieuse* (Paris, 1910–).

SC   *Sources Chrétiennes* (Paris, 1941–).

TRE   *Theologische Realenzyclopädie* (Berlin, 1974–).

ZKG   *Zeitschrift für Kirchengeschichte* (Stuttgart and elsewhere, 1877–).

INTRODUCTION

1. *The Author and his Work*

(a) *Cyril's Place in History*

THE patristic understanding of the Incarnation owes more to
Cyril of Alexandria than to any other individual theologian.
The classic picture of Christ the God-man, as it is delineated
in the formulae of the Church from the Council of Chalcedon
onwards, and as it has been presented to the heart in liturgies
and hymns, is the picture Cyril persuaded Christians was the
true, the only credible, Christ. All subsequent Christology has
proceeded, and must proceed, by way of interpretation or
criticism of this picture; it is the standard by which interpreta-
tions of Christ as God's eternal Son and Word made man and
incarnate are judged, the reference-point for differing pictures.
Cyril's place, therefore, in the intellectual history of mankind
is assured and his perduring relevance to theology as near self-
evident as any such matter can be. Moreover, because men soon
divided over how to express their loyalty to his interpretation of
Christ, with the formation of mutually opposed 'monophysite'
and Chalcedonian churches, and because this division had far-
reaching political and social consequences for the Empire which
are with us yet in the political and religious structures of the
Middle East, Cyril's importance extends outside theology and
what may be thought of as narrowly ecclesiastical. Only Augustine, if the Reformation may be allowed to count as a consequence
of following to their conclusions his leading thoughts about
divine grace and human freedom, has had a comparable significance, at once religious and political, unitive and unwittingly
divisive.

The letters presented here provide a cross-section of Cyril's
theological work. The first seven deal principally with Christology; the last three with the doctrine of man, the spiritual life,
the Eucharist and some specific points of Biblical exegesis as
they arose out of queries addressed to him. All aspects of Cyril's
thought are represented in these letters which speak far more

directly to the reader than do his longer treatises. Cyril himself might fairly complain that they do not do justice to his work as an exegete of the Old Testament he commented upon so extensively or as an apologist for the Christian faith. But it is not in these fields that his main influence has lain and something of his work here is at least included. These letters, too, show Cyril in his role as church-politician, fierce in his initial campaign against Nestorius, willing in victory, if not to compromise (that he would never do), at any rate to attempt an honest peace with men of good will; and the second group (the correspondence with the Palestinian monks and with Calosirius) gives some insight into Cyril as a pastor and spiritual guide. They reveal the man and his characteristic attitudes as well as his message.

(b) *His Career*

To 428. Cyril succeeded his maternal uncle, Theophilus, on the throne of St Mark almost indecently soon after Theophilus' death on Tuesday, 15 October 412. On the Friday of that same week, after rioting between his own faction and supporters of the rival candidate Timothy the archdeacon, Cyril was installed despite opposition from the secular arm.[1] He must have been at least 30 at the time of his consecration and probably in his twenties when (as we know from a rare piece of self-reference) he attended Theophilus at the Synod of the Oak in 403 where John Chrysostom was condemned.[2] His date of birth, then, may be fixed somewhere between 375 and 380.

Little is known about his upbringing. A monastic education for part of the time would be a certainty if we could trust the correspondence of Isidore of Pelusium, who writes to him (or is presented in these letters as writing to him) with the authority of a monk and spiritual mentor.[3] It may be alluded to when

---

[1] Socrates, *Hist. Eccles.* 7, 7.

[2] *Letter to Acacius of Beroea* (= Aleppo) *Ep.* 33 (*ACO* 1, 1, 7 p. 148, 30 ff.): see *Letter to Acacius of Melitene*, para. 3, n. 5.

[3] Cf. *Epp.* 1, 25 and from the same book nos. 310, 324, and 370 (*PG* 78). The corpus of Isidoriana and the manuscript tradition needs to be re-examined; see P. Evieux 'Isidore de Péluse', *RSR* 64 (1976), 322–40. The presence of these letters in sources hostile to Cyril (in Rusticus' *Synodicon*, *ACO* 1, 4; see below, p. xliv) suggests at least the possibility of forgery. No notice is to be taken of Severus ibn Al-Muqaffa's account, according to which Cyril was sent by Theophilus to Nitria where he spent five years with Serapion the Wise

he says: 'from early years we learned the holy scriptures and were nurtured at the hands of holy and orthodox fathers',[4] where 'fathers' may mean monks. But the evidence here is uncertain. It is a plausible conjecture (if no more) that Theophilus played a large part in his intellectual formation and that he intended him to be his successor. He prepared him, we may guess, for high office and ensured the solid grounding in Biblical study and standard Christian authorities appropriate to his future role. The influence he exercised on Cyril was deep and lasting; so we may guess from the continuity of policy between uncle and nephew. The same respect for the monks of Egypt, the same vigorous measures against non-Christians and heretics, the same repudiation of any pretensions by the bishops of the eastern capital to interfere in their see, are to be observed. But there are discontinuities which should warn us not to exaggerate that influence. Cyril relented towards the memory of John Chrysostom (other evidence aside, he calls him a 'holy bishop' and quotes him)[5] and took a precisely contrary view to his uncle over the question of God's 'form' (as we see from the letters to the Palestinian monks and to Calosirius). He was by no means a carbon copy of his uncle and would acknowledge by implication, at any rate, that Theophilus had been wrong.

The qualities and limitations of Cyril's education show in his

as his teacher (*History of the Patriarchs of the Coptic Church of Alexandria*, ed. and trans. B. Evetts, *PO* i, pp. 427 ff.). The rest of his narrative is a tissue of legends and misunderstood facts.

[4] *ACO* i, i, 3 p. 22, 8 ff. It occurs in a personal declaration of faith at the Council of Ephesus at the session on 17 July.

[5] *Oratio ad Dominas* 15 (Cyril's address to the imperial ladies, Arcadia and Marina), *ACO* i, i, 5 p. 67, cf. p. 66, 20. The other evidence: John of Nikiu, *Chronicle*, tr. R. H. Charles (London, 1916), pp. 95 f., says that Cyril was overjoyed to reinstate John Chrysostom's name at Atticus' request; Nestorius says (see F. Loofs, *Nestoriana* (Halle, 1905), p. 300) 'Taceo de Ioanne, cuius nunc cineres adorando veneraris invitus' ('I do not mention John, to whose ashes you now pay unwilling respect'); Cyril's letter to Atticus of Constantinople, Nestorius' predecessor but one, (*Ep.* 76) gives no direct answer to the request for recognition (amongst Cyril's *epp.* no. 75). See *Codex Vaticanus gr. 1431* (Bibliography, p. li below), nos. 48–50, pp. 23–8, with Schwartz's observations, pp. 95 f. However, it looks to me as if the compiler of the dossier (see below, p. lxiv) presumed that Cyril agreed: he puts in this correspondence as an example of a case where it is legitimate to compromise. Finally, Cyril appears to have made no objection to the restoration of John's body to Constantinople by Proclus in 438.

writings. He betrays few signs of interest in, or specialized knowledge of, secular science, philosophy, or history for their own sake. In this he is quite different from his peers in theology, the Cappadocian fathers and Augustine. His literary style, distinctive in its abundance of rare words, archaizing forms and regularly repeated epithets,[6] shows, however, that he aspired to an elegance at home in the ancient Alexandrine tradition of fine writing. It has, it must be confessed, all the studied ugliness of the Albert Memorial or Second Empire furniture. The occasional quotations from Homer[7] and the acknowledgement of a debt to Greek poets for inspiration in describing the beauties of spring[8] tell in the same direction. He valued the forms, but not the content, of ancient culture, turning his expositions of the Trinity and the Incarnation, for the benefit of refined audiences, lay and clerical, into dialogues and forging thus a tenuous, external link with the traditions of Plato. The foundations of his learning were laid by Christian writers and beyond them he seems to have ventured only little. When it came to rebutting the apostate emperor Julian's work *Against the Galileans*, stuffed as it is with a pretentious display of learning, he leaned heavily upon Eusebius for suitable quotations from pagan writers.[9] He

---

[6] See A. Vaccari, 'La grecità di S. Cyrillo d'Alessandria', *Studi dedicati alla memoria di Paolo Ubaldi* (Milan, 1937), pp. 27–39. A project for editing the *Lexicon Cyrillianum* produced in antiquity to explain his unusual words has run into the ground; see the three articles *Cyrilliana* i and ii under the title 'Observations sur deux manuscrits parisiens du Lexique de Cyrille' and *Cyrilliana* iii 'Remarques sur la composition du Lexique de Cyrille', *REA* 63 (1961), 345–51, 64 (1962), 95–108 and 72 (1970), 364–84, by P. Burguière. In antiquity Photius had commented on the poetic style Cyril displayed, especially in his dialogues and *Glaphyra*; see *Bibliotheca* 49, ed. and trans. R. Henry (Paris, 1959), vol. 1, p. 35.

[7] e.g. *Dialogues on the Trinity* 1 (*PG* 75 Aubert 391). *Paschal Homily* 4 (*PG* 77, 460C), *Paschal Homily* 15 (*PG* 77, 744B).

[8] *In Jo.* 4, 4 (Pusey 1, 567). Cf. *Paschal Homily* 9 (*PG* 77, 591A ff.) and R. L. Wilken's remarks in *Judaism and the Early Christian Mind* (New Haven and London, 1971), pp. 176 f. Cyril sometimes displays a surprisingly lyrical turn, not merely when describing spring; cf. *Dialogues on the Trinity* 6 (*PG* 75 Aubert 593), where he explains John 15: 26: 'It is as if a most sweetly smelling flower should say of the perfume it exhales to the senses of the bystanders "he shall take of mine" .' This vocal flower is a refreshing piece of fancy. For a similar development cf. *In Jo.* 11, 2 (Pusey 2, 639).

[9] See R. M. Grant, 'Greek Literature in the Treatise *De Trinitate* and Cyril's *Contra Julianum*', *JTS* 15 (1964), 265–79 and W. J. Malley, *Hellenism and Christianity* (Rome, 1978), pp. 251–61.

certainly went beyond his immediate source to the originals, but it looks as if he were making forays into unfamiliar territory. Cyril's education made him, we may say, a deeply impressive and deeply learned theologian with a daunting knowledge of the Bible and able to cope fluently with the complexities of Trinitarian discussion. It did not give him intellectual curiosity; and, indeed, it is a gift he would have scorned. Instead it gave him beliefs as solid as a pyramid whose mode of expression altered little over the years.

Cyril owed little, then, directly to secular culture. Who amongst Christian writers influenced him most? His clearest debt is to Athanasius and one of his earliest works, the *Thesaurus*, is, in the main, a digest of Athanasius' *Discourses against the Arians*.[10] Other influences are harder to detect. The Cappadocian fathers had some part to play here as had, of course, the old theological tradition of Alexandria stretching back to Clement. Origen as speculative theologian he repudiated, like Theophilus. It was wicked nonsense, he thought (and rightly too) to deny the resurrection of the body, or to dream that embodied existence was a punishment for the soul's sins.[11] But on many points of exegesis and doctrinal argument he produces arguments similar enough to Origen's to suggest that he was their source.[12] His admittedly limited Latin correspondence with Rome and Carthage[13] indicates a passing acquaintance, at least,

[10] See J. Liébaert, *La Doctrine Christologique de Saint Cyrille d'Alexandrie avant la querelle Nestorienne* (Lille, 1951), pp. 22–43.

[11] See *Ep.* 81 to the monks at Phua (for the place see E. Honigmann, 'The monks of Fua, addressees of a letter from St. Cyril of Alexandria', *Studi e Testi* 173 (Vatican, 1953), pp. 52 f.), two fragments of which are preserved in Justinian's edict against Origen *ACO* 3, pp. 201 f.; cf. *In Jo.* 1, 10 (Pusey 1, 115–26) and 6, 1 (Pusey 2, 136–8).

[12] e.g. the camel passing through the eye of a needle is a ship's cable, not an animal: Cyril, frag. *In Matt.* (*PG* 72, 429D) and frag. 21/29 *Contra Julianum* 16 (K. J. Neumann and E. Nestle, *Iuliani Imperatoris Librorum quae supersunt, insunt Cyrilli Alexandri Fragmenta Syriaca* (Leipzig, 1880), pp. 56/75). Cf. Origen, frag. *In Matt.* 19: 24 (cited *PGL* s.v. κάμηλος), where Origen mentions it as a possible interpretation. For another example see below, p. 139 n. 16. The development of the themes of God's omnipresence and spirituality (see below, pp. 140 ff.) seems to owe something to Origen, *De Principiis* 2, 1, 3 and 2, 4, 3.

[13] He must have been able to superintend the translations of his letters to Celestine. See also *Ep.* 86 (*PG* 77, 377D–381A) and cf. B. Krusch, *Studien zur christlich-mittelalterisch Chronologie* (Leipzig, 1880), pp. 344 ff.; and P. Grosjean, *Analecta Bollandiana* 64 (1946), 231. For his letter to Carthage in 419, enclosing

with the language but it is highly unlikely that he knew much Latin theology despite his brief quotations from Cyprian and Ambrose.[14] He may well, though, have learned something from the commentaries of Jerome,[15] who had made himself serviceable to Theophilus as a translator and ally against Origen.

What he brought with him to office were an enviable knowledge of the Bible and orthodox theology and, we may surmise, a grounding in ecclesiastical affairs which was part of the family tradition.

The first years were stormy. The contested election made his position predictably insecure in a city prone to conflict and violence where not even bishops were safe from lynching. Socrates, the Church historian, records a catalogue of outrages: the seizure of Novatianist churches, troubles with Orestes the prefect, mob-violence culminating in the murder of Hypatia the philosopher in 415 and the (temporary) expulsion of some Jews from Alexandria at Cyril's command.[16] The account is partial, for Socrates' sympathies with Novatianists have certainly distorted the picture. But the facts are not to be denied. The picture they yield is not of a fanatical priest, hungry for power, heading a howling mob, but of an untried leader attempting, and initially failing, to master popular forces. In the end he succeeded, and the imperial order restoring to him control over the *parabalani*

---

a dossier of documents from the archives at Alexandria, see C. H. Turner, *Ecclesiae Occidentalis Monumenta Iuris Antiquissima* (Oxford, 1899 ff.), i, 2, 3 pp. 610 f.

[14] Quoted as testimonies at the Council of Ephesus (431), *ACO* i, 1, 2 p. 42.

[15] See F. M. Abel 'Parallélisme exégétique entre S. Jérôme et S. Cyrille d'Alexandrie', *Vivre et Penser* i (1941), 94–119, 212–30; A. Kerrigan, *St. Cyril of Alexandria interpreter of the Old Testament* (Rome, 1952), pp. 435–9; and J.-D. Barthelémy 'Quinta ou version selon les Hébreux?', *Theologische Zeitschrift* 16 (1960), 342–53. The additional evidence from a hagiographical notice in a 9th/10th c. manuscript, to the effect that Cyril 'went through the whole course of Greek and Latin studies', produced by Abel, p. 97, is worthless—such a great man must have known *everything* is what it means. If Barthelémy is right, Cyril may have known Jerome's work in Greek translation by Sophronius (see Jerome, *De Viris Illustribus*, c. 134).

[16] *Hist. Eccles.* 7, 13–16. See R. L. Wilken's observations, op. cit. (n. 8 above), pp. 54–8, on the expulsion of the Jews. They were far too many and too important to be expelled *en bloc* as Socrates suggests. Moreover, they are still to be found at Alexandria not long after. Socrates exaggerates this unpleasant episode.

responsible for Hypatia's death[17] was clearly an admission that
his authority could now be trusted or, at least, could not be
challenged. We hear no more of rioting. But the cost of retaining
control was always to be heavy. The archbishop of Alexandria
could never falter in matters of doctrine, never retract, never
allow authority to pass out of his hands and especially not to
the archbishop of the Eastern capital, whose pretensions to
seniority it was vital for his own security at home to rebut.
There will, again, certainly have been some substance to the
protestations of ill-treatment at Cyril's hands, which played a
part in the controversy with Nestorius. It will always have been
unwise, and sometimes even physically dangerous, to meet Cyril
as an opponent.

We know little of the next thirteen years during which Cyril
was consolidating his authority. Perhaps to this period belongs
the translation of the bones of saints Cyrus and John to the
ancient seat of Isis at Menouthis, where their superior power
quelled the demon-goddess—the place (Aboukir) still registers in
its name the Christian shrine.[18] His earliest literary work is
probably his Old Testament commentaries and these, if they do
not ante-date his episcopate, along with the *Thesaurus*, the *Commentary on John*, and the *Dialogues on the Trinity* were probably
written then.[19] Every year, too, he despatched festal letters to

[17] Control was withdrawn in 416, but restored in 418. See *CT* 16.2.42/43
(Eng. trans. and notes in P. R. Coleman-Norton, *Roman State and Christian
Church* (3 vols., London, 1966), ii, nos. 347 and 349, pp. 577 f. and 579 f.).
The *parabalani* (translated by Coleman-Norton 'sick-nurses') were, properly
speaking, bath-attendants—the word comes from παρὰ βαλανεῖον—under the
direction of the bishop. Strong men, used to lifting the sick, they formed a
kind of guard for him, 500 (or by the later mandate 600) strong. The 'Zeuxip-
pites' of Constantinople, of whom we also hear (*ACO* 1, 1, 3 p. 46, 13) were
evidently a parallel institution belonging to the baths of Zeuxippus at Constantinople, cf. Pauly–Wissowa, *Realencyclopädie* (2nd series 10A, 1972) s.v.
Zeuxippos. *Parabalani* and sailors accompanied Cyril to the Council at
Ephesus and were complained of (*ACO* 1, 1, 3 p. 50, 29). See E. Schwartz,
Cyrill und der Mönch Viktor, pp. 28 f. and 35; W. Schubart 'Parabalani', *The
Journal of Egyptian Archaeology* 40 (1954), 97–101. The connection of these
parabalani with Hypatia's death is certain, I think, though Socrates does not
specifically mention them.

[18] See Sophronius, *Laudes in SS. Cyrum et Joannem* (*PG* 87(3), 3380–3424,
esp. 3412 ff.). Three short addresses by Cyril on the occasion are preserved
(*PG* 77, 1100–1106).

[19] The *Thesaurus* is referred to by name in *In Jo.* 1, 7 (Pusey 1, 81, 17 f.),
and the preface to the *Dialogues on the Trinity* (*PG* 75 Aubert 383BC) implies

his churches announcing the date of Easter and giving a pastoral message; the series begins in 414, Theophilus presumably having composed that for the year 413.[20] These festal letters offer some hints as to Cyril's predominant concerns. The earlier letters (and the Old Testament commentaries) where they press home an attack direct it against Jews and Pagans. In 420 (*Hom. Pasch.* viii) he was moved to write fiercely against some form of christological dualism such as he was later to detect in Nestorius. In 424 (*Hom. Pasch.* xii) it was 'Arianism' which he castigated and the consubstantiality of the Trinity which he defended in unusually technical language. These polemics against Jews, Pagans, and

its existence—Cyril has written again for Nemesinus to whom the *Thesaurus* is dedicated. The *Thesaurus* is thus prior to the other two works. A λόγος on the Holy Trinity and a βίβλιον on the same theme are referred to in *In Jo.* 1, 9 (Pusey 1, 128, 5 f. and 137, 29 f.), and the second reference Pusey connects with the seventh *Dialogue* (because of the theme, the Holy Ghost); see his marginal note. Assuming that Pusey is correct and that the work referred to is not the *Thesaurus* 33 (for in that case we should have expected the work to be named, as before) or an unknown piece, the *Commentary on John* was composed after the *Dialogues*. The sixth *Dialogue* is apparently mentioned by Cyril as having been composed 'whilst Atticus of blessed memory was still alive', i.e. before 10 October 425 (*Ep.* 2 = *First Letter to Nestorius* para. 4, *ACO* 1, 1, 1 p. 24, 29 ff.), but as being (429) not yet published. Certainly the production of the *Dialogues* and of the *Commentary on John* will have gone on over a number of years, and portions of the *Dialogues* were perhaps published separately. The *Commentary* must surely have been completed in all essentials before 428, because the Nestorian controversy finds no explicit mention there, though he attacks 'dualist' accounts of Christ, *In Jo.* 2, 1 (Pusey 1, 224, 14 ff.). As for the Old Testament commentaries, *De Adoratione in spiritu et veritate* was written first, then *Glaphyra* (= polished pieces/studies), followed probably by the commentaries on the *Minor Prophets* and *Isaiah*; see G. Jouassard, 'L'activité littéraire de saint Cyrille d'Alexandrie jusqu'à 428; essai de chronologie et de synthèse', *Mélanges E. Podechard* (Lyon, 1945), pp. 159–74. For further discussion over the dating of the various works, see also N. Charlier 'Le "Thesaurus de Trinitate" de Saint Cyrille d'Alexandrie, questions de critique littéraire' in *RHE* 45 (1950), 25–81; G. Jouassard, 'La date des écrits antiariens de Saint Cyrille d'Alexandrie', *Revue Bénédictine* 87 (1977), 172–8; J. Liébaert, *La Doctrine Christologique de Saint Cyrille d'Alexandrie avant la querelle Nestorienne* (Lille, 1951), pp. 12–16; and G. M. de Durand's introduction to vol. 1 of his edition of the *Dialogues on the Trinity* (*SC* 231, 1976), pp. 38–43. In the debate between Jouassard and the others over the dating of the *Commentary on John* I think Jouassard has the better case.

[20] *PG* 77, 401–981. The table given on p. 395/6 is correct; there is no break in the series (cf. p. 397/8) by the loss of a no. 3. Thus Homily 4 is really the third (for 416). I follow the numbering of Migne.

heretics must reflect in some measure particular problems and conflicts in the diocese of which we otherwise know nothing. Another enterprise, his massive *Against Julian*,[21] was probably begun during this period too, and reflects not so much a particular problem as the continuing struggle with intelligent paganism, a struggle waged, as we have seen, at the popular level with saints' bones.

From 428 to 444, with Special Reference to the First Seven Letters.

We now come to the most significant years of Cyril's episcopate, when he played the part which gives him the assured place in the history of doctrine mentioned at the outset. In 428 Nestorius, a monk from Antioch and keen expositor of the theological emphases characteristic of Diodore and Theodore, was installed as bishop in Constantinople. From now on Cyril's energies were predominantly directed against him and his school of thought. More detailed comments on the origins and course of the controversy will be found in the notes to the letters here edited, but in general it is fair to say here that though the controversy itself was perhaps unavoidable (for it concerned alternative and irreconcilable pictures of Christ) its form, as a controversy affecting the whole Church and involving the defined teaching of the Church rather than the views of particular theologians, was determined by matters of personality and Church politics and in particular by the personality and self-chosen role of Nestorius. We do not have to sit in judgement over figures from ancient history who are not free to stand up and speak for themselves and whom we cannot interrogate in a court of law, to see that Nestorius lost the argument because his picture of Christ was incredible; he lost his throne because he blundered.

The catalogue of these blunders is long. He saw himself as a defender of truth against the errors of Arius and Apollinarius and delivered sermons of a much more controversial character

---

[21] *PG* 76, 504–1064. Further fragments in Neumann/Nestle, see above, n. 12. Cyril sent copies of this along with *Ep.* 41 on the scapegoat (addressed to Acacius of Scythopolis) to John of Antioch for distribution amongst the Eastern bishops—of whom Theodoret was one (his *Ep.* 83, *ACO* 2, 1 p. 247, 9 ff.). Theodoret treats this as a friendly gesture, but I suspect there is a sting in the tail; Cyril is showing how Julian *should* have been rebutted—not as Theodore of Mopsuestia had done (his refutation has not survived, cf. Neumann/ Nestle, pp. 23 ff.).

than usual before a lay public,[22] some of whom probably liked them rather too well. The defence of truth he offered laid him open to criticism not merely from prejudiced critics like Cyril, and the disaffected elements every church always contains, but men of good will from his own side. It was foolish to cast doubt on the propriety of the title 'Mother of God' applied to the Blessed Virgin Mary[23] and deeply offensive to ascend the pulpit one day to denounce as heretical the Marian homily of the previous preacher Proclus,[24] his rival in the election and later to occupy the throne. His utterances at the time of the controversy were *heard* to convey what they were certainly not intended to convey, the idea that Christ was simply an inspired man. In the end, I judge, this is all that Nestorius *was* saying. When the reader has worked through the complexities of transferable functions or presentations which the manhood and Godhead in Christ mutually interchange to produce the unitary function, or presentation, of Christ (this is Nestorius' own language when he came to set his views out systematically),[25] an inspired man is what is left. The people who picked this up from Nestorius' sermons were perfectly correct. Nonetheless, he did not mean to say it. Moreover Nestorius saw himself as a defender of the down-trodden and received favourably refugees from Alexandria and the West complaining of ill-treatment. From the point of view of Rome, what was quite as bad as this was his interference in Macedonia, which was a kind of outpost of the Roman see and enjoyed a special relationship with it.[26] In these ways Nestorius was laying claim, or appearing to lay claim, to rights of jurisdiction which would bring him into conflict with colleagues who, whatever else they might overlook, could never allow such pretensions to go unrebuked. If we look at the matter without reference to the substance of doctrine at all, we can

---

[22] Cf. *Third Letter to Nestorius*, para. 1, '*congregations* not only at Constantinople . . .', not just the learned audiences Cyril addressed on technical matters (cf. *ACO* 1, 1, 1 p. 24, 29 ff.).

[23] Cf. Socrates, *Hist. Eccles.* 7, 32.

[24] *ACO* 1, 5 pp. 37–9. Proclus' sermon is in *ACO* 1, 1, 1 pp. 103–7, probably delivered on Lady Day 430.

[25] See *Liber Heraclidis*, 333 f./*212* f. (See below, n. 27).

[26] Cyril *Ep.* 11 (to Celestine), *ACO* 1, 1, 5 p. 11, 30 ff., and 12, 10 ff. See the account of the establishment of the Roman vicariate in Thessalonica by Charles Pietri, *Roma Christiana* (2 vols., Rome, 1976), esp. ii, pp. 1083–1147.

see that to embroil himself with a well-established colleague like Cyril, even though he was close to the sources of power in the capital, was to lose the war before it had started. His exile and disgrace from 436 onwards are, of course, sad. But sympathy is wasted upon him. The enforced leisure allowed him to order his account of Christ and to write his *apologia vitae*. Modern study of the work, the *Liber Heraclidis*, surviving in translation from the Greek into Syriac and first published in a printed edition in 1910,[27] has removed ancient propagandist distortions. He will never lack friends now, ready to lend an ear to his tale of injustice and perfidy.

The main stages of the controversy are marked by the first seven letters given here. The first two (Cyril's second and third letters to Nestorius) are at the centre of the battle; the next four (the letters to Acacius of Melitene, to Eulogius and to Successus) belong to the aftermath of the war; and *On the Creed* comes at a later stage, when the question of Nestorius' masters, in particular Theodore of Mopsuestia, was becoming acute.

The second letter to Nestorius (dated Mechir = 26 January to 24 February 430) clearly sets out the issues. Nestorius has entertained fugitives from Cyril and has been guilty of heretical teaching contrary to the Nicene Creed; he has taught that there is no real union in Christ and denied that the Blessed Virgin Mary is Mother of God. During the spring and summer Cyril wrote letters to the court[28] and to leading bishops to muster support against Nestorius. He met with some splendid rebuffs.

---

[27] *T^e gurta d^e Heraclidus d^e men Damsoq*, ed. P. Bedjan (Paris, 1910). French translation by F. Nau, *Le Livre d'Héraclide de Damas* (Paris, 1910); in references the translation is underlined. The best accounts of his Christology are to be found in L. I. Scipioni, *Nestorio e il Concilio di Efeso* (Milan, 1974) and Luise Abramowski, *Untersuchungen zum Liber Heraclidis des Nestorius* (*CSCO* 242, *Subsidia* 22, Louvain, 1963). The literary question of the integrity of the book remains unresolved: Luise Abramowski argues against it, Scipioni defends it. There are certainly contrasts between different sections, but maybe he was simply inconsistent. See also the Appendix, 'The Nestorius question in modern study', pp. 559–68 of Alois Grillmeier, *Christ in Christian Tradition*, vol. 1 (London and Oxford, 1975).

[28] The *Oratio ad Theodosium* (*ACO* 1, 1, 1 pp. 42–72), a re-working of an earlier dialogue *On the Incarnation of the Only-begotten*, see G. M. de Durand, *Deux Dialogues Christologiques* (*SC* 97, Paris, 1964), chapter 2 Introduction; and the two treatises, to the princesses *Oratio ad Dominas* (*ACO* 1, 1, 5 pp. 62–118) and the empresses *Oratio ad Augustas* (ibid. pp. 26–61).

Theodosius, the emperor, sharply rebuked him for trying to divide the imperial family.[29] The centenarian Acacius of Aleppo, on whose sympathies Cyril particularly tried to play, refused to be drawn.[30] Far from offering help, he offered a peculiarly pointed reminder of the case of Apollinarius, a hero of the faith who had fallen from grace.[31] Rome however listened. Nestorius was suspected there of being an intriguer. Damaging extracts from Nestorius' sermons (gathered by Cyril's agents in Constantinople and previously despatched to Rome) along with this second letter to Nestorius constituted the main information that Rome had about the doctrinal issues. It was enough to move the pope, Celestine, to action. A Roman synod in August 430 declared against Nestorius, and the pope by an extraordinary move appointed Cyril as his representative to order Nestorius to retract his errors and embrace the faith of Rome and Alexandria within ten days of receiving an ultimatum.[32]

Sufficient stir had now been made to justify the emperor in summoning a council to deal with the issues in dispute. His letter, dated 19 November 430, duly convokes the council at Ephesus for Whitsuntide 431.[33] In the emperor's mind (as in

[29] See his letter to Cyril (*ACO* i, i, i pp. 73 f.). After general observations about the need for peace and for the clergy to resolve their disputes amongst themselves, he goes on (p. 73, 22 ff.): 'What was the point of despatching one letter to me and my partner in life, the most religious empress Eudocia and another to my sister, the most religious Pulcheria? You either thought we disagreed or hoped your Reverence's letters would make us disagree.' At the end he mentions the council he has convoked (see below, n. 33). So he stored up this personal expression of rage till November—but Cyril will have heard about it long before.

[30] *Ep.* 14 (*ACO* i, i, i pp. 98 f.). Nestorius is scandalizing the churches. He has even permitted a bishop, Dorotheus, to stand up in church and anathematize anyone who calls the Blessed Virgin Mary 'Mother of God'—a title well known to Athanasius, Theophilus, Basil, Gregory, and Atticus of blessed memory (most of whom were probably personally known to Acacius). What are we to do, if we find ourselves anathematized along with the fathers? Cyril has been forced to write to his scandalized monks (*Ep.* i, *ACO* i, i, i pp. 10–23—Cyril's initial clarion call, see p. 2 n. 1). As a result, Nestorius is campaigning against him using vagabonds and desperadoes. We must act to check the infection.

[31] *ACO* i, i, i pp. 99 f., esp. p. 99, 11 ff.

[32] *ACO* i, 2 pp. 5 f. (Greek trans. ibid. i, i, i pp. 75 f.), dated 10 August 430.

[33] To Cyril, *ACO* i, i, i pp. 114 ff. Other letters were sent to the parties involved.

Nestorius') the council was to be an occasion for putting Cyril in his place as a disturber of the peace.[34] For the emperor, too, it was an easy way of avoiding his responsibilities for keeping discipline in the Church. The bishops would resolve their differences without his having to do anything and all would be well again. Things did not work out like this, for Cyril now presented his ultimatum: the *Third Letter to Nestorius*, with its twelve anathematisms, delivered 30 November 430. The special significance of this piece I discuss below. The point to note here is that Nestorius, by refusing to accept it, put himself technically in the position of defendant. He would now be on trial.

Even had the council met as planned, Cyril would probably have carried the day. He had the support of the West, of a few leading bishops and of a good number of less important episcopal voices.[35] Councils, of course, were not assemblies subject to the tyranny of the majority vote. Their decisions were always unanimous on questions of doctrine, because the decisions were not theirs but those of the Holy Ghost. Argument went on until everybody agreed. By the time that the president called for individual expressions of opinion from the assembled bishops (which is the nearest thing to a vote) the matter had already been decided. That is the way councils were run. The risk that Cyril ran was that with a sizeable number of bishops supporting Nestorius, the council would never reach a decision. The Church was not yet ready for a technical debate on Christology at a General Council; another twenty years would be needed for that. It is at least possible (though I do not think it the most likely of outcomes) that the council, if it had met as intended, would have cried a plague on both houses and refused to go any further.

However that may be, the council did not meet as planned. June 7th came and went and neither the Eastern delegation favourable to Nestorius, and headed by John of Antioch, nor

[34] See above, n. 29.

[35] On the other hand, 68 bishops, including 20 metropolitans, wrote (*ACO* 1, 4 pp. 27–30) on 21 June, telling him not to start without John of Antioch; see below in text. However, 32 of these (6 metropolitans) came over to Cyril, including the grandfather of his great exponent Severus, patriarch of Antioch, also called Severus and the bishop of Sozopolis; see John of Beth-Aphthonia's life of Severus, ed. and trans. M. Kugener, *PO* 2, 3 (Paris, 1907, repr. 1971, p. 211).

the Roman legates had arrived. The Easterns were held up by bad roads and sickness;[36] what delayed the others we do not know. Cyril had no chance of getting the right decision out of the council without Roman support. So when by 22 June the Roman legates had not arrived, and he knew from outriders that the Easterns would be at Ephesus within the next few days, he took advantage of an imprudent note from John of Antioch, written months beforehand, which politely intimated that if he was not there in time, Cyril might begin the proceedings without him. So Cyril did.[37] Despite the protests of the imperial commissioner,[38] appointed to keep order but clearly left in the lurch by a central government quite out of touch with events, he despatched most of the business, declaring Nestorius deposed and condemning his views.[39] When the Easterns arrived on 26 June they proceeded to complain loudly about what had happened. Cyril and his close associate Memnon, bishop of Ephesus, were declared deposed and all their adherents excommunicated, and letters of protestation were sent off to the capital.[40] The Roman legates eventually arrived and joined forces with Cyril, declaring their agreement with all that had been accomplished at the session on 22 June.[41] After six weeks or so of delay, the Emperor intervened with a letter revelatory of total incomprehension of the business (it is addressed, among others, to Celestine, who had appointed deputies, and Augustine, who was dead) confirming the deposition of Nestorius, Cyril and Memnon, all three of whom were placed under house arrest, and censuring everything else.[42] Both sides replied to this,[43] the Easterns in an

[36] See John's note to Cyril (*ACO* 1, 1, 1 p. 119) written from one of the last staging posts in the overland route, where he asks for 5 or 6 days of delay—he has been travelling for 30 days so far. John's official explanation to the Emperor is in *ACO* 1, 1, 5 p. 125, 14 ff.

[37] The episode is well unmasked by E. Schwartz, *Cyrill und der Mönch Viktor*, pp. 38 ff. For Cyril's justification, see *ACO* 1, 1, 2 p. 67, 8; 1, 1, 3 p. 3, 24 and p. 84, 16 ff.   [38] Candidian. For his protest, see *ACO* 1, 4 pp. 31–3.

[39] *ACO* 1, 1, 2 pp. 3–64.   [40] *ACO* 1, 1, 5 pp. 119–36.

[41] *ACO* 1, 1, 3 pp. 53–63. The sessions were on 10 and 11 July.

[42] *ACO* 1, 1, 3 pp. 31 f. 'We accept the deposition of Nestorius, Cyril and Memnon' (the bishop of Ephesus) 'notified by your reverences, but condemn the rest of your acts, preserving, as we do, the orthodox Christianity we received from our fathers and forebears and the faith which the most holy council in the time of Constantine, of divine appointment, harmoniously thereto decreed' (p. 31, 22 ff.). It is a confession of weakness and incompetence on Theodosius' part, who is chiefly to blame for all the muddle.

Note 43 on facing page.

important submission, which contains their conditions for a
settlement and a draft of the 'formula of reunion'.[44] A conference
of delegates from both sides met and argued their cases before
Theodosius at Chalcedon without result.[45] Meanwhile Nestorius,
nervously exhausted, no doubt, and seeing no future in attempting to continue in office, had resigned and gone back to Antioch,[46]
and Theodosius, veering towards the Cyrilline party, then
summoned the Cyrillines to the consecration of Maximian,
Nestorius' successor, on 25 October.[47] On the Saturday of that
week Cyril entered Alexandria to a personal ovation.[48] There
was neither reason nor will to detain him, and so he left before
the Emperor had officially dismissed the council and released
him and Memnon.[49] His fairly long *Apology* to the Emperor[50]
explains his departure and has as its crowning touch the news
that Victor (one of the original dissidents from Alexandria, about
whose alleged injustices so much fuss had been made) swore at
Ephesus that he had no charges to make against Cyril.[51]

How peaceful relations between Cyril and the Eastern bishops
were restored is told, from Cyril's point of view naturally, in the
letter to Acacius of Melitene. What is left out there is any account
of the effort and money expended by Cyril in the process.[52]
Nothing could happen unless the government pressed for reunion
(because one of the disputing parties, at least, had to give way,
and that was almost intolerable) and the government would not
intervene without payment to the appropriate officials at the
going rate. The hostile dossier which records the transaction
criticizes, by malicious exposure, the size, not the fact, of the
payment. The bankrupting size is the sincerest testimony to
Cyril's wish for a united Church and should, in fairness, bring
him credit. He wanted to find common ground with his opponents now that Nestorius was disposed of, provided there was

---

[43] From the Cyrillines, *ACO* 1, 1, 3 pp. 32 f.

[44] *ACO* 1, 1, 7 pp. 69 f., esp. p. 70, 15 ff.

[45] See *Collectio Atheniensis* (*ACO* 1, 1, 7) items 62 ff.

[46] See *Collectio Atheniensis* (*ACO* 1, 1, 7) items 55 f.

[47] Socrates, *Hist. Eccles.* 7, 37 *ad fin.* for the date; *ACO* 1, 1, 3 p. 67 for the
summons.   [48] See *ACO* 1, 3 p. 179, 11.

[49] *ACO* 1, 1, 7 p. 142. Nestorius says Cyril bribed his way out (*Liber Heraclidis*
pp. 388/*249*).

[50] *ACO* 1, 1, 3 pp. 75–90.

[51] *ACO* 1, 1, 3 p. 90, 7 ff.   [52] See below, *Letter to Eulogius*, n. 8.

no sacrifice of principle. The common ground already existed; it had been mapped in the Easterns' submission mentioned above. With the addition of two vital words, 'the same', and a qualification of one of the anathematisms, Cyril could fairly represent what was in essentials the work of the Easterns as his own conviction, and on the basis of this formula communion was publicly restored on 23 April 433.[53] The letters to Acacius, Eulogius, and Successus tell their own story of the exercise in diplomacy in which Cyril had now to engage. Friends needed to be convinced that he had not sold the pass. In periods of controversy men find curious allies and the views of some, at least, of Cyril's were by later standards heretical. It is a tribute to his skill that he brought these to heel and convinced the genuinely puzzled. John of Antioch, for his part, was not so successful. Fifteen of his bishops declined to conform and were unseated.[54]

The battle broadened over the next years to embrace Nestorius' precursors, Diodore and Theodore. The first mention of Diodore by name appears in the *First Letter to Successus*. Hints and explicit allusions to Theodore had appeared earlier;[55] overt attack was to wait until 438. The story of how this came about is complicated and not entirely clear. The dossiers of letters contain enough material to reconstruct the course of events, but, since the letters are not dated, in several different ways. Besides that, a number of elusive subsidiary figures flit on and off the stage, and their motives are hard to track down.[56] In broad outline what happened was this. Maximian, Nestorius' successor, died in 434. He was succeeded by Proclus, now elected at the third attempt. It was a moment for friendlier relationships and the customary courtesies between Constantinople and Antioch to be resumed. This was to reckon, though, without Acacius of Melitene or the bishop of Edessa, Rabbula. These were not to be pacified by the

[53] A short paragraph was delivered by Cyril in church at Alexandria (*ACO* 1, 1, 7 p. 173) followed by the reading of John's letter to Cyril (*ACO* 1, 1, 4 pp. 7 f.) and Cyril's to John (ibid. pp. 15–20) beginning 'Let the heavens rejoice'. [54] See *ACO* 1, 4 pp. 203 f.

[55] An extract from Theodore, without naming him, was quoted for condemnation by Cyril in his *Commentary on Hebrews* (fragments in Pusey 3, 362–440) belonging to the years 429/30; see P. M. Parvis 'The Commentary on Hebrews and the Contra Theodorum of Cyril of Alexandria' in *JTS* 26 (1975), 415–19.

[56] See Luise Abramowski, 'Der Streit um Diodor und Theodor zwischen den beiden ephesenischen Konzilien', *ZKG* 67 (1955/56), 252–87.

measures against Nestorius. Rabbula had already condemned Theodore before the peace of 433 and Acacius was moved to action a couple of years later.[57] Theodore's writings were circulating, or alleged to be circulating, in Armenian translation.[58] Rabbula died in 436 and was succeeded by Ibas, a man of the opposite persuasion. Something had to be done to stop the rot, and so an unofficial Armenian delegation approached Proclus for a judgement against Theodore. A collection of extracts from Theodore was presented to him for his disapprobation. In response he despatched to the Armenian Patriarch Sahak (i.e. Isaac) the letter known as the *Tome to the Armenians*,[59] a noble exposition of traditional teaching which puts Cyril's thoughts as well as they have ever been put by anyone else. The excerpts from Theodore were condemned, though without naming their author. This letter was circulated to the Eastern bishops. They did not disapprove of the doctrine but would have nothing to do with the condemnation of the revered Theodore.[60]

Cyril had, of course, been kept acquainted with what was going on but had, so far, made no decisive intervention. He was in Palestine, accompanying the empress Eudocia on pilgrimage,[61] when he received in Jerusalem, by the official post, that dossier of damaging extracts from Theodore.[62] A sharp letter went back to John and the Easterns[63] and, on his return to Alexandria, at the request of Maximus, the abbot from Antioch who visited him, he wrote *On the Creed*. It made his position clear on the question: the condemnation of Nestorius' views certainly included

[57] See M. Richard, 'Acace de Mélitène, Proclus de Constantinople et la Grande Arménie, *Opera Minora*, vol. 2 (Leuven, 1977), no. 50, for the interchange of letters between Sahak and Acacius.

[58] See Innocentius of Maronea's remark, *ACO* 4, 2 p. 68, 10 ff.

[59] *ACO* 4, 2 pp. 187–95. It is famous for its line: 'By confessing that God the Word, *one of the Trinity, was incarnate*, we explain to those who ask with faith the purpose of the Incarnation' (p. 192, 7 f.). It should be equally famous for its rejection of the notion that the Incarnation involves a change analogous to the turning of the Nile into blood (p. 190, 10 f.), a view canvassed by Theodotus of Ancyra (see p. xlii). The inexpugnable majesty of God and the mystery of his eternal Son's sufferings are finely placed.

[60] *ACO* 1, 5 pp. 310 ff.—a letter of John of Antioch and his Eastern synod to Cyril.

[61] John of Nikiu, op. cit. (n. 5 above), 87, 20; cf. Socrates, *Hist. Eccles.* 7, 47.

[62] *Ep.* 70, ed. E. Schwartz *Codex Vaticanus gr. 1431*, pp. 16 f.

[63] *Ep.* 67 *ACO* 1, 1, 4 pp. 37–9.

Theodore's, even though he had not been named. Expensive parchment copies of this letter were sent to the Emperor and the royal ladies.[64] Moreover Cyril was moved to write his tripartite treatise *Against Diodore and Theodore* (one part against Diodore, two against Theodore, making use of extracts from them). Only fragments of this survive.[65] Its loss is probably not greatly to be regretted. What survives suggests it contained a few good lines but that their author had exhausted his stock of ideas. The watch dogs of orthodoxy had barked, yet it was a tired shepherd who dutifully responded. Cyril would not press for the condemnation of Christian men's memories. That was to be the work of future generations and the Fifth General Council (553). Theodore was wrong, he wrote to Proclus[66] and to John,[67] but should be left to God's judgement. The court was, no doubt, vastly relieved at this irenic gesture and there, so far as Cyril was concerned, the matter rested. This must be amongst his last acts. He died on 27 June 444.

(c) *The Answers to Tiberius, Doctrinal Questions and Answers, and the Letter to Calosirius*

These pieces come from a milieu quite different from that of the others. The issues involved here do not agitate the Empire or threaten the stability of the imperial household. The storms, such as they are, are storms in tea-cups.

The date of the first probably lies between 431 and 434. Cyril's victory over Nestorius is evidently a recent event, and there is no reference to Diodore or Theodore by the deacon Tiberius, who approached Cyril for guidance on some points which were disturbing his Palestinian brothers. Intruders have appeared in the community, whose location is not given, demanding special privileges for themselves and unsettling the others with various assertions and questions. What their views were can in part be ascertained from the headings to Cyril's answers along

---

[64] See *Epp.* 70 (n. 62 above) and 71 (Latin version only, *ACO* 1, 4 pp. 210 f.); the latter is the dedicatory address, accompanying the copy, to Theodosius.

[65] Pusey 3, 492–537. See M. Richard, 'Les traités de Cyrille d'Alexandrie contre Diodore et Théodore et les fragments dogmatiques de Diodore de Tarse', *Opera Minora* 2 (n. 57 above), no. 51.

[66] *Ep.* 72, *Codex Vaticanus gr. 1431* (n. 62 above), pp. 17–19.

[67] *ACO* 1, 5 pp. 314 f.

with the answers themselves—only in part, because one of the
objections to these intruders is that they roused controversy, so
that we cannot assume that all the answers are directed against
them. Clearly they held that God is human in form, because
man was made in God's image (*Answers* 1, 2, 3, and 10), and that
the consubstantiality of Father and Son had to be understood
in a literal, 'physical' manner. They are not formal heretics,
then, because they accept the 'consubstantiality' of the Nicene
Creed, but they may well be schismatics, since Cyril (*Answer* 11)
is moved to pronounce against the validity of schismatic euchar-
ists. Tiberius is vague about the origins of this group and the
evidence does not permit us to identify them with Audians or
any other sect. Besides disturbing the brethren over the 'form'
of God, questions about the conditions of the Incarnation (*Answers*
4, 5, 6, 7, 9, and 13) are raised, about its effects (*Answer* 8), about
angels and demons (*Answers* 14 f.), and about the possibility of
eliminating the sexual drive (*Answer* 12). No doubt some of
these issues arose out of assertions by the intruders. For example,
it is plausible to suggest, in view of their pretensions to superior
status, that they asserted that it was possible to attain serenity
in this life—and that they had done so. But beyond the fact
that they were 'anthropomorphites' we cannot go for certain.

Some time later the same Palestinian monks headed by Tiberius
(now a priest, if we trust the Armenian version) approached
Cyril again, this time to present for his solution doctrinal questions on which they had been asked to adjudicate but which they
found too difficult. Two groups of questioners are mentioned:
from Abilene and Egypt. It is not clear whether the same points
were at issue for both or not. Probably we are to understand that
they were, since Tiberius speaks of the Egyptians as being
infected with the 'same madness' as the people of Abilene. God's
'form' and the image of God in man are again issues but expressed
in a subtler way than in the preceding series (*Doctrinal Questions
and Answers* 1–4); indeed the intellectual level is a good deal
higher. Questions were posed about the progress of the soul and
its possible regress (no. 5), about the relation between Adam's
transgression and baptismal grace (no. 6), about the resurrection
(nos. 7 f.), about Hosea's marriage and the puzzling figure of
Melchizedek (nos. 9 f.), and finally about the possibility of God's
altering the past. Some of these questions clearly echo debates

between so-called Origenists and anti-Origenists, but Origen's name is never breathed and no defenders of Origen's memory (if there were any at the period) would have allowed their case to go for adjudication to Theophilus' nephew. The Origenism here (such as it is) is that of Evagrius and Gregory of Nyssa perhaps, of standard teaching, or traditional exegesis unconnected in men's minds with its original author. Moreover, there is in the question about sin (no. 6) a whiff of the debate between Augustine and Pelagius, and of contemporary discussions in the monasteries of Egypt in that about Melchizedek (no. 10). The questions, then, are a mixed bag and do not emanate from formal or quasi-formal parties having identifiable slogans, but rather from people of some intelligence and learning, in lively combat over a variety of issues which had been, or were being, debated elsewhere.

The *Letter to Calosirius* is connected only by the theme of anthropomorphism with the other two. Its date is uncertain, and there is nothing to link the anthropomorphites at Calamon with the intruders in Palestine or the contentious Egyptians of the second piece. Cyril's spies in the monastery (this is not simply casual news brought by accidental visitors to Alexandria) told him about the anthropomorphites there, about some odd views on the eucharist being circulated by the same people, about some work-shy monks, and about the indiscriminate communion with Meletians going on there. On all of these matters Cyril delivers a brisk judgement whose wide circulation he requires. The tone of the letter is polite, but there is a touch of rebuke, no doubt, in the very fact that it needed to be sent.

The common theme of these pieces is the 'form' of God and God's image in man. Though the fact that some simple souls took literally the Biblical metaphors would seem to require little comment, there is a background to the phenomenon, as it meets us here in distinct communities, that deserves a brief mention. Anthropomorphism had been a burning issue in Egypt in the time of Theophilus, when disputes between anthropomorphite and Origenist monks, led by the Tall Brothers, produced violent disturbances. Theophilus, we are told,[68] sided at first with the Origenists but, faced with the superior forces of the anthropomorphites, did a *volte face*, declared for the anthropomorphites,

---

[68] Socrates, *Hist. Eccles.* 6, 7 ff.

and proceeded to orchestrate a campaign against Origen. Palestine, through Jerome, Rufinus, and John of Jerusalem, was brought into the disagreement, which eventually caught up John Chrysostom, who unwisely allowed himself to take up the cause of the persecuted Origenists. More than thirty years separate these events from our present documents, and there is certainly no obvious, direct connection. They are background and no more. The Bible, and the Bible only, was the religion of monks and nuns. The consequence of that was the prevalence of bad theology, of which the anthropomorphism we meet in these texts is the most striking example.

There is another reason for not connecting the anthropomorphism we find here closely with the phenomenon in the time of Theophilus. The argument between Origenists and anthropomorphites seems to have been not so much whether God has a human form or not, as whether he may be visualized in prayer as having a form or not. The Origenists were, it would seem, the exponents of the pure, imageless prayer of Evagrius, the anthropomorphites the representatives of a more affective practice. If this is right, there is certainly a difference from the discussions we find here. All our anthropomorphites are convinced that God has something corresponding with a human form because it says so in the Bible. Prayer does not enter into the question.

Cyril moves amongst these questions, some of which are embarrassing in their naïveté, with enviable aplomb. Although his replies are strictly occasional, directed to specific queries from groups with particular intellectual difficulties, they do in fact make up his fullest and most important treatment of the divine image in man, the transmission of sin and man's future hope, amongst other issues.

(d) Cyril's Theology—a Brief Appraisal

Christian theology is, in its essentials, an account of the nature of, and relationship between, three entities or alleged entities: God, Christ, and man. By Cyril's time what had to be said about the first and third, at least so far as their natures were concerned, was long decided. Popular belief lingered behind educated thought, as we can see from the second group of letters, but for trained theologians God was understood as the ground of the world and all existence, true being, absolute reality, the

omnipotent sustainer of all, who cares for man and will bring him to perfection. Man is a compound of naturally transitory body and naturally immortal soul, gifted with freedom of choice and therefore capable of abandoning his destiny and falling into a state of alienation from God, out of which he cannot extricate himself. As for Christ, all recognized after the protracted debate over the Trinity in the preceeding century that he was the means whereby God in person undertakes humanly to undo the wrong man has done himself.

What precisely this meant and how Christ, God in person humanly, was to be understood, was not yet decided. The Nestorian controversy and what Cyril said during its course were to produce a decision. The form of the debate (as we have seen) was determined by the accidents of history but there was no way round the debate itself once the Church had decreed (as it had by the time of the Council of Constantinople in 381) that Godhead admits of no degrees, and that the Son is on the same level of being as, is consubstantial with, his Father. Unless one can say in principle how this affirmation holds good of Jesus son of Mary, the words are idle. To put it in another way, the Nicene Creed, which Cyril loved to expound, contains a paradox: of the Son, who is God in precisely the same sense as his Father, are predicated human experiences—he became flesh, was made man, and suffered. All Catholic theologians of the period saw this as the innermost mystery of the Christian faith, the precondition and cause of man's restoration. All agreed that God is transcendent. Whatever he is like, he is not like Aphrodite wounded with a hero's spear and shrieking with pain.[69] That was pagan myth. God the Son assumes, acquires, or appropriates (various expressions were possible) manhood, or the human condition, or a human body; yet all his acts and experiences rest upon the free agency of a serene and impassible divine subject. All agreed too that no solution to this mystery could count as valid which rejected any component of Christ's humanity to accommodate the divine subject. The matter for debate was how to proceed from there.

Cyril's contribution to this debate was much of it negative, consisting in denials of a series of sharply drawn caricatures, using as a rule Nestorius' own words, whom he accuses of divid-

[69] *Iliad* 5, 335 ff.

ing the natures, of offering a picture of Christ as two beings, a
Son of God and a son of Mary, joined in a union analogous to
prophetic inspiration. It is a legitimate caricature, for it merely
accentuates certain features of the subject. Put in its simplest
form, what Nestorius believed is that the Incarnation is to be
explained as a union of wills—the will of God the Son and the
will of the human being, Jesus. The sufficiency of this explanation
Cyril passionately denies, and along with the denials he variously
and subtly repeats the mystery or paradox, which he did not,
in the end, think could be resolved. It is the descent of the eternal
Word of God into human conditions and limitations in order
radically to alter and restore them, without annihilating them.
God remains God and his manhood is manhood still, but now
charged with divine power and capable of restoring to fullness of
life the believer who shares in it sacramentally. If an analogy is
required for this union, to illustrate its possibility and its conditions, one must look to the relation of soul and body, two
distinct realities, which together constitute a single human being.
This is the only analogy which will do and Cyril brushes aside
all analogies based on mixing elements together or associating
one thing or person with another. It is an analogy which is
perfectly reliable for this one feature alone, namely unity of
distinct elements in a single being. It throws a little light on the
impassibility of God, for there is a sense in which the soul is
impassible because it is the immaterial agent, but only a little.[70]

[70] Cf. *Scholion* 2 (*ACO* 1, 5 p. 220): 'The soul lays claim (οἰκειοῦται) to all
that belongs to the body, though, so far as its own nature is concerned, it has
no share in the body's externally induced physical experiences. The body is
stimulated to natural desires and the soul within feels these along with it
because of the union; but the soul does not share them at all, though it takes
the accomplishment of the desire to be its own enjoyment. Even if the body
be hit by someone, say, or scratched with a knife, though it feels pain along
with the body, because its own body is suffering, it suffers none of these
inflictions itself in its own nature.' (That is to say: the soul is not itself knocked,
scratched, etc.; it is the register of the sensations connected with the body's
functions, whether these be active or passive). 'But we say that the union in the
case of Emmanuel is beyond this. The soul united with it must feel pain along
with its own body, in order that it may shun afflictions and bow in obedience
to God. But in the case of God the Word, it is absurd to speak of feeling the
afflictions along with anything—the divine is impassible and not within our
condition. Yet it was united with flesh possessing a rational soul, and when
the flesh suffers it was impassibly conscious of what happened to the flesh
and, as God, obliterated the weakness of the flesh yet claimed them as belonging

B

It must not be misapplied to mean that the human soul is replaced
by the divine subject; Cyril's disclaimers of the standard heretics
of half a century back, Eunomius and Apollinarius, who denied
Christ a human mind, are repeated and genuine. The Incarnation is a union, not a partnership, voluntary or involuntary on
the human side, of persons or natures. There are not two sons
of God, but one. A man has not become God; God has become
man. The Blessed Virgin Mary must not be refused the title
'Mother of God', therefore, for the same Son of God is also her son.

Cyril's Christology, at the level of philosophical explanation,
will always seem thin. It lacks the barrage of technical jargon to
be developed over the next century—'communication of idioms',
'composite hypostasis', 'enhypostatic humanity', 'hypostatic
union' (he did invent the last, but it was not for him a technical
term and he dropped it quickly). In the end, one will probably
judge that these terms do no more than give a name to a problem
and a comforting illusion that it has thereby gone away. Cyril's
innocence of jargon, his simplicity over against the sophistications
of his opponents and even of his interpreters, is his strength.
What is the use of trying to explain that which, if it were
explained, would cease to be of any religious interest? The
theologian's task must be something different.

There is the way of exploration, of allowing the fancy to range
amongst the poetic symbols, allusions, and metaphors of the Bible.
The ark of the covenant, the burning coal of Isaiah's vision, and
many others direct the heart towards wonder at the Emmanuel,
'God with us', who is the mysterious, paradoxical centre of
theology. Cyril is the only theologian of genius there has ever
been of whom it is true to say, almost without metaphor, that
his theology was 'Christocentric'. He draws the mind always
back to the Jesus Christ who is the point to which all the Bible's
proclamation immediately relates. Whereas for Augustine, as for
most theologians, Jesus Christ recedes in the end to give place
to something else (in Augustine's case, to the inscrutable will of
God), for Cyril the Incarnation is the form and justification of
the faith that the God who is all-powerful and good beyond
imagining has repaired the ravages of sin, given men freedom
and the holiness which is his outpoured Spirit. Christ is, in a

to his own body. This is what it means to say he hungered, was tired and
suffered for us.'

word, for Cyril divine grace. Therefore, for him, Christology and
theology are the same thing. The 'explanation' of Christ is his
connexion with all else that can and must be said.

How this is so can be seen from these letters, where all Cyril's
leading thoughts which give colour to his picture of Christ are
to be found. The inexpressible nature of God, the creation of
man in God's image, his fall into sin and its effects, his present
state of preparation for the life to come where he will enjoy
ultimate security—all these are reflected here and specially in
the less well known second group. They explain a feature which
may otherwise seem absurd: the peculiar passion Cyril brought
to the Nestorian controversy. The disquieting emotion which
meets us so blatantly in the *Third Letter to Nestorius* results from
identifying Christology and theology. By disputing the mode of
God's involvement or engagement with man in Christ, Nestorius
questioned its purpose and so the whole of the Christian message.
For if man's creation, his present condition, and future hope
are all bound up with the divine grace which is Christ, it will not
do to think of Christ as a good man or a very good man, an
inspired man or a very inspired man, an important or a very
important example of divine grace. It will not do to explain the
Incarnation as a union of wills dependent upon the essentially
transitory and fragile responsiveness of the human subject in
Christ. Grace cannot depend upon anything, least of all upon
the waverings of the best even of human wills. Grace must be
unconditional and the Incarnation a binding of the Son of God
with man in a union stronger than, because more basic than,
any human act or choice. To divide the One Christ must be to
divide man from life and grace. Because these were his convictions, he became passionate, angry and unfair to his opponents in
controversy. No one would praise Cyril for his open-mindedness
or his ability to hold in fruitful tension, for the Church's good,
views which were at odds with one another and with his whole
understanding of the faith. But he would not have wished, nor
should any wise man wish, for such praise.

(e) *A Note on the Anathematisms*

These twelve striking 'chapters' deserve a note to themselves.
Attached to his ultimatum to Nestorius, they were essential to

Cyril's strategy, but they were a tricky piece of weaponry and nearly lost him the war.

Their immediate aim was to secure the conviction of Nestorius on doctrinal grounds. Cyril's second letter had not been enough. On being told there to affirm the Nicene Creed, Nestorius had constructed a reasoned and subtly sarcastic reply. Yes, of course he accepted the Nicene Creed, but ought not his colleague to take a closer look at the text of that document which by no means favoured his Arian and Apollinarian misconceptions?[71] Cyril needed to put a document before Nestorius about which he could not equivocate, and so he sent him for his immediate signature an exposition of the faith, to which was annexed this set of propositions, which, starting with an assertion of the human birth of the Word such that the Blessed Virgin Mary can be called 'Mother of God', moves through a series of rejections of any distinct human agent in Christ to culminate in assertions of the divine efficacy of Christ's eucharistic body and of the fleshly suffering and death of the Word of God. He wrote these chapters with passion, and he cast them deliberately in the strongest and most uncompromising terms, which cut across all the delicate provisos Nestorius had learned to make.

Nestorius was outraged and promptly spread the outrage all over the East. Copies of the offensive chapters were sent to John of Antioch, who galvanized all the pamphleteers he could find (the most important were bishops Andreas of Samosata and Theodoret, the distinguished theologian and Church historian, of Cyrrhus)[72] to write rebuttals. Cyril had put Nestorius in the wrong, but at the price of enflaming the East. Nestorius now had a breadth of support he would otherwise never have enjoyed. For when the controversy was still brewing John had written a warning letter to Nestorius advising caution and reminding

---

[71] *ACO* 1, 1, 1 pp. 29–32, esp. para. 2: The Nicene fathers declared that the Only-begotten Son came down, was incarnate, made man, suffered, and rose again. But attend to what they said. 'Because reading the tradition of these holy men superficially, as you do, you show a pardonable ignorance by supposing that they said that the Word, co-eternal with the Father, was passible. Please to look more closely at the words, and you will discover that this same choir of fathers did not declare the consubstantial Godhead passible or newly born the Godhead co-eternal with the Father, nor the Godhead which raised up the dissolved temple did they say rose again.'

[72] *ACO* 1, 1, 7 pp. 33–65; *ACO* 1, 1, 6 pp. 107–46.

him that even their master Theodore of Mopsuestia had admitted freely and publicly to error. Without the chapters Nestorius could have expected no help from John or from men of judgement. Now they would make common cause with him.

When the Easterns arrived at Ephesus, seething with indignation over the contents of these chapters, they were deprived of the satisfaction of debating them with their author. Cyril, at the meeting of his assembly on 22 June 431, had already dealt with all that part of the business and inserted the *Third Letter to Nestorius* in the minutes along with evidence from the bearers of the letter telling how they had handed it over to Nestorius with Celestine's letter at the bishop's house after Sunday morning service, had been invited back for discussion the following day, and had then had the doors shut on them.[73] The doors remained shut for obvious reasons. The point of including the letter in the minutes with the accompanying evidence is legal. Nestorius' acceptance of the letters and his refusal to sign the anathematisms convict him of knowingly committing the offence of failing to retract his errors and affirm the faith of Alexandria and Rome within the specified time. Their role, therefore, was strictly limited, and their specific doctrine was not officially discussed at the Council, though Cyril's *Solutio* (an explanation, without dedication or address, designed to explain them in a sober manner) may well be an unofficial contribution to the assembly.[74] The doctrinal stand of the Council was taken upon the *Second Letter to Nestorius*, a copy of which had been sent to Rome. No copy of the *Third Letter to Nestorius* was sent, and the chapters were unknown until the reign of Justin (518–27).[75] Assuming that the minutes of the Council of 431 are a fair record, the Roman delegates, when they arrived, ratified the previous

---

[73] *ACO* 1, 1, 2 pp. 36 f.

[74] *ACO* 1, 1, 5 pp. 15–25, headed in some manuscripts: Explanation of the 12 Chapters delivered at Ephesus by Archbishop Cyril of Alexandria, the holy Council having asked him for a plainer explanation of them to be set out clearly.

[75] The evidence is usefully drawn together by N. M. Haring, 'The Character and Range of the Influence of St. Cyril of Alexandria on Latin Theology (430–1260)' *Medieval Studies* 12 (1950), 1–19. For Dionysius Exiguus' claim to present the first Latin version see *ACO* 1, 5 p. 236, 9 ff., with Schwartz's observations, pp. IIII *et seq*. See also P. Galtier, 'Les anathématismes de Saint Cyrille et le Concile de Chalcédoine', *RSR* 23 (1933), 45–57.

business, which included the deposition of Nestorius and the account of the evidence, the failure to obey Celestine and Cyril, on which that had been based, and approved in an indefinite way the content of the chapters.

Rome had no interest in the chapters. The Eastern bishops, though, had—it was what united them in opposition to Cyril. Their complaints were loud, persistent, and widely circulated. There could be no doctrinal agreement unless the chapters were nullified.[76] It was impossible for Cyril to do that, not only because they expressed his convictions, but because the deposition of Nestorius rested upon their validity.[77] A modification of the fourth is conceded in the Formula of Reunion, and Cyril explains carefully to Acacius that this involves no sacrifice of principle.[78] But though he never withdrew the chapters, Cyril could not and would not insist upon them.

Cyril's immediate successors, who with no real justification announced themselves as the bearers of the master's message, were not so wise. At the *Latrocinium* (449) Dioscorus had them promulgated,[79] and their opponents Theodoret and Ibas of Edessa, author of a letter to a certain Maris containing astringent observations about them and about Cyril, condemned and

---

[76] See *ACO* 1, 1, 5 pp. 121 ff. and 124 ff.

[77] Cf. his letter to Acacius of Beroea, *Ep.* 33 § 2, written in 432: 'It is a perverse zeal shown by people, who ought to anathematize Nestorius' foul dogmas and separate themselves from his irreligion, to seek the nullification of what was written against him. What rationale does that have? Your holiness must appreciate the absurdity of the thing were we writers on behalf of orthodoxy to deny our own words and condemn our own faith instead. Unless, therefore, the writings against Nestorius or his unhallowed dogmas are sound, his deposition is empty, his sentiments are somehow orthodox and it is we who are in the wrong . . .'. When peace and harmony were restored he was willing, he said, to satisfy, not enemies, but brethren that 'what we have written in opposition to Nestorius' dogmas is all sound and absolutely consonant with the holy and inspired scriptures' and the Nicene Creed. See *ACO* 1, 1, 7 pp. 147 ff. Nothing came of the last undertaking.

[78] See para. 13.

[79] *Akten der ephesinischen Synode vom Jahre 449*, ed. J. Flemming, *Abh. der Kgl. Ges. der Wiss. zu Göttingen*, Phil.-hist Kl., N.S. 15 (1917), 146/*147*. There is a break in the manuscript at this point, but it is clear that they were read after the announcement. Dioscorus thus brutally upset the balance established by the Formula of Reunion, for the Eastern bishops had never accepted the Chapters. (In Domnus' letter to Dioscorus, ibid. pp. 144/*145*, we are certainly to read, against the manuscript, that the twelve chapters were *not* accepted by the Easterns.)

deprived. The Council of Chalcedon (451) reversed the verdicts on Theodoret and Ibas[80] (a move which would ensure that the Council was rejected by many loyal Cyrillines), and the Church, in no mood to offer aid or comfort to Dioscorus, did not go beyond asserting the general validity of the *Third Letter to Nestorius* as part of the faith affirmed at Ephesus (431).[81] The norms decreed by the Council of Chalcedon were: the Creeds of Nicaea (325) and Constantinople (381); Cyril's *Second Letter to Nestorius* and *Letter to John* containing the Formula of Reunion; and Pope Leo's *Tome*. This last was admitted only after a probing which involved quotations from the *Tome* including the lines: 'For each form effects what belongs to it, in communion with the other, i.e. whilst the Word does what pertains to the Word and the flesh accomplishes what pertains to the flesh, one of them shines with wonders and the other falls victim to pains.'[82] Such dualist language could be justified by comparison with the *Letter to Acacius* (of which p. 52 below, lines 14 ff., were quoted, along with other passages, to prove the point), but it would have been very unwise to test it by the standard of Anathemas 3 and 4. Bishop Atticus of Nicopolis nearly succeeded in opening the can of worms, but the discussion he asked for was postponed for five days and never took place.[81]

The inconsistency, though, was unlikely to be overlooked by opponents of Chalcedon. The years following 451 saw the end of 'Antiochene' Christology—indeed, this Christology was the work of Theodore and his immediate pupils and did not long survive them in the Greek-speaking world; Cyril's status was almost unchallenged. East and West were divided politically with the collapse of the Western empire. Rome's views had no political significance, and the Emperor Zeno, advised by Acacius, Patriarch of Constantinople, sacrificed Western agreement for Eastern harmony by issuing on his own authority an *Edict of Union* (Henoticon) in 482. In this the dogmatic decisions of the Council of Chalcedon were by-passed, the *Tome* of Leo implicitly set aside, the Chapters of Cyril accepted as authoritative.[84]

---

[80] Actio XI.

[81] *ACO* 2, 1 p. 196, 2 ff.

[82] 94 f. in the edition by C. Silva-Tarouca in *Textus et Documenta Series Theologica* 9 (Rome, 1959).

[83] *ACO* 2, 1 pp. 279, 3 ff.

[84] *Codex Vaticanus gr. 1431* (above, n. 62), pp. 52–4, esp. p. 53, 27–54, 6.

A schism, the Acacian, between East and West resulted. The emperor Anastasius, careless of Roman reactions, reinforced this judgement in a letter of 505, in which he rejected Chalcedon, along with Leo's *Tome*, on the ground that they were incompatible with Cyril's chapters.[85]

The reign of Justin introduced a new era in ecclesiastical affairs. The unity of the empire, and the unity of the Church, East and West, was to be a renewed theme of imperial policy. And more than that, Justinian (Justin's nephew, close counsellor, and successor) cared for doctrinal truth. That meant the end of the mediating theology of the *Henoticon* and a restoration of the authority of Leo's *Tome* and of the Council which had canonized it. The chapters of Cyril could not conceivably have been set aside. By now they were too well known, too authoritative for that. This new doctrinal settlement presented a challenge. How was the non-acceptance of the chapters at Chalcedon to be accounted for? Why did that Council instead implicitly reject them by restoring their opponents Theodoret and Ibas to office? These were the questions pressed by theologians of the *ancien régime*. To the first question conflicting answers were given. At a conference in the capital in 533 between Catholics and followers of Severus, distinguished theologian and former Patriarch of Antioch, now an exiled victim of the change of policy, the reply was given: that the chapters are inconsistent in their terminology with Cyril's ordinary usage, for in the chapters he speaks of two hypostases; the Council of Chalcedon had therefore refrained from accepting them to avoid the inconsistency.[86] The answer had a certain plausibility, no doubt, for people who had not read the *Acta*, and at least this much truth that the Council had *not* received the chapters. The false assumption that ruled at the *Fifth General Council* in 553 was that they had been received as authoritative from the very beginning by all parties and had been ratified at the Council of Chalcedon. Justinian writes in 549/550 to defenders of the Three Chapters (i.e. the works of Theodore of Mopsuestia *en bloc*, Theodoret's writings against the

---

[85] See F. C. Conybeare's translation, *American Journal of Theology* 9 (1905), 739 f. (reproduced in P. R. Coleman-Norton, *Roman State and Christian Church* (London, 1966), no. 542, p. 951) and 'Un fragment du Type de l'empereur Anastase I', by C. Moeller, *Studia Patristica* III (Berlin, 1961), pp. 240–7.

[86] See Innocentius of Maronea, *On the conference with the Severians* (*ACO* 4, 2, p. 173, 19 ff.). The reference is to the 3rd Anathematism (p. 28, line 29).

Chapters, and Ibas' *Letter to Maris*) that 'sainted Celestine, the first Council of Ephesus, sainted Leo, and the holy Council of Chalcedon accepted and ratified these very chapters of sainted Cyril and sought no further interpretation of them'.[87] As for the second question, the answer given by the Council of 553 was in effect a practical one, doing what might well have been done at Chalcedon itself had the chapters there been received (as the current myth supposed). Their most notable opponents were condemned, and Theodore, the father of 'Antiochene' Christology, the Nestorius before Nestorius and so indirect object of the anathematisms, condemned *in toto*.

Their structure. A later rumour was current that Cyril had written the anathematisms first and afterwards prefixed the letter.[88] The rumour is surely false, but almost certainly the chapters circulated independently. Their opponents, Theodoret and Andreas, make no allusion to the rest of the letter even when their case would have been strengthened by so doing. There is, for example, no mention of the phrase the 'one incarnate subject (ὑπόστασις) of the Word', although that was open to all the objections raised by Succensus' questioners against its equivalent, 'the one incarnate nature (φύσις) of the Word', as we see in Cyril's second letter to him. The number of the chapters, 12, has relation with the tribes of Israel and the Apostles rather than with theology, of course. The relationship between the chapters and the rest of the letter has a few oddities, which can best be explained on the assumption that both were not, so to say, written in the same breath—and this despite the fact that the chapters go over almost all the ground covered in the letter: (1) the order is unrelated to the rest of the letter; (2) no. 7 has no counterpart in the letter; (3) qualifications are made in the letter which are not made in the chapters. The arrangement of the chapters is without significance, and their text contains a large number of small variants, even in their different appearances in Cyril in the replies to Theodoret and Andreas, the *Solutio*, the *Third Letter to Nestorius*, and *Letter to Acacius*.

[87] *Drei dogmatische Schriften Iustinians*, ed. E. Schwartz (*Abh. der Bay. Akad. der Wiss.* N.F. 18 (1939), 62, 24 ff.). The piece is to be dated 549/550, cf. Schwartz's notes, p. 115.

[88] See R. Y. Ebied/L. R. Wickham, 'An unknown letter of Cyril of Alexandria in Syriac', *JTS* 22 (1971), 420–34.

Their intention and theology. The sharpness and clarity of these chapters—a consequence of the intense emotion which lies behind them—made them eventually a standard of orthodoxy for Catholic Christians and rightly, because talk about Incarnation slips into vagueness without these reminders that Christ is not only, not simply, a special case of divine immanence.

The complaint made by the Easterns was that they are replete with Apollinarian and Eunomian blasphemies. What they meant is that the chapters imply that Christ had no human mind, that the Word's 'coming down from heaven' and 'being made man' is not an act of grace in which there is a confluence of divine and human wills but the animation by impersonal process of an inert human body. Christ is then a hybrid, neither impassible God nor passible man but an obscene mixture of both. The complaint is vain and unsubstantiated by any reading of the text. Yet we can sympathize to some extent with the charge. The chapters will always shock timid minds. The delicate veil of nuanced provisos is torn away, and we are presented with the logical consequences of what we have been saying all along, if, that is, we have been speaking of Incarnation. Moreover, Apollinarianism (to which the Easterns believed they alone had the answer) is a wicked and destructive belief because it cuts away the ground of redemption by denying Christ's healing presence at the point where it is most needed—in the human mind. Obsessed with the need to preserve that difference between God and man which is the premise of all theology, including most certainly Cyril's, Antiochene theologians were bound to see Apollinarianism in the chapters.

Cyril's answers to these 'refutations', produced rapidly and probably before the Council met in June 431, concede nothing real, for there was nothing he needed to concede. To some extent his explanations draw the string from the anathematisms (his deepest concern being to demonstrate that he had said nothing new); a phrase like καθ' ὑπόστασιν, which has a technical ring to it, is interpreted along prosaic lines.

Potentially more damaging to his cause in the long run than anything he wrote in the chapters was the company he kept. His allies were odd. Theodotus of Ancyra, for example, a principal associate of Cyril in the Nestorius affair, preached that the mode of the incarnation was analogous to the turning of the

Nile to blood and that no duality was to be observed in Christ even at the level of speculation.[89] Moreover Cyril certainly appealed to 'Apollinarian' texts circulating under venerable names to support his teaching. In the end, these had little effect upon his cause. The charge of 'Apollinarianism' did not stick. By the time it had become accepted in the sixth century that Cyril had drawn on 'Apollinarian' sources[90] his reputation was, in any case, unassailable. Cyril himself would probably not have been perturbed by the discovery of his sources. 'There is no obligation', he tells Eulogius (p. 63), 'to shun and reject everything heretics say—they affirm many of the points we too affirm'. A certain shared concern, a certain community of terminology between 'Apollinarian' writings and these chapters shows itself. One could go further, perhaps, and say that Cyril here presents in sharply defined form the core of all that was of serious religious importance in Apollinarius' thought: the unity of God and man in Christ Jesus, the Saviour. Yet that assertion would only be a damaging admission were one to allow guilt by association. Nor, perhaps, ought it to influence (though that is a wider issue) any estimate of Apollinarius himself.

2. *The Text*

The Letters to Nestorius, Acacius, Eulogius, Succensus and *On the Creed*

Our primary sources for most of Cyril's letters, including these here, are the large ancient collections of documents relating to the Council of Ephesus (431). Besides these there are abundant quotations in florilegia, doctrinal treatises, and subsequent councils of the Church. These witnesses formed the basis for

---

[89] See his second sermon on Christ's birth, read at the Council of Ephesus (431), *ACO* 1, 1, 2 pp. 80–90, esp. p. 83, 36–85, 10. The Latin version (*ACO* 1, 3 p. 156) has the marginal note: 'Here you will get very bad illustrations from mutable and perishable things.'

[90] A great deal has been written about this. For the facts and some sensible observations, see P. Galtier, 'Saint Cyrille et Apollinaire', *Gregorianum* 37 (1956), 584–609. With this compare and contrast H.-M. Diepen, 'Stratagèmes contre la théologie de l'Emmanuel: à propos d'une nouvelle comparaison entre Saint Cyrille et Apollinaire', *Divinitas* 1 (1957), 444–78. Diepen has written extensively on Cyril. With the negative critique of his opponents, as with the general vigour of his approach, all admirers of Cyril will sympathize. Like Hamlet's lady, though, he protests too much.

Eduard Schwartz's edition in Tome 1 of *Acta Conciliorum Oecumenicorum*, an edition superseding Aubert's of 1638 (reprinted in Migne *PG* 77). The text here presented is substantially that established by Schwartz, and I acknowledge with gratitude the permission granted by the publishers, Walter de Gruyter and Co, and by Schwartz's successor as editor of the series, Professor Dr Johannes Straub of Bonn, to reproduce his text. I have thought it unnecessary to reproduce Schwartz's apparatus. On the rare occasions when I have selected a reading different from his I have indicated the fact. An editor of these documents rapidly discovers, after reading through the main manuscripts which Schwartz used, that he has little to do. The textual problems, almost without exception, have been solved as well as they are likely to be. The one or two cases of radical textual corruption are ancient and must go back to the first copies.

A few lines must suffice to describe the primary sources. The details are to be found in Schwartz's various prefaces to the volumes of *ACO* Tome 1.[91] The Council of Ephesus (431) is the first general council whose minutes and accompanying papers survive. These conciliar records are not neutral documents. They are collections with a propagandist tendency, as it belongs to Schwartz to have shown clearly. This is most obviously true of collections dealing with Ephesus (431). Each of the two opposing groups, headed by Cyril and John of Antioch, produced its own. The doctrinal battle was lost by the Easterns in the long run, and only a few of their documents survive in Greek. However, they did not perish entirely. A good number survive in a Latin translation made by Rusticus, the nephew of Pope Vigilius, at the time of the Three Chapters controversy in the reign of Justinian. Justinian and Eastern Christianity decreed the official condemnation of Nestorius' teacher, Theodore, and of opponents of Cyril's anathematisms, Theodoret and Ibas. The Pope vacillated and eventually agreed, but with loud protestations in the West, especially from Africa. Rusticus, one of the protesters, in producing his Synodicon drew upon material he found in the monastery of the Acoimeti at Constantinople, including a work called *The Tragedy of Irenaeus* by Irenaeus, bishop of Tyre, who had been a loyal friend of Nestorius. Its 'tendency' is to defend

[91] A convenient summary will be found in P. Galtier, 'Le Centenaire d'Ephèse', *RSR* 21 (1931), 169–99.

the condemned theologians; it does so partly by quotation from Cyril's opponents. This collection of documents bears the title *Collectio Casinensis* in Schwartz's edition (from the connexion with the library of the abbey at Monte Cassino). It is to be found in *ACO* 1, 3 and 1, 4. The minutes of Cyril's Council were kept, and Cyril himself was responsible for circulating an edited version of them widely. These, together with large numbers of related papers, are to be found in three big Greek collections, named in accordance with the libraries they belonged in, *Collectio Vaticana* (V), *Collectio Seguierana* (S),[92] and *Collectio Atheniensis* (A). The fullest in material here is V, 172 items in all, ending with the two epistles to Successus. S was in origin a short collection to which items from V were subsequently added. A is a collection basically of Alexandrine provenance but containing material found in Irenaeus' *Tragedy* and in an important collection of documents made in the time of the Emperor Zeno as directed against the Council of Chalcedon in *Codex Vaticanus gr. 1431* (R) (edited by Schwartz also). Each collection has its history which can in part be traced; each has a nucleus to which further documents have been added. Latin collections were comparatively late in arriving. Though some of the most significant documents were made available in Latin versions almost immediately (Cyril's Second Letter to Nestorius, for example, and extracts from Nestorius' sermons) the West remained in many ways badly informed about, and indifferent towards, the Council. About a century was to elapse before Latin collections (of which the *Casinensis* mentioned above is the most important example) began to make their appearance. All are concerned in one way or another with the *Three Chapters* controversy, which gave an impetus to examining the history of the controversy's origins. The first important stage in the establishment of these Latin collections came with the translation, about the end of the fifth century, of the *Third Letter to Nestorius*, by Dionysius Exiguus. When the controversy was well under way the *Collectio Palatina*

---

[92] Named after Pierre Séguier, Chancellor of France (d. 1672), whose grandson Coislin presented his collection of manuscripts, including Codex Parisinus Coislinianus 32 which contains it to the abbey of S. Germain des Prés, whence it passed to the Bibliothèque Nationale in Paris. Another version of this collection was also used by Schwartz; see *ACO* 1, 1, 1 p. ii and 1, 1, 2 p. v; cf. also 4, 3, 1 p. 18.

(*ACO* 1, 5)[93] was produced. The documents selected here were designed to attack the Eastern bishops, and specially Theodoret. It is a collection whose apparent aim was to propagate the monist Christology of the Scythian (Gothic) monks, strong opponents of the Acoimeti; their formula was 'one of the Trinity suffered in the flesh'. It is this slant which largely prevailed at the Council of Constantinople (553). To the same period belongs the *Collectio Turonenis* (*ACO* 1, 3), used evidently by Liberatus writing shortly after 553. Its stance is Cyrilline. The *Collectio Veronensis* (*ACO* 1, 2), evidently compiled after 553, has as its aim the demonstration that the Holy See fully concurred in the decisions of the Council of Ephesus (431). It is a justification, on the basis of past history, of the policy eventually adopted by Vigilius. Volume 5 of Tome 1 of *ACO* also contains three smaller collections of varying provenance, named after their first editors: Sichardiana,[94] Quesneliana,[95] and Winteriana.[96] These ancient Latin translations are of some help in establishing the text. They vary though in literalness and literacy and not unusually fudge a difficult phrase.

Ancient quotations are notoriously unreliable. Schwartz thought it worth while to include readings from *Doctrina Patrum de incarnatione Verbi*, a seventh-century florilegium, and the *Florilegium Cyrillianum*, a collection of texts containing many passages from the letters here edited, designed to show the conformity of the Council of Chalcedon with the mind of Cyril and rebutted by Severus of Antioch in his *Philalethes*. Other citations figure in his apparatus. The evidence here is overwhelming in extent and fundamentally valueless for the text, however important it may be for the history of how later generations understood Cyril. I have made occasional reference also to the Syriac of Brit. Lib. Add. MS 14557 (*Σ*) for the last five letters. Its general testimony I have not thought worth reproducing here; that can be found in the apparatus to the edition printed in *CSCO* vols. 359/360, Scriptores Syri vols. 157/*158*, under the title *A Collection of*

---

[93] So named after the Vatican codex, Palatinus 234, which contains it.
[94] Johannes Sichardt (Sichardus), the German jurist and humanist (d. 1552), Basle, 1528. See *ACO* 1, 5, 2 pp. i ff.
[95] The French scholar Paschasius (Pasquier) Quesnel (d. 1719), 1675. See *ACO* 1, 5, 2 pp. XIIII ff.
[96] Robert Winter, Basle, 1542. See *ACO* 1, 5, 2 pp. XVII f.

Unpublished Syriac Letters of Cyril of Alexandria, ed. R. Y. Ebied/L. R. Wickham.

The Answers to Tiberius, Doctrinal Questions and Answers, and *Letter to Calosirius*

These pieces found no place in collections of conciliar texts and were transmitted separately.

The *Answer to Tiberius*, which includes an introductory address and a letter of explanation from the Palestinian monks, survives complete only in a Syriac version, Brit. Lib. Add. MS 14531, folios 119r–141r, dated by Wright to the seventh or eighth centuries. The Greek original which is printed here is based primarily on two manuscripts: the Florentine Laurentianus plut. vi. 17 (11th cent.), folios 210 *et seqq.*, starting, through loss of a folio, with the second *Answer*; and the Vatican Cod. gr. 447 (12th cent.), folios 302r–312r, also beginning with the second *Answer*.

The *Doctrinal Questions and Answers* likewise survives in its original layout, so far as I know uniquely, in a translation, this time into Armenian, found in two manuscripts in the Bodleian Library at Oxford (Arm.e.20, dated 1394, folios 37v–48r; and Arm.e.36, dated 1689, folios 33v–42v).[97] A printed edition of this version was produced at the press of Karapet in Constantinople in 1717.[98] A third manuscript, San Lazzaro 308 (14th cent.), whose contents are identical with Bodleian Arm.e.20, I have not consulted. According to F. C. Conybeare,[99] the translation belongs to the eighth century. It was evidently made from a good Greek text, which it renders with painful literalness. The primary witnesses to the original Greek are again contained in the Florentine and Vatican manuscripts mentioned above. The Florentine manuscript contains the introductory letter starting

---

[97] See G. Zarbhanalian, *Catalogue des anciennes traductions arméniennes (siècles IV–XIII)* (Venice, 1889), p. 510.

[98] See Vrej Nersessian, *Catalogue of Early Armenian Books 1512–1850* (British Library, 1980), no. 96, for the British Library copy (defective). The copy I used is in the possession of Wadham College, Oxford, whom I thank for permission to consult it, as I also thank Mr. D. Barrett of the Bodleian Library for drawing my attention to it.

[99] F. C. Conybeare, *The Armenian Version of Revelation and Cyril of Alexandria's Scholia on the Incarnation and Epistle on Easter* (Oxford, 1907), pp. 165 ff.

on folio 206v and ending on folio 209v with the fifth *Answer*;
the Vatican manuscript has no introductory letter but is otherwise complete in folios 295r–302r.

The Letter to Calosirius is complete in its original independent
form, apparently uniquely, in folios 214v *et seq.* of the Florentine
manuscript. A small fragment is found also in the sixteenth-
century Berlin manuscript Phillipicus gr. 1475, folios 21r and v.[100]

Selected chapters from the *Answers to Tiberius* and *Doctrinal
Questions and Answers* are found in folios 116v–121r of the Paris
manuscript Cod. gr. 1115 (dated 1276), where they appear as
part of a florilegium of unknown authorship. This is a useful
additional witness, despite its numerous mistakes.

Neither the Armenian version of the *Doctrinal Questions and
Answers* nor the Vatican manuscript was known to Philip Pusey
who first edited these three pieces under their correct designation
and genuine form in 1872.[101] In 1903 Cardinal G. Mercati
published from the Vatican manuscript the two paragraphs of
the *Doctrinal Questions and Answers* missing from the Florentine
manuscript but without collating the whole text of this or of the
Answers to Tiberius.[102] The present is the first complete edition
of the Greek text.

Before Pusey these pieces had been known, from Bonaventura
Vulcanius' edition of 1605,[103] as a single treatise by Cyril *Against
the Anthropomorphites* in twenty-eight chapters, preceded by the
Letter to Calosirius, the last five chapters being drawn from
Gregory of Nyssa's *Christmas Sermon*.[104] The first twenty-three
chapters present most of the *Answers to Tiberius* and the *Doctrinal
Questions and Answers* though in a jumbled order.[105] A number of
manuscripts, the most ancient of which is the fourteenth-century
Venetian Marcianus graecus 2.122 (= 295), present this extra-

---

[100] See *Byzantinische Zeitschrift* 9 (1900), 43 n. 1, and the catalogue by W.
Stundemund and L. Cohn (1890), vol. 1, no. 71, pp. 23 f.

[101] Pusey 3, 545–607.

[102] *Varia Sacra*, fasc. 1 (*Studi e Testi* 11; Rome, 1903), pp. 83–6: 'Un nuovo
frammento del 1. "de dogmatum solutione" di S. Cirillo Alessandrino.'

[103] Printed at Leiden. It was reproduced by Aubert in vol. 6 of his complete
edition of Cyril's works (Paris, 1638) and taken over into *PG* 76, 1065–1132.

[104] *PG* 46, 1128–1149. Now properly edited by F. Mann, *Die Weihnachts-
predigt Gregors von Nyssa: Überlieferungsgeschichte und Text*, Doctoral Dissertation,
Münster (Westf.), 1976.

[105] See Pusey 3, 545 for a table of comparisons for his edition.

ordinarily free re-working of patristic texts.[106] When this version was produced we do not know, except that the heading to the *Answer to Tiberius* 4 has κατὰ ἀγνοητῶν, implying the existence of the Agnoete sect which emerged in the sixth century; it will post-date the sixth century, then. The text-form of this version contains a substantial number of variants from that otherwise known, mostly in the order of words, and its evidence may safely be disregarded, seeing that it is in effect a fresh work *based upon* Cyril of Alexandria and not a text *of* Cyril of Alexandria. I have accordingly made only rare references to it in the apparatus.[107]

I have mentioned in this edition only the ancient quotations found in the *Florilegium Cyrillianum*.

Where the Greek text is lost Pusey printed the Syriac version. Here I have given only an English translation. The complete Syriac text of the *Answers to Tiberius* with an earlier translation, the known mistakes in which I have now here rectified, will be found in R. Y. Ebied and L. R. Wickham, 'The Letter of Cyril of Alexandria to Tiberius the Deacon', *Le Muséon* 83 (1970), 433–82.

---

[106] Besides this I know of

(i) a Basle University manuscript, Codex gr. 32 (A III 4) folios 117 *et seqq.* (14th cent.). It is mutilated at the end and terminates with chapter 17 (= *Answers to Tiberius* 15); see H. Omont, *Catalogue des Manuscrits Grecs des Bibliothèques de Suisse*, Extrait du Centralblatt für Bibliothekwesen (Leipzig, 1886), pp. 16 f.;

(ii) a Munich manuscript Codex gr. 65, folios 100 *et seqq.* (16th cent.); see I. Hardt's catalogue, vol. 1 (1806), pp. 378 ff.;

(iii) Vulcanius' own manuscript in the University Library at Leiden, Vulc. 5, folios 2 *et seqq.* (15th cent. for this part of the manuscript); see *Codices Manuscripti Bibliothecae Universitatis Leidensis I: Codices Vulcaniani* (Leiden, 1910), p. 3, and P. C. Molhuysen, 'De Cyrillus-Handschriften van Bonaventura Vulcanius', *Tijdschrift voor Boek en Bibliothekwesen* 3 (1905), 71–4.

I have collated these manuscripts, which are closely similar. The Basle and the Venetian manuscripts are not transcripts one of the other, but both derive, I suspect, from a common source, perhaps at one remove, since both include an explanation of Hebrew letters Aleph, Beth, etc. Otherwise there is no over-lap of contents. For the Venetian manuscript see the catalogue of Zanetti and Bongiovanni (1740), p. 70.

[107] Where I have referred to it, I have mentioned the readings of the Basle manuscript, which has some claim, I think, to be the purest version of this work. It can only, of course, be the relative purity of one harlot to another, seeing that this is an adulterous piece.

BIBLIOGRAPHY

All standard textbooks on Church history and doctrine in this period include accounts of the Nestorian controversy. That of L. Duchesne in vol. III translated under the title *The Early History of the Christian Church* (London, 1924) is perhaps the liveliest. For a survey of Christology A. Grillmeier, *Christ in Christian Tradition*, vol. 1: *From the Apostolic Age to Chalcedon* (451) (2nd revised edition, London, 1975) is indispensable. A full but uninspiring analysis of Cyril's theology as a whole is to be found in H. Du Manoir de Juaye, *Dogme et Spiritualité chez S. Cyrille d'Alexandrie* (Paris, 1944). A short, vivid account is given of Cyril in G. L. Prestige, *Fathers and Heretics* (London, 1940) as also of Apollinarius and Nestorius in the same work. The articles on Cyril in *DTC* (J. Mahé) and, *RAC* (G. Jouassard) are still useful, and to these may now be added the article by E. R. Hardy in *TRE*. The fullest and most sympathetic recent discussion of Nestorius is that of L. Scipioni, *Nestorio e il concilio di Efeso* (Milan, 1974). Much valuable information and a fine insight into Cyril is found in the notes and introductions to G. M. de Durand's editions of the two dialogues *De incarnatione unigeniti* and *Quod unus sit Christus* in *Cyrille d'Alexandrie Deux Dialogues Christologiques* (*SC* 97; Paris, 1964) and in those to his edition of the Dialogues on the Trinity in *Dialogues sur la Trinité* (*SC* 231, 237, and 246; Paris, 1976 ff.). The monograph by W. J. Burghardt, *The Image of God in Man according to Cyril of Alexandria* The Catholic University of America Studies in Christian Antiquity 14; Washington D.C., 1957), deals clearly and concisely with a prominent theme in the second group of letters. Perhaps the best commentary on Cyril's Christology, because it uses Cyril's own words, is the seventh-century florilegium *Doctrina Patrum* edited by F. Diekamp (Münster, 1907). Here the reader will find clearly set out what Cyril was claimed to have taught on all the main points in dispute.

Important notices on historical and literary-critical questions by E. Schwartz are to be found scattered amongst the prefaces and annotations to *ACO* 1 and to *Codex Vaticanus gr. 1431, eine*

antichalkedonische Sammlung aus der Zeit Kaiser Zenos (Abhandlungen der Bayerischen Akademie der Wissenschaften, Philosophisch philologische und historische Klasse XXXII; Munich, 1927). Important here too are the same author's *Cyrill und der Mönch Viktor* (Sitzungsberichte der Wissenschaften in Wien, Philosophisch-historische Klasse, 208, 4; Vienna, 1928) and *Konzilstudien I, Cassian und Nestorius, II, Über echte und unechte Schriften des Bischofs Proklos von Konstantinopel* (Strasburg, 1914). An invaluable guide to the complexities of the latest phase in the controversy is 'Der Streit um Diodor und Theodor zwischen den beiden ephesenischen Konzilien', *ZKG* 67 (1955/56), 252–87 by Professor Luise Abramowski.

There is a large literature dealing with aspects of Cyril's thought. All that is of importance will be found listed in the works by Grillmeier, Jouassard, Scipioni, and Hardy mentioned above, and in that of Wilken mentioned below. Further references will be found in the notes, but the following demand mention here:

Books

Diepen, H.-M. *Douze dialogues de Christologie ancienne* (Rome, 1960).

Gebremedhin, E. *Life-giving Blessing. An Inquiry into the Eucharistic Doctrine of Cyril of Alexandria* (Uppsala, 1977).

Kerrigan, A. *St. Cyril of Alexandria, Interpreter of the Old Testament* (Rome, 1952).

Liébaert, J. *La Doctrine Christologique de Saint Cyrille d'Alexandrie avant la querelle Nestorienne* (Lille, 1951).

Malley, W. J. *Hellenism and Christianity. The Conflict between Hellenic and Christian Wisdom in the* Contra Galilaeos *of Julian the Apostate and the* Contra Julianum *of St. Cyril of Alexandria* (Analecta Gregoriana 210; Rome, 1978).

Struckmann, A. *Die Eucharistielehre des heiligen Cyrill von Alexandrien* (Paderborn, 1910).

Wilken, R. L. *Judaism and the early Christian Mind: A Study of Cyril of Alexandria's Exegesis and Theology* (Yale U.P., 1971).

Articles

Cyril's language and style
Vaccari, A.   'La grecità di S. Cirillo d'Alessandria',
                           Studi dedicati alla memoria di P. Ubaldi
                           (Milan, 1937), pp. 23–39.

Points of Chronology
Jouassard, G.   'L'activité littéraire de S. Cyrille d'Alex-
                           andrie jusqu'en 428', *Mélanges Podechard*
                           (Lyons, 1945), pp. 159–74.
— —   'La date des écrits antiariens de Saint
                           Cyrille d'Alexandrie', *Revue Bénédictine*
                           87 (1977), 172–8.
Charlier, N.   'Le "Thesaurus de Trinitate" de Saint
                           Cyrille d'Alexandrie, questions de cri-
                           tique littéraire', *RHE* 45 (1950), 25–81.
Parvis, P. M.   'The Commentary on Hebrews and the
                           Contra Theodorum of Cyril of Alex-
                           andria', *JTS* 26 (1975), 415–19.

Cyril and Hellenism
Liébaert, J.   'Saint Cyrille d'Alexandrie et la culture
                           antique', *Mélanges de Science Religieuse* 12
                           (1955), 5–21.
Grant, R. M.   'Greek Literature in the Treatise *De
                           Trinitate* and Cyril *Contra Julianum*',
                           JTS 15 (1964), 265–79.

Aspects of Cyril's Career and Influence
Abel, F. M.   'S. Cyrille d'Alexandrie dans ses rap-
                           ports avec la Palestine', *Kyrilliana*
                           (Cairo, 1947), pp. 203–30.
Batiffol, P.   'Les présents de Saint Cyrille à la cour
                           de Constantinople', *Études de Liturgie et
                           d'Archéologie Chrétienne* (Paris, 1919).
Diepen, H.-M.   *Les Trois Chapitres au Concile de Chalcé-
                           doine* (Oosterhout, 1953).
Galtier, P.   'Les anathématismes de Saint Cyrille et
                           le Concile de Chalcédoine, *RSR* 23
                           (1933), 45–57.

Galtier, P.   'Le Centenaire d'Ephèse', *RSR* 21 (1931), 169–99.

Haring, N. M.   'The Character and Range of the Influence of St. Cyril of Alexandria on Latin Theology (430–1260)', *Medieval Studies* 12 (1950), 1–19.

Liébaert, J.   Article 'Ephèse (Concile d'), 431' in *DHGE* i, cols. 561–74.

Richard, M.   'Les traités de Cyrille d'Alexandrie contre Diodore et Theodore et les fragments dogmatiques de Diodore de Tarse', *Mélanges F. Grat* (Paris, 1946), vol. i, pp. 99–116 = *Opera Minora* 2 no. 51 (Leuven, 1977).

— —   'Acace de Mélitène, Proclus de Constantinople et la Grande Arménie', *Mémorial L. Petit, Mélanges d'histoire et d'archéologie byzantines* (Bucharest, 1948), pp. 393–412 = *Opera Minora* 2 no. 50 (Leuven, 1977).

Cyril's Christology

Galtier, P.   'L' "Unio secundum Hypostasim" chez Saint Cyrille', *Gregorianum* 33 (1952), 351–98.

— —   'Saint Cyrille et Apollinaire', *Gregorianum* 37 (1956), 584–609.

Jouassard, G.   ' "Impassibilité" du Logos et "Impassibilité" de l'âme humaine chez Saint Cyrille d'Alexandrie', *RSR* 45 (1957), 209–24.

Cyril's Eucharistic Doctrine

Chadwick, H.   'Eucharist and Christology in the Nestorian Controversy', *JTS* 2 (1951), 145–64.

Texts

The editions used here are those of *PGL* = G. W. H. Lampe, *A Patristic Greek Lexicon* (Oxford, 1961). Nestorius' *Liber Heraclidis* is cited with reference to Bedjan's edition of the text and (in

italics) the translation of F. Nau, *Le Livre d'Héraclide de Damas*
(Paris, 1910).

Reference works referred to in notes and Introduction

Coleman-Norton, P. R.   *Roman State and Christian Church: A Collection of Legal Documents to 535* (3 vols.;
                         London, 1966).
Hahn, A.   *Bibliothek der Symbole und Glaubensregeln
                         der Alten Kirche* (Breslau, 1897).
Jones, A. H. M.   *The Later Roman Empire 284–602* (3 vols.;
                         Oxford, 1964).

SIGNS USED IN THE APPARATUS

V   *Collectio Vaticana*: Codex Vaticanus 830, 15th cent.
S   *Collectio Seguierana*: Codex Parisinus Coislinianus 32,
            11th cent.
A   *Collectio Atheniensis*: Codex Atheniensis societatis
            archaeologiae Christianae 9, 13th cent.
R   Codex Vaticanus graecus 1431, 11th cent.
Σ   Syriac version: B.L. Additional MS 14557, c. 10th
            cent., ed. R. Y. Ebied/L. R. Wickham, *CSCO*, Scrip-
            tores Syri vol. 157 (Louvain, 1975).
G   Codex Vaticanus graecus 447, 12th cent.
C   Codex Laurentianus graecus Plu. vi, 17, 11th cent.
O   Codex Parisinus graecus 1115, A.D. 1276.
N   Codex Basiliensis Bibliothecae Universitatis graecus
            32 (A. III. 4), 14th cent.
B   Codex Berolensis Phillipicus graecus 1475, 16th cent.
Arm.   Armenian version (see Introduction, p. xlvii).
Flor. Cyr. Florilegium Cyrillianum, ed. R. Hespel, *Le Florilège
            Cyrillien réfuté par Sévère d'Antioche* (*Bibliothèque du
            Muséon* 37; Louvain, 1955).
Syr   B.L. Additional MS 14531, 7th/8th cents., ed. R. Y.
            Ebied/L. R. Wickham, *Le Muséon* 83 (1970), 438–82.

TEXTS AND TRANSLATIONS

1

SECOND LETTER TO NESTORIUS

1. Τῷ εὐλαβεστάτῳ καὶ θεοφιλεστάτῳ συλλειτουργῷ Νεστορίῳ
Κύριλλος ἐν κυρίῳ χαίρειν.

Καταφλυαροῦσι μέν, ὡς μανθάνω, τινὲς τῆς ἐμῆς ὑπολήψεως ἐπὶ
τῆς σῆς θεοσεβείας, καὶ τοῦτο συχνῶς, τὰς τῶν ἐν τέλει συνόδους
καιροφυλακοῦντες μάλιστα, καὶ τάχα που καὶ τέρπειν οἰόμενοι τὴν 5
σὴν ἀκοὴν καὶ ἀβουλήτους πέμπουσι φωνάς, ἠδικημένοι μὲν οὐδέν,
ἐλεγχθέντες δέ, καὶ τοῦτο χρηστῶς, ὃ μὲν ὅτι τυφλοὺς ἠδίκει καὶ
πένητας, ὃ δὲ ὡς μητρὶ ξίφος ἐπανατείνας, ὃ δὲ θεραπαίνη συγκε-
κλοφὼς χρυσίον ἀλλότριον καὶ τοιαύτην ἐσχηκὼς ἀεὶ τὴν ὑπόληψιν,
ἣν οὐκ ἂν εὔξαιτό τις συμβῆναί τισι καὶ τῶν λίαν ἐχθρῶν. πλὴν οὐ 10
πολὺς τῶν τοιούτων ὁ λόγος ἐμοί, ἵνα μήτε ὑπὲρ τὸν δεσπότην
καὶ διδάσκαλον μήτε μὴν ὑπὲρ τοὺς πατέρας τὸ τῆς ἐνούσης ἐμοὶ
βραχύτητος ἐκτείνοιμι μέτρον. οὐ γὰρ ἐνδέχεται τὰς τῶν φαύλων
διαδρᾶναι σκαιότητας, ὡς ἂν ἕλοιτό τις διαβιοῦν.

Witnesses: V S A R + *Acta* of the Council of Chalcedon, Latin versions,
smaller collections, and citations   *ACO* 1, 1, 1 pp. 25–8

---

1 Without title in most mss. Dated Mechir (= 26 Jan–24 Feb), Indiction
13 (= 430) in the acts of Chalcedon (*ACO* 2, 1 p. 104). The letter was for
Chalcedon, along with the letter to John of Antioch containing the Formula
of Reunion, the authoritative expression of Cyril's teaching. Three works of
Cyril, important in the progress of the controversy, preceded this: (1) Cyril's
Paschal Letter 17 (*PG* 77, 768 ff.) announcing the date of Easter 429; (2) Cyril's
Letter to the Monks (*Ep.* 1) (*ACO* 1, 1, 1 pp. 10 ff.) written at the same time;
and (3) the *First Letter to Nestorius* (*Ep.* 2) (*ACO* ibid. pp. 23 ff.) written a few
months later. (1) and (2) attack Nestorius' doctrine anonymously and in
particular the denial of the title 'Mother of God' (see below, n. 10). (2) was

1

SECOND LETTER TO NESTORIUS[1]

1. Greetings in the Lord from Cyril to his most pious and divinely favoured fellow minister Nestorius.

I understand that certain parties are conducting before your Reverence an intensive campaign of gossip against my good name, that they look out especially for meetings of high officials and that they then give vent to reckless language in the expectation, I daresay, of gratifying your ears—parties, I say, who have sustained no injuries but who have been convicted, fairly convicted, one on the grounds that he was ill-treating the blind and poor, the second that he had brandished a sword over his mother, the third that he has stolen gold belonging to someone else in company with a female servant and enjoys a standing reputation one would not wish on one's dearest enemies.[2] However, I pay little attention to people like this in case I exaggerate my own small measure of importance beyond the Master and Teacher, or beyond the fathers[3] either. It is, indeed, impossible to avoid mean men's mischief however one chooses to live one's life.

widely circulated and publicly attacked in Constantinople, fomenting the discord there between Nestorius and dissident clergy (see below, Third Letter to Nestorius, n. 4). Meanwhile Cyril wrote to Rome sending extracts from Nestorius. On receipt of Celestine's disturbed reply Cyril wrote (3) whose aim was 'to frighten him by his reports of scandalized Romans' (Schwartz). Peace is still possible if he will drop the attack on the title 'Mother of God'. Nestorius was now hoping for a council to vindicate him and would not budge. He sent back a brief, pained note (*ACO* 1, 1, 1 p. 25) to what was a declaration of war.

[2] Four complainants, 'the scum of Alexandria', are named in Cyril's letter (*Ep.* 10) to his representatives at Constantinople: Chairemon, Victor, Sophronas, and the bankrupt Flavian's slave (*ACO* 1, 1, 1 p. 111). Victor eventually abjured any intention of complaining (see above, p. xxv). For a brilliant, if perverse, account of this aspect of the controversy, see E. Schwartz, *Cyrill und der Mönch Viktor*. Nestorius alludes to the affair (*Liber Heraclidis*, p. 153/92): 'The news gained strong currency that I was not one to overlook the downtrodden. . . . It encouraged Cyril's critics to make mentionable and unmentionable reports about him to the Emperor, requesting me to be judge.'

[3] The 'fathers', for Cyril, are dead, orthodox bishops of unblemished life; see E. Nacke, *Das Zeugnis der Väter in der theologischen Beweisführung Cyrills von Alexandrien* (Münster, 1964).

2. Ἀλλ' ἐκεῖνοι μὲν ἀρᾶς καὶ πικρίας μεστὸν ἔχοντες τὸ στόμα[a]
τῷ πάντων ἀπολογήσονται κριτῇ· τετράψομαι δὲ πάλιν ἐγὼ πρὸς
τὸ ὅτι μάλιστα πρέπον ἐμαυτῷ καὶ ὑπομνήσω καὶ νῦν ὡς ἀδελφὸν
ἐν Χριστῷ τῆς διδασκαλίας τὸν λόγον καὶ τὸ ἐπὶ τῇ πίστει φρόνημα
μετὰ πάσης ἀσφαλείας ποιεῖσθαι πρὸς τοὺς λαοὺς ἐννοεῖν τε ὅτι τὸ 5
σκανδαλίσαι καὶ μόνον ἕνα τῶν μικρῶν τῶν πιστευόντων εἰς
Χριστὸν ἀφόρητον ἔχει τὴν ἀγανάκτησιν.[b] εἰ δὲ δὴ πληθὺς εἴη
τοσαύτη τῶν λελυπημένων, πῶς οὐχ ἁπάσης εὐτεχνίας ἐν χρείᾳ
καθεστήκαμεν πρός γε τὸ δεῖν ἐμφρόνως περιελεῖν τὰ σκάνδαλα καὶ
τὸν ὑγιᾶ τῆς πίστεως κατευρῦναι λόγον τοῖς ζητοῦσι τὸ ἀληθές; 10
ἔσται δὲ τοῦτο καὶ μάλα ὀρθῶς, εἰ τοῖς τῶν ἁγίων πατέρων περιτυγ-
χάνοντες λόγοις περὶ πολλοῦ τε αὐτοὺς ποιεῖσθαι σπουδάζοιμεν καὶ
δοκιμάζοντες ἑαυτοὺς εἰ ἐσμὲν ἐν τῇ πίστει κατὰ τὸ γεγραμμένον,[c]
ταῖς ἐκείνων ὀρθαῖς καὶ ἀνεπιλήπτοις δόξαις τὰς ἐν ἡμῖν ἐννοίας εὖ
μάλα συμπλάττοιμεν. 15

3. Ἔφη τοίνυν ἡ ἁγία καὶ μεγάλη σύνοδος αὐτὸν τὸν ἐκ θεοῦ
πατρὸς κατὰ φύσιν γεννηθέντα υἱὸν μονογενῆ, τὸν ἐκ θεοῦ ἀληθινοῦ
θεὸν ἀληθινόν, τὸ φῶς τὸ ἐκ τοῦ φωτός, τὸν δι' οὗ τὰ πάντα
πεποίηκεν ὁ πατήρ, κατελθεῖν σαρκωθῆναι ἐνανθρωπῆσαι παθεῖν
ἀναστῆναι τῇ τρίτῃ ἡμέρᾳ καὶ ἀνελθεῖν εἰς οὐρανούς. τούτοις καὶ 20
ἡμᾶς ἕπεσθαι δεῖ καὶ τοῖς λόγοις καὶ τοῖς δόγμασιν, ἐννοοῦντας τί
τὸ σαρκωθῆναι καὶ ἐνανθρωπῆσαι δηλοῖ τὸν ἐκ θεοῦ λόγον. οὐ γὰρ
φαμὲν ὅτι ἡ τοῦ λόγου φύσις μεταποιηθεῖσα γέγονε σάρξ, ἀλλ' οὐδὲ
ὅτι εἰς ὅλον ἄνθρωπον μετεβλήθη τὸν ἐκ ψυχῆς καὶ σώματος,
ἐκεῖνο δὲ μᾶλλον ὅτι σάρκα ἐψυχωμένην ψυχῇ λογικῇ ἑνώσας ὁ 25

[a] cf. Rom. 3: 14, Ps. 9(10): 27(7)   [b] cf. Matt. 18: 6   [c] cf. 2
Cor. 13: 5

---

4 Nicaea (325).
5 That is, he *was* made flesh, he *is* a complete man body and soul, but he
did not change.
6 The expression was favoured by Cyril in this stage of the controversy and
probably introduced by him into the theological vocabulary. It had no technical meaning for Cyril and does not designate a *type* of union. It is equivalent

2. These, though, have their mouth full of cursing and bitterness and will give an account of themselves to the Judge of all. I, for my part, will revert to my own special task and will now remind you, as my brother in Christ, to be absolutely reliable in setting out your teaching and interpretation of the faith to lay people and to take note of the fact that causing even just one of the little ones who believe in Christ to stumble brings wrath unendurable. How much more, then, if there be a vast number of people in pain, must we not need all our skill to strip away the snares and give a broad, wholesome interpretation of the faith to seekers after truth? This can be done quite straightforwardly if we review the declarations of the holy fathers, taking them with full seriousness and testing ourselves, as the Bible says, to see if we are in the faith, and thoroughly frame our own minds to agree with their orthodox and irreproachable views.

3. The holy and great Council[4] stated that 'the only-begotten Son', 'begotten' by nature 'of the Father', 'true God from true God', 'light from light', 'through whom' the Father made all things did himself 'come down, was incarnate, made man, suffered, rose again the third day, and ascended into heaven'. These declarations and these doctrines we too must follow, taking note of the Word of God's 'being incarnate' and 'being made man'. We do not mean that the nature of the Word was changed and made flesh or, on the other hand, that he was transformed into a complete man consisting of soul and body,[5] but instead we affirm this: that the Word substantially[6] united to himself flesh,

to ἕνωσις φυσική and both expressions in Cyril have an exclusive and negative sense, i.e. they rule out every explanation which Nestorius proposed of the union, without offering any explanation themselves. Cyril says, in reply to Theodoret's fuss about this novel expression (*ACO* 1, 1, 6 p. 115): '. . . "substantial" (καθ᾽ ὑπόστασιν) simply means that the nature (φύσις) or being (ὑπόστασις) of the Word, i.e. the Word himself, was really (κατ᾽ ἀλήθειαν) united to human nature without change or merger and, as we have frequently said, is seen to be and is one Christ, the same both God, and man'. The same sort of explanation of ἕνωσις φυσική is given to the Orientals (*ACO* 1, 1, 7 p. 40): 'If we term the union "natural" (φυσικήν) we mean that it is real (ἀληθῆ), it being the practice of inspired Scripture to use this expression. Inspired Paul writes: "We too were naturally (φύσει) children of wrath, even as the rest." Nobody could mean that divine wrath has a physical being (ὑφεστάναι κατὰ φύσιν) so that sinners would be thought of as its offspring or we should have to be sick, crazy Manichees. No, "naturally" (φύσει) means really (κατ᾽ ἀλήθειαν) . . .' Cyril's usage of καθ᾽ ὑπόστασιν is that of 'Aristotle' *De Mundo* (cited *LSJ* s.v. ὑπόστασις III, 2): 'Some atmospheric images are appearances (κατ᾽ ἔμφασιν), some are substantial (καθ᾽ ὑπόστασιν)'. See P. Galtier, 'L' "unio secundum Hypostasim" chez Saint Cyrille', *Gregorianum* 33 (1952), 351–98.

λόγος ἑαυτῷ καθ᾽ ὑπόστασιν ἀφράστως τε καὶ ἀπερινοήτως
γέγονεν ἄνθρωπος καὶ κεχρημάτικεν υἱὸς ἀνθρώπου, οὐ κατὰ
θέλησιν μόνην ἢ εὐδοκίαν, ἀλλ᾽ οὐδὲ ὡς ἐν προσλήψει προσώπου
μόνου, καὶ ὅτι διάφοροι μὲν αἱ πρὸς ἑνότητα τὴν ἀληθινὴν συν-
ενεχθεῖσαι φύσεις, εἰς δὲ ἐξ ἀμφοῖν Χριστὸς καὶ υἱός, οὐχ ὡς τῆς 5
τῶν φύσεων διαφορᾶς ἀνῃρημένης διὰ τὴν ἕνωσιν, ἀποτελεσασῶν δὲ
μᾶλλον ἡμῖν τὸν ἕνα κύριον καὶ Χριστὸν καὶ υἱὸν θεότητός τε καὶ
ἀνθρωπότητος διὰ τῆς ἀφράστου καὶ ἀπορρήτου πρὸς ἑνότητα
συνδρομῆς.

4. Οὕτω τε λέγεται, καίτοι πρὸ αἰώνων ἔχων τὴν ὕπαρξιν καὶ 10
γεννηθεὶς ἐκ πατρός, γεννηθῆναι καὶ κατὰ σάρκα ἐκ γυναικός, οὐχ
ὡς τῆς θείας αὐτοῦ φύσεως ἀρχὴν τοῦ εἶναι λαβούσης ἐν τῇ ἁγίᾳ
παρθένῳ οὔτε μὴν δεηθείσης ἀναγκαίως δι᾽ ἑαυτὴν δευτέρας
γεννήσεως μετὰ τὴν ἐκ πατρός (ἔστι γὰρ εἰκαῖόν τε ὁμοῦ καὶ
ἀμαθὲς τὸν ὑπάρχοντα πρὸ παντὸς αἰῶνος καὶ συναΐδιον τῷ πατρὶ 15
δεῖσθαι λέγειν ἀρχῆς τῆς εἰς τὸ εἶναι δευτέρας), ἐπειδὴ δὲ δι᾽ ἡμᾶς
καὶ διὰ τὴν ἡμετέραν σωτηρίαν ἑνώσας ἑαυτῷ καθ᾽ ὑπόστασιν τὸ
ἀνθρώπινον προῆλθεν ἐκ γυναικός, ταύτῃ τοι λέγεται γεννηθῆναι
σαρκικῶς. οὐ γὰρ πρῶτον ἄνθρωπος ἐγεννήθη κοινὸς ἐκ τῆς ἁγίας
παρθένου, εἶθ᾽ οὕτως καταπεφοίτηκεν ἐπ᾽ αὐτὸν ὁ λόγος, ἀλλ᾽ ἐξ 20
αὐτῆς μήτρας ἑνωθεὶς ὑπομεῖναι λέγεται γέννησιν σαρκικήν, ὡς
τῆς ἰδίας σαρκὸς τὴν γέννησιν οἰκειούμενος.

5. Οὕτω φαμὲν αὐτὸν καὶ παθεῖν καὶ ἀναστῆναι, οὐχ ὡς τοῦ
θεοῦ λόγου παθόντος εἰς ἰδίαν φύσιν ἢ πληγὰς ἢ διατρήσεις ἥλων ἢ
γοῦν τὰ ἕτερα τῶν τραυμάτων (ἀπαθὲς γὰρ τὸ θεῖον, ὅτι καὶ 25
ἀσώματον), ἐπειδὴ δὲ τὸ γεγονὸς αὐτοῦ ἴδιον σῶμα πέπονθε ταῦτα,
πάλιν αὐτὸς λέγεται παθεῖν ὑπὲρ ἡμῶν· ἦν γὰρ ὁ ἀπαθὴς ἐν τῷ
πάσχοντι σώματι. κατὰ τὸν ἴσον δὲ τρόπον καὶ ἐπὶ τοῦ τεθνάναι

---

[7] πρόσωπον had at this time a fixed meaning in trinitarian doctrine as the
equivalent of ὑπόστασις. In 'Antiochene' Christology, and in Nestorius especially, it meant something like 'outward aspect'. Cyril either intentionally, or out

endowed with life and reason, in a manner mysterious and incon-
ceivable, and became man, and was called 'Son of Man' uniting
it substantially, not merely by way of divine favour or good will,
yet neither with the assumption merely of an outward appearance;[7] and that though the natures joined together to form a
real unity are different, it is one Christ and Son coming from
them—not implying that the difference between the natures was
abolished through their union[8] but that instead Godhead and
manhood have given us the one Lord, Christ and Son by their
mysterious and inexpressible unification.

4. This is what it means to say that he was also born of woman
in the flesh though owning his existence before the ages and
begotten of the Father: not that his divine nature originated in
the holy Virgin or necessarily required for its own sake a second
birth subsequent to that from the Father (to say that one existing
before every epoch, co-eternal with the Father needed a second
start to his existence is idle and stupid)—no, it means that he
had fleshly birth because he issued from woman for us and for
our salvation having united humanity substantially to himself.
The point is that it was not the case that initially an ordinary
man was born of the holy Virgin and then the Word simply
settled on him—no, what is said is that he underwent fleshly
birth united from the very womb, making the birth of his flesh
his very own.

5. This is what we mean when we say he suffered and rose
again; not that God the Word suffered blows, nail-piercings or
other wounds in his own nature (the divine is impassible because
it is incorporeal)[9] but what is said is that since his own created
body suffered these things he himself 'suffered' for our sake, the
point being that within the suffering body was the Impassible.
We interpret his dying along exactly comparable lines. The

of ignorance, caricatures this as 'mere outward aspect', 'role'. See § 7 below.
Cf. *PGL* s.v. πρόσωπον XD.

[8] Cf. the formula of the Council of Chalcedon (451)—οὐδαμοῦ τῆς τῶν
φύσεων διαφορᾶς ἀνῃρημένης διὰ τὴν ἕνωσιν (*ACO* 2, 1 p. 325, 31 f.)—elsewhere
indebted mostly to the Formula of Reunion.

[9] Cf. *Scholia* 2 (*ACO* 1, 5 p. 220) where Cyril uses the admittedly imperfect
analogy of the union of soul and body to explain the union of impassible Word
and flesh in Christ. The soul is not itself cut by the blade which lacerates the
body, though it feels the pain as its own. So in a far higher degree, the Word
is impassibly conscious (πασχούσης ἀπαθῶς) of the body's sufferings which are
his because the body is his. Beyond these (in context) carefully qualified
commonplaces Cyril could not, or would not, go; cf. Introduction p. xxxiii and
n. 70.

νοοῦμεν. ἀθάνατος μὲν γὰρ κατὰ φύσιν καὶ ἄφθαρτος καὶ ζωὴ καὶ
ζωοποιός ἐστιν ὁ τοῦ θεοῦ λόγος· ἐπειδὴ δὲ πάλιν τὸ ἴδιον αὐτοῦ
σῶμα χάριτι θεοῦ, καθά φησιν ὁ Παῦλος, ὑπὲρ παντὸς ἐγεύσατο
θανάτου,[d] λέγεται παθεῖν αὐτὸς τὸν ὑπὲρ ἡμῶν θάνατον, οὐχ ὡς
εἰς πεῖραν ἐλθὼν τοῦ θανάτου τό γε ἧκον εἰς τὴν αὐτοῦ φύσιν 5
(ἀποπληξία γὰρ τοῦτο λέγειν ἢ φρονεῖν), ἀλλ' ὅτι, καθάπερ ἔφην
ἀρτίως, ἡ σὰρξ αὐτοῦ ἐγεύσατο θανάτου. οὕτω καὶ ἐγηγερμένης
αὐτοῦ τῆς σαρκός, πάλιν ἡ ἀνάστασις αὐτοῦ λέγεται, οὐχ ὡς
πεσόντος εἰς φθοράν, μὴ γένοιτο, ἀλλ' ὅτι τὸ αὐτοῦ πάλιν ἐγήγερ-
ται σῶμα. 10

6. Οὕτω Χριστὸν ἕνα καὶ κύριον ὁμολογήσομεν, οὐχ ὡς ἄνθρωπον
συμπροσκυνοῦντες τῷ λόγῳ, ἵνα μὴ τομῆς φαντασία παρεισκρίνηται
διὰ τοῦ λέγειν τὸ "σύν", ἀλλ' ὡς ἕνα καὶ τὸν αὐτὸν προσκυνοῦντες,
ὅτι μὴ ἀλλότριον τοῦ λόγου τὸ σῶμα αὐτοῦ, μεθ' οὗ καὶ αὐτῷ
συνεδρεύει τῷ πατρί, οὐχ ὡς δύο πάλιν συνεδρευόντων υἱῶν, ἀλλ' ὡς 15
ἑνὸς καθ' ἕνωσιν μετὰ τῆς ἰδίας σαρκός. ἐὰν δὲ τὴν καθ' ὑπόστασιν
ἕνωσιν ἢ ὡς ἀνέφικτον ἢ ὡς ἀκαλλῆ παραιτώμεθα, ἐμπίπτομεν εἰς
τὸ δύο λέγειν υἱούς· ἀνάγκη γὰρ πᾶσα διορίσαι καὶ εἰπεῖν τὸν μὲν
ἄνθρωπον ἰδικῶς τῇ τοῦ υἱοῦ κλήσει τετιμημένον, ἰδικῶς δὲ πάλιν
τὸν ἐκ θεοῦ λόγον υἱότητος ὄνομά τε καὶ χρῆμα ἔχοντα φυσικῶς. οὐ 20
διαιρετέον τοιγαροῦν εἰς υἱοὺς δύο τὸν ἕνα κύριον Ἰησοῦν Χριστόν.

7. Ὀνήσει δὲ κατ' οὐδένα τρόπον τὸν ὀρθὸν τῆς πίστεως λόγον
εἰς τὸ οὕτως ἔχειν, κἂν εἰ προσώπων ἕνωσιν ἐπιφημίζωσί τινες.
οὐ γὰρ εἴρηκεν ἡ γραφὴ ὅτι ὁ λόγος ἀνθρώπου πρόσωπον ἥνωσεν
ἑαυτῷ, ἀλλ' ὅτι γέγονε σάρξ.[e] τὸ δὲ σάρκα γενέσθαι τὸν λόγον 25
οὐδὲν ἕτερόν ἐστιν εἰ μὴ ὅτι παραπλησίως ἡμῖν μετέσχεν αἵματος
καὶ σαρκὸς[f] ἴδιόν τε σῶμα τὸ ἡμῶν ἐποιήσατο καὶ προῆλθεν
ἄνθρωπος ἐκ γυναικός, οὐκ ἀποβεβληκὼς τὸ εἶναι θεὸς καὶ τὸ ἐκ
θεοῦ γεννηθῆναι πατρός, ἀλλὰ καὶ ἐν προσλήψει σαρκὸς μεμενηκὼς
ὅπερ ἦν. τοῦτο πρεσβεύει πανταχοῦ τῆς ἀκριβοῦς πίστεως ὁ λόγος· 30
οὕτως εὑρήσομεν τοὺς ἁγίους πεφρονηκότας πατέρας· οὕτως
τεθαρσήκασι θεοτόκον εἰπεῖν τὴν ἁγίαν παρθένον, οὐχ ὡς τῆς τοῦ

---

[d] Heb. 2:9   [e] cf. John 1:14   [f] cf. Heb. 2:14

Word of God is by nature immortal and incorruptible, is Life and life-giving, but since, again, his own body '*tasted death for every man*', as Paul says, '*by the grace of God*', he himself suffered death for our sake, not as though he had experience of death with respect to his nature (to assert or imagine that is lunacy) but because his flesh, as I have just said, tasted death. This again too is what is meant by his resurrection with the raising up of his flesh: not (God forbid!) that he succumbed to corruption but that it is *his* body which was raised.

6. In this way we shall confess one Christ and Lord, not 'worshipping' a man 'along with' the Word (in case the idea of division should be brought in through the use of the phrase 'along with') but worshipping one and the same Christ because the Word's body is not dissociated from him; with it he presides jointly with the Father himself—not that there are *two* jointly presiding sons, but that there is one in union with his own flesh. Deny substantial union as a crass impossibility and we fall into talk of two sons, for we shall be forced to assert a distinction between the particular man honoured with the title 'Son' on the one hand, and the Word from God, natural possessor of both the name and the reality of sonship, on the other. The one Lord Jesus Christ must not therefore be divided into two sons.

7. Talk, by certain parties, of a union of roles will *not* help an orthodox account of the faith in the case as it stands. Scripture, after all, has not asserted that the Word united a man's role to himself but that he has become flesh. But the Word's 'becoming flesh' is just the fact that he shared flesh and blood like us, made our body his own and issued as man from woman without abandoning his being God and his being begotten of God the Father but remaining what he was when he assumed flesh as well. This is the universal representation of carefully framed theology. This is the key to the holy fathers' thinking. This is why they dare to call the holy Virgin 'mother of

λόγου φύσεως ἤτοι τῆς θεότητος αὐτοῦ τὴν ἀρχὴν τοῦ εἶναι λαβούσης ἐκ τῆς ἁγίας παρθένου, ἀλλ' ὡς γεννηθέντος ἐξ αὐτῆς τοῦ ἁγίου σώματος ψυχωθέντος λογικῶς, ᾧ καὶ καθ' ὑπόστασιν ἑνωθεὶς ὁ λόγος γεγεννῆσθαι λέγεται κατὰ σάρκα.

Ταῦτα καὶ νῦν ἐξ ἀγάπης τῆς ἐν Χριστῷ γράφω, παρακαλῶν 5 ὡς ἀδελφὸν καὶ διαμαρτυρόμενος ἐνώπιον τοῦ Χριστοῦ καὶ τῶν ἐκλεκτῶν ἀγγέλων ταῦτα μεθ' ἡμῶν καὶ φρονεῖν καὶ διδάσκειν, ἵνα σώζηται τῶν ἐκκλησιῶν ἡ εἰρήνη καὶ τῆς ὁμονοίας καὶ ἀγάπης ὁ σύνδεσμος ἀρραγὴς διαμένοι τοῖς ἱερεῦσι τοῦ θεοῦ.

Πρόσειπε τὴν παρὰ σοὶ ἀδελφότητα. σὲ ἡ σὺν ἡμῖν ἐν Χριστῷ 10 προσαγορεύει.

God'[10]—not because the Word's nature, his Godhead, originated from the holy Virgin but because his holy body, endowed with life and reason was born from her and the Word was 'born' in flesh because united to this body substantially.

Christian love prompts me to write this even at this stage and I call on you as my brother and entreat you before Christ and the elect angels to join us in holding and teaching it, so that the peace of the churches may be preserved and God's priests may have an abiding bond of unbroken love and harmony.

Greet the brethren with you. Those with us greet you in Christ.

[10] The term occurs once only in Cyril's writings before the Nestorian controversy (*Commentary on Isaiah* IV, 4, *PG* 70, 1036D, in explanation of 'Emmanuel') and it may well be a gloss even there. Cyril had no interest in the dogmatic significance of the term before his *Letter to the Monks* (*Ep.* 1). In defending its aptness, he creates the impression that the term was constantly on the lips of 'the fathers'. The surviving literature suggests otherwise. Origen, Eusebius, Alexander of Alexandria, Athanasius, and the Council of Antioch (324) used the term. Julian the Apostate reproaches the Galileans for its frequent repetition (ed. Neumann, p. 214). The Apollinarian *De Fide et Incarnatione* (allegedly by Julius of Rome) uses it in a context of learned Christology (ed. Lietzmann, pp. 195 ff.). It is used too by Gregory of Nyssa and Epiphanius. But its most significant appearance is in Gregory Nazianzen's *First Letter to Cledonius*—'anyone who does not accept saint Mary as 'Mother of God' is outside his Godhead' (*PG* 37, 177C)—a text quoted by Cyril in his brief patristic florilegia (*ACO* 1, 1, 2 p. 43; 1, 1, 7 p. 93). Antiochene criticism of the term, never amounting even with Nestorius when in cautious mood to outright rejection, goes back to Diodore. It may be that in origin the term was a learned creation of respect for the BVM, only later becoming a term of Christology. It was exclusively such for Cyril.

2
THIRD LETTER TO NESTORIUS

1. Τῷ εὐλαβεστάτῳ καὶ θεοφιλεστάτῳ συλλειτουργῷ Νεστορίῳ Κύριλλος καὶ ἡ συνελθοῦσα σύνοδος ἐν Ἀλεξανδρείᾳ ἐκ τῆς Αἰγυπτιακῆς διοικήσεως ἐν κυρίῳ χαίρειν.

Τοῦ σωτῆρος ἡμῶν λέγοντος ἐναργῶς ὁ φιλῶν πατέρα ἢ μητέρα ὑπὲρ ἐμὲ οὔκ ἐστί μου ἄξιος καὶ ὁ φιλῶν υἱὸν ἢ 5 θυγατέρα ὑπὲρ ἐμὲ οὔκ ἐστί μου ἄξιος,[a] τί πάθωμεν ἡμεῖς οἱ παρὰ τῆς σῆς εὐλαβείας ἀπαιτούμενοι τὸ ὑπεραγαπᾶν σε τοῦ πάντων ἡμῶν σωτῆρος Χριστοῦ; τίς ἡμᾶς ἐν ἡμέρᾳ κρίσεως ὀνῆσαι δυνήσεται ἢ ποίαν εὑρήσομεν τὴν ἀπολογίαν, σιωπὴν οὕτω τιμήσαντες τὴν μακρὰν ἐπὶ ταῖς παρὰ σοῦ γενομέναις κατ' αὐτοῦ 10 δυσφημίαις; καὶ εἰ μὲν σαυτὸν ἠδίκεις μόνον τὰ τοιαῦτα φρονῶν καὶ διδάσκων, ἥττων ἂν ἦν ἡ φροντίς· ἐπειδὴ δὲ πᾶσαν ἐσκανδάλισας ἐκκλησίαν καὶ ζύμην αἱρέσεως ἀήθους καὶ ξένης ἐμβέβληκας τοῖς λαοῖς καὶ οὐχὶ τοῖς ἐκεῖσε μόνοις, ἀλλὰ γὰρ καὶ τοῖς ἀπανταχοῦ (περιηνέχθη γὰρ τῶν σῶν ἐξηγήσεων τὰ βιβλία), ποῖος ἔτι ταῖς 15 παρ' ἡμῶν σιωπαῖς ἀρκέσει λόγος ἢ πῶς οὐκ ἀνάγκη μνησθῆναι λέγοντος τοῦ Χριστοῦ μὴ νομίσητε ὅτι ἦλθον βαλεῖν εἰρήνην ἐπὶ τὴν γῆν, ἀλλὰ μάχαιραν. ἦλθον γὰρ διχάσαι ἄνθρωπον κατὰ τοῦ πατρὸς αὐτοῦ καὶ θυγατέρα κατὰ τῆς μητρὸς αὐτῆς·[b] πίστεως γὰρ ἀδικουμένης, ἐρρέτω μὲν ὡς ἔωλος καὶ 20 ἐπισφαλὴς ἡ πρὸς γονέας αἰδώς, ἠρεμείτω δὲ καὶ ὁ τῆς εἰς τέκνα καὶ ἀδελφοὺς φιλοστοργίας νόμος καὶ τοῦ ζῆν ἀμείνων ἔστω λοιπὸν τοῖς εὐσεβέσιν ὁ θάνατος, ἵνα κρείττονος ἀναστάσεως τύχωσι[c] κατὰ τὸ γεγραμμένον.

2. Ἰδοὺ τοίνυν ὁμοῦ τῇ ἁγίᾳ συνόδῳ τῇ κατὰ τὴν μεγάλην 25 Ῥώμην συνειλεγμένῃ προεδρεύοντος τοῦ ὁσιωτάτου καὶ θεοσεβεστάτου ἀδελφοῦ καὶ συλλειτουργοῦ ἡμῶν Κελεστίνου τοῦ ἐπισκόπου καὶ τρίτῳ σε τούτῳ διαμαρτυρόμεθα γράμματι, συμβουλεύοντες ἀποσχέσθαι τῶν οὕτω σκαιῶν καὶ ἐξεστραμμένων δογμάτων ἃ καὶ

---

[a] Matt. 10:37   [b] Matt. 10:34 f.   [c] Heb. 11:35

Witnesses: V S A R + Latin versions, smaller collections, and citations   ACO 1, 1, 1 pp. 33–42

2

THIRD LETTER TO NESTORIUS[1]

1. Greetings in the Lord from Cyril and the council assembled at Alexandria from the diocese of Egypt to his most pious and divinely favoured fellow minister Nestorius.

When our Saviour plainly tells us that *'he who loves father or mother more than me is not worthy of me and he who loves son or daughter more than me is not worthy of me'*, what will be our fate when your Piety requires us to love you more than Christ the saviour of us all? Who can help us on the day of judgement or what excuse are we to invent for having set store by silence, long silence in the face of the blasphemies you have directed against him? Were you only damaging yourself by teaching these ideas of yours we should be less concerned. As it is, seeing you have scandalized the whole Church, have injected the ferment of bizarre and outlandish heresy into congregations not only at Constantinople but all over the world (indeed volumes of your sermons have been put into circulation) what sort of satisfactory explanation would further silence on our part have? How could we fail to recall Christ saying *'do not think I came to bring peace on earth but a sword—I came to set a man against his father and a daughter against her mother'*? When the faith is being injured, away with stale and slippery parental reverence, an end to the rule of cherishing children and brothers! Men of true religion must henceforth prefer death to life *'that they may obtain'*, as the Bible says, *'a better resurrection'*.

2. Accordingly we, in company with the holy council assembled at great Rome under the presidency of bishop Celestine[2] our most holy and religious brother and fellow minister, charge you presently by this third letter, warning you to dissociate yourself from the utterly mischievous and distorted doctrines you hold

---

[1] No heading in most mss. The letter was delivered to Nestorius after morning service on Sunday, 30 November 430 (*ACO* 1, 2 p. 51, 33; cf. 1, 5 p. 39, 19 ff.) along with Celestine's letter (*ACO* 1, 2 pp. 7–12) dated 10 August.

[2] Pope (422–32). The council at Rome must have met at the beginning of August.

φρονεῖς καὶ διδάσκεις, ἀνθελέσθαι δὲ τὴν ὀρθὴν πίστιν τὴν ταῖς
ἐκκλησίαις παραδοθεῖσαν ἐξ ἀρχῆς διὰ τῶν ἁγίων ἀποστόλων καὶ
εὐαγγελιστῶν, οἳ καὶ αὐτόπται καὶ ὑπηρέται τοῦ λόγου[d]
γεγόνασιν. καὶ εἰ μὴ τοῦτο δράσειεν ἡ σὴ εὐλάβεια κατὰ τὴν
ὁρισθεῖσαν προθεσμίαν ἐν τοῖς γράμμασι τοῦ μνημονευθέντος 5
ὁσιωτάτου καὶ θεοσεβεστάτου ἐπισκόπου καὶ συλλειτουργοῦ ἡμῶν
τῆς Ῥωμαίων Κελεστίνου, γίνωσκε σαυτὸν οὐδένα κλῆρον ἔχοντα
μεθ᾽ ἡμῶν οὐδὲ τόπον ἢ λόγον ἐν τοῖς ἱερεῦσιν τοῦ θεοῦ καὶ ἐπισκόποις. οὐ γὰρ ἐνδέχεται περιιδεῖν ἡμᾶς ἐκκλησίας οὕτω τεθορυ-
βημένας καὶ σκανδαλισθέντας λαοὺς καὶ πίστιν ὀρθὴν ἀθετουμένην 10
καὶ διασπώμενα παρὰ σοῦ τὰ ποίμνια τοῦ σώζειν ὀφείλοντος, εἴπερ
ἦσθα καθ᾽ ἡμᾶς ὀρθῆς δόξης ἐραστὴς τὴν τῶν ἁγίων πατέρων
ἰχνηλατῶν εὐσέβειαν. ἅπασι δὲ τοῖς παρὰ τῆς σῆς εὐλαβείας
κεχωρισμένοις διὰ τὴν πίστιν ἢ καθαιρεθεῖσι λαϊκοῖς τε καὶ
κληρικοῖς κοινωνικοὶ πάντες ἐσμέν. οὐ γάρ ἐστι δίκαιον τοὺς ὀρθὰ 15
φρονεῖν ἐγνωκότας σαῖς ἀδικεῖσθαι ψήφοις, ὅτι σοὶ καλῶς ποιοῦντες
ἀντειρήκασιν. τοῦτο γὰρ αὐτὸ καταμεμήνυκας ἐν τῇ ἐπιστολῇ τῇ
γραφείσῃ παρὰ σοῦ πρὸς τὸν τῆς μεγάλης Ῥώμης ἁγιώτατον καὶ
συνεπίσκοπον ἡμῶν Κελεστῖνον. οὐκ ἀρκέσει δὲ τῇ σῇ εὐλαβείᾳ
τὸ συνομολογῆσαι μόνον τὸ τῆς πίστεως σύμβολον τὸ ἐκτεθὲν κατὰ 20
καιροὺς ἐν ἁγίῳ πνεύματι παρὰ τῆς ἁγίας καὶ μεγάλης συνόδου
τῆς κατὰ καιροὺς συναχθείσης ἐν τῇ Νικαέων (νενόηκας γὰρ καὶ
ἡρμήνευσας οὐκ ὀρθῶς αὐτό, διεστραμμένως δὲ μᾶλλον, κἂν
ὁμολογῇς τῇ φωνῇ τὴν λέξιν), ἀλλὰ γὰρ ἀκόλουθον ἐγγράφως καὶ
ἐνωμότως ὁμολογῆσαι ὅτι καὶ ἀναθεματίζεις μὲν τὰ σαυτοῦ μιαρὰ 25
καὶ βέβηλα δόγματα, φρονήσεις δὲ καὶ διδάξεις ἃ καὶ ἡμεῖς ἅπαντες
οἵ τε κατὰ τὴν Ἑσπέραν καὶ τὴν Ἑῴαν ἐπίσκοποι καὶ διδάσκαλοι
καὶ λαῶν ἡγούμενοι. συνέθετο δὲ καὶ ἡ κατὰ τὴν Ῥώμην ἁγία
σύνοδος καὶ ἡμεῖς ἅπαντες ὡς ὀρθῶς ἐχούσαις καὶ ἀνεπιλήπτως
ταῖς γραφείσαις ἐπιστολαῖς πρὸς τὴν σὴν εὐλάβειαν παρὰ τῆς 30
Ἀλεξανδρέων ἐκκλησίας. ὑπετάξαμεν δὲ τούτοις ἡμῶν τοῖς
γράμμασιν ἅ σε δεῖ φρονεῖν καὶ διδάσκειν καὶ ὧν ἀπέχεσθαι
προσήκει. αὕτη γὰρ τῆς καθολικῆς καὶ ἀποστολικῆς ἐκκλησίας ἡ

[d] Luke 1: 2

and teach and to embrace instead the orthodox faith transmitted
originally to the churches by the holy apostles and evangelists
who were made the *'eyewitnesses and stewards of the Word'*. Unless
your Piety does so by the date appointed in the letter[3] of the
afore-mentioned most holy and religious bishop of Rome Celestine our fellow minister, you are to recognize yourself as having
no appointment, official position or status along with us amongst
God's priests and bishops. We cannot turn a blind eye to churches
in utter turmoil, congregations scandalized, right faith nullified
and flocks scattered by you who would have the duty of safeguarding them, were you like us a lover of orthodoxy faithfully
following the true religion of the holy fathers. We are all of us
in communion with all the laity and clergy excommunicated or
deprived by your Piety on account of the faith.[4] For men of
sound views should not be damaged by your condemnation for
proper opposition to you—the fact itself you supply in your
letter written to our most holy fellow bishop Celestine of great
Rome.[5] It will not be sufficient for your Piety simply to confess
the Creed duly set out with the authority of the Holy Ghost by
the holy and great Council assembled in time past at Nicaea
(you interpret it not in an orthodox but in a twisted sense even
though you confess it verbally);[6] consistency demands that you
make a written acknowledgement on oath that you anathematize
your foul, unhallowed dogmas and that you will hold and teach
what all we bishops, teachers and leaders of congregations
throughout the West and East do. The holy council at Rome and
all of us agree on the irreproachable orthodoxy of the letters
addressed to your Piety by the Church of Alexandria. We subjoin
to this letter of ours the propositions you are to hold and teach
and those you must dissociate yourself from.

[3] Ten days from receipt; see *ACO* 1, 2 p. 12.

[4] These include: *Eusebius* (then a layman, but subsequently bishop of
Dorylaeum), vociferous opponent of Nestorius as a new 'Paul of Samosata'
and leading figure in the contention, which led eventually to the Council of
Chalcedon (451), over *Eutyches* a monk, subsequently archimandrite, also
deprived by Nestorius now; *Basil*, another monk (for whose complaint to
the emperors of brutal treatment see *ACO* 1, 1, 5 pp. 9–10); *Philip of Side*,
priest and Church historian, three times candidate for the throne of Constantinople, accused first by Celestius (the Pelagian) of being a Manichee
(i.e. of holding to some idea of original sin) but when the charge did not
stick deprived for celebrating the eucharist at home (*ACO* 1, 1, 7 pp. 171, 31–
172, 8).

[5] First Letter to Celestine, *ACO* 1, 2 pp. 12–14, para 2.

[6] See Nestorius' Second Letter to Cyril, *ACO* 1, 1, 1 pp. 29–32, his reply to
Cyril's Second Letter.

πίστις, ᾗ συναινοῦσιν ἅπαντες οἵ τε κατὰ τὴν Ἑσπέραν καὶ τὴν Ἑῴαν ὀρθόδοξοι ἐπίσκοποι.

3. Πιστεύομεν εἰς ἕνα θεὸν πατέρα παντοκράτορα, πάντων ὁρατῶν τε καὶ ἀοράτων ποιητήν· καὶ εἰς ἕνα κύριον Ἰησοῦν Χριστὸν τὸν υἱὸν τοῦ θεοῦ, γεννηθέντα ἐκ τοῦ πατρὸς μονογενῆ, τουτέστιν 5 ἐκ τῆς οὐσίας τοῦ πατρός, θεὸν ἐκ θεοῦ, φῶς ἐκ φωτός, θεὸν ἀληθινὸν ἐκ θεοῦ ἀληθινοῦ, γεννηθέντα, οὐ ποιηθέντα, ὁμοούσιον τῷ πατρί, δι' οὗ τὰ πάντα ἐγένετο τά τε ἐν τῷ οὐρανῷ καὶ τὰ ἐν τῇ γῇ, τὸν δι' ἡμᾶς τοὺς ἀνθρώπους καὶ τὴν ἡμετέραν σωτηρίαν κατελθόντα καὶ σαρκωθέντα καὶ ἐνανθρωπήσαντα, παθόντα καὶ 10 ἀναστάντα τῇ τρίτῃ ἡμέρᾳ, ἀνελθόντα εἰς τοὺς οὐρανούς, ἐρχόμενον κρῖναι ζῶντας καὶ νεκρούς· καὶ εἰς τὸ ἅγιον πνεῦμα.

Τοὺς δὲ λέγοντας "ἦν ποτε ὅτε οὐκ ἦν" καὶ "πρὶν γεννηθῆναι οὐκ ἦν" καὶ ὅτι ἐξ οὐκ ὄντων ἐγένετο, ἢ ἐξ ἑτέρας ὑποστάσεως ἢ οὐσίας φάσκοντας εἶναι ἢ τρεπτὸν ἢ ἀλλοιωτὸν τὸν υἱὸν τοῦ θεοῦ, 15 τούτους ἀναθεματίζει ἡ καθολικὴ καὶ ἀποστολικὴ ἐκκλησία.

Ἑπόμενοι δὲ πανταχῇ ταῖς τῶν ἁγίων πατέρων ὁμολογίαις αἷς πεποίηνται λαλοῦντος ἐν αὐτοῖς τοῦ ἁγίου πνεύματος καὶ τῶν ἐν αὐτοῖς ἐννοιῶν ἰχνηλατοῦντες τὸν σκοπὸν καὶ βασιλικὴν ὥσπερ ἐρχόμενοι τρίβον φαμὲν ὅτι αὐτὸς ὁ μονογενὴς τοῦ θεοῦ λόγος ὁ 20 ἐξ αὐτῆς γεννηθεὶς τῆς οὐσίας τοῦ πατρός, ὁ ἐκ θεοῦ ἀληθινοῦ θεὸς ἀληθινός, τὸ φῶς τὸ ἐκ τοῦ φωτός, ὁ δι' οὗ τὰ πάντα ἐγένετο τά τε ἐν τῷ οὐρανῷ καὶ τὰ ἐν τῇ γῇ τῆς ἡμετέρας ἕνεκα σωτηρίας κατελθὼν καὶ καθεὶς ἑαυτὸν εἰς κένωσιν[e] ἐσαρκώθη τε καὶ ἐνηνθρώπησε, τουτέστι σάρκα λαβὼν ἐκ τῆς ἁγίας παρθένου καὶ ἰδίαν αὐτὴν 25 ποιησάμενος ἐκ μήτρας τὴν καθ' ἡμᾶς ὑπέμεινε γέννησιν καὶ προῆλθεν ἄνθρωπος ἐκ γυναικός, οὐχ ὅπερ ἦν ἀποβεβληκώς, ἀλλ' εἰ καὶ γέγονεν ἐν προσλήψει σαρκὸς καὶ αἵματος, καὶ οὕτω μεμενηκὼς ὅπερ ἦν, θεὸς δηλονότι φύσει τε καὶ ἀληθείᾳ. οὔτε δὲ τὴν σάρκα φαμὲν εἰς θεότητος τραπῆναι φύσιν οὔτε μὴν εἰς φύσιν 30 σαρκὸς τὴν ἀπόρρητον τοῦ θεοῦ λόγου παρενεχθῆναι φύσιν. ἄτρεπτος γάρ ἐστι καὶ ἀναλλοίωτος παντελῶς ὁ αὐτὸς ἀεὶ μένων[f] κατὰ τὰς γραφάς, ὁρώμενος δὲ καὶ βρέφος καὶ ἐν σπαργάνοις ὢν ἔτι καὶ ἐν κόλπῳ τῆς τεκούσης παρθένου πᾶσαν ἐπλήρου τὴν κτίσιν ὡς θεὸς καὶ σύνεδρος ἦν τῷ γεγεννηκότι· τὸ γὰρ θεῖον ἄποσόν τέ ἐστι καὶ 35 ἀμέγεθες καὶ περιορισμῶν οὐκ ἀνέχεται.

[e] cf. Phil. 2: 7   [f] cf. Mal. 3: 6

This is the faith of the Catholic and Apostolic Church to which all orthodox bishops throughout West and East assent:

3. We believe in one God, Father almighty, maker of all things visible and invisible; and in one Lord Jesus Christ the Son of God, begotten of the Father, only-begotten, that is from the Father's substance, God from God, light from light, true God from true God, begotten not made, consubstantial with the Father, and through him were made all things both in heaven and earth, who for us men and for our salvation came down, was incarnate and made man, suffered and rose again the third day, ascended into heaven and is coming to judge quick and dead; and in the Holy Ghost.

But as for those who say 'there was a time when he did not exist' and 'he did not exist before being begotten' and that he was made of nothing, or declare that God's Son comes from a different basis or substance, or that he is mutable or changeable —these the Catholic and Apostolic Church anathematizes.

We follow at every point the confession of the holy fathers which they have drawn up with the Holy Ghost speaking by them and we keep close to their intentions taking the royal highway, as it were; and we declare that the only-begotten Word of God, begotten from the very substance of the Father, true God from true God, light from light, the one through whom all things both in heaven and earth were made, who came down for our salvation, emptying himself, he it is who was incarnate and made man, that is to say, took flesh of the holy Virgin, making it his own from the womb, and underwent our human birth and came forth as man from woman without abandoning what he was but remaining, even when he has assumed flesh and blood, what he was, God, that is, in nature and truth. We declare that the flesh was not changed into the nature of Godhead and that neither was the inexpressible nature of God the Word converted into the nature of flesh. He is, indeed, utterly unchangeable and immutable ever remaining, as the Bible says, the same; even when a baby seen in swaddling clothes at the bosom of the Virgin who bore him, he still filled the whole creation as God and was co-regent with his sire—for deity is measureless, sizeless and admits of no bounds.[7]

---

[7] Cf. the noble lines in Proclus' Lady Day Sermon (430): 'The same in the Father's bosom and the Virgin's womb, in his mother's arms and on the wings of the winds, was being worshipped by angels and was sitting with publicans' (*ACO* 1, 1, 1 p. 107). For Nestorius' (frigid) reply to the sermon see *ACO* 1, 5 pp. 37–39.

4. Ἡνῶσθαί γε μὴν σαρκὶ καθ᾽ ὑπόστασιν ὁμολογοῦντες τὸν λόγον, ἕνα προσκυνοῦμεν υἱὸν καὶ κύριον Ἰησοῦν Χριστόν, οὔτε ἀνὰ μέρος τιθέντες καὶ διορίζοντες ἄνθρωπον καὶ θεὸν ὡς συνημμένους ἀλλήλοις τῇ τῆς ἀξίας καὶ αὐθεντίας ἑνότητι (κενοφωνία γὰρ τοῦτο καὶ ἕτερον οὐδέν) οὔτε μὴν Χριστὸν ἰδικῶς ὀνομάζοντες τὸν ἐκ 5 θεοῦ λόγον καὶ ὁμοίως ἰδικῶς Χριστὸν ἕτερον τὸν ἐκ γυναικός, ἀλλ᾽ ἕνα μόνον εἰδότες Χριστὸν τὸν ἐκ θεοῦ πατρὸς λόγον μετὰ τῆς ἰδίας σαρκός. τότε γὰρ ἀνθρωπίνως κέχρισται μεθ᾽ ἡμῶν, καίτοι τοῖς ἀξίοις τοῦ λαβεῖν τὸ πνεῦμα διδοὺς αὐτὸς καὶ οὐκ ἐκ μέτρου,[g] καθά φησιν ὁ μακάριος εὐαγγελιστὴς Ἰωάννης. ἀλλ᾽ οὐδὲ ἐκεῖνο 10 φαμὲν ὅτι κατῴκηκεν ὁ ἐκ θεοῦ λόγος ὡς ἐν ἀνθρώπῳ κοινῷ τῷ ἐκ τῆς ἁγίας παρθένου γεγεννημένῳ, ἵνα μὴ θεοφόρος ἄνθρωπος νοοῖτο Χριστός. εἰ γὰρ καὶ ἐσκήνωσεν ἐν ἡμῖν[h] ὁ λόγος, εἴρηται δὲ καὶ ἐν Χριστῷ κατοικῆσαι πᾶν τὸ πλήρωμα τῆς θεότητος σωματικῶς,[i] ἀλλ᾽ οὖν ἐννοοῦμεν ὅτι γενόμενος σάρξ, οὐχ ὥσπερ 15 ἐν τοῖς ἁγίοις κατοικῆσαι λέγεται, κατὰ τὸν ἴσον καὶ ἐν αὐτῷ τρόπον γενέσθαι διοριζόμεθα τὴν κατοίκησιν· ἀλλ᾽ ἑνωθεὶς κατὰ φύσιν καὶ οὐκ εἰς σάρκα τραπείς, τοιαύτην ἐποιήσατο τὴν κατοίκησιν, ἣν ἂν ἔχειν λέγοιτο καὶ ἡ τοῦ ἀνθρώπου ψυχὴ πρὸς τὸ ἴδιον ἑαυτῆς σῶμα. 20

5. Εἷς οὖν ἄρα Χριστὸς καὶ υἱὸς καὶ κύριος, οὐχ ὡς συνάφειαν ἁπλῶς τὴν ὡς ἐν ἑνότητι τῆς ἀξίας ἢ γοῦν αὐθεντίας ἔχοντος ἀνθρώπου πρὸς θεόν· οὐ γὰρ ἑνοῖ τὰς φύσεις ἡ ἰσοτιμία. καὶ γοῦν Πέτρος τε καὶ Ἰωάννης ἰσότιμοι μὲν ἀλλήλοις καθὸ καὶ ἀπόστολοι καὶ ἅγιοι μαθηταί, πλὴν οὐχ εἷς οἱ δύο. οὔτε μὴν κατὰ παράθεσιν 25 τὸν τῆς συναφείας νοοῦμεν τρόπον (οὐκ ἀπόχρη γὰρ τοῦτο πρὸς ἕνωσιν φυσικήν) οὔτε μὴν ὡς κατὰ μέθεξιν σχετικήν, ὡς καὶ ἡμεῖς κολλώμενοι τῷ κυρίῳ κατὰ τὸ γεγραμμένον ἓν πνεῦμά ἐσμεν πρὸς αὐτόν,[j] μᾶλλον δὲ τὸ τῆς συναφείας ὄνομα παραιτούμεθα ὡς οὐκ

---

[g] John 3: 34   [h] John 1: 14   [i] Col. 2: 9   [j] cf. 1 Cor. 6: 17

8 Cf. *Scholia* i, an exposition of the term 'Christ' (*ACO* 1, 5 pp. 219 f.). On the human level (ἀνθρωπίνως) the Word incarnate is anointed with the Holy Ghost whose presence with him is, unlike his presence with anointed prophets of the O.T., permanent; on the divine level (θεϊκῶς) he anoints believers in him with his own Spirit. Cf. *Answers to Tiberius* 9 and n. 42.

4. Because we acknowledge that the Word has been substantially *united* with flesh it is *one* Son and Lord Jesus Christ we worship without separating and parting man and God as though they were mutually connected by unity of rank and sovereignty (pure nonsense that!) or applying the name 'Christ' in parallel fashion both to the Word of God on his own and to a second woman-born 'Christ', but recognizing the Word of God the Father with his own flesh as one Christ and one only. For it was then that he was anointed humanly alongside us,[8] giver though he is (as blessed John the Evangelist says) of the Spirit *'without measure'* to worthy recipients. We do not say either that the Word of God has made his home in an ordinary man born of the holy Virgin lest Christ should be deemed a divinely inspired man.[9] Though the Word *'dwelt amongst us'*, indeed, and *'all the fulness of the Godhead'* is asserted to have made its *'bodily'* home in Christ, yet we recognize that 'being made flesh' is not to be defined by us as meaning a residence of the Word in him precisely comparable with his residence in the saints. No, he was actually[10] united with flesh, without being changed into it, and brought about the sort of residence in it which a man's soul can be said to have in relation to its body.

5. There is, then, one Christ, Son and Lord. There is no question of his being a man simply possessing a connection with God by way of unity of rank or sovereignty—equality of honour does not unite real things. Why, Peter and John are equal in honour as apostles and holy disciples, yet the two are not one person! Moreover we do not interpret the manner of connection as involving juxtaposition (this is insufficient for actual union) or a relationship of participation in the way that, according to the Bible, by 'sticking to the Lord we are one Spirit' with him.

---

[9] Theodoret, apparently falsely, claimed this as a classic designation of Christ (see *ACO* 1, 1, 6 p. 126) in reply to Cyril's fifth Chapter (see below). *PGL* records no examples. θεοφόρος is used often of saints, prophets, etc. According to Gregory of Nazianzus, *Second Letter to Cledonius* (*PG* 37, 200B) it was the Apollinarian article of orthodoxy 'not to worship an inspired (God-bearing) man but God clad in flesh (σαρκοφόρον)'. The casual use of the expression, without any reference to the dilemma (ἄνθρωπος θεοφόρος or θεὸς σαρκοφόρος), shows how far removed Cyril is from systematic Apollinarianism, close though he is to its anti-dualist intention.

[10] κατὰ φύσιν means the same thing, for Cyril, as καθ' ὑπόστασιν. See p. 4 n. 6. Cf. the similar phrase ἕνωσις φυσική below, § 5 and *Anathema* 3.

ἔχον ἱκανῶς σημῆναι τὴν ἔνωσιν. ἀλλ' οὐδὲ θεὸν ἢ δεσπότην τοῦ
Χριστοῦ τὸν ἐκ θεοῦ πατρὸς λόγον ὀνομάζομεν, ἵνα μὴ πάλιν
ἀναφανδὸν τέμνωμεν εἰς δύο τὸν ἕνα Χριστὸν καὶ υἱὸν καὶ κύριον
καὶ δυσφημίας ἐγκλήματι περιπέσωμεν, θεὸν ἑαυτοῦ καὶ δεσπότην
ποιοῦντες αὐτόν. ἐνωθεὶς γάρ, ὡς ἤδη προείπομεν, ὁ τοῦ θεοῦ 5
λόγος σαρκὶ καθ' ὑπόστασιν θεὸς μέν ἐστι τῶν ὅλων, δεσπόζει δὲ
τοῦ παντός, οὔτε δὲ αὐτὸς ἑαυτοῦ δοῦλός ἐστιν οὔτε δεσπότης.
εὔηθες γάρ, μᾶλλον δὲ ἤδη καὶ δυσσεβὲς τὸ οὕτω φρονεῖν ἢ λέγειν.
ἔφη μὲν γὰρ θεὸν ἑαυτοῦ τὸν πατέρα,[k] καίτοι θεὸς ὢν φύσει καὶ ἐκ
τῆς οὐσίας αὐτοῦ· ἀλλ' οὐκ ἠγνοήκαμεν ὅτι μετὰ τοῦ εἶναι θεὸς καὶ 10
ἄνθρωπος γέγονεν ὑπὸ θεῷ κατά γε τὸν πρέποντα νόμον τῇ τῆς
ἀνθρωπότητος φύσει. αὐτὸς δὲ ἑαυτοῦ πῶς ἂν γένοιτο θεὸς ἢ
δεσπότης; οὐκοῦν ὡς ἄνθρωπος καὶ ὅσον ἧκεν εἴς γε τὸ πρέπον
τοῖς τῆς κενώσεως μέτροις, ὑπὸ θεῷ μεθ' ἡμῶν ἑαυτὸν εἶναί φησιν.
οὕτω γέγονε καὶ ὑπὸ νόμον,[l] καίτοι λαλήσας αὐτὸς τὸν νόμον καὶ 15
νομοθέτης ὑπάρχων ὡς θεός.

6. Παραιτούμεθα δὲ λέγειν ἐπὶ Χριστοῦ "διὰ τὸν φοροῦντα τὸν
φορούμενον σέβω· διὰ τὸν ἀόρατον προσκυνῶ τὸν ὁρώμενον".
φρικτὸν δὲ πρὸς τούτῳ κἀκεῖνο εἰπεῖν "ὁ ληφθεὶς τῷ λαβόντι
συγχρηματίζει θεός". ὁ γὰρ ταῦτα λέγων διατέμνει πάλιν εἰς δύο 20
Χριστοὺς καὶ ἄνθρωπον ἵστησιν ἀνὰ μέρος ἰδικῶς καὶ θεὸν ὁμοίως.
ἀρνεῖται γὰρ ὁμολογουμένως τὴν ἔνωσιν, καθ' ἣν οὐχ ὡς ἕτερος
ἑτέρῳ συμπροσκυνεῖταί τις οὔτε μὴν συγχρηματίζει θεός, ἀλλ' εἷς
νοεῖται Χριστὸς Ἰησοῦς υἱὸς μονογενής, μιᾷ προσκυνήσει τιμώμενος
μετὰ τῆς ἰδίας σαρκός. ὁμολογοῦμεν δὲ ὅτι αὐτὸς ὁ ἐκ θεοῦ πατρὸς 25
γεννηθεὶς υἱὸς καὶ θεὸς μονογενής, καίτοι κατὰ φύσιν ἰδίαν ὑπάρχων
ἀπαθής, σαρκὶ πέπονθεν[m] ὑπὲρ ἡμῶν κατὰ τὰς γραφὰς καὶ ἦν ἐν
τῷ σταυρωθέντι σώματι, τὰ τῆς ἰδίας σαρκὸς ἀπαθῶς οἰκειούμενος
πάθη. χάριτι δὲ θεοῦ καὶ ὑπὲρ παντὸς ἐγεύσατο θανάτου,[n]
διδοὺς αὐτῷ τὸ ἴδιον σῶμα, καίτοι κατὰ φύσιν ὑπάρχων ζωὴ καὶ 30
αὐτὸς ὢν ἡ ἀνάστασις.[o] ἵνα γὰρ ἀρρήτῳ δυνάμει πατήσας τὸν
θάνατον ὡς ἔν γε δὴ πρώτῃ τῇ ἰδίᾳ σαρκὶ γένηται πρωτότοκος
ἐκ νεκρῶν[p] καὶ ἀπαρχὴ τῶν κεκοιμημένων[q] ὁδοποιήσῃ τε

---

[k] cf. Matt. 26: 39, etc.   [l] cf. Gal. 4: 4   [m] cf. 1 Peter 4: 1
[n] Heb. 2: 9   [o] cf. John 11: 25   [p] Col. 1: 18   [q] 1 Cor. 15: 20

Instead we deprecate the term 'connection'[11] as inadequate to designate the union. We do not term the Word of God the Father Christ's 'God' or 'Master'—again to avoid the obvious division of the one Christ, Son and Lord into two, and a charge of blasphemy for making him his own God and Master. The Word of God, as we have already said, substantially united with flesh is God of the universe and rules the whole world; he is neither slave nor master of himself. To think or speak like this, indeed, is more than stupid, it is blasphemous. Though actually being God and of his Father's substance he called his Father his 'God'. Nevertheless we bear in mind the fact that along with his being God he was made man subject to God in accordance with the law belonging to man's nature. How could he be his own God or Master? Accordingly as man and with due regard to the conditions of his self-emptying he declared himself subject to God along with us. In this way he is even under law though he himself pronounced the law and is as God law-giver.

6. We refuse to say of Christ 'I venerate the possessed because of the possessor; I revere the one visible because of the invisible'. It is a horrible thing to add to this, 'the assumed is called God along with the assumer'.[12] To say this is once more to divide him into two Christs and to posit man separately on his own and to do the same with God. It is expressly to deny the union by virtue of which the one is not somehow worshipped or called 'God' along with another but recognition is given to one Christ Jesus, Only-begotten Son, venerated with his flesh in a single worship.[13] We confess that the very Son begotten of God the Father, the Only-begotten God, impassible though he is in his own nature, has (as the Bible says) suffered in flesh for our sake and that he was in the crucified body claiming the sufferings of his flesh as his own impassibly. By nature Life and personally the Resurrection though he exists and is, '*by God's grace* he tasted *death for every man*' in surrendering his body to it. With unspeakable power he trampled on death to become in his own flesh first the '*first-born of the dead*' and '*first fruits of those asleep*' in order that

---

[11] A quite classical term, used by Cyril himself before the Nestorian controversy (*Dialogues* vi, *PG* 75 Aubert 605) of the union. It was favoured by Theodore, Nestorius, and Theodoret because of its implicit denial of a merger of deity and humanity.

[12] Loofs, *Nestoriana*, p. 262, cf. *Contra Nestorium* ii, 12, 13 (*ACO* 1, 1, 6 pp. 50 f.).

[13] Cf. (Ps.)Athanasius, *Ad Jovianum*: προσκυνουμένην μετὰ τῆς σαρκὸς αὐτοῦ μίᾳ προσκυνήσει (Lietzmann, *Apollinaris*, etc. p. 251, 2 f.), see p. 63 n. 3.

τῇ ἀνθρώπου φύσει τὴν εἰς ἀφθαρσίαν ἀναδρομήν, χάριτι θεοῦ,
καθάπερ ἔφημεν ἀρτίως, ὑπὲρ παντὸς ἐγεύσατο θανάτου τριήμε-
ρός τε ἀνεβίω σκυλεύσας τὸν ᾅδην. ὥστε κἂν λέγηται δι' ἀνθρώπου
γενέσθαι ἡ ἀνάστασις τῶν νεκρῶν,ʳ ἀλλὰ νοοῦμεν ἄνθρωπον τὸν ἐκ
θεοῦ γεγονότα λόγον καὶ λελύσθαι δι' αὐτοῦ τοῦ θανάτου τὸ κράτος. 5
ἥξει δὲ κατὰ καιροὺς ὡς εἰς υἱὸς καὶ κύριος ἐν τῇ δόξῃ τοῦ πατρός,
ἵνα κρίνῃ τὴν οἰκουμένην ἐν δικαιοσύνῃ,ˢ καθὰ γέγραπται.

7. Ἀναγκαίως δὲ κἀκεῖνο προσθήσομεν. καταγγέλλοντες γὰρ τὸν
κατὰ σάρκα θάνατον τοῦ μονογενοῦς υἱοῦ τοῦ θεοῦ, τουτέστιν
Ἰησοῦ Χριστοῦ τήν τε ἐκ νεκρῶν ἀναβίωσιν καὶ τὴν εἰς οὐρανοὺς 10
ἀνάληψιν ὁμολογοῦντες, τὴν ἀναίμακτον ἐν ταῖς ἐκκλησίαις τελοῦμεν
λατρείαν πρόσιμέν τε οὕτω ταῖς μυστικαῖς εὐλογίαις καὶ ἁγιαζόμεθα
μέτοχοι γινόμενοι τῆς τε ἁγίας σαρκὸς καὶ τοῦ τιμίου αἵματος τοῦ
πάντων ἡμῶν σωτῆρος Χριστοῦ καὶ οὐχ ὡς σάρκα κοινὴν δεχόμενοι,
μὴ γένοιτο, οὔτε μὴν ὡς ἀνδρὸς ἡγιασμένου καὶ συναφθέντος τῷ 15
λόγῳ κατὰ τὴν ἑνότητα τῆς ἀξίας ἢ γοῦν ὡς θείαν ἐνοίκησιν
ἐσχηκότος, ἀλλ' ὡς ζωοποιὸν ἀληθῶς καὶ ἰδίαν αὐτοῦ τοῦ λόγου.
ζωὴ γὰρ ὢν κατὰ φύσιν ὡς θεός, ἐπειδὴ γέγονεν ἓν πρὸς τὴν
ἑαυτοῦ σάρκα, ζωοποιὸν ἀπέφηνεν αὐτήν, ὥστε κἂν λέγῃ πρὸς
ἡμᾶς ἀμὴν λέγω ὑμῖν, ἐὰν μὴ φάγητε τὴν σάρκα τοῦ υἱοῦ 20
τοῦ ἀνθρώπου καὶ πίητε αὐτοῦ τὸ αἷμα,ᵗ οὐχ ὡς ἀνθρώπου
τῶν καθ' ἡμᾶς ἑνὸς καὶ αὐτὴν εἶναι λογιούμεθα (πῶς γὰρ ἡ
ἀνθρώπου σὰρξ ζωοποιὸς ἔσται κατὰ φύσιν τὴν ἑαυτῆς;), ἀλλ' ὡς
ἰδίαν ἀληθῶς γενομένην τοῦ δι' ἡμᾶς καὶ υἱοῦ ἀνθρώπου γεγονότος
τε καὶ χρηματίσαντος. 25

8. Τὰς δέ γε ἐν τοῖς εὐαγγελίοις τοῦ σωτῆρος ἡμῶν φωνὰς οὔτε
ὑποστάσεσι δυσὶν οὔτε μὴν προσώποις καταμερίζομεν. οὐ γάρ ἐστι
διπλοῦς ὁ εἰς καὶ μόνος Χριστός, κἂν ἐκ δύο νοῆται καὶ διαφόρων
πραγμάτων εἰς ἑνότητα τὴν ἀμέριστον συνενηνεγμένος, καθάπερ
ἀμέλει καὶ ἄνθρωπος ἐκ ψυχῆς νοεῖται καὶ σώματος καὶ οὐ διπλοῦς 30
μᾶλλον, ἀλλ' εἰς ἐξ ἀμφοῖν. ἀλλὰ τάς τε ἀνθρωπίνας καὶ πρός γε
τούτῳ τὰς θεϊκὰς παρ' ἑνὸς εἰρῆσθαι διακεισόμεθα, φρονοῦντες
ὀρθῶς. ὅταν μὲν γὰρ θεοπρεπῶς λέγῃ περὶ ἑαυτοῦ ὁ ἑωρακὼς
ἐμὲ ἑώρακε τὸν πατέραᵘ καὶ ἐγὼ καὶ ὁ πατὴρ ἓν ἐσμέν,ᵛ τὴν

ʳ cf. 1 Cor. 15: 21   ˢ Acts 17: 31   ᵗ John 6: 53   ᵘ John 14: 9
ᵛ John 10: 30

he might blaze the trail for human nature's return to incorruptibility; '*by God's grace*' (as we have just said) he tasted death for every man, harrowed Hell and came back to life the third day. The result is that though the resurrection of the dead is asserted to have been brought about '*through man*' we nonetheless interpret the phrase as meaning the Word of God made man and death's power as having been broken through him. He shall come in due time, one Son and Lord in his Father's glory to judge '*the world in righteousness*', as the Bible says.

7. This too we must add. We proclaim the fleshly death of God's only-begotten Son, Jesus Christ, we confess his return to life from the dead and his ascension into heaven when we perform in church the unbloody service, when we approach the sacramental gifts and are hallowed participants in the holy flesh and precious blood of Christ, saviour of us all, by receiving not mere flesh (God forbid!) or flesh of a man hallowed by connection with the Word in some unity of dignity or possessing some divine indwelling, but the personal, truly vitalizing flesh of God the Word himself. As God he is by nature Life and because he has become one with his own flesh he rendered it vitalizing; and so, though he tells us '*verily I say unto you, unless you eat the flesh of the Son of Man and drink his blood*', we must not suppose it belongs to one of us men (how could man's flesh be vitalizing by its own nature?) but that it was made the truly personal possession of him who for us has become and was called 'Son of Man'.[14]

8. As for our Saviour's statements in the Gospels, we do not divide them out to two subjects or persons. The one, unique Christ has no duality though he is seen as compounded in inseparable unity out of two differing elements in the way that a human being, for example, is seen to have no duality but to be one, consisting of the pair of elements, body and soul. We must take the right view and maintain that human as well as divine expressions are from one speaker. When he talks of himself in terms appropriate to God: '*He who has seen me has seen the Father*' and '*The Father and I are one*', we understand his divine

---

[14] The argument from the eucharist is regular in Cyril's anti-Nestorian polemic, cf. *Contra Nestorium* iv, 4 ff. It is perhaps the most revelatory of the religious feelings he appealed to; cf. H. Chadwick, 'Eucharist and Christology in the Nestorian controversy', *JTS* 2 (1951), esp. 153 ff.

θείαν αὐτοῦ καὶ ἀπόρρητον ἐννοοῦμεν φύσιν, καθ᾽ ἣν καὶ ἕν ἐστι
πρὸς τὸν ἑαυτοῦ πατέρα διὰ τὴν ταυτότητα τῆς οὐσίας εἰκών τε
καὶ χαρακτὴρ καὶ ἀπαύγασμα τῆς δόξης αὐτοῦ.[w] ὅταν δὲ τὸ τῆς
ἀνθρωπότητος μέτρον οὐκ ἀτιμάζων τοῖς Ἰουδαίοις προσλαλῇ νῦν
δέ με ζητεῖτε ἀποκτεῖναι, ἄνθρωπον ὃς τὴν ἀλήθειαν   5
ὑμῖν λελάληκα,[x] πάλιν οὐδὲν ἧττον αὐτὸν τὸν ἐν ἰσότητί τε καὶ
ὁμοιότητι τοῦ πατρὸς θεὸν λόγον καὶ ἐκ τῶν τῆς ἀνθρωπότητος
αὐτοῦ μέτρων ἐπιγινώσκομεν. εἰ γάρ ἐστιν ἀναγκαῖον τὸ πιστεύειν
ὅτι θεὸς ὢν φύσει γέγονε σὰρξ ἢ γοῦν ἄνθρωπος ἐψυχωμένος ψυχῇ
λογικῇ, ποῖον ἂν ἔχοι λόγον τὸ ἐπαισχύνεσθαί τινα ταῖς παρ᾽ αὐτοῦ   10
φωναῖς, εἰ γεγόνασιν ἀνθρωποπρεπῶς; εἰ γὰρ παραιτοῖτο τοὺς
ἀνθρώπῳ πρέποντας λόγους, τίς ὁ ἀναγκάσας γενέσθαι καθ᾽ ἡμᾶς
ἄνθρωπον; ὁ δὲ καθεὶς ἑαυτὸν δι᾽ ἡμᾶς εἰς ἑκούσιον κένωσιν διὰ
ποίαν αἰτίαν παραιτοῖτο ἂν τοὺς τῇ κενώσει πρέποντας λόγους;
ἑνὶ τοιγαροῦν προσώπῳ τὰς ἐν τοῖς εὐαγγελίοις πάσας ἀναθετέον   15
φωνάς, ὑποστάσει μιᾷ τῇ τοῦ λόγου σεσαρκωμένῃ. κύριος γὰρ εἷς
Ἰησοῦς Χριστὸς[y] κατὰ τὰς γραφάς.

9. Εἰ δὲ δὴ καλοῖτο καὶ ἀπόστολος καὶ ἀρχιερεὺς τῆς ὁμολογίας
ἡμῶν,[z] ὡς ἱερουργῶν τῷ θεῷ καὶ πατρὶ τὴν πρὸς ἡμῶν αὐτῷ τε
καὶ δι᾽ αὐτοῦ τῷ θεῷ καὶ πατρὶ προσκομιζομένην τῆς πίστεως   20
ὁμολογίαν καὶ μὴν καὶ εἰς τὸ ἅγιον πνεῦμα, πάλιν αὐτὸν εἶναι
φαμὲν τὸν ἐκ θεοῦ κατὰ φύσιν υἱὸν μονογενῆ καὶ οὐκ ἀνθρώπῳ
προσνεμοῦμεν παρ᾽ αὐτὸν ἑτέρῳ τό τε τῆς ἱερωσύνης ὄνομα καὶ
αὐτὸ δὲ τὸ χρῆμα. γέγονε γὰρ μεσίτης θεοῦ καὶ ἀνθρώπων[a] καὶ
διαλλακτὴς εἰς εἰρήνην,[b] ἑαυτὸν ἀναθεὶς εἰς ὀσμὴν εὐωδίας τῷ θεῷ   25
καὶ πατρί.[c] τοιγάρτοι καὶ ἔφασκε θυσίαν καὶ προσφορὰν οὐκ
ἠθέλησας, σῶμα δὲ κατηρτίσω μοι. ὁλοκαυτώματα καὶ
περὶ ἁμαρτίας οὐκ εὐδόκησας. τότε εἶπον· ἰδοὺ ἥκω· ἐν
κεφαλίδι βιβλίου γέγραπται περὶ ἐμοῦ τοῦ ποιῆσαι, ὁ
θεός, τὸ θέλημά σου.[d] προσκεκόμικε γὰρ ὑπὲρ ἡμῶν εἰς ὀσμὴν   30
εὐωδίας τὸ ἴδιον σῶμα καὶ οὐχ ὑπέρ γε μᾶλλον ἑαυτοῦ. ποίας γὰρ
ἂν ἐδεήθη προσφορᾶς ἢ θυσίας ὑπὲρ ἑαυτοῦ, κρείττων ἁπάσης

---

[w] cf. Heb. 1 : 3   [x] John 8 : 40   [y] cf. 1 Cor. 8 : 6   [z] cf.
Heb. 3 : 1   [a] cf. 1 Tim. 2 : 5   [b] cf. Acts 7 : 26   [c] cf. Eph. 5 : 2
[d] Heb. 10 : 5 ff.

and inexpressible nature in virtue of which he is one with his
Father by identity of substance, is image, stamp and effulgence
of his Father's glory. When on the other hand he respects the
limitations of humanity and tells the Jews: '*Now you are seeking
to kill me, a man who has told you the truth*', the limitations of his
humanity do not make us any less conscious of him as God the
Word in equality and parity with the Father. For if it is essential
to believe that whilst being God by nature he has become flesh,
that is to say man endowed with life and reason,[15] what ground
is there for anybody to be ashamed of sayings on his part if they
are expressed in terms appropriate to man? If he had refused
the conditions appropriate to man, could anyone have forced
him to be made man like us? Why should one who condescends
to voluntary abasement for us refuse the conditions appropriate
to that abasement? Accordingly all the sayings contained in the
Gospels must be referred to a single person, to the one incarnate
subject of the Word.[16] For according to the Bible there is one
Lord, Jesus Christ.

9. Moreover when he is styled 'Apostle and High-Priest of
our confession'[17] on the grounds that he renders our confession
of faith, as it is proffered to him and through him to God the
Father and to the Holy Ghost as well, in sacrifice to God the
Father, we reaffirm him to be by nature the Only-begotten Son
of God and do not allocate the title and reality of priesthood to
a different 'man'. He has been made mediator between God and
men, agent of peaceful reconciliation, by offering himself as a
fragrant sacrifice to God the Father. That is why he said:
'*Sacrifice and offering thou didst not desire, but thou didst prepare a body
for me. Whole offerings and sin-offerings thou didst not delight in. Then
I said, "Here I come; it is written of me in the scroll to do thy will, O
God."* ' He proffered his own body as a fragrant sacrifice for us
and not for himself. What need had he, God as he is, utterly
transcending sin, of offering or sacrifice on his own behalf?

[15] Cf. *Answers to Tiberius* 7, below p. 159, and *On the Creed* § 14.
[16] The phrase is equivalent to μία φύσις κ.τ.λ.
[17] For the development of the argument cf. *Fragmenta Homiliarum* 10 (Pusey 3,
466 ff.) and *In Ep. ad Hebr.* (ibid, 400 ff.). Cyril understands by 'our confession'
the acknowledgement of faith in the Trinity which Christ creates in us as an
offering both to himself and to Father and Holy Ghost. See further for a
related discussion J.-C. Dhôtel 'La "sanctification" du Christ d'après *Hébreux*,
2, 11', *RSR* 47 (1959), 515–43, esp. 525 ff.

ὑπάρχων ἁμαρτίας ὡς θεός; εἰ γὰρ πάντες ἥμαρτον καὶ ὑστε-
ροῦνται τῆς δόξης τοῦ θεοῦ,[e] καθὸ γεγόναμεν ἡμεῖς ἕτοιμοι
πρὸς παραφορὰν καὶ κατηρρώστησεν ἡ ἀνθρώπου φύσις τὴν
ἁμαρτίαν, αὐτὸς δὲ οὐχ οὕτως καὶ ἡττώμεθα διὰ τοῦτο τῆς δόξης
αὐτοῦ, πῶς ἂν εἴη λοιπὸν ἀμφίβολον ὅτι τέθυται δι' ἡμᾶς καὶ ὑπὲρ 5
ἡμῶν ὁ ἀμνὸς ὁ ἀληθινός; καὶ τὸ λέγειν ὅτι προσκεκόμικεν ἑαυτὸν
ὑπέρ τε ἑαυτοῦ καὶ ἡμῶν, ἀμοιρήσειεν ἂν οὐδαμῶς τῶν εἰς δυσσέβειαν
ἐγκλημάτων. πεπλημμέληκε γὰρ κατ' οὐδένα τρόπον οὔτε μὴν
ἐποίησεν ἁμαρτίαν· ποίας οὖν ἐδεήθη προσφορᾶς, ἁμαρτίας οὐκ
οὔσης ἐφ' ᾗπερ ἂν γένοιτο καὶ μάλα εἰκότως; 10

10. Ὅταν δὲ λέγῃ περὶ τοῦ πνεύματος ἐκεῖνος ἐμὲ δοξάσει,[f]
νοοῦντες ὀρθῶς οὐχ ὡς δόξης ἐπιδεᾶ τῆς παρ' ἑτέρου φαμὲν τὸν
ἕνα Χριστὸν καὶ υἱὸν τὴν παρὰ τοῦ ἁγίου πνεύματος δόξαν ἑλεῖν,
ὅτι μηδὲ κρεῖττον αὐτοῦ καὶ ὑπὲρ αὐτὸν τὸ πνεῦμα αὐτοῦ. ἐπειδὴ
δὲ εἰς ἔνδειξιν τῆς ἑαυτοῦ θεότητος ἐχρῆτο τῷ ἰδίῳ πνεύματι πρὸς 15
μεγαλουργίας, δεδοξάσθαι παρ' αὐτοῦ φησιν, ὥσπερ ἂν εἰ καί τις
λέγοι τῶν καθ' ἡμᾶς περὶ τῆς ἐνούσης ἰσχύος αὐτῷ τυχὸν ἢ γοῦν
ἐπιστήμης τῆς ἐφ' ὁτῳοῦν ὅτι δοξάσουσί με. εἰ γὰρ καὶ ἔστιν ἐν
ὑποστάσει τὸ πνεῦμα ἰδικῇ καὶ δὴ καὶ νοεῖται καθ' ἑαυτό, καθὸ
πνεῦμά ἐστιν καὶ οὐχ υἱός, ἀλλ' οὖν ἐστιν οὐκ ἀλλότριον αὐτοῦ. 20
πνεῦμα γὰρ ἀληθείας[g] ὠνόμασται καὶ ἔστιν Χριστὸς ἡ ἀλήθεια[h]
καὶ προχεῖται παρ' αὐτοῦ καθάπερ ἀμέλει καὶ ἐκ τοῦ θεοῦ καὶ
πατρός. ἐνεργῆσαν τοιγαροῦν τὸ πνεῦμα καὶ διὰ χειρὸς τῶν ἁγίων
ἀποστόλων τὰ παράδοξα μετὰ τὸ ἀνελθεῖν τὸν κύριον ἡμῶν Ἰησοῦν
Χριστὸν εἰς τὸν οὐρανὸν ἐδόξασεν αὐτόν. ἐπιστεύθη γὰρ ὅτι θεὸς 25
κατὰ φύσιν ἐστίν, πάλιν αὐτὸς ἐνεργῶν διὰ τοῦ ἰδίου πνεύματος.
διὰ τοῦτο καὶ ἔφασκεν ὅτι ἐκ τοῦ ἐμοῦ λήψεται καὶ ἀπαγγελεῖ
ὑμῖν.[i] καὶ οὔτι που φαμὲν ὡς ἐκ μετοχῆς τὸ πνεῦμά ἐστι σοφόν τε
καὶ δυνατόν. παντέλειον γὰρ καὶ ἀπροσδεές ἐστι παντὸς ἀγαθοῦ.
ἐπειδὴ δὲ τῆς τοῦ πατρὸς δυνάμεως καὶ σοφίας,[j] τουτέστι τοῦ υἱοῦ, 30
πνεῦμά ἐστιν, αὐτόχρημα σοφία ἐστὶ καὶ δύναμις.

11. Ἐπειδὴ δὲ θεὸν ἑνωθέντα σαρκὶ καθ' ὑπόστασιν ἡ ἁγία
παρθένος ἐκτέτοκε σαρκικῶς, ταύτῃ τοι καὶ θεοτόκον εἶναι φαμὲν
αὐτήν, οὐχ ὡς τῆς τοῦ λόγου φύσεως τῆς ὑπάρξεως τὴν ἀρχὴν

---

[e] Rom. 3: 23   [f] John 16: 14   [g] John 16: 13   [h] cf. John 14: 6
[i] John 16: 14   [j] cf. 1 Cor. 1: 24

If '*all sinned and are deprived of God's glory*' in the sense that we have
become prone to stray and that man's nature became utterly
sick with sin but if this is not *his* condition and that is why we
yield to his glory, what doubt remains that the true Lamb has
been sacrificed on our account and our behalf? To say that he
proffered himself on his own behalf as well as ours cannot fail
to incur the charge of blasphemy. He has not offended in any
way and he committed no sin. Did he need any sort of offering
in the absence of the sin for which it should properly have been
made?

10. When he says of the Spirit: '*He will glorify me*', we rightly
interpret him as not meaning that the one Christ and Son was
deficient in glory and acquired glory from the Holy Ghost,
because his Spirit has no superiority over him. He talks of having
been glorified by him because he used his own Spirit in the
performance of great acts to show his personal Godhead; in
the same way an ordinary person might talk of the physical
strength or particular skill he has as 'bringing glory' to him.
Though, indeed, the Spirit exists as a distinct subject and is
recognized specifically as Spirit and not Son, yet the Spirit is
not alien to him. He is called '*Truth's Spirit*' and Christ is the
Truth; he is poured out by Christ just as he is poured forth from
God the Father. The Spirit, then, worked miracles through the
agency of the holy apostles and glorified our Lord Jesus Christ
after his ascension into heaven. For it was by acting personally
through his own Spirit that he was believed to be God in nature.
That is why he said: '*He will take what belongs to me and proclaim
it to you.*' Not for one moment do we assert that the Spirit is
wise and powerful by participation. He is utterly perfect and
complete in goodness. Since he is the Spirit of the Father's
wisdom and power (that is to say, the Son) he is absolute wisdom
and power.

11. For the very reason that the holy Virgin gave fleshly birth
to God substantially united with flesh we declare her to be
'Mother of God', not because the Word's nature somehow

ἐχούσης ἀπὸ σαρκός (ἦν γὰρ ἐν ἀρχῇ καὶ θεὸς ἦν ὁ λόγος καὶ
ὁ λόγος ἦν πρὸς τὸν θεὸν[k] καὶ αὐτός ἐστι τῶν αἰώνων ὁ ποιητής,
συναΐδιος τῷ πατρὶ καὶ τῶν ὅλων δημιουργός), ἀλλ' ὡς ἤδη
προείπομεν, ἐπειδὴ καθ' ὑπόστασιν ἑνώσας ἑαυτῷ τὸ ἀνθρώπινον
καὶ ἐκ μήτρας αὐτῆς γέννησιν ὑπέμεινε σαρκικήν, οὐχ ὡς δεηθεὶς 5
ἀναγκαίως ἤτοι διὰ τὴν ἰδίαν φύσιν καὶ τῆς ἐν χρόνῳ καὶ ἐν ἐσχάτοις
τοῦ αἰῶνος καιροῖς γεννήσεως, ἀλλ' ἵνα καὶ αὐτὴν τῆς ὑπάρξεως
ἡμῶν εὐλογήσῃ τὴν ἀρχὴν καὶ τεκούσης γυναικὸς αὐτὸν ἑνωθέντα
σαρκὶ παύσηται λοιπὸν ἡ κατὰ παντὸς τοῦ γένους ἀρὰ πέμπουσα
πρὸς θάνατον τὰ ἐκ γῆς ἡμῶν σώματα καὶ τὸ ἐν λύπαις τέξῃ 10
τέκνα[l] δι' αὐτοῦ καταργούμενον ἀληθὲς ἀποφήνῃ τὸ διὰ τῆς τοῦ
προφήτου φωνῆς κατέπιεν ὁ θάνατος ἰσχύσας καὶ πάλιν
ἀφεῖλεν ὁ θεὸς πᾶν δάκρυον ἀπὸ παντὸς προσώπου.[m]
ταύτης γὰρ ἕνεκα τῆς αἰτίας φαμὲν αὐτὸν οἰκονομικῶς καὶ αὐτὸν
εὐλογῆσαι τὸν γάμον καὶ ἀπελθεῖν κεκλημένον ἐν Κανᾷ τῆς Γαλι- 15
λαίας ὁμοῦ τοῖς ἁγίοις ἀποστόλοις.[n]

12. Ταῦτα φρονεῖν δεδιδάγμεθα παρά τε τῶν ἁγίων ἀποστόλων
καὶ εὐαγγελιστῶν, καὶ πάσης δὲ τῆς θεοπνεύστου γραφῆς καὶ ἐκ
τῆς τῶν μακαρίων πατέρων ἀληθοῦς ὁμολογίας· τούτοις ἅπασιν καὶ
τὴν σὴν εὐλάβειαν συναινέσαι χρὴ καὶ συνθέσθαι δίχα δόλου παντός. 20
ἃ δέ ἐστιν ἀναγκαῖον ἀναθεματίσαι τὴν σὴν εὐλάβειαν, ὑποτέτακται
τῇδε ἡμῶν τῇ ἐπιστολῇ.

α΄ Εἴ τις οὐχ ὁμολογεῖ θεὸν εἶναι κατὰ ἀλήθειαν τὸν Ἐμμανουὴλ
καὶ διὰ τοῦτο θεοτόκον τὴν ἁγίαν παρθένον (γεγέννηκε γὰρ σαρκικῶς σάρκα γεγονότα τὸν ἐκ θεοῦ λόγον), ἀνάθεμα ἔστω. 25

β΄ Εἴ τις οὐχ ὁμολογεῖ σαρκὶ καθ' ὑπόστασιν ἡνῶσθαι τὸν ἐκ
θεοῦ πατρὸς λόγον ἕνα τε εἶναι Χριστὸν μετὰ τῆς ἰδίας σαρκός, τὸν
αὐτὸν δηλονότι θεόν τε ὁμοῦ καὶ ἄνθρωπον, ἀνάθεμα ἔστω.

γ΄ Εἴ τις ἐπὶ τοῦ ἑνὸς Χριστοῦ διαιρεῖ τὰς ὑποστάσεις μετὰ τὴν
ἕνωσιν, μόνῃ συνάπτων αὐτὰς συναφείᾳ τῇ κατὰ τὴν ἀξίαν ἢ γοῦν 30
αὐθεντίαν ἢ δυναστείαν καὶ οὐχὶ δὴ μᾶλλον συνόδῳ τῇ καθ' ἕνωσιν
φυσικήν, ἀνάθεμα ἔστω.

[k] John 1:1   [l] Gen. 3:16   [m] Is. 25:8   [n] cf. John 2:1 f.

derived its origin from flesh (he was, after all, '*in the beginning*', '*the Word was God*', '*the Word was with God*' and is personally the creator of the worlds, co-eternal with the Father and artificer of the universe) but because, as we previously affirmed, he substantially united humanity with himself, and underwent fleshly birth from her womb. He had no need of temporal birth, in the last days of the world, for his own nature. No, he meant to bless the very origin of our existence, through a woman's giving birth to him united with flesh, meant too that the curse on the whole race which dispatches our earthly bodies to death should cease as well as the words (from now on rendered null and void by him) '*in sorrow you shall bear children*', and he intended to prove true the prophet's utterance '*Death waxed strong and swallowed and again God took away every tear from every countenance*'. This is our reason for affirming of him that he personally blessed marriage by his incarnation as well as by responding to the invitation to leave for Cana in Galilee along with the holy apostles.[18]

12. These are the views we have been taught to hold both by the holy apostles and evangelists and by inspired Scripture in its entirety and from the true confession of the blessed fathers. Your Piety must assent to all this and give it your entire unfeigned concurrence. What your Piety must anathematize, is set down here in our letter:

1. Whoever does not acknowledge Emmanuel to be truly God and hence the holy Virgin 'Mother of God' (for she gave fleshly birth to the Word of God made flesh) shall be anathema.[19]

2. Whoever does not acknowledge the Word of God the Father to have been substantially united with flesh and to be one Christ along with his own flesh, that is the same at once God and man, shall be anathema.[20]

3. Whoever divides the subjects in respect to the one Christ after the union, joining them together just in a conjunction involving rank i.e. sovereignty or authority instead of a combination involving actual union shall be anathema.[21]

---

[18] Cf. *In Jo.* 2, 1 (Pusey 1, 200 f.), where the reason for Christ's presence at Cana is explained—to perform a miracle, sanctify the bodily aspect of human generation, and reverse Eve's curse. His own birth is here added as a reason for these effects.

[19] See above, § 11. (Note the qualifications omitted in the anathematisms but present in the preceding letter.)

[20] See above, §§ 4 f.

[21] See above, § 5 n. 11.

δ' Εἴ τις προσώποις δυσὶν ἢ γοῦν ὑποστάσεσι τάς τε ἐν τοῖς
εὐαγγελικοῖς καὶ ἀποστολικοῖς συγγράμμασι διανέμει φωνὰς ἢ ἐπὶ
Χριστῷ παρὰ τῶν ἁγίων λεγομένας ἢ παρ' αὐτοῦ περὶ ἑαυτοῦ
καὶ τὰς μὲν ὡς ἀνθρώπῳ παρὰ τὸν ἐκ θεοῦ λόγον ἰδικῶς νοουμένῳ
προσάπτει, τὰς δὲ ὡς θεοπρεπεῖς μόνῳ τῷ ἐκ θεοῦ πατρὸς λόγῳ, 5
ἀνάθεμα ἔστω.

ε' Εἴ τις τολμᾷ λέγειν θεοφόρον ἄνθρωπον τὸν Χριστὸν καὶ οὐχὶ
δὴ μᾶλλον θεὸν εἶναι κατὰ ἀλήθειαν ὡς υἱὸν ἕνα καὶ φύσει, καθὸ
γέγονε σὰρξ ὁ λόγος καὶ κεκοινώνηκε παραπλησίως ἡμῖν αἵματος
καὶ σαρκός,[o] ἀνάθεμα ἔστω.   10

ϛ' Εἴ τις λέγει θεὸν ἢ δεσπότην εἶναι τοῦ Χριστοῦ τὸν ἐκ θεοῦ
πατρὸς λόγον καὶ οὐχὶ δὴ μᾶλλον τὸν αὐτὸν ὁμολογεῖ θεόν τε ὁμοῦ
καὶ ἄνθρωπον, ὡς γεγονότος σαρκὸς τοῦ λόγου[p] κατὰ τὰς γραφάς,
ἀνάθεμα ἔστω.

ζ' Εἴ τίς φησιν ὡς ἄνθρωπον ἐνηργῆσθαι παρὰ τοῦ θεοῦ λόγου 15
τὸν Ἰησοῦν καὶ τὴν τοῦ μονογενοῦς εὐδοξίαν περιῆφθαι ὡς ἑτέρῳ
παρ' αὐτὸν ὑπάρχοντι, ἀνάθεμα ἔστω.

η' Εἴ τις τολμᾷ λέγειν τὸν ἀναληφθέντα ἄνθρωπον συμπροσ-
κυνεῖσθαι δεῖν τῷ θεῷ λόγῳ καὶ συνδοξάζεσθαι καὶ συγ-
χρηματίζειν θεὸν ὡς ἕτερον ἑτέρῳ (τὸ γὰρ "σύν" ἀεὶ προστιθέμενον 20
τοῦτο νοεῖν ἀναγκάσει) καὶ οὐχὶ δὴ μᾶλλον μιᾷ προσκυνήσει τιμᾷ
τὸν Ἐμμανουὴλ καὶ μίαν αὐτῷ τὴν δοξολογίαν ἀνάπτει, καθὸ
γέγονε σὰρξ ὁ λόγος, ἀνάθεμα ἔστω.

θ' Εἴ τίς φησι τὸν ἕνα κύριον Ἰησοῦν Χριστὸν δεδοξάσθαι παρὰ
τοῦ πνεύματος, ὡς ἀλλοτρίᾳ δυνάμει τῇ δι' αὐτοῦ χρώμενον καὶ 25
παρ' αὐτοῦ λαβόντα τὸ ἐνεργεῖν δύνασθαι κατὰ πνευμάτων ἀκαθάρ-
των καὶ τὸ πληροῦν εἰς ἀνθρώπους τὰς θεοσημείας, καὶ οὐχὶ δὴ
μᾶλλον ἴδιον αὐτοῦ τὸ πνεῦμά φησιν, δι' οὗ καὶ ἐνήργηκε τὰς
θεοσημείας, ἀνάθεμα ἔστω.

ι' Ἀρχιερέα καὶ ἀπόστολον τῆς ὁμολογίας ἡμῶν γεγενῆσθαι 30
Χριστὸν[q] ἡ θεία λέγει γραφή, προσκεκόμικε δὲ ὑπὲρ ἡμῶν ἑαυτὸν
εἰς ὀσμὴν εὐωδίας τῷ θεῷ καὶ πατρί.[r] εἴ τις τοίνυν ἀρχιερέα καὶ

---

[o] cf. Heb. 2: 14   [p] cf. John 1: 14   [q] cf. Heb. 3: 1   [r] cf.
Eph. 5: 2

4. Whoever allocates the terms contained in the gospels and apostolic writings and applied to Christ by the saints or used of himself by himself to two persons or subjects and attaches some to the man considered separately from the Word of God, some as divine to the Word of God the Father alone, shall be anathema.[22]

5. Whoever has the temerity to state that Christ is a divinely inspired man instead of saying that he is truly God as being one Son by nature, because the Word was made flesh and shared in flesh and blood like us, shall be anathema.[23]

6. Whoever says the Word of God the Father is Christ's God or Master instead of acknowledging the same Christ at once God and man on the scriptural ground of the Word's having been made flesh, shall be anathema.[24]

7. Whoever says that the man Jesus is under the control of God the Word and that the glory of the Only-begotten attaches to a different entity from the Only-begotten shall be anathema.[25]

8. Whoever has the temerity to assert that the assumed man should be worshipped along with God the Word, that one should be praised and be styled 'God' along with another (the addition of 'along with' will always entail this interpretation) instead of venerating Emmanuel with a single worship and ascribing to him a single act of praise because the Word has been made flesh, shall be anathema.[26]

9. Whoever says that the one Lord Jesus Christ has been glorified by the Spirit, Christ using the force mediated by the Spirit as an alien force and having acquired from him the ability to act against foul spirits and to perform miracles on human beings instead of saying that the Spirit whereby he effected the miracles is Christ's own, shall be anathema.[27]

10. Divine Scripture says Christ has been made 'High Priest and Apostle of our confession' and 'gave himself up for us as a fragrant offering to God the Father'. So whoever says that it

---

[22] See above, § 8 and *To Acacius of Melitene* 13.
[23] See above, § 4.
[24] See above, § 5.
[25] Without counterpart.
[26] See above, § 6.
[27] See above, § 10 and *Answers to Tiberius* 4 with n. 28.

ἀπόστολον ἡμῶν γεγενῆσθαί φησιν οὐκ αὐτὸν τὸν ἐκ θεοῦ λόγον, ὅτε γέγονε σὰρξ καὶ καθ᾽ ἡμᾶς ἄνθρωπος, ἀλλ᾽ ὡς ἕτερον παρ᾽ αὐτὸν ἰδικῶς ἄνθρωπον ἐκ γυναικός, ἢ εἴ τις λέγει καὶ ὑπὲρ ἑαυτοῦ προσενεγκεῖν αὐτὸν τὴν προσφορὰν καὶ οὐχὶ δὴ μᾶλλον ὑπὲρ μόνων ἡμῶν (οὐ γὰρ ἂν ἐδεήθη προσφορᾶς ὁ μὴ εἰδὼς ἁμαρτίαν), 5 ἀνάθεμα ἔστω.

ια΄ Εἴ τις οὐχ ὁμολογεῖ τὴν τοῦ κυρίου σάρκα ζωοποιὸν εἶναι καὶ ἰδίαν αὐτοῦ τοῦ ἐκ θεοῦ πατρὸς λόγου, ἀλλ᾽ ὡς ἑτέρου τινὸς παρ᾽ αὐτὸν συνημμένου μὲν αὐτῷ κατὰ τὴν ἀξίαν ἢ γοῦν ὡς μόνην θείαν ἐνοίκησιν ἐσχηκότος, καὶ οὐχὶ δὴ μᾶλλον ζωοποιόν, ὡς 10 ἔφημεν, ὅτι γέγονεν ἰδία τοῦ λόγου τοῦ τὰ πάντα ζωογονεῖν ἰσχύοντος, ἀνάθεμα ἔστω.

ιβ΄ Εἴ τις οὐχ ὁμολογεῖ τὸν τοῦ θεοῦ λόγον παθόντα σαρκὶ καὶ ἐσταυρωμένον σαρκὶ καὶ θανάτου γευσάμενον σαρκὶ γεγονότα τε πρωτότοκον ἐκ τῶν νεκρῶν, καθὸ ζωή τέ ἐστι καὶ ζωοποιὸς ὡς 15 θεός, ἀνάθεμα ἔστω.

was not the Word of God personally who was made our High Priest and Apostle when he became flesh and man as we are, but another woman-born man separate from him, or whoever asserts he made the offering for himself too instead of for us alone (for he who knew no sin did not need an offering) shall be anathema.[28]

11. Whoever does not acknowledge the Lord's flesh to be vitalizing and to belong to the very Word of God the Father but says it belongs to somebody different joined to him by way of rank or merely possessing divine indwelling instead of being vitalizing, as we said, because it has come to belong to the Word who has power to vivify everything, shall be anathema.[29]

12. Whoever does not acknowledge God's Word as having suffered in flesh, been crucified in flesh, tasted death in flesh and been made first-born from the dead because as God he is Life and life-giving, shall be anathema.[30]

[28] See above, § 9.   [29] See above, § 7.   [30] See above, § 6.

3

TO ACACIUS OF MELITENE

Τοῦ αὐτοῦ πρὸς Ἀκάκιον ἐπίσκοπον Μελιτηνῆς

1. Κυρίῳ μου ἀγαπητῷ ἀδελφῷ καὶ συλλειτουργῷ Ἀκακίῳ
Κύριλλος ἐν κυρίῳ χαίρειν.

Χρῆμα μὲν ἀδελφοῖς ἡ πρόσρησις γλυκύ τε καὶ ἀξιάγαστον καὶ
τοῦ παντὸς ἄξιον λόγου παρά γε τοῖς ἀρτίφροσιν ἀληθῶς· χρῆναι 5
δὲ φημὶ τοὺς ὁμοπίστους τε καὶ ὁμοψύχους ἀδιαλείπτως ἐπείγεσθαι
τοῦτο δρᾶν, οὐδενὸς ὄντος ἐμποδὼν οὔτε μὴν ἀνακόπτοντος τὴν εἰς
γε τοῦτο θερμὴν ἔφεσίν τε καὶ προθυμίαν. ἀλλ᾽ ἔσθ᾽ ὅτε βασκαίνει
καὶ οὐχ ἑκοῦσιν ἡμῖν ἢ τῶν μεταξὺ διαστημάτων τὸ μῆκος ἢ τῶν
τοῦ γράμματος διακομιστῶν ἡ σπάνις· καιροῦ δὲ τὸ δύνασθαι 10
προσειπεῖν εἰσφέροντος, εὕρεμα ποιεῖσθαι προσήκει τὸ πρᾶγμα καὶ
τοῖς τριποθήτοις ἀσμένως ἐπιπηδᾶν. ἡσθεὶς δὴ οὖν ἄγαν ἐπὶ τοῖς
παρὰ τῆς σῆς τελειότητος ἐπεσταλμένοις καὶ τεθαυμακὼς τὴν
διάθεσιν, δεῖν ᾠήθην τῆς τῶν ἐκκλησιῶν εἰρήνης καταμηνῦσαι τὸν
τρόπον ἕκαστά τε ὅπως γέγονε διειπεῖν. 15

2. Ὁ εὐσεβέστατος καὶ φιλόχριστος βασιλεὺς τὴν ὑπὲρ τῶν
ἁγίων ἐκκλησιῶν φροντίδα πλείστην τε ὅσην καὶ ἀναγκαίαν ποιούμενος οὐ φορητὴν ἡγεῖτο τὴν τούτων διχόνοιαν· μεταπεμψάμενος

Witnesses: V S A R + Latin versions, smaller collections, Σ, and citations
ACO 1, 1, 4 pp. 20–31

---

[1] Acacius was bishop of Melitene (present-day Malatya) in Armenia
Secunda before 431 and died before 449; he was amongst the group dominating
the Council of Ephesus, viz. Cyril, Juvenal of Jerusalem, Theodotus of Ancyra,
Firmus of Caesarea, Palladius of Amasea, Flavian of Philippi. At the colloquy
before the emperor at Chalcedon he shocked the emperor with some 'theopaschite' remarks (gleefully reported back by the Oriental delegation, *ACO*
1, 1, 7 p. 77). Apart from the letter to Cyril (see below) which gave rise to
this reply, there survives a sermon delivered at Ephesus, *ACO* 1, 1, 2 pp. 90–2.
It emphasizes sharply the sufferings of 'the slave's form'. 'For the Godhead
which assumed the slave's form in no way shunned all these things' (i.e. the
insults of Christ's passion) 'which belonged to it, in order that through each

3

TO ACACIUS OF MELITENE

By the same to Acacius, Bishop of Melitene[1]

1. To my lord, dear brother and fellow minister Acacius, Cyril sends greeting in the Lord.

The pleasure brothers have of speaking to each other is an admirable one, worthy of all esteem from men of real intelligence; it is, I feel, the duty of those of one faith and one soul to pursue it constantly when there is no bar to interrupt their keen and eager desire for it. At times, though, long distances or scarcity of mail-bearers thwarts our will; but when the opportunity to speak comes round, we should treat the thing as a piece of special good fortune and joyfully seize what we have longed for time and time again. I was therefore exceedingly pleased at your Perfection's letter[2] and admiring your tone I thought it my duty to indicate to you the form of the peace between the Churches and recount its origin in detail.

2. The most devout and Christian Emperor,[3] who takes his responsibility for the Churches with the earnestness it demands, considered their dissension intolerable. Accordingly he sum-

particular feature I have mentioned, it might remove the barriers to salvation and might bestow on us a benefit worthy of so great a self-limitation. I will not make void the grace of God! I will not forbear telling what he endured for me! Impassible he did not cease from being, but he united himself to the passible and thus took on sufferings on my behalf.' Two other letters (*Epp.* 68 and 69) were written to him by Cyril in connexion with the refutation of Theodore (see pp. xxvi f.).

[2] Extant in Latin, *ACO* 1, 4 pp. 118 f. and (a second version) p. 232. It links the name of Theodore with that of Nestorius as one whose impious doctrines were to be anathematized by imperial command and urges Cyril to ensure that each (bishop) publicly denounces these doctrines and 'those who speak of two natures after the union'. Acacius has found people in Germanicia who reject 'two sons' but not 'two natures', one passible, the other impassible, acting individually—which amounts to talking of 'two sons'. The burden of Cyril's letter is to dampen his excess of ardour by expounding the agreed solution.

[3] Theodosius II (408–50).

τοίνυν τὸν εὐλαβέστατον καὶ θεοσεβέστατον ἐπίσκοπον τῆς ἁγίας
Κωνσταντινουπολιτῶν ἐκκλησίας Μαξιμιανόν, καὶ ἑτέρους δὲ
πλείστους τῶν αὐτόθι κατειλημμένων, τίνα δὴ τρόπον ἐκ μέσου μὲν
γένοιτ᾽ ἂν τῶν ἐκκλησιῶν ἡ διαφορά, κεκλήσονται δὲ πρὸς εἰρήνην
οἱ τῶν θείων μυστηρίων ἱερουργοί, διεσκέπτετο. οἱ δὲ ἔφασκον ὡς 5
οὐκ ἂν ἑτέρως γένοιτο τοῦτό ποτε οὐδ᾽ ἂν εἰς ὁμοψυχίαν ἔλθοιεν
τὴν πρὸς ἀλλήλους οἱ περὶ ὧν ὁ λόγος, μὴ προανατείλαντος αὐτοῖς
καὶ οἰονεὶ προεισκεκομισμένου τοῦ συνδέσμου τῆς ὁμοπιστίας,
ἔφασκόν τε ὅτι τὸν τῆς Ἀντιοχείας θεοσεβέστατον ἐπίσκοπον
Ἰωάννην ἀναθεματίσαι χρὴ τὰ Νεστορίου δόγματα καὶ ἐγγράφως 10
ὁμολογῆσαι τὴν καθαίρεσιν αὐτοῦ καὶ τό γε ἧκον εἰς λύπας ἰδίας ὁ
τῆς Ἀλεξανδρείας ἐπίσκοπος ἀμνημονήσει τε διὰ τὴν ἀγάπην καὶ
παρ᾽ οὐδὲν ἡγήσεται τὸ ὑβρίσθαι κατὰ τὴν Ἐφεσίων, καίτοι
παγχάλεπόν τε καὶ δύσοιστον ὄν.

3. Συναινέσαντος τοίνυν καὶ ἡσθέντος ἄγαν ἐπὶ τούτοις τοῦ 15
εὐσεβεστάτου βασιλέως, ἀπεστάλη τοῦτο αὐτὸ κατορθώσων ὁ
θαυμασιώτατος τριβοῦνος καὶ νοτάριος Ἀριστόλαος. ἐπειδὴ δὲ τοῖς
κατὰ τὴν Ἑῴαν τὸ βασιλικὸν ἐνεφανίσθη θέσπισμα καὶ ὡς μετὰ
γνώμης γεγονὸς τῶν εὑρεθέντων ἐπισκόπων κατὰ τὴν μεγάλην
Κωνσταντινούπολιν, οὐκ οἶδ᾽ ὅτι σκοπήσαντες συνήχθησαν μὲν 20
πρὸς τὸν ὁσιώτατον καὶ θεοσεβέστατον τῆς Βεροιαίων ἐπίσκοπον
Ἀκάκιον γράψαι τε πρός με παρεσκεύασαν ὅτι τὸν τῆς συμβάσεως[1]
τρόπον ἤτοι τὸν τῆς εἰρήνης τῶν ἁγίων ἐκκλησιῶν οὐχ ἑτέρως
γενέσθαι προσήκει, εἰ μὴ κατὰ τὸ αὐτοῖς δοκοῦν. ἦν δὲ δὴ ἄρα
τοῦτο φορτικὸν καὶ βαρὺ τὸ αἴτημα. ἤθελον γὰρ ἀργῆσαι μὲν 25
σύμπαντα τὰ παρ᾽ ἐμοῦ γραφέντα ἔν τε ἐπιστολαῖς καὶ τόμοις καὶ
βιβλιδίοις, μόνῃ δὲ ἐκείνῃ συνθέσθαι τῇ ἐν Νικαίᾳ παρὰ τῶν ἁγίων
ἡμῶν πατέρων ὁρισθείσῃ πίστει. ἐγὼ δὲ πρὸς ταῦτα ἔγραφον ὅτι

---

[1] συμβιβάσεως V+one other witness, perh. rightly

4 Consecrated 21 October 431, died 12 April 434.
5 This is the 'Home Synod' (σύνοδος ἐνδημοῦσα) of bishops temporarily
resident in Constantinople. It formed a permanent consultative and judicial
committee on ecclesiastical affairs.

moned the most pious and religious Maximian[4] bishop of the holy Church of Constantinople, and a large number of others who happened to be there,[5] and examined the method by which the division between the Churches could be removed and the priests of the divine mysteries be recalled to peace. They answered that this could never happen nor could the persons in question ever attain to mutual harmony except by the prior dawn, so to say, and pre-establishment of a bond of common faith between them; they said too that the most religious John bishop of Antioch must anathematize the doctrines of Nestorius and affirm his deposition in writing and that the bishop of Alexandria should overlook what pertains to personal injuries and, for charity's sake, disregard the insults done him at Ephesus, grave and difficult to bear though they were.

3. The most devout Emperor, accordingly, concurred thoroughly satisfied with these proposals and my lord, the most admirable tribune and notary Aristolaus[6] was despatched to effect this very business. After the imperial decree,[7] which had also been given with the sanction of the bishops on hand at great Constantinople, was published to the Easterns, they assembled for some purpose or other with the most holy and religious Acacius, bishop of Beroea,[8] and got him to write to me that it was improper for the form of agreement or peace between the holy Churches to be brought about in any other way except along the lines they approved.[9] This was indeed a burdensome and heavy demand. For they wanted everything written by me in letters, treatises and books to be null and void and they wanted me to give my support to the faith defined at Nicaea by our holy fathers and that alone. In answer to this

[6] 'Tribune and notary' (see A. H. M. Jones, *Later Roman Empire* (Oxford, 1964), vol. ii, pp. 572 ff.)—a senior officer in the Imperial Secretariat ('most admirable' is, of course, an honorific address).

[7] *ACO* 1, 1, 4 pp. 3–5. Trans. in P. R. Coleman-Norton, *Roman State and Christian Church. A Collection of Legal Documents to A.D. 535* (London, 1966), vol. ii, 412.

[8] Beroea = present-day Aleppo. The venerable Acacius, now 110 years old, had consistently stayed aloof from the controversy, despite Cyril's attempts to engage his support. He was free then to act as honest broker between the dissidents.

[9] *ACO* 1, 1, 7 p. 146; Latin version *ACO* 1, 4 p. 92. It affirms 3 points: (1) The sole sufficiency of the Nicene Creed; (2) Athanasius' *Ad Epictetum* as guide to the creed; (3) rejection of doctrines, disruptive of communion, recently introduced through epistles or chapters, i.e. Cyril's to Nestorius and especially the third. Cf. Cyril's following words.

τῇ μὲν ἐκθέσει τῆς πίστεως τῇ ὁρισθείσῃ παρὰ τῶν ἁγίων πατέρων
κατὰ τὴν Νικαέων πόλιν ἑπόμεθα πάντες, οὐδὲν τὸ παράπαν τῶν
ἐν αὐτῇ κειμένων παρασημαίνοντες² (ἔχει γὰρ πάντα ὀρθῶς καὶ
ἀλήπτως καὶ τὸ περίεργον ἔτι μετ᾽ ἐκείνην οὐκ ἀσφαλές), ἃ δὲ
γεγράφαμεν ὀρθῶς κατὰ τῶν Νεστορίου δυσφημιῶν, οὐδεὶς ἡμᾶς 5
ἀναπείσει λόγος ὡς οὐκ εὖ γεγόνασιν, εἰπεῖν, χρῆναι δὲ μᾶλλον
αὐτοὺς κατά γε τὸ δόξαν καὶ τῷ εὐσεβεστάτῳ καὶ φιλοχρίστῳ
βασιλεῖ, καὶ αὐτῇ δὲ τῇ ἁγίᾳ συνόδῳ τῇ κατὰ τὴν Ἐφεσίων πόλιν
συναγηγερμένῃ ποιεῖσθαι μὲν ἀποκήρυκτον τὸν τῇ τοῦ σωτῆρος
δόξῃ μεμαχημένον, ἀναθεματίσαι δὲ τὰς ἀνοσίους αὐτοῦ δυσφημίας 10
ὁμολογῆσαί τε τὴν καθαίρεσιν αὐτοῦ καὶ συναινέσαι τῇ χειροτονίᾳ
τοῦ ὁσιωτάτου καὶ θεοσεβεστάτου ἐπισκόπου Μαξιμιανοῦ.

4. Τούτων τοίνυν αὐτοῖς τῶν γραμμάτων ἀποδοθέντων, πεπόμ-
φασιν εἰς τὴν Ἀλεξάνδρειαν τὸν εὐλαβέστατον καὶ θεοσεβέστατον
ἐπίσκοπον Παῦλον τῆς Ἐμεσηνῶν· πρὸς ὃν πλεῖστοι μὲν ὅσοι καὶ 15
μακροὶ γεγόνασι λόγοι περὶ τῶν κατὰ τὴν Ἐφεσίων ὠμῶς καὶ
ἀκαθηκόντως εἰρημένων τε καὶ πεπραγμένων. ἐπειδὴ δὲ τούτων
ἀμνημονήσαντας τῶν ἀναγκαιοτέρων ἔχεσθαι μᾶλλον ἐχρῆν σπου-
δασμάτων, ἠρώτων εἰ ἐπικομίζεται γράμματα τοῦ θεοσεβετάτου
ἐπισκόπου Ἰωάννου. εἶτά μοι προεκόμισεν ἐπιστολήν, ἃ μὲν ἐχρῆν 20
ἔχειν, οὐκ ἔχουσαν, ὑπαγορευθεῖσαν δὲ μᾶλλον οὐ καθ᾽ ὃν ἔδει
τρόπον (παροξυσμοῦ γάρ, οὐ παρακλήσεως εἶχε δύναμιν, καὶ ταύτην
οὐ προσηκάμην), καίτοι γε δέον ταῖς ἀπολογίαις τὴν ἐμὴν κατα-
γοητεῦσαι λύπην τὴν ἐπί γε τοῖς φθάσασι καὶ παρ᾽ αὐτῶν γεγονόσι
κατὰ τὴν Ἐφεσίων. καὶ εὐαφόρμως ἔφασκον παρωξύνθαι κατ᾽ ἐμοῦ 25
διά τοι τὸν ζῆλον τὸν ὑπέρ γε τῶν ἱερῶν δογμάτων. ἀλλ᾽ ἤκουον ὅτι
οὔτε ζῆλος αὐτοὺς κεκίνηκε θεῖος οὔτε τῶν τῆς ἀληθείας δογμάτων

---

² παρασαλεύοντες SR+others

¹⁰ *ACO* 1, 1, 7 pp. 147–50; Latin version *ACO* 1, 4 pp. 94–8. The letter, the
main points of which Cyril recapitulates, reminds Acacius *inter alia* of what he
had heard Acacius say at the Synod of the Oak at Constantinople (403) before
the vote against John Chrysostom was taken: 'If I knew that John pardoned
would improve upon himself and abandon his present obduracy I would have
pleaded for him.' Approval of Maximian's ordination (in addition to the
deposition of Nestorius) is not specifically laid down in the letter but is no
doubt implied. Cyril also undertakes to clarify the meaning of the chapters
(which, so far as we know, he never did) when peaceful relations are resumed
and affirms his life-long opposition to Apollinarianism and Arianism repudiat-
ing the notions mentioned in § 20 below.

I wrote:[10] that we all followed the statement of the faith defined by the holy fathers at Nicaea, without any misconstruction of its propositions whatsoever (for it is orthodox and irreproachable on all points and thereafter curious inquiry is dangerous); that no argument would induce us to declare what we had written in sound belief against Nestorius' blasphemies had been done amiss; but that it was up to them rather to disown the man who had opposed the Saviour's glory, to anathematize his profane blasphemies, affirm his deposition and approve the ordination of the most holy and religious bishop Maximian, in conformity with the decision of the most devout and Christian Emperor and also the holy synod assembled at Ephesus itself.

4. This letter, accordingly, was despatched to them and they sent to Alexandria the most pious and religious bishop Paul of Emesa,[11] with whom very many long discussions took place about the brutal and unseemly statements and acts at Ephesus. Since it was our duty to overlook these and rather keep firmly to more vital business, I enquired whether he brought with him a letter from the most religious bishop John. Thereupon he produced for me a letter[12] not containing the points it ought to have contained but framed rather in an improper tone (it bore the tenor of provocation not of entreaty and I did not accept it) despite the fact that there was an obligation to assuage the injury done me in their previous dealings at Ephesus by satisfactory explanations. Their excuse was that they had been goaded to anger against me by fervour for holy doctrine. But they were given to understand[13] that it was not godly fervour which had moved them nor had they conspired against me because they

[11] Emesa = present-day Homs. Notes of three homilies delivered at Alexandria 25 December 432, 1 January 433, and the last undated are preserved, ACO 1, 1, 4 pp. 9 f. and 11 f.; 1, 1, 7 pp. 173 f. Besides the letter mentioned below, a Latin version exists of another letter to the *Magister Militiae* Anatolius ACO 1, 4 pp. 139 f. telling him briefly of events immediately after Cyril's letter to Acacius of Beroea.

[12] ACO 1, 1, 7 pp. 151 f.; Latin version ACO 1, 4 pp. 115–17. The letter makes the excuse Cyril goes on to mention; says that the schism was caused by Cyril's publication of the chapters though Cyril's answer goes a good way to meet their objections and John welcomes the offer of further clarification after peace has been made; John is pleased to hear that Cyril accepts *Ad Epictetum* (acceptance unmentioned by Cyril, perhaps implied by his repudiation of Apollinarianism and Arianism, but most probably John is prodding Cyril into a specific avowal), which is to be a sufficient guide to the meaning of the Nicene creed; John urges the desirability of an end to mutual hostilities.

[13] i.e. orally.

ὑπερμαχόμενοι συνεφράττοντο κατ' ἐμοῦ, ἀλλὰ ταῖς ἀνθρώπων
εἴξαντες κολακείαις καὶ τὰς τῶν ἰσχυόντων τὸ τηνικάδε φιλίας ἐφ'
ἑαυτοὺς ἁρπάζοντες. ὅμως τοῦ θεοσεβεστάτου Παύλου ἐπισκόπου
φάσκοντος ἑτοίμως ἔχειν ἀναθεματίζειν τὰς Νεστορίου δυσφημίας
καὶ ὁμολογεῖν αὐτοῦ τὴν καθαίρεσιν ἐγγράφως καὶ τοῦτο δρᾶν ὑπὲρ   5
πάντων καὶ ὡς ἐκ προσώπου πάντων τῶν κατὰ τὴν Ἀνατολὴν
θεοσεβεστάτων ἐπισκόπων, ἀντενήνεγμαι λέγων τὸν παρ' αὐτοῦ
περὶ τούτου προκομιζόμενον χάρτην ἀρκέσειν αὐτῷ καὶ μόνῳ πρὸς
τὸ χρῆναι τυχεῖν τῆς παρὰ πάντων ἡμῶν κοινωνίας, διεβεβαιούμην
δὲ ὅτι πάντῃ τε καὶ πάντως ἔγγραφον ὁμολογίαν περὶ τούτων 10
ἐκθέσθαι προσήκει τὸν εὐλαβέστατον καὶ θεοσεβέστατον τῆς
Ἀντιοχέων ἐπίσκοπον Ἰωάννην· ὃ δὴ καὶ γέγονε, καὶ πέπαυται τὸ
μεσολαβοῦν καὶ ἀποφοιτᾶν ἀλλήλων ἀναπεῖθον τὰς ἐκκλησίας.

5. Ἀλλ' ἦν οὐδαμόθεν ἀμφίβολον ὅτι τῶν Νεστορίου δυσφημιῶν
τοὺς ὑπασπιστὰς κατατήξειν ἔμελλε τῶν ἁγίων ἐκκλησιῶν ἡ εἰρήνη. 15
καί μοι δοκοῦσι τοιοῦτόν τι παθεῖν ὁποῖόν τι συμβαίνειν ἔθος τοῖς
νήχεσθαι μὲν οὐκ εἰδόσι, νεώς γε μὴν ἀδοκήτως ἀπολισθήσασιν·
οἳ ἐπειδὰν καταπνίγωνται, πόδας τε καὶ χεῖρας ὧδε κἀκεῖσε
διαρριπτοῦντες ἀτάκτως τοῦ παρατυχόντος ἁπλῶς ἐπιδράττονται
φιλοψυχοῦντες οἱ δείλαιοι. ἢ οὐκ ἀληθὲς εἰπεῖν ὡς τεθορύβηνται 20
λίαν, ἐκπεσόντες καὶ μεμονωμένοι καὶ ἔξω γεγονότες ἐκκλησιῶν, ἃς
ἐνόμιζον ἔσεσθαι πρὸς ἐπικουρίαν αὐτοῖς; ἢ οὐκ ἀσχάλλουσι, καὶ
τοῦτο οὐ φορητῶς, ἀποπηδῶντας αὐτῶν τοὺς ἠπατημένους ὁρῶντες
καὶ λοιπὸν ἀνανήφοντας εἰς ἀλήθειαν τοὺς ταῖς παρ' αὐτῶν βεβήλοις
κενοφωνίαις οἱονεί πως ἐκμεμεθυσμένους; καίτοι φαίη τις ἂν αὐτοῖς 25
καὶ λίαν ἐπὶ καιροῦ τὸ διὰ τῆς τοῦ προφήτου φωνῆς συνάχθητε
καὶ συνδέθητε, τὸ ἔθνος τὸ ἀπαίδευτον, πρὸ τοῦ γενέσθαι
ὑμᾶς ὡσεὶ ἄνθος παραπορευόμενον.[a] διὰ τί γὰρ ὅλως
γεγόνασιν ἀλλοτρίων ἐμέτων παράσιτοι, οὐκ αἰσχύνονται δὲ τοῖς

[a] Zeph. 2: 1

[14] *ACO* 1, 1, 4 pp. 6 f.; Latin version *ACO* 1, 3 pp. 184 f.; cf. also *Ep.* 37.
It rehearses briefly the events preceding Paul's despatch and his purpose as
an ambassador seeking to find the necessary conditions for peace; declares
that Paul has had conversations with Cyril [hence the document was written
during the visit] and found Cyril irenically disposed to the business in hand;
Cyril has given him a document presenting the orthodox faith handed down
from the fathers, and getting this was the chief object of his labours; Paul, in
turn, herein declares that 'we' accept the appointment of Maximian, declare

were championing dogmatic truth, but because they had succumbed to the blandishments of men and were seeking to gain
the regard of current authority. All the same, when the most
religious bishop Paul declared himself ready to anathematize
Nestorius' blasphemies, affirm his deposition in writing and to
do this on behalf of, and as representative of, all the most religious
bishops of the East, my response was that the document[14] produced by him on the subject did suffice for him but for him
alone as a necessary condition for obtaining communion with
all of us. I insisted, though, that it was absolutely essential that
the most pious and religious bishop John of Antioch should
issue a written affirmation[15] on these points—which has indeed
occurred and the obstacle causing the mutual withdrawal of the
Churches from communion is over and done with.

5. However, there was no doubt at all that peace between the
holy Churches was going to weaken the defenders of Nestorius'
blasphemies. They seem to me to have suffered somewhat the
same sort of fate as habitually overtakes non-swimmers who
suddenly slide overboard—when the poor creatures begin to
drown they thrash out at random with arms and legs all over
the place and simply grasp hold for dear life of anyone who
happens to be by. Would it not be true to describe them as in
utter confusion—banished, isolated, excluded as they are from
Churches they counted on for help? Are they not dismayed past
bearing, as they see their dupes hastily abandoning them and
men once drunk, so to say, on their impure nonsense now sobering
up to the truth? Indeed one could quote to them, and very aptly,
the prophet's utterance: '*Be gathered and bound together, O ignorant
people, before you become like grass which passes away.*' Why have
they become complete toadies taking a meal off others' vomit?

Nestorius deposed, anathematize his impious utterances, and 'welcome the
pure and sincere communion with us based on the brief exposition of the incarnation of God the Word given by us to your Reverence, with which you concurred, which you accepted as your own, and a copy of which is included in the
present writing' [viz. the 'Formula of Reunion', which is not actually included
in the document]. Notice the diplomatic way in which this is recounted; Cyril
is not represented as bowing to the demands of the Easterns, though the formula
is the Easterns'. Nevertheless it is to leave Cyril open to the charge of accepting
a new creed, something ruled out by the 'Ephesine decree' (cf. below, § 7 nn.).

[15] *ACO* 1, 1, 4 pp. 7–9; Latin version *ACO* 1, 3 pp. 185–87. Cyril experienced
delay in extracting this from John, and his famous letter Εὐφραινέσθωσαν οἱ
οὐρανοί (*ACO* 1, 1, 4 pp. 15–20) was written and despatched but not delivered
till John had been finally induced to make it. Cyril published it together with
his own on (Sunday) 23 April 433 in Alexandria. For a translation of the
Formula of Reunion see below, Appendix.

ἑτέρου βορβόροις τὰς ἑαυτῶν καρδίας καταμιαίνοντες; οἱ κωφοὶ
ἀκούσατε καὶ οἱ τυφλοὶ ἀναβλέψατε ἰδεῖν.[b] φρονήσατε
περὶ τοῦ κυρίου ἀληθῆ καὶ ἐν ἁπλότητι καρδίας ζητήσατε
αὐτόν.[c] ποία γὰρ χρεία πολυπλόκων ὑμῖν εὑρημάτων καὶ λόγων
διεστραμμένων; τί τὴν ἐπ᾽ εὐθὺ περιυβρίζοντες τρίβον καμπύλας 5
ποιεῖτε τὰς ἑαυτῶν τροχιάς; νεώσατε ἑαυτοῖς νεώματα καὶ
μὴ σπείρετε ἐπ᾽ ἀκάνθαις.[d]

6. Ἀλύοντες γάρ, ὡς ἔφην, ἐπὶ τῇ εἰρήνῃ τῶν ἁγίων ἐκκλησιῶν,
τοὺς μὴ ἀνασχομένους τὰ ἴσα φρονεῖν αὐτοῖς κακουργότατα δια-
σύρουσι καὶ καταγορεύουσι πικρῶς τῆς ἀπολογίας τῶν ἁγίων 10
ἐπισκόπων, τῶν ἀπό γε τῆς Ἑῴας φημί· εἶτα περιέλκοντες αὐτὴν
πρὸς τὸ αὐτοῖς ἡδύ τε καὶ φίλον καὶ νοοῦντες οὐκ ὀρθῶς, οὐκ
ἀπᾳδόντως γενέσθαι φασὶ ταῖς Νεστορίου κενοφωνίαις. συγκατα-
ψέγουσι δὲ καὶ ἡμᾶς ὡς οἷς ἤδη γεγράφαμεν, πεφρονηκότας τὰ
ἐναντία. μανθάνω δὲ ὅτι κἀκεῖνό φασιν ὅτι πίστεως ἔκθεσιν ἤτοι 15
σύμβολον καινὸν ἀρτίως κατεδεξάμεθα, τάχα που τὸ ἀρχαῖον ἐκεῖνο
καὶ σεπτὸν ἀτιμάσαντες. καὶ ὁ μὲν μωρὸς μωρὰ λαλήσει καὶ ἡ
καρδία αὐτοῦ μάταια νοήσει,[e] πλὴν ἐκεῖνο φαμέν· οὐ πίστεως
ἔκθεσιν ἢ ἐξῄτηνται παρ᾽ ἡμῶν τινες ἢ γοῦν καινοτομηθεῖσαν παρ᾽
ἑτέρων κατεδεξάμεθα. ἀπόχρη γὰρ ἡμῖν ἡ θεόπνευστος γραφὴ καὶ 20
τῶν ἁγίων πατέρων ἡ νῆψις καὶ τὸ πρὸς πᾶν ὁτιοῦν τῶν ἐχόντων
ὀρθῶς ἐκτετορνευμένον τῆς πίστεως σύμβολον.

7. Ἐπειδὴ δὲ ἦσαν οἱ κατὰ τὴν Ἀνατολὴν ὁσιώτατοι ἐπίσκοποι
διχονοήσαντες πρὸς ἡμᾶς κατὰ τὴν Ἐφεσίων καὶ γεγόνασί πως ἐν
ὑποψίαις τοῦ καὶ ἑναλῶναι βρόχοις τῶν Νεστορίου δυσφημιῶν, 25
ταύτῃ τοι καὶ μάλα ἐμφρόνως ἀπαλλάττοντες ἑαυτοὺς τῆς ἐπὶ τούτοις
αἰτίας καὶ τοὺς τῆς ἀμωμήτου πίστεως ἐραστὰς πληροφορεῖν
σπουδάζοντες ὅτι τῆς ἐκείνου βδελυρίας ἀμοιρεῖν ἐγνώκασι,
πεποίηνται τὴν ἀπολογίαν, καὶ τὸ χρῆμά ἐστι ψόγου τε παντὸς καὶ
μώμου μακράν. ἆρα γὰρ εἰ καὶ αὐτὸς Νεστόριος κατ᾽ ἐκεῖνο καιροῦ 30

[b] Is. 42 : 18   [c] Wisdom 1 : 1   [d] Jer. 4 : 3   [e] Is. 32 : 6

16 This is very much what Nestorius himself says in the *Liber Heraclidis*,
pp. 404–52/*259–90*, where he gives an extended critique of Cyril's explanation
to Acacius. In sum, Nestorius objects that Cyril deliberately distorts the
Formula of Reunion; that he distorts Nestorius' own utterances and is guilty
of self-contradiction. The most telling of Nestorius' points about the Formula
of Reunion (relevant to the whole of Cyril's explanation) are: (p. 405/*260*)

Why are they not ashamed to foul their own hearts with another's excrement? *'Hear you deaf and look, you blind, that you may see.' 'Consider the Lord in truth and seek him in simplicity of heart.'* What use to you are tricks and twisted arguments? Why do you rail against the straight road and make your paths crooked? *'Break up your fallows and do not sow on thorns.'*

6. For, as I have said, distraught at the peace between the holy Churches they disparage those who refuse to entertain their mischievous notions and make bitter accusations against the explanation of the holy bishops—the Easterns, I mean. Consequently wresting that explanation in their favourite direction and misinterpreting it they are asserting that it is not out of key with Nestorius' vanities. Us too they stigmatize as thinking the opposite of what we have written.[16] I learn that they are even asserting that we have just accepted a statement of faith or new symbol,[17] as if we had somehow lost respect for the old and venerable one.[18] *'The fool will speak folly and his heart think vanity'*; nevertheless this do we say: none have required of us a statement of faith nor indeed did we accept one newly formulated by others. Enough for us are the inspired Scripture, the sober vigilance of the holy fathers, and the Creed carved out to meet absolutely every detail of orthodoxy.

7. Since there were most holy Eastern bishops who had been in disagreement with us at Ephesus and were even under some suspicion of being caught in the toils of Nestorius' blasphemies, they very wisely avoided accusation on that score and were eager to satisfy the lovers of the spotless faith that they had no conscious share in that man's coarseness, by producing a justification[19]—and no hint of criticism or blame attaches to their action. For if Nestorius too had himself produced a written

Nestorius does not deny the title $\theta \epsilon o \tau \acute{o} \kappa o s$ but does deny a 'natural' and 'hypostatic' union; the formula calls the B.V.M. $\theta \epsilon o \tau \acute{o} \kappa o s$ not in the sense that God the Word was born of her, but that he united to himself the temple which was born of her. Nestorius no more confesses 'two Christs' than does Cyril when Cyril says that Christ is of two natures (p. 409/*262*). Cyril distorts the meaning of the division of expressions in the New Testament—the Easterns mean a real distinction of expressions and of natures, Cyril does not (p. 438/*280 f.*). Though not all the Easterns would have accepted Nestorius' positive affirmations, Nestorius shows us how they understood the Formula which he himself could have accepted.

[17] This is an important gloss. The formula is certainly an $\check{\epsilon} \kappa \theta \epsilon \sigma \iota s \ \tau \hat{\eta} s \ \pi \acute{\iota} \sigma \tau \epsilon \omega s$ (Paul of Emesa, quoted above, so designates it), but it is not a creed like that of Nicaea. [18] Sc. of Nicaea.

[19] An unusual, not to say Pickwickian, way of describing a formula dictated by John and the Easterns.

καθ᾽ ὃν αὐτῷ προετείνετο παρὰ πάντων ἡμῶν τὸ χρῆναι κατα-
ψηφίσασθαι τῶν ἑαυτοῦ δογμάτων καὶ ἀνθελέσθαι τὴν ἀλήθειαν,
ἔγγραφον ἐποιήσατο τὴν ἐπὶ τούτοις ὁμολογίαν, καὶ αὐτὸν ἄν τις
ἔφη πίστεως ἡμῖν καινοτομῆσαι σύμβολον; τί τοίνυν διαλοιδορεῖται
μάτην, ἔκθεσιν συμβόλου καινὴν ὀνομάζοντες τὴν συναίνεσιν τῶν 5
κατὰ τὴν Φοινίκην θεοσεβεστάτων ἐπισκόπων, ἣν πεποίηνται
χρησίμως τε καὶ ἀναγκαίως ἀπολογούμενοί τε καὶ θεραπεύοντες
τοὺς οἰηθέντας ὅτι ταῖς Νεστορίου κατακολουθοῦσι φωναῖς; ἡ μὲν
γὰρ ἁγία καὶ οἰκουμενικὴ σύνοδος ἡ κατὰ τὴν Ἐφεσίων πόλιν
συνειλεγμένη προενόησεν ἀναγκαίως τοῦ μὴ δεῖν ταῖς ἐκκλησίαις 10
τοῦ θεοῦ πίστεως ἔκθεσιν ἑτέραν εἰσκρίνεσθαι παρά γε τὴν οὖσαν,
ἣν οἱ τρισμακάριοι πατέρες ἐν ἁγίῳ πνεύματι λαλοῦντες ὡρίσαντο.
οἵ γε μὴν ἅπαξ οὐκ οἶδ᾽ ὅπως πρὸς αὐτὴν διχονοήσαντες, γεγονότες
δὲ καὶ ἐν ὑποψίαις τοῦ μὴ ὀρθῶς ἑλέσθαι φρονεῖν μήτε μὴν τοῖς
ἀποστολικοῖς τε καὶ εὐαγγελικοῖς ἕπεσθαι δόγμασιν ἆρα σιωπῶντες 15
ἀπηλλάγησαν ἂν τῆς ἐπὶ τούτῳ δυσκλείας ἢ μᾶλλον ἀπολογούμενοι
καὶ τῆς ἐνούσης αὐτοῖς δόξης τὴν δύναμιν ἐμφανίζοντες; καίτοι
γέγραφεν ὁ θεσπέσιος μαθητής· ἕτοιμοι ἀεὶ πρὸς ἀπολογίαν
παντὶ τῷ αἰτοῦντι ὑμᾶς λόγον περὶ τῆς ἐν ὑμῖν ἐλπίδος·ᶠ
ὁ δὲ τοῦτο δρᾶν ᾑρημένος καινουργεῖ μὲν οὐδέν, ἀλλ᾽ οὐδὲ πίστεως 20
ἔκθεσιν ὁρᾶται καινοτομῶν, ἐναργῆ δὲ μᾶλλον καθίστησι τοῖς
ἐρομένοις αὐτὸν ἣν ἂν ἔχοι πίστιν περὶ Χριστοῦ.

8. Ἐπυθόμην δὲ πρὸς τούτοις ὅτι ταῖς τῶν θεοσεβεστάτων
ἐπισκόπων ὁμοψυχίαις οὐ μετρίως ἐπιστυγνάζοντες οἱ τῆς ἀληθείας
ἐχθροὶ ἄνω τε καὶ κάτω διακυκῶσι τὰ πάντα καὶ τοῖς ἀνοσίοις 25
ἑαυτῶν εὑρήμασι συμβῆναί φασι τῆς παρ᾽ αὐτῶν γεγενημένης
ὁμολογίας τὴν δύναμιν, ἣν ἐπὶ τῇ ὀρθῇ πεποίηνται πίστει, καινο-
τομοῦντες μέν, ὡς ἔφην, ἢ γοῦν προσεπάγοντες τοῖς πάλαι δι-
ωρισμένοις τὸ σύμπαν οὐδέν, ἑπόμενοι δὲ μᾶλλον τοῖς τῶν ἁγίων
πατέρων ἀνεπιπλήκτοις δόγμασιν. ἵνα δὲ ψευδοποιοῦντας ἐλέγχωμεν, 30
φέρε, παραγάγωμεν εἰς μέσον τὰς Νεστορίου φλυαρίας καὶ τὰς
τούτων φωνάς. ἐκδείξειε γὰρ ἂν ὧδέ τε καὶ οὐχ ἑτέρως τὸ ἀληθὲς
ἡ βάσανος.

9. Οὐκοῦν Νεστόριος μὲν ἀναιρῶν εἰς ἅπαν εὑρίσκεται τοῦ
μονογενοῦς υἱοῦ τοῦ θεοῦ τὴν κατὰ σάρκα γέννησιν· οὐ γάρ τοι 35

ᶠ 1 Peter 3: 15

affirmation on these points at the time the obligation to denounce his own doctrines and embrace instead the truth was being proposed to him by us all, could anybody have said he had produced us a novel creed? Why then do they offer idle abuse, calling the joint statement of the most religious Phoenician bishops[20] a new credal exposition, a joint statement which they helpfully produced as a matter of duty to justify themselves and set right those who thought they followed Nestorius' utterances? For the holy, ecumenical synod assembled at Ephesus of course foresaw that it was essential no other statement of faith should be introduced into God's Churches in addition to the existing one,[21] which the thrice-blessed fathers defined in words inspired by the Holy Ghost. Would those who in some way or other once disagreed with it, coming under suspicion of failure to take the orthodox view and follow apostolic and gospel doctrine, would they, I say, have cleared themselves by silence from this disgrace or by explaining themselves and bringing to light the meaning of their inner conviction? And indeed the inspired disciple has written: *'Always be ready to make your defence to everyone who asks you the reason for the hope that is in you.'* The man who chooses to do this makes no innovation neither is he regarded as the proponent of a new statement of faith. No, he is clarifying his belief about Christ in response to questioners.

8. I hear furthermore that the enemies of the truth, chagrined more than a little by the common mind of the most religious bishops, are turning everything topsy-turvy and asserting that the bishops' affirmation agrees in meaning with their own unhallowed inventions—an affirmation which they produced on the question of orthodoxy, innovating, as I said, or adding to long-standing definitions not a whit but rather following the irreproachable doctrines of the holy fathers. Well then, to refute liars let us introduce Nestorius' nonsense alongside their utterances. Scrutiny and scrutiny alone can demonstrate the truth.

9. Nestorius then, on the one hand, is discovered to be totally destroying the incarnate birth of the Only-begotten Son of God—

---

[20] A way of referring to the Eastern bishops of John's jurisdiction (which included Phoenicia), if it is not simply an error for 'Eastern bishops'.

[21] See *ACO* 1, 1, 7 p. 105—the so-called 'Ephesine decree', see *To Eulogius* n. 10.

τετέχθαι φησὶν αὐτὸν ἐκ γυναικὸς κατὰ τὰς γραφάς. ἔφη γὰρ
οὕτως· τὸ παρελθεῖν τὸν θεὸν ἐκ τῆς Χριστοτόκου παρθένου παρὰ
τῆς θείας ἐδιδάχθην γραφῆς· τὸ δὲ γεννηθῆναι θεὸν ἐξ αὐτῆς
οὐδαμοῦ ἐδιδάχθην. ἐν ἑτέρᾳ δὲ πάλιν ἐξηγήσει· Οὐδαμοῦ τοίνυν ἡ
θεία γραφὴ θεὸν ἐκ τῆς Χριστοτόκου παρθένου λέγει γεγεννῆσθαι, 5
ἀλλὰ Ἰησοῦν Χριστὸν υἱὸν κύριον.
Ὅτι δὲ ταῦτα λέγων εἰς υἱοὺς δύο μερίζει τὸν ἕνα καὶ ἕτερον
μὲν ἰδικῶς εἶναί φησιν υἱὸν καὶ Χριστὸν καὶ κύριον, τὸν ἐκ θεοῦ
πατρὸς γεννηθέντα λόγον, ἕτερον δὲ πάλιν ἀνὰ μέρος τε καὶ ἰδικῶς
υἱὸν καὶ Χριστὸν καὶ κύριον, τὸν ἐκ τῆς ἁγίας παρθένου, πῶς ἂν 10
ἐνδοιάσειέ τις, αὐτὸ δὴ τοῦτο σαφῶς μόνον οὐχὶ βοῶντος ἐκείνου;

10. Οἱ δὲ θεοτόκον ὀνομάζουσι τὴν ἁγίαν παρθένον ἕνα τε εἶναί
φασιν υἱὸν καὶ Χριστὸν καὶ κύριον, τέλειον ἐν θεότητι, τέλειον ἐν
ἀνθρωπότητι, ἅτε δὴ καὶ ἐψυχωμένης αὐτοῦ τῆς σαρκὸς ψυχῇ
νοερᾷ. ὅτι γὰρ οὐχ ἕτερον εἶναί φασιν υἱὸν τὸν ἐκ θεοῦ πατρὸς λόγον, 15
ἕτερον δὲ πάλιν τὸν ἐκ τῆς ἁγίας παρθένου, καθὰ Νεστορίῳ δοκεῖ,
ἕνα δὲ μᾶλλον καὶ τὸν αὐτόν, σαφὲς ἂν γένοιτο καὶ μάλα ῥᾳδίως διά
γε τῶν ἐφεξῆς. προσεπάγουσι γάρ, τίς ἂν εἴη σημαίνοντες ὁ τέλειος
ὡς θεός, τέλειος δὲ καὶ ἄνθρωπος, "τὸν πρὸ αἰώνων μὲν ἐκ τοῦ
πατρὸς γεννηθέντα κατὰ τὴν θεότητα, ἐπ᾽ ἐσχάτου δὲ τῶν ἡμερῶν 20
δι᾽ ἡμᾶς καὶ διὰ τὴν ἡμετέραν σωτηρίαν ἐκ Μαρίας τῆς ἁγίας
παρθένου κατὰ τὴν ἀνθρωπότητα, ὁμοούσιον τῷ πατρὶ τὸν αὐτὸν
κατὰ τὴν θεότητα καὶ ὁμοούσιον ἡμῖν κατὰ τὴν ἀνθρωπότητα".
οὐκοῦν ἥκιστα μὲν εἰς δύο διαιροῦσι τὸν ἕνα υἱὸν καὶ Χριστὸν καὶ
κύριον Ἰησοῦν, τὸν αὐτὸν δὲ εἶναί φασι τὸν πρὸ αἰῶνος καὶ ἐν 25
ἐσχάτοις, δῆλον δὲ ὅτι τὸν ἐκ θεοῦ πατρὸς ὡς θεὸν καὶ ἐκ γυναικὸς
κατὰ σάρκα ὡς ἄνθρωπον.

11. Πῶς γὰρ ἂν νοοῖτο πρὸς ἡμᾶς ὁμοούσιος εἶναι κατὰ τὴν ἀνθρωπότητα, καίτοι γεννηθεὶς ἐκ πατρός, κατά γε φημὶ τὴν θεότητα, εἰ
μὴ νοοῖτο καὶ λέγοιτο θεός τε ὁμοῦ καὶ ἄνθρωπος ὁ αὐτός; ἀλλ᾽ 30
οὐχ ὧδε ταῦτ᾽ ἔχειν Νεστορίῳ δοκεῖ, τέτραπται δὲ μᾶλλον ὁ
σκοπὸς αὐτῷ πρὸς πᾶν τοὐναντίον. ἔφη γοῦν ἐπ᾽ ἐκκλησίας ἐξηγού-
μενος· διὰ τοῦτο καὶ Χριστὸς ὁ θεὸς λόγος ὀνομάζεται, ἐπειδήπερ
ἔχει τὴν συνάφειαν τὴν πρὸς τὸν Χριστὸν διηνεκῆ. καὶ πάλιν·
Ἀσύγχυτον τοίνυν τὴν τῶν φύσεων τηρῶμεν συνάφειαν· ὁμολογῶμεν 35

he denies that he was born of a woman in accordance with the Scriptures. This is what he said: 'That God entered from the Virgin Mother of Christ I was taught by divine Scripture; that God was born of her was I nowhere taught.'[22] And again in another sermon: 'Accordingly nowhere does divine Scripture say God was born of the Virgin Mother of Christ, but Jesus Christ Son and Lord.'[23] How can anyone doubt when he all but shouts the very thing out clearly, that when he says these things he is dividing the one into two sons and is asserting the personally distinct existence of a Son, Christ and Lord, the Word begotten of God the Father and in addition that of a different separate and personally distinct Son, Christ and Lord, born of the holy Virgin?

10. They, on the other hand, call the holy Virgin 'Mother of God' and assert the existence of one Son, Christ and Lord, perfect in Godhead, perfect in manhood, since his flesh is endowed with life and reason.[24] That they are not asserting the existence of a Son, the Word of God the Father and also of a different Son born from the holy Virgin (the doctrine of Nestorius) but rather that he is one and the same Son can be very simply made plain by what follows. For they add, indicating who the perfect as God and perfect as man is: 'Who was begotten of the Father before the ages in respect of his Godhead and in the last days for us and for our salvation of Mary the holy Virgin in respect of his manhood, the same consubstantial with the Father in Godhead and consubstantial with us in manhood.' In no way, therefore, do they divide the one Son, Christ and Lord Jesus into two, but assert that the same existed before the world and in the last days, namely he who is of God the Father as God and of woman incarnate as man.

11. How can he be seen as consubstantial with us in respect of his manhood though begotten (I mean in his Godhead) of the Father unless they mean to say that the same is at once God and man? But this is not Nestorius' opinion of the case; his aim rather is quite the reverse. Preaching in church he declared: 'For this reason also God the Word is called "Christ", since he has continuous connection with Christ.'[25] And again: 'Let us, then, keep the connection of natures unconfused! Let us confess God in

[22] Loofs, *Nestoriana*, pp. 277 f.; cf. *Contra Nestorium* I, 1, 2 (*ACO* 1, 1, 6 p. 20).
[23] Loofs, *Nestoriana*, p. 278; cf. *Contra Nestorium* I, 1, 2 (*ACO* 1, 1, 6 p. 18).
[24] For the whole of the Formula see below, Appendix.
[25] Loofs, *Nestoriana*, p. 275; cf. *Contra Nestorium* II, 7, 8 (*ACO* 1, 1, 6 p. 45).

τὸν ἐν ἀνθρώπῳ θεόν· σέβωμεν τὸν τῇ θείᾳ συναφείᾳ τῷ παντοκράτορι
θεῷ συμπροσκυνούμενον ἄνθρωπον.

Ὁρᾷς οὖν ὅσον ἔχει τὸ ἀπηχὲς ὁ λόγος αὐτῷ; δυσσεβείας γὰρ
τῆς ἀνωτάτω μεμέστωται. Χριστὸν μὲν γὰρ ἰδικῶς ὠνομάσθαι
φησὶ τὸν τοῦ θεοῦ λόγον, ἔχειν δὲ τὴν συνάφειαν τὴν πρὸς τὸν 5
Χριστὸν διηνεκῆ. ἆρ' οὖν οὐ δύο Χριστοὺς ἐναργέστατα λέγει; οὐκ
ἄνθρωπον θεῷ συμπροσκυνούμενον σέβειν οὐκ οἶδ' ὅπως ὁμολογεῖ;
ταῦτ' οὖν ἀδελφὰ τοῖς παρ' ἐκείνων ὁρᾶται; οὐκ ἀντεξάγουσαν ἔχει
πρὸς ἄλληλα τῶν ἐννοιῶν τὴν δύναμιν; ὁ μὲν γὰρ δύο φησὶν ἐναργῶς,
οἱ δὲ Χριστὸν ἕνα καὶ υἱὸν καὶ θεὸν καὶ κύριον ὁμολογοῦσι προσ- 10
κυνεῖν, τὸν αὐτὸν ἐκ πατρὸς κατὰ τὴν θεότητα καὶ ἐκ τῆς ἁγίας
παρθένου κατὰ τὴν ἀνθρωπότητα. δύο μὲν γὰρ φύσεων ἕνωσιν γενέσθαι
φασί, πλὴν ἕνα Χριστόν, ἕνα υἱόν, ἕνα κύριον ὁμολογοῦσι σαφῶς.
γέγονε γὰρ σὰρξ ὁ λόγος κατὰ τὰς γραφὰς[g] καὶ σύμβασιν οἰκονο-
μικὴν καὶ ἀπόρρητον ἀληθῶς πεπρᾶχθαι φαμὲν ἀνομοίων πραγ- 15
μάτων εἰς ἕνωσιν ἀδιάσπαστον.

12. Οὐ γάρ τοι κατά τινας τῶν ἀρχαιοτέρων αἱρετικῶν ἐξ ἰδίας
λαβόντα φύσεως, τουτέστι τῆς θεϊκῆς ἑαυτῷ κατασκευάσαι τὸ
σῶμα τὸν τοῦ θεοῦ λόγον ὑπονοήσομεν, ἑπόμενοι δὲ πανταχῇ ταῖς
θεοπνεύστοις γραφαῖς ἐκ τῆς ἁγίας παρθένου λαβεῖν αὐτὸν δια- 20
βεβαιούμεθα. ταύτῃ τοι τὰ ἐξ ὧν ἐστιν ὁ εἷς καὶ μόνος υἱὸς καὶ
κύριος Ἰησοῦς Χριστός, ὡς ἐν ἐννοίαις δεχόμενοι, δύο μὲν φύσεις
ἠνῶσθαί φαμεν, μετὰ δέ γε τὴν ἕνωσιν, ὡς ἀνῃρημένης ἤδη τῆς
εἰς δύο διατομῆς, μίαν εἶναι πιστεύομεν τὴν τοῦ υἱοῦ φύσιν, ὡς
ἑνός, πλὴν ἐνανθρωπήσαντος καὶ σεσαρκωμένου. εἰ δὲ δὴ λέγοιτο 25
σαρκωθῆναί τε καὶ ἐνανθρωπῆσαι θεὸς ὢν ὁ λόγος, διερρίφθω που
μακρὰν τροπῆς ὑποψία (μεμένηκε γὰρ ὅπερ ἦν), ὁμολογείσθω δὲ
πρὸς ἡμῶν καὶ ἀσύγχυτος παντελῶς ἡ ἕνωσις.

13. Ἀλλὰ γὰρ ἴσως ἐκεῖνο φαῖεν ἂν οἱ δι' ἐναντίας· ἰδοὺ δὴ
σαφῶς οἱ τῆς ὀρθῆς πίστεως τὴν ὁμολογίαν ποιούμενοι δύο μὲν 30
ὀνομάζουσι φύσεις, διῃρῆσθαι δὲ τὰς τῶν θεηγόρων φωνὰς διατείνονται κατά γε τὴν διαφορὰν αὐτῶν· εἶτα πῶς οὐκ ἐναντία ταῦτα
τοῖς σοῖς; οὐδὲ γὰρ ἀνέχῃ προσώποις δυσὶν ἢ γοῦν ὑποστάσεσι τὰς
φωνὰς διανέμειν. ἀλλ', ὦ βέλτιστοι, φαίην ἄν, γεγράφαμεν[3] ἐν τοῖς

[g] cf. John 1 : 14

3 γέγραφα μὲν one Lat. version, perh. rightly

Man! Let us worship the man adored along with the omnipotent God in divine connection!'[26]

Do you see, then, the extent his thinking fails to accord with theirs? It is stuffed with the last degree of blasphemy. He says, on the one hand, that the personally distinct Word of God is called 'Christ', but, on the other hand, that he has continuous connection with Christ. Then is he not very clearly saying 'two Christs'? Is he not affirming some sort of worship of a man adored along with God? Do these ideas look akin to theirs, then? Are they not mutually contradictory? He plainly says 'two'; they affirm they worship one Christ, both Son and God and Lord, the same being of the Father in respect of Godhead and of the holy Virgin in respect of manhood. For they say that a union of two natures came into being, yet they plainly affirm one Christ, one Son, one Lord. The Word, according to the Scriptures, became flesh and we declare that there was truly created a divinely planned and mysterious concurrence of dissimilar realities in indissoluble union.

12. We will not imagine, like some of the more primitive heretics,[27] that the Word of God took from his own (that is, his divine) nature and fashioned himself a body, but follow at every point the inspired Scriptures in insisting that he took it from the holy Virgin. In this way, when we have the idea of the elements of the one and unique Son and Lord Jesus Christ, we speak of two natures being united; but after the union, the duality has been abolished and we believe the Son's nature to be one, since he is one Son, yet become man and incarnate.[28] Though we affirm that the Word is God on becoming incarnate and made man, any suspicion of change is to be repudiated entirely because he remained what he was, and we are to acknowledge the union as totally free from merger.

13. However, the opposition may say perhaps: 'Look here, the makers of this affirmation of orthodoxy use the words "two natures" and maintain that the terms of the Scriptural writers are distinguished in accordance with their particular mark. This must then be the opposite of your position. You, after all, do not allow of allocating the terms to two persons or subjects.' But, my friends, I should answer, we have written in the

---

[26] Loofs, *Nestoriana*, p. 249.
[27] Gnostics like Apelles, Valentinus, and Marcion.
[28] The μία φύσις formula—see *To Eulogius* p. 62 line 17 and n. 3.

κεφαλαίοις· εἴ τις προσώποις δυσὶν ἢ γοῦν ὑποστάσεσι διανέμει τὰς
φωνὰς καὶ τὰς μὲν ὡς ἀνθρώπῳ παρὰ τὸν ἐκ θεοῦ λόγον ἰδικῶς
νοουμένῳ προσάπτει, τὰς δὲ ὡς θεοπρεπεῖς μόνῳ τῷ ἐκ θεοῦ πατρὸς
λόγῳ, οὗτος ἔστω κατάκριτος· φωνῶν δὲ διαφορὰν κατ᾽ οὐδένα
τρόπον ἀνῃρήκαμεν, εἰ καὶ ἀπόβλητον πεποιήμεθα τὸ μερίζειν αὐτὰς 5
ὡς υἱῷ κατὰ μόνας ἐκ πατρὸς λόγῳ καὶ ὡς ἀνθρώπῳ πάλιν κατὰ
μόνας υἱῷ νοουμένῳ τῷ ἐκ γυναικός. μία γὰρ ὁμολογουμένως ἡ τοῦ
λόγου φύσις, ἴσμεν δὲ ὅτι σεσάρκωταί τε καὶ ἐνηνθρώπησε,
καθάπερ ἤδη προεῖπον.

14. Τίνα δὲ τρόπον ἐσαρκώθη τε καὶ ἐνηνθρώπησεν, εἰ περι- 10
εργάζοιτό τις, καταθρήσειεν ἂν τὸν ἐκ θεοῦ θεὸν λόγον δούλου τε
λαβόντα μορφὴν καὶ ἐν ὁμοιώματι ἀνθρώπων γενόμενον, καθὰ
γέγραπται.ʰ καὶ κατ᾽ αὐτὸ δὴ τουτὶ καὶ μόνον νοηθείη ἂν ἡ τῶν
φύσεων ἢ γοῦν ὑποστάσεων διαφορά· οὐ γάρ τοι ταὐτὸν ὡς ἐν
ποιότητι φυσικῇ θεότης τε καὶ ἀνθρωπότης. ἐπεὶ πῶς κεκένωται 15
θεὸς ὢν ὁ λόγος, καθεὶς ἑαυτὸν ἐν μείοσι, τουτέστιν ἐν τοῖς καθ᾽
ἡμᾶς; ὅταν τοίνυν ὁ τῆς σαρκώσεως πολυπραγμονῆται τρόπος, δύο
τὰ ἀλλήλοις ἀπορρήτως τε καὶ ἀσυγχύτως συνενηνεγμένα καθ᾽
ἕνωσιν ὁρᾷ δὴ πάντως ὁ ἀνθρώπινος νοῦς, ἑνωθέντα γε μὴν διίστησιν
οὐδαμῶς, ἀλλ᾽ ἕνα τὸν ἐξ ἀμφοῖν καὶ θεὸν καὶ υἱὸν καὶ Χριστὸν 20
καὶ κύριον εἶναί τε πιστεύει καὶ ἀραρότως εἰσδέχεται.

15. Ἑτέρα δὲ παντελῶς παρὰ ταύτην ἡ Νεστορίου κακοδοξία.
ὑποκρίνεται μὲν γὰρ ὁμολογεῖν ὅτι καὶ ἐσαρκώθη καὶ ἐνηνθρώπησε
θεὸς ὢν ὁ λόγος, τὴν δέ γε τοῦ σεσαρκῶσθαι δύναμιν οὐκ εἰδὼς δύο
μὲν ὀνομάζει φύσεις, ἀποδιίστησι δὲ ἀλλήλων αὐτάς, θεὸν ἰδίᾳ 25
τιθεὶς καὶ ὁμοίως ἄνθρωπον ἀνὰ μέρος συναφθέντα θεῷ σχετικῶς
κατὰ μόνην τὴν ἰσοτιμίαν ἢ γοῦν αὐθεντίαν. ἔφη γὰρ οὕτως·
ἀχώριστος τοῦ φαινομένου θεός. διὰ τοῦτο τοῦ μὴ χωριζομένου τὴν
τιμὴν οὐ χωρίζω· χωρίζω τὰς φύσεις, ἀλλ᾽ ἑνῶ τὴν προσκύνησιν.

ʰ cf. Phil. 2 : 7

---

²⁹ See p. 30.
³⁰ Cyril here equates φύσις and ὑπόστασις, having equated πρόσωπον and
ὑπόστασις in the 'chapter' quoted above. The terminology is loose and not to
be judged by the standards of neo-Chalcedonian orthodoxy. For Cyril ὑπόστασις
only has a technical meaning within the context of 'theology' (i.e. the doctrine
of God in Trinity) where it means distinguishable and distinct 'person'. When
we look at the actual Jesus Christ, according to Cyril, we see one πρόσωπον,

Chapters:[29] 'Whoever allocates the terms to two persons or subjects and attaches some to the man considered separately from the Word of God, some as divine to the Word of God the Father alone, shall be anathema.' By no manner of means have we abolished the difference between the terms though we have caused their separate division to a Son, the Word of the Father, and to a man thought of as a separate woman-born son, to be discarded. The nature of the Word is, by general consent, one but we recognize that he is incarnate and became man, as I have already stated.

14. The inquisitive as to the mode of his incarnation and becoming man may contemplate God the Word of God who, as Scripture has it, 'took the form of a slave and was made in the likeness of men'. By this very fact alone the difference between the natures or subjects[30] will be appreciated; for Godhead and manhood are not the same thing in quality of nature. Otherwise what is the point of the Word's becoming empty, though being God, and abasing himself among inferiors that is to say us men? Accordingly when the mode of the incarnation is the object of curiosity the human mind is bound to observe two things joined together in union with each other mysteriously and without merger, yet it in no way divides what are united but believes and firmly accepts that the product of both elements is one God, Son, Christ and Lord.

15. Nestorius' mischievous doctrine is quite different from this. He, for his part, makes a pretence of affirming that the Word was incarnate and became man whilst being God, and failing to recognize the meaning of being incarnate he uses the words 'two natures' but sunders them from each other, isolating God and a separate man connected with God in a relation only of equal honour or sovereignty. He spoke as follows: 'God is indivisible from the manifestation. Therefore I do not divide the honour of him who is undivided; I divide the natures but unite the adoration.'[31]

ὑπόστασις, φύσις, or πρᾶγμα; if we enter into metaphysical subtleties about the mode of union of Godhead and manhood in Christ we are bound to think in terms of two φύσεις, πράγματα, or ὑποστάσεις (Cyril never speaks of two πρόσωπα) in mysterious union like the union of body and soul. The precise term to designate either the one or the two does not matter. Cyril's casualness worried his interpreters later—see Innocentius of Maronea, *On the conference with the Severians* (above, Introduction, p. xl and n. 24; cf. *Doctrina Patrum* 22, 13 f. [31] Loofs, *Nestoriana*, p. 262.

Οἱ δέ γε κατὰ τὴν Ἀντιόχειαν ἀδελφοὶ τὰ μὲν ἐξ ὧν νοεῖται
Χριστός, ὡς ἐν ψιλαῖς καὶ μόναις ἐννοίαις δεχόμενοι, φύσεων μὲν
εἰρήκασι διαφοράν, ὅτι μὴ ταὐτόν, ὡς ἔφην, ἐν ποιότητι φυσικῇ
θεότης τε καὶ ἀνθρωπότης, ἕνα γε μὴν υἱὸν καὶ Χριστὸν καὶ κύριον
καί, ὡς ἑνὸς ὄντος ἀληθῶς, ἐν αὐτοῦ καὶ πρόσωπον εἶναί φασι, 5
μερίζουσι δὲ κατ᾿ οὐδένα τρόπον τὰ ἡνωμένα οὔτε μὴν φυσικὴν
παραδέχονται τὴν διαίρεσιν, καθὰ φρονεῖν ἔδοξε τῷ τῶν ἀθλίων
εὑρημάτων εἰσηγητῇ. [16] διαιρεῖσθαι δὲ μόνας διατείνονται τὰς
ἐπὶ τῷ κυρίῳ φωνὰς πρέπειν τέ φασιν αὐτὰς οὐ τὰς μὲν ὡς υἱῷ
κατὰ μόνας τῷ ἐκ θεοῦ πατρὸς λόγῳ, τὰς δὲ ὡς ἑτέρῳ πάλιν 10
υἱῷ τῷ ἐκ γυναικός, ἀλλὰ τὰς μὲν τῇ θεότητι αὐτοῦ, τὰς δὲ τῇ αὐτοῦ
πάλιν ἀνθρωπότητι (θεὸς γάρ ἐστιν ὁ αὐτὸς καὶ ἄνθρωπος), εἶναι δέ
φασιν καὶ ἑτέρας κοινοποιηθείσας τρόπον τινὰ καὶ οἷον ἐπ᾿ ἄμφω
βλεπούσας, θεότητά τε καὶ ἀνθρωπότητα λέγω, οἷον δή τι φημί· αἱ
μὲν γάρ εἰσι τῶν φωνῶν ὅτι μάλιστα θεοπρεπεῖς, αἱ δὲ οὕτω πάλιν 15
ἀνθρωποπρεπεῖς, αἱ δὲ μέσην τινὰ τάξιν ἐπέχουσιν, ἐμφανίζουσαι
τὸν υἱὸν θεὸν ὄντα καὶ ἄνθρωπον ὁμοῦ τε καὶ ἐν ταὐτῷ. ὅταν μὲν
γὰρ τῷ Φιλίππῳ λέγῃ τοσοῦτον χρόνον μεθ᾿ ὑμῶν εἰμι, καὶ
οὐκ ἔγνωκάς με, Φίλιππε; οὐ πιστεύεις ὅτι ἐγὼ ἐν τῷ
πατρὶ καὶ ὁ πατὴρ ἐν ἐμοί ἐστιν; ὁ ἑωρακὼς ἐμὲ ἑώρακε 20
τὸν πατέρα.[i] ἐγὼ καὶ ὁ πατὴρ ἕν ἐσμεν,[j] θεοπρεπεστάτην εἶναι
διαβεβαιούμεθα τὴν φωνήν. ὅταν δὲ τοῖς Ἰουδαίων ἐπιπλήττῃ δήμοις,
ἐκεῖνο λέγων εἰ τέκνα τοῦ Ἀβραὰμ ἦτε, τὰ ἔργα τοῦ Ἀβραὰμ
ἐποιεῖτε ἄν· νῦν δὲ ζητεῖτέ με ἀποκτεῖναι, ἄνθρωπον
ὃς τὴν ἀλήθειαν ὑμῖν λελάληκα· τοῦτο Ἀβραὰμ οὐκ 25
ἐποίησεν,[k] ἀνθρωποπρεπῶς εἰρῆσθαι τὰ τοιάδε φαμέν, πλὴν τοῦ
ἑνὸς υἱοῦ τὰς θεοπρεπεῖς καὶ μέντοι τὰς ἀνθρωπίνας. θεὸς γὰρ ὢν
γέγονεν ἄνθρωπος, οὐ τὸ εἶναι θεὸς ἀφείς, ἐν προσλήψει δὲ μᾶλλον
σαρκὸς καὶ αἵματος γεγονώς· ἐπειδὴ δὲ εἷς ἐστι Χριστὸς καὶ υἱὸς
καὶ κύριος, ἐν αὐτοῦ καὶ πρόσωπον εἶναί φαμεν ἡμεῖς τε κἀκεῖνοι. 30
[17] μέσας δὲ εἶναι φωνὰς ἐκείνας διαβεβαιούμεθα, οἷον ὅταν ὁ
μακάριος γράφῃ Παῦλος Ἰησοῦς Χριστὸς χθὲς καὶ σήμερον,
ὁ αὐτὸς καὶ εἰς τοὺς αἰῶνας.[l] καὶ πάλιν· εἴπερ εἰσὶ θεοὶ
πολλοὶ καὶ κύριοι πολλοὶ ἔν τε τῷ οὐρανῷ καὶ ἐπὶ τῆς γῆς,
ἀλλ᾿ ἡμῖν εἷς θεὸς ὁ πατήρ, ἐξ οὗ τὰ πάντα καὶ ἡμεῖς ἐξ 35

---

[i] John 14: 9, 10, 9   [j] John 10: 30   [k] John 8: 39 f.
[l] Hebr. 13: 8

The Antiochene brethren, on the other hand, taking the recognized elements of Christ at the level only of mere ideas, have mentioned a difference of natures, because, as I have said, Godhead and manhood are not the same thing in quality of nature, yet they do declare there is one Son and Christ and Lord, and, since he is actually one in reality, that his person too is one; by no manner of means do they divide what are in union nor do they accept the physical division of that proponent of pitiful ingenuities. [16] They maintain that it is only the terms applied to the Lord which are divided; they do not mean that some of these apply to a Son in isolation, the Word of God, some again to a different woman-born son, but instead that some apply to his Godhead some to his manhood (for the same Son is God and man); others too they assert, much as I do, are to be applied in some way jointly, those looking, so to say, to both aspects (Godhead and manhood, I mean). The point is that some of the terms are specially appropriate to God, some are specially appropriate to man and some occupy an intermediate position, indicating the Son who is at one and the same time God and man. For when he says to Philip: *'Have I been with you so long, and yet you do not know me, Philip? Do you not believe that I am in the Father and the Father in me? He who has seen me has seen the Father. I and the Father are one'*—when he says this we maintain that the language applies most fittingly to God. When, though, he rebukes the crowds of Jews, saying *'If you were Abraham's children you would be doing the deeds of Abraham, but now you are seeking to kill me, a man who has told you the truth; this Abraham did not do'*— things like this we say are spoken humanly, nevertheless the divine and human words are the one Son's. For whilst being God he has become man, not ceasing to be God but rather becoming man by assumption of flesh and blood; since he is one Christ, Son and Lord both they and we declare his person also to be one. [17] The sort of terms we maintain to be intermediate occur when blessed Paul writes: *'Jesus Christ, the same yesterday, today, and for ever'*. And again: *'Although there are many gods and many lords in heaven and on earth, yet to us there is one God the Father,*

αὐτοῦ, καὶ εἷς κύριος Ἰησοῦς Χριστός, δι' οὗ τὰ πάντα καὶ
ἡμεῖς δι' αὐτοῦ.ᵐ καὶ πάλιν· ηὐχόμην γὰρ αὐτὸς ἐγὼ ἀνάθεμα
εἶναι ἀπὸ τοῦ Χριστοῦ ὑπὲρ τῶν ἀδελφῶν μου τῶν συγ-
γενῶν μου κατὰ σάρκα, οἵτινές εἰσιν Ἰσραηλῖται, ὧν
ἐστιν ἡ υἱοθεσία καὶ ἡ νομοθεσία καὶ ἡ διαθήκη καὶ ἡ   5
δόξα, ὧν οἱ πατέρες καὶ ἐξ ὧν ὁ Χριστὸς τὸ κατὰ σάρκα
ὁ ὢν ἐπὶ πάντων θεὸς εὐλογητὸς εἰς τοὺς αἰῶνας. ἀμήν.ⁿ
ἰδοὺ γὰρ ἰδοὺ Χριστὸν Ἰησοῦν ὀνομάσας, χθὲς καὶ σήμερον τὸν
αὐτὸν εἶναί φησι καὶ εἰς τοὺς αἰῶνας καὶ δι' αὐτοῦ γενέσθαι τὰ
πάντα καὶ τὸν κατὰ σάρκα ἐξ Ἰουδαίων ἐπὶ πάντων ὀνομάζει   10
θεὸν καὶ μὴν καὶ εὐλογητὸν εἶναί φησιν εἰς τοὺς αἰῶνας. μὴ
τοίνυν διέλῃς ἐν τούτοις τὰς ἐπὶ τῷ κυρίῳ φωνάς (ἔχουσι γὰρ ἐν
ταὐτῷ τὸ θεοπρεπὲς καὶ τὸ ἀνθρώπινον), ἐφάρμοσον δὲ μᾶλλον
αὐτὰς ὡς ἑνὶ τῷ υἱῷ, τουτέστι τῷ θεῷ λόγῳ σεσαρκωμένῳ. ἕτερον
τοίνυν ἐστὶ τὸ διαιρεῖν τὰς φύσεις, καὶ τοῦτο μετὰ τὴν ἕνωσιν, καὶ   15
κατὰ μόνην ἰσοτιμίαν συνῆφθαι λέγειν ἄνθρωπον θεῷ καὶ ὁμοίως
ἕτερον τὸ φωνῶν εἰδέναι διαφοράν.

18. Ποῦ τοιγαροῦν ταῖς Νεστορίου κενοφωνίαις τὰ ἐκείνων
συντρέχει; εἰ γὰρ καί τισι δοκεῖ τῶν λέξεων ἡ συνθήκη καὶ τῶν
ῥημάτων ἡ προφορὰ τῆς ἰσχύης ἄγαν ἀκριβείας ἀπολιμπάνεσθαι,   20
θαυμαστὸν οὐδέν· δυσεκφώνητα γὰρ τὰ τοιάδε λίαν. ταύτῃ τοι καὶ
ὁ θεσπέσιος Παῦλος ἐζήτει παρὰ θεοῦ λόγον ἐν ἀνοίξει τοῦ
στόματος αὐτοῦ.ᵒ ὅτι γὰρ οὐ μερίζουσιν εἰς δύο τὸν ἕνα κύριον
Ἰησοῦν Χριστόν, χρῆναι λέγοντες ἐφαρμόζεσθαι τὰς φωνάς, τῇ
μὲν θεότητι αὐτοῦ τὰς θεοπρεπεῖς, τῇ δὲ ἀνθρωπότητι πάλιν αὐτοῦ   25
τὰς ἀνθρωπίνας, πῶς οὐχ ἅπασιν ἐναργές; διαβεβαιοῦνται γάρ, ὡς
ἔφην, ὅτι αὐτὸς ὁ ἐκ θεοῦ πατρὸς λόγος, γεννηθεὶς πρὸ αἰώνων,
καὶ ἐν ἐσχάτοις καιροῖς ἐγεννήθη κατὰ σάρκα ἐκ τῆς ἁγίας παρ-
θένου· προσεπάγουσι δὲ ὅτι διὰ τὴν ἄφραστόν τε καὶ ἀσύγχυτον
ἕνωσιν καὶ θεοτόκον εἶναι πιστεύουσι τὴν ἁγίαν παρθένον, καὶ ἕνα   30
υἱὸν καὶ Χριστὸν καὶ κύριον ὁμολογοῦσι σαφῶς. ἀπίθανον δὲ
παντελῶς τὸ καὶ ἕνα λέγειν καὶ διατέμνειν εἰς δύο τὸν ἕνα νομίζειν
αὐτούς. οὐ γὰρ ἂν εἰς τοῦτο προῆλθον ἀποπληξίας, ὡς παραβάτας
ἑαυτοὺς συνιστάνειν, ἃ κατέλυσαν ὀρθῶς, οἰκοδομοῦντες ἀβούλως.
εἰ γὰρ ταῖς Νεστορίου συμφέρονται δόξαις, πῶς αὐτὰς ἀναθεμα-   35

ᵐ 1 Cor. 8: 5 f.   ⁿ Rom. 9: 3 ff.   ᵒ Eph. 6: 19

*from whom are all things and we from him, and one Lord Jesus Christ,
through whom are all things and we through him.'* And again: *'For
I myself was praying to be anathema from Christ for the sake of my
brethren and my kinsfolk in the flesh, who are Israelites; whose are the
adoption, the lawgiving, the covenant, and the glory, whose the fathers
and from whom is the Christ in flesh who is God over all blessed for ever,
Amen.'* For mark you, he uses the words 'Christ Jesus' and declares
him *'the same yesterday, today, and for ever'* and that *'through him all
things'* were made; him who is of the Jews *'in the flesh'* he calls
'God over all' and moreover indeed declares him *'blessed for ever'.*
Do not then divide the terms applied to the Lord here (for they
possess at the same time divine and human application) but
attribute them rather to the one Son, that is God the Word
incarnate. It is, then, one thing to divide the natures even after
the union and to say a man has been connected with God only
in equality of honour, and quite another thing to acknowledge
a difference of terms.

18. So where do their opinions coincide with Nestorius' nonsense? Though for some the phraseology and choice of language
may lack the last degree of refinement and precision, there is no
cause for surprise—things like this are very hard to put into words.
That is why even inspired Paul sought a word from God *'to open
his mouth'.* Must it not be clear to everyone that they are not
dividing the one Lord Jesus Christ into two when they assert
that the divine terms must be attached to his Godhead, and the
human in turn to his manhood? For they insist, as I said, that
the very Word of God the Father, begotten before the ages, was
born in the last times in flesh of the holy Virgin; they add that
because of the mysterious union free from merger they believe
the holy Virgin to be Mother of God and plainly affirm one Son
and Christ and Lord. The suggestion that they are saying 'one'
and also in the same breath dividing the one into two is utterly
incredible. They could not have reached such a pitch of madness
as to render themselves renegades, recklessly building up what
they rightly destroyed. If they agree with Nestorius' doctrines,
how can they be anathematizing them as unhallowed and

τίζουσιν ὡς βεβήλους καὶ μυσαράς; [19] οἶμαι δὲ δεῖν καὶ τὰς
αἰτίας εἰπεῖν, δι' ἃς εἰς τοῦτο προῆλθον ἰσχνομυθίας. ἐπειδὴ γὰρ οἱ
τῆς Ἀρείου δυσσεβείας ὑπασπισταί, τῆς ἀληθείας τὴν δύναμιν
ἀνοσίως ἐκκαπηλεύοντες, τὸν ἐκ θεοῦ φασι λόγον γενέσθαι μὲν
ἄνθρωπον, πλὴν ἀψύχῳ προσχρήσασθαι σώματι (πράττουσι δὲ τοῦτο 5
φιλοκακούργως, ἵνα τὰς ἀνθρωπίνας φωνὰς αὐτῷ προσνέμοντες ὡς
ἐν μείοσιν ὄντα τῆς τοῦ πατρὸς ὑπεροχῆς τοῖς παρ' αὐτῶν πλανω-
μένοις καταδεικνύωσιν ἑτεροφυᾶ τε αὐτὸν εἶναι λέγωσι), ταύτῃ
τοι δεδιότες οἱ ἐκ τῆς Ἀνατολῆς, μὴ ἄρα πως ἡ τοῦ θεοῦ λόγου
κατασμικρύνοιτο δόξα τε καὶ φύσις ἀπό γε τῶν ἀνθρωπίνως 10
εἰρημένων διὰ τὴν μετὰ σαρκὸς οἰκονομίαν, διορίζουσι τὰς φωνάς,
οὐκ εἰς⁴ δύο τέμνοντες, ὡς ἔφην, τὸν ἕνα υἱὸν καὶ κύριον, ἀλλὰ τὰς
μὲν τῇ θεότητι αὐτοῦ προσνέμοντες, τὰς δὲ τῇ ἀνθρωπότητι πάλιν
τῇ αὐτοῦ, πλὴν τὰς πάσας ἑνός.

20. Ἐπυθόμην δὲ ὅτι γέγραφέ τισι τῶν ἐπιτηδείων ὁ εὐ- 15
λαβέστατος καὶ θεοσεβέστατος ἐπίσκοπος Ἰωάννης ὡσανεὶ ἐμοῦ
σαφῶς διδάξαντος καὶ λαμπρᾷ τῇ φωνῇ ὁμολογεῖν μὲν τῶν φύσεων
τὸ διάφορον, διαιρεῖν δὲ τὰς φωνὰς καταλλήλως ταῖς φύσεσι, καὶ
ἐπ' αὐτῷ δὴ τούτῳ σκανδαλίζονταί τινες. ἦν οὖν ἀναγκαῖον καὶ
πρός γε τοῦτο ἡμᾶς εἰπεῖν. οὐκ ἠγνόησεν ἡ σὴ τελειότης ὅτι τῆς 20
Ἀπολιναρίου δόξης τὸν μῶμον τῶν ἐμῶν καταχέοντες ἐπιστολῶν
ᾠήθησαν ὅτι καὶ ἄψυχον εἶναί φημι τὸ ἅγιον σῶμα Χριστοῦ καὶ
ὅτι κρᾶσις ἢ σύγχυσις ἢ φυρμὸς ἢ μεταβολὴ τοῦ θεοῦ λόγου γέγονεν
εἰς τὴν σάρκα ἢ γοῦν τῆς σαρκὸς μεταφοίτησις εἰς φύσιν θεότητος,
ὡς μηδὲν ἔτι σώζεσθαι καθαρῶς μήτε μὴν εἶναι ὅ ἐστιν. ᾠήθησαν 25
δὲ πρὸς τούτῳ καὶ ταῖς Ἀρείου με συμφέρεσθαι δυσφημίαις διά τοι
τὸ μὴ θέλειν διαφορὰν εἰδέναι φωνῶν καὶ τὰς μὲν εἶναι λέγειν
θεοπρεπεῖς, τὰς δὲ ἀνθρωπίνας καὶ πρεπούσας μᾶλλον τῇ οἰκονομίᾳ
τῇ μετὰ σαρκός. ἐγὼ δὲ ὅτι τῶν τοιούτων ἀπήλλαγμαι, μαρτυρήσειεν
ἂν ἑτέροις ἡ σὴ τελειότης, πλὴν ἔδει σκανδαλισθεῖσιν ἀπολογή- 30
σασθαι. ταύτῃ τοι γέγραφα πρὸς τὴν θεοσέβειαν αὐτοῦ ὡς οὔτε
πεφρόνηκά ποτε τὰ Ἀρείου τε καὶ Ἀπολιναρίου οὔτε μὴν μεταπεποιῆσθαι τὸν τοῦ θεοῦ λόγον εἰς σάρκα φημί, ἀλλ' οὐδὲ εἰς φύσιν
θεότητος μεταφῦναι τὴν σάρκα διὰ τὸ ἄτρεπτον εἶναι καὶ ἀναλ-
λοίωτον τὸν τοῦ θεοῦ λόγον· ἀνέφικτον δὲ καὶ τὸ ἕτερον οὔτε μὴν 35

⁴ πρόσωπα add. AR+others

loathsome? [19] I feel I had better explain their motives in descending to this level of subtlety. It is due to the fact that the defenders of Arius' profanity, make a blasphemous counterfeit of the truth, by asserting that the Word of God was made man but employed an inanimate body.[32] Their mischievous aim in ascribing the human expressions to him is to prove him to their dupes inferior in being to the transcendence of the Father and categorize him as belonging to a different stock. The Easterns, fearing therefore that the glory and nature of God the Word might be diminished by the human expressions employed for the incarnate dispensation, distinguish the terms, not, as I have said, by dividing the one Son and Lord into two, but by ascribing some terms to his Godhead, some in turn to his manhood; nevertheless all belong to one.

20. I hear that the most pious and religious bishop John has written to certain friends to the effect that I have told people clearly and in strong language to affirm the difference between the natures and divide the terms in conformity with the natures;[33] and that this has caused scandal. Our answer here must be this: your Perfection is not unaware that they had cast the aspersion of Apollinarianism on my letters and believed that I declared the holy body of Christ inanimate and that a mixture, merger, mingling or change of God the Word into the flesh or transition of flesh into the nature of deity had occurred, so that nothing would remain intact or be what it is. They believed besides that a refusal to recognize a difference in expressions and declare some to be divine and some human belonging rather to the incarnate dispensation would mean my sympathy with Arius' blasphemies. That I am free of such things your Perfection can testify to others; nevertheless I had an obligation to explain myself to those who had taken offence. I have accordingly written to his Reverence[34] that I have never entertained the views of Arius and Apollinarius, nor do I assert that God's Word was converted into flesh, or again, that the flesh changed its nature into the nature of deity, because God's Word is immutable and unchangeable; as for

[32] Not attested for Arius himself *in ipsissimis verbis* (though certainly his view) but for the 'Arian' Eudoxius (see Hahn, *Bibliothek der Symbole* 191) and the Anomoean Eunomius in his Ἔκθεσις—true text of passage preserved in Gregory of Nyssa, *Refutatio Confessionis Eunomii* 172, *Opera* ii, ed. W. Jaeger, pp. 384 f. = οὐκ ἀναλαβόντα τὸν ἐκ ψυχῆς καὶ σώματος ἄνθρωπον.

[33] *ACO* 1, 1, 7 p. 156, lines 34 ff.

[34] *ACO* 1, 1, 4 pp. 15–31; see pp. 17 ff. for the sentiments but not the precise expressions.

ἀνήρηκά ποτε φωνῶν διαφοράς, ἀλλ᾽ οἶδα τὸν κύριον θεοπρεπῶς τε
ἅμα καὶ ἀνθρωπίνως διαλεγόμενον, ἐπείπερ ἐστὶν ἐν ταὐτῷ θεὸς
καὶ ἄνθρωπος. οὐκοῦν αὐτὸ δὴ τουτὶ κατασημῆναι θέλων γέγραφεν
ὅτι ἐδίδαξεν ὁμολογεῖν τῶν φύσεων τὸ διάφορον καὶ διαιρεῖν τὰς
φωνὰς καταλλήλως ταῖς φύσεσιν· αἱ δὲ τοιαῦται διαλέξεις ἐμαὶ μὲν 5
οὔκ εἰσιν, ἐξεφωνήθησαν δὲ παρ᾽ αὐτοῦ.

21. Κἀκεῖνο δέ, οἶμαι, τοῖς εἰρημένοις προσεπενεγκεῖν ἀναγκαῖον. ἀφίκετο γὰρ πρός με ὁ θεοσεβέστατος ἐπίσκοπος Παῦλος
τῆς Ἐμεσηνῶν, εἶτα λόγου κεκινημένου περὶ τῆς ὀρθῆς τε καὶ
ἀμωμήτου πίστεως διεπυνθάνετό μου καὶ μάλα ἐσπουδασμένως εἰ 10
συναινῶ τοῖς γραφεῖσι παρὰ τοῦ ἀοιδίμου μνήμης καὶ τρισμακαρίου
πατρὸς ἡμῶν Ἀθανασίου πρὸς Ἐπίκτητον ἐπίσκοπον τῆς Κορινθίων.
ἐγὼ δὲ ἔφην ὅτι εἰ σῴζεται παρ᾽ ὑμῖν οὐ νενοθευμένον τὸ γράμμα
(παραπεποίηται γὰρ τῶν ἐν αὐτῷ πολλὰ παρὰ τῶν τῆς ἀληθείας
ἐχθρῶν), συναινέσαιμι ἂν πάντη τε καὶ πάντως. ὁ δὲ πρὸς τοῦτο 15
ἔφασκεν ἔχειν μὲν καὶ αὐτὸς τὴν ἐπιστολήν, βούλεσθαι δὲ ἐκ τῶν
παρ᾽ ἡμῖν ἀντιγράφων πληροφορηθῆναι καὶ μαθεῖν πότερόν ποτε
παρεποιήθη τὰ αὐτῶν βιβλία ἢ μή. καὶ δὴ καὶ λαβὼν ἀντίγραφα
παλαιὰ καὶ οἷς ἐπεφέρετο, συμβαλών, ηὕρισκε ταῦτα νενοθευμένα
καὶ προέτρεψεν ἐκ τῶν παρ᾽ ἡμῖν βιβλίων ἴσα ποιῆσαι πέμψαι τε 20
τῇ Ἀντιοχέων ἐκκλησίᾳ· ὃ δὴ καὶ γέγονε.

Καὶ τοῦτό ἐστιν ὃ γέγραφεν ὁ εὐλαβέστατος καὶ θεοσεβέστατος
ἐπίσκοπος Ἰωάννης τῷ Καρρηνῷ[5] περὶ ἐμοῦ ὅτι "ἐξέθετο τὰ περὶ
τῆς ἐνανθρωπήσεως, συνυφάνας ἡμῖν καὶ τὴν πατρῴαν παράδοσιν,
μικροῦ καὶ ἐξ ἀνθρώπων, ἵν᾽ οὕτως εἴπω, γενέσθαι κινδυνευσάσαν". 25

22. Ἐὰν δὲ περικομίζωσί τινες ἐπιστολὴν ὡς γραφεῖσαν παρὰ
τοῦ εὐλαβεστάτου πρεσβυτέρου τῆς Ῥωμαίων ἐκκλησίας Φιλίππου

---

[5] καρίνῳ V+others: καρήνῳ 2 witnesses: Careno pontifici Latin versions:
Ḥarrīna(?) Σ

---

[35] PG 26 pp. 1049–69, also ed. G. Ludwig (Jena, 1911). The date of the
letter is uncertain but belongs to the later years of Athanasius. Amongst the
reasons why John chose to make acceptance of this work a condition of peace
may be assumed: (1) the unimpeachable orthodoxy of its author; (2) its
claim to interpret the Nicene faith; (3) its clear distinction between Godhead

the second absurd allegation, I have never rejected differences in terms, but I recognize the Lord speaking both divinely and humanly since he is at once God and man. Meaning therefore to make this very point he has written of me that 'he told people to affirm the difference between the natures and distinguish the terms in conformity with the natures'; these phrases, though, are not mine, they were voiced by him.

21. I think I ought to add to what has been said this further point. The most religious bishop Paul of Emesa came to me and after discussion about the orthodox and spotless faith he enquired of me very earnestly whether I hold with what was written by our thrice-blessed father Athanasius of celebrated memory to Epictetus[35] bishop of Corinth. I answered: 'If an uncorrupted text is in your safekeeping (for much of its content has been altered by enemies of the truth) I should be in total and entire agreement with it.' To this he replied that he himself also had the letter and wanted to use our copies to get a sure answer to the question whether their texts had ever been altered or not. He took ancient manuscripts, compared them with what he had brought and on finding them corrupt urged us to make and send copies from our texts to the Church of Antioch; which in fact was done.

This is what bishop John has written to the bishop of Harran[36] about me: 'He has interpreted the facts of the incarnation, drawing together the threads of the fathers' tradition for us, a tradition in danger, if I may so put it, of being well-nigh lost to mankind.'

22. Any who may circulate a letter allegedly written by Philip,[37] the most pious priest of the Church of Rome, implying

and manhood in Christ; (4) its affirmation that the Word assumed a complete humanity. No trace can now be found of any text falsified in a 'Nestorian' direction, if it ever was more than a product of Cyril's wishful thinking. (For further discussion, see Schwartz's observations, *ACO* 1, 5, 2 p. xv; J. Lebon, 'Altération doctrinale de la *Lettre à Epictète* de S. Athanase', *Revue d'Histoire Ecclésiastique* 31 (1935), 713–61; R. Y. Ebied/L. R. Wickham, 'A note on the Syriac version of Athanasius' *Ad Epictetum* in M.S. B.M. Add. 14557', *JTS* 23 (1972), 144–54.)

[36] Text uncertain, but this is the probable meaning whether we read Καρήνῳ or Καρρήνῳ (cf. ὁ τῆς Ἀλεξανδρείας in *Letter to Eulogius*, p. 62). The versions take 'Carrenus' as a personal name, apparently. The heading of the letter in *ACO* 1, 1, 7 p. 156 lacks any corresponding term, and the Latin version, *ACO* 1, 4 p. 3, has a lacuna in the title. The identity of the bishop of Harran at this time is unknown.

[37] Legate of the Apostolic See and signatory of the Acta of Ephesus.

ὡσανεὶ τοῦ ὁσιωτάτου ἐπισκόπου Ξύστου χαλεπήναντος ἐπὶ τῇ
Νεστορίου καθαιρέσει καὶ ἐνρήξαντος αὐτῷ, μὴ πιστευέτω ἡ σὴ
ὁσιότης· σύμφωνα γὰρ τῇ ἁγίᾳ συνόδῳ γέγραφε καὶ πάντα ἐβεβαίωσε
τὰ παρ᾽ αὐτῆς πραχθέντα καί ἐστιν ὁμόφρων ἡμῖν. εἰ δὲ δὴ καὶ ὡς
παρ᾽ ἐμοῦ γραφεῖσα παρακομίζοιτο πρός τινων ἐπιστολὴ ὡς 5
μετανοοῦντος ἐφ᾽ οἷς πεπράχαμεν κατὰ τὴν Ἐφεσίων, γελάσθω καὶ
τοῦτο· ἐσμὲν γὰρ διὰ τὴν τοῦ σωτῆρος χάριν ἐν καλῷ φρενὸς καὶ
τοῦ εἰκότος οὐκ ἐκπεφορήμεθα λογισμοῦ.

Πρόσειπε τὴν παρὰ σοὶ ἀδελφότητα. σὲ ἡ σὺν ἡμῖν ἐν κυρίῳ
προσαγορεύει. 10

that the most holy bishop Xystus[38] was indignant at the deposition of Nestorius and upbraided him, your Holiness is to give no credence to. He has, in fact, written his agreement with the holy synod, confirmed all its acts and is of one mind with us. If a letter allegedly written by me be brought by anybody implying that I have changed my mind about what we did at Ephesus, this too should be treated with derision; for we are, through our Saviour's grace, sound in mind and have not wandered away from true reasoning.

Salute the brotherhood with you. The brotherhood here with us greets you in the Lord.

[38] Sixtus III, Pope 31 July 432–19 August 440. Legates from Cyril and Maximian were present by chance at his consecration and stayed on to confer with him. He wrote to Cyril (*ACO* 1, 1, 7 pp. 143–45), siding with Cyril against John and intimating that John, along with the followers of Nestorius, should be allowed back into the Church if they 'rejected everything which the holy synod (sc. of Ephesus) ourselves confirming, rejected'. He wrote to Cyril and John (*ACO* 1, 2 pp. 107–10) when the terms of peace had been communicated to him by both parties, expressing satisfaction. The dissident Easterns, Eutherius of Tyana and Helladius of Tarsus, wrote to him to ask him to intervene after this betrayal of principle (as they deemed it) on John's part (*ACO* 1, 4 pp. 145–48), presumably without success. M. Richard in 'Le Pape saint Léon le Grand et les "Scholia de Incarnatione Unigeniti" de saint Cyrille d'Alexandrie' (*Opera Minora* 2, no. 53, esp. pp. 126 f.) suggests that there may be substance in this report of disquiet on the part of Sixtus (perhaps over the Chapters) and that Cyril sent the *Scholia* to him to allay it. Only fragments of Cyril's *Ep.* 53 to Sixtus survive (*PG* 77, 285c, cf. 86, 1832A) but there is some suggestion here perhaps of a misunderstanding which has to be resolved.

4

TO EULOGIUS

Ὑπομνηστικὸν Εὐλογίῳ πρεσβυτέρῳ Ἀλεξανδρείας παραμένοντι ἐν
Κωνσταντινουπόλει παρὰ τοῦ ἁγιωτάτου ἐπισκόπου Κυρίλλου[1]

Ἐπιλαμβάνονταί τινες τῆς ἐκθέσεως ἧς πεποίηνται οἱ Ἀνατολικοί,
καί φασι· διὰ τί δύο φύσεις ὀνομαζόντων αὐτῶν ἠνέσχετο ἢ καὶ
ἐπήνεσεν ὁ τῆς Ἀλεξανδρείας; οἱ δὲ τὰ Νεστορίου φρονοῦντες 5
λέγουσι κἀκεῖνον οὕτω φρονεῖν, συναρπάζοντες τοὺς οὐκ εἰδότας
τὸ ἀκριβές.

Χρὴ δὲ τοῖς μεμφομένοις ἐκεῖνα λέγειν ὅτι οὐ πάντα ὅσα
λέγουσιν οἱ αἱρετικοί, φεύγειν καὶ παραιτεῖσθαι χρή· πολλὰ γὰρ
ὁμολογοῦσιν ὧν καὶ ἡμεῖς ὁμολογοῦμεν. οἷον Ἀρειανοὶ ὅταν λέγωσι 10
τὸν πατέρα ὅτι δημιουργός ἐστι τῶν ὅλων καὶ κύριος, μὴ διὰ τοῦτο
φεύγειν ἡμᾶς ἀκόλουθον τὰς τοιαύτας ὁμολογίας; οὕτω καὶ ἐπὶ
Νεστορίου, κἂν λέγῃ δύο φύσεις τὴν διαφορὰν σημαίνων τῆς
σαρκὸς καὶ τοῦ θεοῦ λόγου· ἑτέρα γὰρ ἡ τοῦ λόγου φύσις καὶ ἑτέρα
ἡ τῆς σαρκός. ἀλλ᾽ οὐκέτι τὴν ἕνωσιν ὁμολογεῖ μεθ᾽ ἡμῶν. ἡμεῖς 15
γὰρ ἑνώσαντες ταῦτα ἕνα Χριστόν, ἕνα υἱόν, τὸν αὐτὸν ἕνα κύριον
ὁμολογοῦμεν καὶ λοιπὸν μίαν τὴν τοῦ υἱοῦ φύσιν σεσαρκωμένην,
ὁποῖόν ἐστι καὶ ἐπὶ τοῦ κοινοῦ εἰπεῖν ἀνθρώπου· ἔστι μὲν γὰρ ἐκ

Witnesses : V S A R + Latin versions, Σ, and citations   *ACO* 1, 1, 4 pp. 35–7

[1] Headings vary with mss. This is Schwartz's composite title

[1] Cyril's agent at Constantinople. Called 'priest of Alexandria' in the
notorious letter of Epiphanius, archdeacon and syncellus at Alexandria, to
archbishop Maximian (see below, n. 8), *Casinensis* 293 [203] (*ACO* 1, 4 p. 223
line 28), which together with the following item (294) tell us about Cyril's
moves in Constantinople to initiate reunion. Mentioned also *ACO* 1, 1, 7
p. 154 line 14.

[2] The Formula of Reunion, see Appendix.

[3] See *PGL* s.v. φύσις iv C. The phrase is quoted by Cyril, *Oratio ad Dominas*,
§ 9 (*ACO* 1, 1, 5 pp. 65 f.) in a longish extract from a λόγος (allegedly) by
Athanasius περὶ σαρκώσεως and again in *Apologia xii Capitulorum contra Orientales*
(*ACO* 1, 1, 7 pp. 48 f.) in the first of a series of short quotations from the same
piece ascribed (but without more specific reference) to Athanasius. A striking

4

TO EULOGIUS

Note from the most Holy Bishop Cyril to Eulogius,[1]
Priest of Alexandria, resident in Constantinople

The doctrinal statement[2] which the Easterns have produced
is under attack in certain quarters and it is being asked why
the bishop of Alexandria tolerated, even applauded it, seeing
that they use the words 'two natures'. The Nestorians are
saying that he shares their view and are winning those who do
not know the precise facts over to their side.

To these critics it must be said that there is no obligation to
shun and reject everything heretics say—they affirm many of
the points we too affirm. When, for example, Arians declare the
Father to be creator of the universe and lord, must we, on that
account, shun these affirmations? The same holds good of
Nestorius if he says 'two natures' to indicate the difference between
the flesh and God the Word—the point being that the nature
of the Word is other than that of the flesh. However, he fails
to affirm the union along with us. We unite these, acknowledging
one Christ, one Son, the same one Lord and, further, one incarnate nature of the Son[3] in the same way that the phrase can be
used of ordinary man. The point is that man results from two

phrase for Cyril, it was to become a watch-word of Cyrilline, non-Chalcedonian
orthodoxy ('Monophysitism'). The Athanasian provenance of the text in
which it occurs was to be denied by 'Leontius', *De Sectis* (*PG* 86, i pp. 1253C ff.),
Leontius of Jerusalem, *Contra Monophysitas* (*PG* 86, ii pp. 1864 f.), Justinian,
Tractatus Contra Monophysitas (ed. Schwartz p. 18), and *Doctrina Patrum* 9, 10
(ed. F. Diekamp, p. 62); and their ascription of the text to Apollinaris has been
generally accepted—see H. Lietzmann, *Apollinaris von Laodicea und seine Schule*
(Tübingen, 1904, repr. Hildesheim/New York, 1970), pp. 250–53 [*ΠΡΟΣ
IOBIANON*, text], pp. 119 ff. and 146 f. [discussion]. He only began to use
it during the Nestorian controversy; see *Contra Nest.* 2 *Proëmion* (*ACO* 1, 1, 6
p. 33, 6 f.), *Christ is One* (*PG* 75 Aubert 737), and *To Acacius* 12 and the two
Letters to Succensus (*passim*), which last give his clear explanation of its meaning
for him. Christ is, for Cyril, a single nature compounded of two natures. This
equivocal use of φύσις was bound to cause trouble, but what Cyril means to
say and what he does *not* mean are crystal clear. The one prosopon
and hypostasis of the Chalcedonian definition is its exact equivalent, as was
eventually to become clear to supporters of Chalcedon.

διαφόρων φύσεων, ἀπό τε σώματός φημι καὶ ψυχῆς, καὶ ὁ μὲν
λόγος καὶ ἡ θεωρία οἶδε τὴν διαφοράν, ἑνώσαντες δέ, τότε μίαν
ποιοῦμεν ἀνθρώπου φύσιν. οὐκοῦν οὐ τὸ εἰδέναι τῶν φύσεων τὴν
διαφορὰν διατέμνειν ἐστὶν εἰς δύο τὸν ἕνα Χριστόν. ἐπειδὴ δὲ
πάντες οἱ ἐκ τῆς Ἀνατολῆς νομίζουσιν ἡμᾶς τοὺς ὀρθοδόξους ταῖς 5
Ἀπολιναρίου δόξαις ἀκολουθεῖν καὶ φρονεῖν ὅτι σύγκρασις ἐγένετο ἢ
σύγχυσις (τοιαύταις γὰρ αὐτοὶ κέχρηνται φωναῖς, ὡς τοῦ θεοῦ
λόγου μεταβεβηκότος εἰς φύσιν σαρκὸς καὶ τῆς σαρκὸς τραπείσης εἰς
φύσιν θεότητος), συγκεχωρήκαμεν αὐτοῖς οὐ διελεῖν εἰς δύο τὸν ἕνα
υἱόν, μὴ γένοιτο, ἀλλ᾽ ὁμολογῆσαι μόνον ὅτι οὔτε σύγχυσις ἐγένετο 10
οὔτε κρᾶσις, ἀλλ᾽ ἡ μὲν σὰρξ σὰρξ ἦν ὡς ἐκ γυναικὸς ληφθεῖσα,
ὁ δὲ λόγος ὡς ἐκ πατρὸς γεννηθεὶς λόγος ἦν· πλὴν εἷς ὁ Χριστὸς
καὶ υἱὸς καὶ κύριος κατὰ τὴν Ἰωάννου φωνὴν ὡς γεγονότος σαρκὸς
τοῦ λόγου.[a] παρασκεύαζε δὲ αὐτοὺς προσέχειν τῇ ἀναγνώσει τῆς
ἐπιστολῆς τοῦ μακαρίου πάπα Ἀθανασίου, ὅτι ἐκεῖ φιλονεικούντων 15
τινῶν καὶ λεγόντων ὅτι ἐκ τῆς ἰδίας φύσεως ὁ θεὸς λόγος μετε-
ποίησεν ἑαυτῷ σῶμα, ἄνω καὶ κάτω ἰσχυρίζεται ὅτι οὐχ ὁμοούσιον
ἦν τῷ λόγῳ τὸ σῶμα. εἰ δὲ οὐχ ὁμοούσιον, ἑτέρα πάντως καὶ ἑτέρα
φύσις, ἐξ ὧν ὁ εἷς καὶ μόνος νοεῖται υἱός. κἀκεῖνο δὲ μὴ ἀγνοείτω-
σαν· ὅπου γὰρ ἕνωσις ὀνομάζεται, οὐχ ἑνὸς πράγματος σημαίνεται 20
σύνοδος, ἀλλ᾽ ἢ δύο ἢ καὶ πλειόνων καὶ διαφόρων ἀλλήλοις κατὰ
τὴν φύσιν. εἰ τοίνυν λέγομεν ἕνωσιν, ὁμολογοῦμεν ὅτι σαρκὸς
ἐψυχωμένης νοερῶς καὶ λόγου, καὶ οἱ δύο λέγοντες φύσεις οὕτω
νοοῦσι· πλὴν τῆς ἑνώσεως ὁμολογουμένης οὐκέτι διίστανται
ἀλλήλων τὰ ἑνωθέντα, ἀλλ᾽ εἷς λοιπὸν υἱός, μία φύσις αὐτοῦ, ὡς 25
σαρκωθέντος τοῦ λόγου. ταῦτα ὡμολόγησαν οἱ ἐκ τῆς Ἀνατολῆς,
εἰ καὶ περὶ τὴν λέξιν ὀλίγον ἐσκοτίσθησαν. οἱ γὰρ ὁμολογοῦντες
ὅτι ὁ ἐκ θεοῦ πατρὸς γεννηθεὶς μονογενὴς λόγος ἐγεννήθη ὁ αὐτὸς
καὶ κατὰ σάρκα ἐκ γυναικός, καὶ ὅτι θεοτόκος ἐστὶν ἡ ἁγία παρθένος, καὶ ὅτι ἐν αὐτοῦ τὸ πρόσωπον, καὶ ὅτι οὐ δύο υἱοί, οὐ δύο 30
Χριστοί, ἀλλ᾽ εἷς, πῶς ταῖς Νεστορίου συμφέρονται δόξαις;
Νεστόριος μὲν γὰρ ἐν ταῖς ἑαυτοῦ ἐξηγήσεσι προσποιεῖται λέγειν
"εἷς υἱὸς καὶ εἷς κύριος", ἀλλ᾽ ἀναφέρει τὴν υἱότητα καὶ τὴν
κυριότητα ἐπὶ μόνον τὸν τοῦ θεοῦ λόγον, ὅταν δὲ ἔλθῃ εἰς τὴν

[a] cf. John 1 : 14

natures—body and soul, I mean—and intellectual perception recognizes the difference; but we unite them and then get one nature of man. So, recognizing the difference of natures is not dividing the one Christ into two.[4]

Since all the Easterns reckon us orthodox as following the opinions of Apollinarius in thinking that there occurred a mixture or merger (such are the terms they have employed, implying that God the Word changed into the nature of flesh and the flesh was turned into the nature of deity) we yielded to them not to the extent of dividing the one Son into two—far from it!—but only to that of affirming that no merger or mixing occurred: the flesh was flesh assumed of woman and the Word was Word begotten of the Father. Nevertheless the Christ, Son and Lord is one, the Word having, in John's phrase, become flesh. Get them to read blessed Pope Athanasius' letter[5] and note that in that work, when people were contending that God the Word had refashioned himself a body out of his own nature, he maintains with the full gamut of argument that the body was not consubstantial with the Word. If it is not consubstantial, there must be different natures out of which the one and unique Christ is understood to have his being. This too they should not overlook: where 'union' is mentioned, it is not the joining together of a single entity that is meant, but of two or more, mutually different in nature. So if we speak of 'union' we are affirming that it is a union of flesh, endowed with mental life and reason, and Word and this is how those who say 'two natures' understand it; yet, with the acknowledgement of union the united elements no longer stand apart from each other but from then on there is one Son, one nature of him, the Word incarnate. These truths the Easterns acknowledged, even if they were somewhat in the dark about the phraseology. How can men who affirm that it is the same only-begotten Word of God the Father who was begotten in flesh of a woman, that the holy Virgin is Mother of God and that his person is one, and that there are not two Sons or two Christs but one—how can they, I say, be in agreement with the opinions of Nestorius? For in his sermons Nestorius pretends to say 'one Son and one Lord' but attributes the sonship and lordship to the Word of God only and when he

---

[4] The significance of these two sentences was to be debated heatedly by Severus (and his followers) and Chalcedonians. The passage affirms a real distinction of natures for thought—and hence the ground for disagreement, for in what respect is the duality *actual*?

[5] i.e. to Epictetus. See esp. *PG* 26 pp. 1052C–1053A. On the use of this letter see above, p. 58 n. 35.

οἰκονομίαν, πάλιν ὡς ἕτερον κύριον τὸν ἐκ γυναικὸς ἰδίᾳ ἄνθρωπόν φησιν συναφθέντα τῇ ἀξίᾳ ἢ τῇ ἰσοτιμίᾳ.² τὸ γὰρ λέγειν ὅτι διὰ τοῦτο ὁ θεὸς λόγος Χριστὸς ὀνομάζεται, ὅτι ἔχει τὴν συνάφειαν τὴν πρὸς τὸν Χριστόν, πῶς οὐκ ἐναργῶς ἐστι δύο λέγειν Χριστούς, εἰ Χριστὸς πρὸς Χριστὸν ἔχει συνάφειαν ὡς ἄλλος πρὸς ἄλλον; οἱ 5 δὲ ἐκ τῆς Ἀνατολῆς οὐδὲν εἰρήκασι τοιοῦτον, τὰς δὲ φωνὰς διαιροῦσι μόνον. διαιροῦσι δὲ κατὰ τοῦτον τὸν τρόπον, ὡς τὰς μὲν θεοπρεπεῖς εἶναι λέγειν, τὰς δὲ ἀνθρωπίνας, τὰς δὲ κοινοποιηθείσας, ὡς ἐχούσας ὁμοῦ καὶ τὸ θεοπρεπὲς καὶ τὸ ἀνθρώπινον, πλὴν εἰρημένας παρ' ἑνὸς καὶ τοῦ αὐτοῦ καὶ οὐχ ὡς Νεστόριος τὰς μὲν τῷ θεῷ 10 λόγῳ ἰδικῶς ἀπονέμει, τὰς δὲ τῷ ἐκ γυναικὸς ὡς ἑτέρῳ υἱῷ. ἕτερον δέ ἐστι τὸ φωνῶν εἰδέναι διαφορὰν καὶ ἕτερον τὸ μερίζειν δύο προσώποις, ὡς ἑτέρῳ καὶ ἑτέρῳ.

Ἡ δὲ ἐπιστολὴ ἡ πρὸς Ἀκάκιον μάλιστα ἧς ἡ ἀρχὴ "Χρῆμα μὲν ἀδελφοῖς ἡ πρόσρησις γλυκύ τε καὶ ἀξιάγαστον" καλὴν ἀπολογίαν 15 ἔχει περὶ πάντων. ἔχεις δὲ πλείστας ἐπιστολὰς ἐν τῷ γλωσσοκόμῳ, ἃς ὀφείλεις σπουδαίως δοῦναι. προσάγαγε δὲ τῷ μεγαλοπρε- πεστάτῳ πραιποσίτῳ τὰ ἀποσταλέντα παρ' ἐμοῦ δύο βιβλία, ἓν μὲν κατὰ τῶν Νεστορίου δυσφημιῶν, ἕτερον δὲ ἔχον τὰ ἐν τῇ συνόδῳ πεπραγμένα κατὰ Νεστορίου καὶ τῶν τὰ αὐτοῦ φρονούντων καὶ 20 ἀντιρρήσεις παρ' ἐμοῦ γενομένας πρὸς τοὺς γράψαντας κατὰ τῶν κεφαλαίων· δύο δέ εἰσιν ἐπίσκοποι, Ἀνδρέας καὶ Θεοδώρητος. ἔχει δὲ ἐπὶ τέλει τὸ αὐτὸ βιβλίον καὶ συντόμους ἐκθέσεις περὶ τῆς κατὰ Χριστὸν οἰκονομίας, σφόδρα καλὰς καὶ ὠφελῆσαι δυναμένας.

---

² ἢ τῇ ἰσοτιμίᾳ] Schwartz brackets as an ancient dittography

6 See above p. 53. What Cyril omits to say is that for the Easterns the distinction indicates and arises from an actual and permanent (not merely a theoretical) distinction of 'natures' in Christ.

7 See pp. 34 ff.

8 The eunuch Chryseros (probably this is the correct form rather than 'Chrysoretes') who was *praepositus sacri cubiculi*. His support had to be obtained by suitably grand *largesses* which drained the coffers of the Church of Alexandria, as maliciously exposed by Irenaeus (see *Casinensis* 293 [203] and 294, *ACO* 1, 4 pp. 222 ff.), viz. 200 lbs of gold and quantities of furnishings: *nacotapita* (carpets or perhaps hassocks) *maiora sex, nacotapita mediocria quattuor, tapeta* (rugs) *maiora quattuor, accubitabilia* (sofa-covers) *octo, mensalia* (table-cloths) *sex, bila* (curtains) *grandia tapetes sex, bila mediocria sex, scamnalia* (upholsterings) *sex, in cathedris xii, cortinas* (curtains) *maiores quattuor, cathedras eburneas quattuor, scamna* (stools) *eburnea quattuor, persoina* (pews/benches?) *sex, tabulas maiores quattuor, struthiones* ('ostriches' literally, but some piece of furniture or upholstery must be meant)

comes to the dispensation speaks of another 'lord', the woman-born man on his own, connected with the Word by dignity or equality of honour. Is it not clear that to say that God the Word is called 'Christ' on the ground that he has a connection with Christ is to say 'two Christs', if one Christ has connection with another Christ? The Easterns have said nothing of that sort; they only distinguish the expressions. They distinguish them in this way:[6] some they assert to be appropriate to God, some human, and some common as having simultaneously a divine and human character, nevertheless they have a single, identical author; whereas by contrast Nestorius allots some to God the Word on his own, some to another woman-born son. It is one thing to recognize difference of expressions and another thing to divide them out to two different and distinct persons.

The letter to Acacius especially, beginning 'The pleasure brothers have of speaking to each other is an admirable one',[7] gives a good account of all matters. You have a large number of letters in the file which you ought to be active in giving out. Take the most venerable Chamberlain[8] the two books sent by me: the one against Nestorius' blasphemies,[9] and the other containing the acts of the synod against Nestorius and his sympathizers[10] and refutations produced by me in reply to those who wrote against the Chapters—two are bishops, Andreas and Theodoret.[11] The same book has very good and helpful summary expositions of the dispensation in Christ at the end.[12] Present

sex. For the episode see P. Batiffol, 'Les présents de Saint Cyrille à la cour de Constantinople', *Études de Liturgie et d'Archéologie Chrétienne* (Paris, 1919), and A. H. M. Jones, *Later Roman Empire* (Oxford, 1964) i, p. 346.

[9] *Contra Nestorium* (*ACO* 1, 1, 6 pp. 13–106).

[10] Cyril evidently circularized a version of the acts of the Council dated (Wednesday) 22 July 431 (*ACO* 1, 1, 7 pp. 84–117). These acts (for which see Schwartz's discussion, *ACO* 1, 1, 4 pp. xvii ff.) contain the 'Ephesine decree', viz. the prohibition of any creed other than the Nicene, and a general condemnation of Nestorius' supporters. Their relationship to an actual session of the Council is debatable. There are suspicious overlaps with the records of the session of 22 June, suggestive of a propagandist publication. See *On the Creed*, n. 3.

[11] *Apologia xii capitulorum contra Orientales* (*ACO* 1, 1, 7 pp. 33–65) and *Apologia xii capitulorum contra Theodoretum* (*ACO* 1, 1, 6 pp. 107–46).

[12] Perhaps to be identified with the *Scholia*—so M. Richard, 'Le Pape saint Léon le Grand et les "Scholia de Incarnatione Unigeniti" de saint Cyrille d'Alexandrie', *Opera Minora* 2, no. 53, esp. pp. 122 f.

προσάγαγε δὲ ὁμοίως αὐτῷ ἐκ τῶν ἐχουσῶν δέρμα ἐπιστολὰς
πέντε, μίαν μὲν τοῦ μακαρίου πάπα Ἀθανασίου πρὸς Ἐπίκτητον
καὶ ἄλλην πρὸς Ἰωάννην παρ' ἡμῶν καὶ πρὸς Νεστόριον δύο, μίαν
τὴν μικρὰν καὶ μίαν τὴν μεγάλην, καὶ τὴν πρὸς Ἀκάκιον. ταῦτα
γὰρ ἐζήτησε παρ' ἡμῶν.   5

him likewise with five of the parchment letters: blessed Pope
Athanasius' to Epictetus,[13] ours to John,[14] our two to Nestorius—
the short and the long[15]—and ours to Acacius.[16] He requested
them of us.

[13] See above, p. 59.

[14] *Ep.* 39 (*ACO* 1, 1, 4 pp. 15–20) beginning 'Let the heavens rejoice' and
containing the Formula of Reunion.

[15] The second and third letters to Nestorius, pp. 2 ff.

[16] See pp. 34 ff.

5

FIRST LETTER TO SUCCENSUS

Ὑπομνηστικὸν τοῦ θεοφιλεστάτου καὶ ἁγιωτάτου ἀρχιεπισκόπου
Κυρίλλου πρὸς τὸν μακαριώτατον Σούκενσον ἐπίσκοπον τῆς
Διοκαισαρέων κατὰ τὴν Ἰσαύρων ἐπαρχίαν[1]

1. Ἐνέτυχον μὲν τῷ ὑπομνηστικῷ τῷ παρὰ τῆς σῆς ὁσιότητος
ἀποσταλέντι, ἤσθην δὲ ἄγαν ὅτι καίτοι δυνάμενος ἡμᾶς τε καὶ 5
ἑτέρους ὠφελεῖν ἐκ πολλῆς φιλομαθείας προτρέπειν ἀξιοῖς, ἃ εἰς
νοῦν ἔχομεν καὶ εὖ ἔχειν ὑπειλήφαμεν, ταῦτα καὶ γράψαι. φρο-
νοῦμεν τοίνυν περὶ τῆς τοῦ σωτῆρος ἡμῶν οἰκονομίας ἃ καὶ οἱ πρὸ
ἡμῶν ἅγιοι πατέρες· ἀναγνόντες γὰρ τοὺς ἐκείνων πόνους τὸν
ἑαυτῶν νοῦν καταρυθμίζομεν, ὥστε κατόπιν αὐτῶν ἰέναι καὶ μηδὲν 10
τῇ τῶν δογμάτων ὀρθότητι καινὸν ἐπεισφρῆσαι.

2. Ἐπειδὴ δὲ ἡ σὴ τελειότης διαπυνθάνεται, πότερόν ποτε χρὴ
λέγειν ἐπὶ Χριστοῦ δύο φύσεις ἢ μή, δεῖν ᾠήθην πρὸς τοῦτο εἰπεῖν.
Διόδωρός τις, πνευματομάχος ὢν κατὰ καιρούς, ὥς φασι, κεκοινώνηκε τῇ τῶν ὀρθοδόξων ἐκκλησίᾳ· οὗτος ἀποθέμενος, ὥσπερ οὖν 15
ἐνόμισε, τὸν τῆς Μακεδονιανῆς αἱρέσεως σπίλον, εἰς ἑτέραν
ἐμπέπτωκεν ἀρρωστίαν. πεφρόνηκε γὰρ καὶ γέγραφεν ὅτι ἕτερος
μὲν υἱὸς κατ᾽ ἰδίαν ἐστὶν ὁ ἐκ σπέρματος Δαυὶδ γεννηθεὶς ἐκ τῆς
ἁγίας παρθένου, ἕτερος δὲ πάλιν ἰδικῶς υἱὸς ὁ ἐκ θεοῦ πατρὸς
λόγος. κωδίῳ δὲ ὥσπερ προβάτου κατασκιάζων τὸν λύκον,[a] 20
προσποιεῖται μὲν Χριστὸν ἕνα λέγειν, ἀναφέρων τὸ ὄνομα ἐπὶ

---

[a] cf. Matt. 7: 15

Witnesses : V A R + Latin versions, Σ, and citations   ACO 1, 1, 6 pp. 151–7

[1] The headings vary with mss. This is Schwartz's composite title

[1] Nothing more is known of Succensus, whose theology clearly differs from
that of his metropolitan Dexianus of Seleucia, a loyal supporter of John of
Antioch. A Syriac version of parts of Succensus' two letters to Cyril survives;
for an English translation see R. Y. Ebied/L. R. Wickham, 'A Collection of
Unpublished Syriac Letters of Cyril of Alexandria', *CSCO*, Scriptores Syri
vol. 157, pp. xvi ff. The date of the correspondence is uncertain but probably

5

FIRST LETTER TO SUCCENSUS

Note from the most divinely favoured and holy archbishop Cyril to most blessed Succensus, bishop of Diocaesarea in the province of Isauria[1]

1. I read the note sent by your Holiness and was exceedingly delighted by the fact that, though you have the power to offer us and others aid from your fine store of learning, you see fit to invite us to set down our solid convictions in writing. The view we take of our Saviour's dispensation is the view of the holy fathers who preceded us. By reading their works we equip our own mind to follow them and to introduce no innovation into orthodoxy.

2. Since your Perfection, though, puts the question whether or not one should ever speak of two natures in respect of Christ,[2] I feel bound to make the following point. Somebody called Diodore,[3] one who had previously been a foe of the Spirit (according to general report), joined the communion of the orthodox Church. Having rid himself, as he therefore supposed, of the contamination of Macedonianism, he went down with another illness. He thought and wrote that David's descendant through the holy Virgin was one distinct son and the Word begotten of God the Father was yet another distinct son. He masked the wolf by a sheep's fleece. He pretends to call Christ

falls somewhere between the reunion in April 433 and Cyril's overt attacks on Diodore and Theodore in 438. The references in § 11 to the negotiations over reunion suggest that this was still news, and hence an earlier, rather than later, date.

[2] The puzzlement of Succensus and of his clergy in the face of arguments from apparently successful Cilician propagandists was genuine evidently. Two natures, two hypostases, and one prosopon is the characteristic formula of 'Antiochene' Christology. 'Two natures' appears in the *Formula of Reunion*.

[3] Diodore's dates are uncertain. He left Antioch to become bishop of Tarsus in 378 and was dead by 394. Nestorius cannot have been his direct pupil. Diodore's Macedonianism also (i.e. teachings of the ontological inferiority of the Holy Ghost, after Macedonius, bishop of Constantinople from 342 to 360) exists solely in Cyril's imagination so far as we know.

E

μόνον τὸν ἐκ θεοῦ πατρὸς λόγον γεννηθέντα υἱὸν μονογενῆ, ὡς ἐν
χάριτος δὲ τάξει προσνέμων αὐτό, καθά φησιν αὐτός, καὶ τῷ ἐκ
σπέρματος Δαυὶδ καὶ υἱὸν ἀποκαλεῖ, ὡς ἐνωθέντα, φησίν, τῷ κατὰ
ἀλήθειαν υἱῷ, ἐνωθέντα δὲ οὐχ ὥσπερ ἡμεῖς δοξάζομεν, ἀλλὰ κατὰ
μόνην τὴν ἀξίαν καὶ κατὰ αὐθεντίαν καὶ κατὰ ἰσοτιμίαν. [3] τούτου 5
γέγονεν μαθητὴς Νεστόριος καὶ ἐκ τῶν ἐκείνου βιβλίων ἐσκοτι-
σμένος προσποιεῖται μὲν Χριστὸν ἕνα καὶ υἱὸν καὶ κύριον ὁμολογεῖν,
μερίζει δὲ καὶ αὐτὸς εἰς δύο τὸν ἕνα καὶ ἀμέριστον, ἄνθρωπον
συνῆφθαι λέγων τῷ θεῷ λόγῳ τῇ ὁμωνυμίᾳ, τῇ ἰσοτιμίᾳ, τῇ ἀξίᾳ.
καὶ γοῦν τὰς φωνὰς τὰς ἐν τοῖς εὐαγγελικοῖς καὶ ἀποστολικοῖς 10
κηρύγμασιν περὶ Χριστοῦ κειμένας διορίζει καί φησι τὰς μὲν
ἐφορμίζεσθαι δεῖν τῷ ἀνθρώπῳ, δηλονότι τὰς ἀνθρωπίνας, τὰς δὲ
πρέπειν κατὰ μόνας τῷ θεῷ λόγῳ, δηλονότι τὰς θεοπρεπεῖς. καὶ
ἐπειδὴ διίστησι πολλαχῶς καὶ ἀνὰ μέρος τίθησιν ὡς ἄνθρωπον
ἰδικῶς τὸν ἐκ τῆς ἁγίας παρθένου γεγεννημένον καὶ ὁμοίως ἰδικῶς 15
καὶ ἀνὰ μέρος υἱὸν τὸν ἐκ θεοῦ πατρὸς λόγον, διὰ τοῦτο τὴν ἁγίαν
παρθένον οὐ θεοτόκον εἶναί φησιν, ἀνθρωποτόκον δὲ μᾶλλον.

4. Ἡμεῖς δὲ οὐχ οὕτως ταῦτ᾽ ἔχειν διακείμεθα, ἀλλ᾽ ἐδιδάχθημεν
παρὰ τῆς θείας γραφῆς καὶ τῶν ἁγίων πατέρων ἕνα υἱὸν καὶ
Χριστὸν καὶ κύριον ὁμολογεῖν, τουτέστιν τὸν ἐκ θεοῦ πατρὸς λόγον, 20
γεννηθέντα μὲν ἐξ αὐτοῦ πρὸ αἰώνων θεοπρεπῶς καὶ ἀρρήτως, ἐν
ἐσχάτοις δὲ τοῦ αἰῶνος καιροῖς τὸν αὐτὸν δι᾽ ἡμᾶς γεννηθέντα κατὰ
σάρκα ἐκ τῆς ἁγίας παρθένου, καὶ ἐπειδὴ θεὸν ἐνανθρωπήσαντα καὶ
σαρκωθέντα γεγέννηκε, διὰ τοῦτο καὶ ὀνομάζομεν θεοτόκον αὐτήν.
εἷς οὖν ἐστιν υἱός, εἷς κύριος Ἰησοῦς Χριστὸς καὶ πρὸ τῆς σαρ- 25
κώσεως καὶ μετὰ τὴν σάρκωσιν. οὐ γὰρ ἕτερος ἦν υἱὸς ὁ ἐκ θεοῦ
πατρὸς λόγος, ἕτερος δὲ πάλιν ὁ ἐκ τῆς ἁγίας παρθένου· ἀλλ᾽
αὐτὸς ἐκεῖνος ὁ προαιώνιος καὶ κατὰ σάρκα ἐκ γυναικὸς γεγεννῆσθαι
πιστεύεται, οὐχ ὡς τῆς θεότητος αὐτοῦ λαβούσης ἀρχὴν εἰς τὸ
εἶναι ἢ γοῦν εἰς ἀρχὴν ὑπάρξεως κεκλημένης διὰ τῆς ἁγίας παρ- 30
θένου, ἀλλ᾽ ὅτι μᾶλλον, ὡς ἔφην, προαιώνιος ὢν λόγος ἐξ αὐτῆς
γεγεννῆσθαι λέγεται κατὰ σάρκα. ἰδία γὰρ ἦν αὐτοῦ ἡ σὰρξ
καθάπερ ἀμέλει καὶ ἡμῶν ἑκάστου τὸ ἴδιον αὐτοῦ σῶμα.

---

4 This is a caricature, but texts from Diodore are to be found for each point.
The title 'Son of God' belongs in the proper sense to God the Word and by
way of metaphor to the Word's temple, the Son of David's stock (fr. 27); the

'one' and restricts the name 'Son' to the Only-begotten Son, the Word begotten of God the Father, yet he also styles David's descendant 'son', awarding him the term (as he says himself) 'by way of the category of grace' on the grounds, he declares, of being united with the real Son—united, though, not in our sense of the term but merely in rank, sovereignty and equality of honour.[4] [3] Nestorius was Diodore's pupil and got befogged by the latter's books. He claims to confess one Christ, Son and Lord but he also divides the one and indivisible into two, alleging that a man has been joined to God the Word by a shared name, by equality of honour, by rank. Why, he even separates out the terms used about Christ in the Gospels and apostolic deliverances, declaring that some of them must be referred to the man (i.e. the human terms) whereas others (i.e. the divine) apply in isolation to God the Word! It is because he makes manifold distinctions, because he isolates the individual man born of the holy Virgin and likewise the individual Son, the Word from God the Father, that he declares the holy Virgin is not mother of God but mother of the man.

4. Our conviction is that this is not the case. No, we have learned from holy Scripture and from the holy fathers to acknowledge one Son, Christ and Lord, I mean the Word from God the Father, begotten of him in mysterious and divine manner before the ages yet the self-same born in the last days of the world in flesh of the holy Virgin; for the very reason that she gave birth to God made man and incarnate we name her 'Mother of God'. One is Son, one Lord Jesus Christ, both before the incarnation and after the incarnation. There are not different sons, one the Word from God the Father and another from the holy Virgin. No, that self-same pre-eternal Son was, we believe, born of woman's flesh, meaning not that his Godhead started to exist or was summoned into being for the first time by means of the holy Virgin, but that, as I said, whilst being pre-eternal Word he was born of her in flesh. His flesh, indeed, was his own just as, for example, each of us has his own body.

two constitute a single indissolubly united Son (fr. 30); the human is honoured from association with the divine (fr. 38) by grace (fr. 31). Diodore's Christology is an attempt to reply to pagan critics (like the emperor Julian) and to Apollinarius. It is Cyril's selection which produces the caricature. (The Fragments of Diodore are edited by R. Abramowski, *Der theologische Nachlass der Diodor von Tarsus, Zeitschrift für neutestamentliche Wissenschaft* XLII (1949), 16–69; M. Brière, *Quelques fragments syriaques de Diodore*, etc., *Revue de l'Orient chrétien* XXX (1946), 231–83.)

5. Ἐπειδὴ δέ τινες ἐπιπλέκουσιν ἡμῖν τὰς Ἀπολιναρίου δόξας καί
φασιν ὅτι εἰ ἕνα λέγετε καθ' ἕνωσιν ἀκριβῆ καὶ συνεσταλμένην υἱὸν
τὸν ἐκ θεοῦ πατρὸς λόγον ἐνανθρωπήσαντα καὶ σεσαρκωμένον, τάχα
που κἀκεῖνο φαντάζεσθε καὶ φρονεῖν ἐγνώκατε ὅτι σύγχυσις ἤτοι
σύγκρασις ἢ φυρμὸς ἐγένετο τοῦ λόγου πρὸς τὸ σῶμα ἢ γοῦν τοῦ 5
σώματος εἰς φύσιν θεότητος μεταβολή, ταύτῃ τοι καὶ μάλα ἐμφρόνως ἡμεῖς ἀποκρουόμενοι τὴν συκοφαντίαν φαμὲν ὅτι ὁ ἐκ θεοῦ
πατρὸς λόγος ἀπερινοήτως τε καὶ ὡς οὐκ ἔστιν εἰπεῖν, ἥνωσεν
ἑαυτῷ σῶμα ἐψυχωμένον ψυχῇ νοερᾷ καὶ προῆλθεν ἄνθρωπος ἐκ
γυναικός, οὐ μεταβολῇ φύσεως καθ' ἡμᾶς γεγονώς, ἀλλ' εὐδοκίᾳ 10
μᾶλλον οἰκονομικῇ. ἠθέλησε γὰρ ἄνθρωπος γενέσθαι τὸ εἶναι θεὸς
κατὰ φύσιν οὐκ ἀποβαλών, ἀλλ' εἰ καὶ ἐν τοῖς καθ' ἡμᾶς καθίκετο
μέτροις καὶ πεφόρηκε τὴν τοῦ δούλου μορφήν, καὶ οὕτως μεμένηκεν
ἐν ταῖς τῆς θεότητος ὑπεροχαῖς καὶ ἐν κυριότητι τῇ φυσικῇ.

6. Ἑνοῦντες τοίνυν ἡμεῖς τῇ ἁγίᾳ σαρκὶ ψυχὴν ἐχούσῃ τὴν 15
νοερὰν ἀπορρήτως τε καὶ ὑπὲρ νοῦν τὸν ἐκ θεοῦ πατρὸς λόγον
ἀσυγχύτως ἀτρέπτως ἀμεταβλήτως, ἕνα υἱὸν καὶ Χριστὸν καὶ
κύριον ὁμολογοῦμεν, τὸν αὐτὸν θεὸν καὶ ἄνθρωπον, οὐχ ἕτερον
καὶ ἕτερον, ἀλλ' ἕνα καὶ τὸν αὐτὸν τοῦτο κἀκεῖνο ὑπάρχοντα καὶ
νοούμενον. τοιγάρτοι ποτὲ μὲν ὡς ἄνθρωπος οἰκονομικῶς ἀνθρω- 20
πίνως διαλέγεται, ποτὲ δὲ ὡς θεὸς μετ' ἐξουσίας τῆς θεοπρεποῦς
ποιεῖται τοὺς λόγους. φαμὲν δὲ κἀκεῖνο· βασανίζοντες εὐτεχνῶς
τῆς μετὰ σαρκὸς οἰκονομίας τὸν τρόπον καὶ περιαθροῦντες ἰσχνῶς
τὸ μυστήριον, ὁρῶμεν ὅτι ὁ ἐκ θεοῦ πατρὸς λόγος ἐνηνθρώπησέν
τε καὶ ἐσαρκώθη καὶ οὐκ ἐκ τῆς θείας ἑαυτοῦ φύσεως τὸ ἱερὸν 25
ἐκεῖνο πεπλαστούργηκε σῶμα, ἀλλ' ἐκ παρθένου μᾶλλον ἔλαβεν
αὐτό, ἐπεὶ πῶς γέγονεν ἄνθρωπος, εἰ μὴ σῶμα πεφόρηκε τὸ
ἀνθρώπινον; ἐννοοῦντες τοίνυν, ὡς ἔφην, τῆς ἐνανθρωπήσεως τὸν
τρόπον ὁρῶμεν ὅτι δύο φύσεις συνῆλθον ἀλλήλαις καθ' ἕνωσιν
ἀδιάσπαστον ἀσυγχύτως καὶ ἀτρέπτως· ἡ γὰρ σὰρξ σάρξ ἐστι καὶ 30
οὐ θεότης, εἰ καὶ γέγονε θεοῦ σάρξ, ὁμοίως δὲ καὶ ὁ λόγος θεός
ἐστι καὶ οὐ σάρξ, εἰ καὶ ἰδίαν ἐποιήσατο τὴν σάρκα οἰκονομικῶς.
ὅταν οὖν ἐννοῶμεν τοῦτο, οὐδὲν ἀδικοῦμεν τὴν εἰς ἑνότητα συν-
δρομὴν ἐκ δύο φύσεων γεγενῆσθαι λέγοντες· μετὰ μέντοι τὴν ἕνωσιν

---

5 The first two adverbs are repeated in the Chalcedonian definition, *ACO*
2, 1 [325], 30 f., ἐν δύο φύσεσιν, ἀσυγχύτως ἀτρέπτως ἀδιαιρέτως γνωριζόμενον,

5. Seeing, though, that certain people are implicating us in Apollinarianism alleging that: If your calling the Word from God the Father who became man and incarnate 'one Son' means a strict and tight union, you may well have some fanciful notion that there occurred a merger, mixture or mingling of the Word with the body or a change of the body into the nature of Godhead, we are fully conscious of rebutting this slander when we affirm that the Word from God the Father united to himself in some inscrutable and ineffable manner, a body endowed with mental life and that he came forth, man from woman, become what we are, not by change of nature but in gracious fulfilment of God's plan. In willing to become man he did not abandon his being God by nature; though he descended to our limited level and wore the form of a slave, even in that state he remained in the transcendent realms of Godhead and in the Lordship belonging to his nature.

6. So we unite the Word from God the Father without merger, alteration or change[5] to holy flesh owning mental life in a manner inexpressible and surpassing understanding, and confess one Son, Christ and Lord, the self-same God and man, not a diverse pair but one and the same, being and being seen to be both things. That is why as man in fulfilment of the divine plan he sometimes discourses humanly whilst at other times he utters words as God with the authority of Godhead. Our affirmation is this: if we carefully examine the mode of the scheme of incarnation, if we make a close survey of the mystery, we see that the Word from God the Father became man and was incarnate and that he did not mould that sacred body from his own nature but took it from the Virgin, because how could he have become man unless he wears a human body? So if we consider, as I said, the mode of his becoming man we see that two natures have met without merger and without alteration in unbreakable mutual union— the point being that flesh is flesh and not Godhead even though it has become God's flesh and equally the Word is God and not flesh even though in fulfilment of God's plan he made the flesh his own. Whenever we take this point into consideration, therefore, we do not damage the concurrence into unity by declaring it was effected out of two natures;[6] however, after the union

perhaps with an eye on this passage—'recognized in two natures without confusion, alteration, separation, or division'.

[6] Subsequent generations were to make this 'out of' a point of heated dispute, for the whole section shows Cyril at his most 'dualistic'. Does 'out of' take away what the talk of two mentally distinguishable basic elements in Christ grants,

οὐ διαιροῦμεν τὰς φύσεις ἀπ' ἀλλήλων οὐδὲ εἰς δύο τέμνομεν υἱοὺς
τὸν ἕνα καὶ ἀμέριστον, ἀλλ' ἕνα φαμὲν υἱὸν καὶ ὡς οἱ πατέρες
εἰρήκασι, μίαν φύσιν τοῦ λόγου σεσαρκωμένην. [7] οὐκοῦν ὅσον
μὲν ἧκεν εἰς ἔννοιαν καὶ εἰς μόνον τὸ ὁρᾶν τοῖς τῆς ψυχῆς ὄμμασι
τίνα τρόπον ἐνηνθρώπησεν ὁ μονογενής, δύο τὰς φύσεις εἶναι φαμὲν 5
τὰς ἑνωθείσας, ἕνα δὲ Χριστὸν καὶ υἱὸν καὶ κύριον, τὸν τοῦ θεοῦ
λόγον ἐνανθρωπήσαντα καὶ σεσαρκωμένον. καὶ εἰ δοκεῖ, δεξώμεθα
πρὸς παράδειγμα τὴν καθ' ἡμᾶς αὐτοὺς σύνθεσιν καθ' ἣν ἐσμὲν
ἄνθρωποι. συντεθείμεθα γὰρ ἐκ ψυχῆς καὶ σώματος καὶ ὁρῶμεν
δύο φύσεις, ἑτέραν μὲν τὴν τοῦ σώματος, ἑτέραν δὲ τὴν τῆς 10
ψυχῆς· ἀλλ' εἷς ἐξ ἀμφοῖν καθ' ἕνωσιν ἄνθρωπος καὶ οὐχὶ τὸ ἐκ
δύο συντεθεῖσθαι φύσεων ἀνθρώπους δύο τὸν ἕνα παρασκευάζει,
ἀλλ' ἕνα τὸν ἄνθρωπον κατὰ σύνθεσιν, ὡς ἔφην, τὸν ἐκ ψυχῆς καὶ
σώματος. ἐὰν γὰρ ἀνέλωμεν τὸ ὅτι ἐκ δύο καὶ διαφόρων φύσεων ὁ
εἷς καὶ μόνος ἐστὶ Χριστός, ἀδιάσπαστος ὢν μετὰ τὴν ἕνωσιν, 15
ἐροῦσιν οἱ τῇ ὀρθῇ δόξῃ μαχόμενοι· εἰ μία φύσις τὸ ὅλον, πῶς
ἐνηνθρώπησεν ἢ ποίαν ἰδίαν ἐποιήσατο σάρκα;

8. Ἐπειδὴ δὲ εὗρον ἐν τῷ ὑπομνηστικῷ ἔμφασίν τινα λόγου
τοιαύτην ὅτι μετὰ τὴν ἀνάστασιν τὸ ἅγιον σῶμα τοῦ πάντων ἡμῶν
σωτῆρος Χριστοῦ εἰς θεότητος φύσιν μετακεχώρηκεν, ὡς εἶναι τὸ 20
ὅλον θεότητα μόνην, δεῖν ᾠήθην καὶ πρός γε τοῦτο εἰπεῖν. ὁ
μακάριος γράφει Παῦλος, τῆς ἐνανθρωπήσεως τοῦ μονογενοῦς υἱοῦ
τοῦ θεοῦ τὰς αἰτίας ἡμῖν ἐξηγούμενος, ποτὲ μὲν ὅτι τὸ γὰρ
ἀδύνατον τοῦ νόμου ἐν ᾧ ἠσθένει διὰ τῆς σαρκός, ὁ θεὸς
τὸν ἑαυτοῦ υἱὸν πέμψας ἐν ὁμοιώματι σαρκὸς ἁμαρτίας 25
καὶ περὶ ἁμαρτίας, κατέκρινε τὴν ἁμαρτίαν ἐν τῇ σαρκί,
ἵνα τὸ δικαίωμα τοῦ νόμου πληρωθῇ ἐν ἡμῖν τοῖς μὴ
κατὰ σάρκα περιπατοῦσιν, ἀλλὰ κατὰ πνεῦμα.[b] ποτὲ δὲ
πάλιν ἐπειδὴ γὰρ τὰ παιδία κεκοινώνηκεν αἵματος καὶ
σαρκός, καὶ αὐτὸς παραπλησίως μετέσχε τῶν αὐτῶν, ἵνα 30
διὰ τοῦ θανάτου καταργήσῃ τὸν τὸ κράτος ἔχοντα τοῦ
θανάτου, τουτέστι τὸν διάβολον, καὶ ἀπαλλάξῃ τούτους
ὅσοι φόβῳ θανάτου διὰ παντὸς τοῦ ζῆν ἔνοχοι ἦσαν
δουλείας. οὐ γὰρ δήπου ἀγγέλων ἐπιλαμβάνεται, ἀλλὰ

[b] Rom. 8: 3 f.

we do not divide the natures from each other and do not sever
the one and indivisible into two sons but say 'one Son' and, as
the fathers have put it, 'one incarnate nature of the Word'.[7]
[7] So far, then, as the question of the manner of the Only-
begotten's becoming man appears for purely mental consideration by the mind's eye, our view is that there are two united
natures but one Christ, Son and Lord, the Word of God become
man and incarnate.[8] May we illustrate the case from the composition which renders us human beings? We are composed out
of soul and body and observe two different natures, the body's
and the soul's; yet the pair yields a single united human being,
and composition out of two natures does not turn the one man
into two men but, as I said, produces a single man, a composite
of soul and body. If we repudiate the fact that the one and
unique Christ is from two different natures, existing, as he does,
indivisible after the union, opponents of orthodoxy will ask how
he could have been made man or appropriated any flesh if the
entirety is a single nature.

8. Now seeing that I find in your note a suggestion of the
thought that after the resurrection our universal Saviour Christ's
holy body has changed into the nature of Godhead so that it is
entirely Godhead and Godhead only, I feel obliged to make
a further observation. Blessed Paul, expounding the reasons for
the Only-begotten Son of God's becoming man, writes at one
point: '*For the Law's impotence wherein it was feeble throughout the
flesh [has ceased, for] God, by sending his own Son in the likeness of
sinful flesh and for sin, condemned sin in the flesh, in order that the requirement of the Law might be fulfilled in us who do not behave in accord with
flesh but in accord with spirit.*'[9] Moreover he writes elsewhere: '*For
since the children share blood and flesh, he too shared these on equal terms,
in order that by death he might destroy him who has the power of death
(that is, the Devil) and liberate all who throughout their whole living
were subject to servitude by fear of death. For, indeed, he does not lay*

eliminating all dangerous ambiguity (as Severus of Antioch argued regularly,
cf. *c. Grammaticum* III, 1 *passim*)? It is Cyril's customary mode of expression
and has no *particular* force here.

   [7] See *To Eulogius*, n. 3.
   [8] This is the plain answer Cyril makes to Succensus' original question
whether it was possible to speak of two natures. At the level of abstract thought,
he answers, 'yes'.
   [9] Cf. *In Ep. ad Rom.* (Pusey 3, 211 ff.) where Cyril comments on the passage
after complaining about the syntax of its opening.

σπέρματος Ἀβραὰμ ἐπιλαμβάνεται· ὅθεν ὤφειλε κατὰ
πάντα τοῖς ἀδελφοῖς ὁμοιωθῆναι.ᶜ

9. Φαμὲν οὖν ὅτι ἐκ τῆς παραβάσεως τῆς ἐν Ἀδὰμ τῆς ἀνθρωπίνης
φύσεως παθούσης τὴν φθορὰν καὶ τυραννουμένης τῆς ἐν ἡμῖν
διανοίας ἐκ τῶν τῆς σαρκὸς ἡδονῶν ἤτοι κινημάτων ἐμφύτων, ἀναγ- 5
καῖον γέγονεν εἰς σωτηρίαν ἡμῖν τοῖς ἐπὶ τῆς γῆς τὸ ἐνανθρωπῆσαι
τὸν τοῦ θεοῦ λόγον, ἵνα τὴν σάρκα τὴν ἀνθρωπίνην ὑπενηνεγμένην
τῇ φθορᾷ καὶ νοσήσασαν τὸ φιλήδονον ἰδίαν ποιήσηται καὶ ἐπειδήπερ
ἐστὶ ζωὴ καὶ ζωοποιός, καταργήσῃ μὲν τὴν ἐν αὐτῇ φθοράν,
ἐπιτιμήσῃ δὲ καὶ τοῖς ἐμφύτοις κινήμασι, τοῖς εἰς φιληδονίαν 10
δηλαδή. ἣν γὰρ οὕτως νεκρωθῆναι τὴν ἁμαρτίαν ἐν αὐτῇ· μεμνήμεθα
δὲ καὶ τοῦ μακαρίου Παύλου νόμον ἁμαρτίας καλέσαντος τὸ ἐν
ἡμῖν ἔμφυτον κίνημα.ᵈ οὐκοῦν ἐπειδήπερ ἡ ἀνθρωπίνη σὰρξ γέγονεν
ἰδία τοῦ λόγου, πέπαυται μὲν τοῦ ὑποφέρεσθαι τῇ φθορᾷ καὶ ἐπειδὴ
ἁμαρτίαν οὐκ οἶδεν ὡς θεὸς ὁ οἰκειωσάμενος αὐτὴν καὶ ἰδίαν 15
ἀποφήνας, ὡς ἔφην, πέπαυται καὶ τοῦ νοσεῖν τὸ φιλήδονον. καὶ οὐχ
ἑαυτῷ τοῦτο κατώρθωκεν ὁ μονογενὴς τοῦ θεοῦ λόγος (ἔστι γὰρ ὅ
ἐστιν, ἀεί), ἀλλ᾽ ἡμῖν δηλονότι. εἰ γὰρ ὑπενηνέγμεθα τοῖς ἐκ
παραβάσεως τῆς ἐν Ἀδὰμ κακοῖς, ἥξει πάντως ἐφ᾽ ἡμᾶς καὶ τὰ ἐν
Χριστῷ, τουτέστιν ἡ ἀφθαρσία καὶ τῆς ἁμαρτίας ἡ νέκρωσις. 20
οὐκοῦν γέγονεν ἄνθρωπος, οὐκ ἄνθρωπον ἀνέλαβεν, ὡς Νεστορίῳ
δοκεῖ, καὶ ἵνα πιστευθῇ γεγονὼς ἄνθρωπος, καίτοι μεμενηκὼς ὅπερ
ἦν, δῆλον δὲ ὅτι θεὸς κατὰ φύσιν, ταύτῃ τοι καὶ πεινῆσαιᵉ λέγεται
καὶ καμεῖν ἐξ ὁδοιπορίας,ᶠ ἀνασχέσθαι δὲ καὶ ὕπνουᵍ καὶ ταραχῆς
καὶ λύπηςʰ καὶ τῶν ἄλλων ἀνθρωπίνων καὶ ἀδιαβλήτων παθῶν. ἵνα 25
δὲ πάλιν πληροφορῇ τοὺς ὁρῶντας αὐτὸν ὅτι μετὰ τοῦ εἶναι
ἄνθρωπος καὶ θεός ἐστιν ἀληθινός, εἰργάζετο τὰς θεοσημείας, θαλάσ-
σαις ἐπιτιμῶν,ⁱ νεκροὺς ἐγείρωνʲ καὶ τὰ ἕτερα παράδοξα κατορθῶν.
ὑπέμεινε δὲ καὶ σταυρόν, ἵνα σαρκὶ παθὼν τὸν θάνατον καὶ οὐ
φύσει θεότητος γένηται πρωτότοκος ἐκ νεκρῶνᵏ καὶ ὁδοποιήσῃ τῇ 30
ἀνθρώπου φύσει τὴν εἰς ἀφθαρσίαν ὁδὸν καὶ σκυλεύσας τὸν ᾅδην
τὰς αὐτόθι καθειργμένας ἐλεήσῃ ψυχάς.

ᶜ Heb. 2: 14 ff. ᵈ cf. Rom. 7: 23 etc. ᵉ cf. Matt. 4: 2 etc.
ᶠ cf. John 4: 6 etc. ᵍ cf. Matt. 8: 24 etc. ʰ cf. Matt. 26: 38 etc.
ⁱ cf. Matt. 8: 26 etc. ʲ cf. John 11: 43 f. etc. ᵏ cf. Col. 1: 18

*hold of angels but of Abraham's race, which is why he had to be made
like his brethren in all respects.'*

9. We affirm, then, that because human nature underwent
corruption as a result of the transgression in Adam and our
understanding was being dominated by the pleasures, the innate
impulses, of the flesh, it was vital for the Word of God to become
man for the salvation of us earthly men and to make human flesh,
subject to decay and infected with sensuality as it was, his own
and (since he is Life and Life-giver) that he should destroy the
corruption within it and curb the innate, the sensual, impulses.
In this way the sin within it could be done to death—and we
bear in mind blessed Paul's calling the innate impulse 'sin's law'.
In view of the fact, then, that human flesh has become the Word's
own flesh it has stopped being burdened with corruption, and
since as God, conscious of no sin, he appropriated it and displayed it as his own (as I have said) it has ceased to be infected
with sensuality. Not for his own benefit has God's Only-begotten
Word accomplished this (he is, indeed, ever what he is), but
clearly for ours. If we have been subject to the evils following
upon the sin in Adam the benefits in Christ must attend us
also —I mean, incorruption and the doing to death of sin.[10] That
is why he has become man; he has not, as Nestorius thinks, assumed a man. It is for the very reason that he should be credited
with having become man whilst yet remaining what he was
(i.e. God by nature) that he is reported as having been hungry,
tired with travelling and to have borne sleep, anxiety, pain and
other innocent human experiences. Moreover, to assure those
who saw him that he was true God along with being man, he
worked divine miracles, curbing seas, raising dead, accomplishing
further different marvels. He even endured the cross, so that he
might, after suffering death not in the Godhead's nature but in
the flesh, be made first-born of the dead, might open the way
for man's nature to incorruption, might harrow Hell of the souls
there held fast and take pity on them.

---

[10] Mortality, corruption and the disharmony between intentions and desires
which leads to sin are the consequences of Adam's transgression, according to
Cyril. See *Answers to Tiberius* 12 and *Doctrinal Questions and Answers*.

10. Μετὰ δέ γε τὴν ἀνάστασιν ἦν μὲν αὐτὸ τὸ σῶμα τὸ πεπονθός,
πλὴν οὐκέτι τὰς ἀνθρωπίνας ἀσθενείας ἔχον ἐν ἑαυτῷ. οὐ γὰρ ἔτι
πείνης ἢ κόπου ἢ ἑτέρου τινὸς τῶν τοιούτων δεκτικὸν εἶναί φαμεν
αὐτό, ἀλλὰ λοιπὸν ἄφθαρτον καὶ οὐχὶ τοῦτο μόνον, ἀλλὰ γὰρ καὶ
ζωοποιόν· ζωῆς γὰρ σῶμά ἐστι, τουτέστι τοῦ μονογενοῦς, κατελαμ-   5
πρύνθη δὲ καὶ δόξῃ τῇ θεοπρεπεστάτῃ καὶ νοεῖται θεοῦ σῶμα.
τοιγάρτοι κἂν εἴ τις αὐτὸ λέγοι θεῖον, ὥσπερ ἀμέλει τοῦ ἀνθρώπου
ἀνθρώπινον,[2] οὐκ ἂν ἁμάρτοι τοῦ πρέποντος λογισμοῦ· ὅθεν οἶμαι
καὶ τὸν σοφώτατον Παῦλον εἰπεῖν· εἰ καὶ ἐγνώκαμεν κατὰ
σάρκα Χριστόν, ἀλλὰ νῦν οὐκέτι γινώσκομεν.[1] θεοῦ γάρ,   10
ὡς ἔφην, ἴδιον σῶμα ὑπάρχον, ὑπερέβη πάντα τὰ ἀνθρώπινα,
μεταβολὴν δὲ τὴν εἰς τὴν τῆς θεότητος φύσιν οὐκ ἐνδέχεται παθεῖν
σῶμα τὸ ἀπὸ γῆς· ἀμήχανον γάρ, ἐπεὶ καταγορεύσομεν τῆς
θεότητος ὡς γενητῆς καὶ ὡς προσλαβούσης τι ἐν ἑαυτῇ ὃ μή ἐστι
κατὰ φύσιν ἴδιον αὐτῆς. ἴσον γάρ ἐστιν εἰς ἀτοπίας λόγον τὸ εἰπεῖν   15
ὅτι μετεβλήθη τὸ σῶμα εἰς θεότητος φύσιν, καὶ μὴν κἀκεῖνο ὅτι
μετεβλήθη ὁ λόγος εἰς τὴν τῆς σαρκὸς φύσιν. ὥσπερ γὰρ τοῦτο
ἀμήχανον (ἄτρεπτος γὰρ καὶ ἀναλλοίωτός ἐστιν), οὕτως καὶ τὸ
ἕτερον· οὐ γάρ ἐστι τῶν ἐφικτῶν εἰς θεότητος οὐσίαν ἤτοι φύσιν
μεταχωρῆσαί τι δύνασθαι τῶν κτισμάτων· κτίσμα δὲ καὶ ἡ σάρξ.   20
οὐκοῦν θεῖον μὲν εἶναί φαμεν τὸ σῶμα Χριστοῦ, ἐπειδὴ καὶ θεοῦ
σῶμά ἐστι, καὶ ἀρρήτῳ δόξῃ κατηγλαϊσμένον, ἄφθαρτον ἅγιον
ζωοποιόν· ὅτι δὲ εἰς φύσιν θεότητος μετεβλήθη, οὔτε τῶν πατέρων
τις τῶν ἁγίων ἢ πεφρόνηκεν ἢ εἴρηκεν οὔτε ἡμεῖς οὕτω διακείμεθα.

11. Μὴ ἀγνοείτω δὲ κἀκεῖνο ἡ σὴ ὁσιότης ὅτι ὁ τῆς μακαρίας   25
μνήμης ὁ πατὴρ ἡμῶν Ἀθανάσιος ὁ γενόμενος κατὰ καιροὺς τῆς
Ἀλεξανδρέων ἐπίσκοπος, κεκινημένων τινῶν κατ᾽ ἐκεῖνο καιροῦ,
γέγραφεν ἐπιστολὴν πρὸς Ἐπίκτητον ἐπίσκοπον τῆς Κορίνθου
πάσης ὀρθοδοξίας μεστήν· ἐπειδὴ δὲ ἠλέγχετο καὶ ἐξ αὐτῆς

―――――――――

[1] 2 Cor. 5: 16

[2] τὸ ἀνθρώπινον VR: τὸ ἀνθρώπειον A: ἀνθρώπειον one witness

10. After the resurrection there existed the very body which had experienced suffering, no longer though containing in itself human infirmities. For we declare it capable no more of hunger, weariness or anything of that kind, but declare it to be incorruptible—and not only that, but life-giving as well. It is, indeed, Life's (that is, the Only-begotten's) body; it has been made resplendent with divinest glory and is conceived of as God's body. That is why anyone calling it 'divine' in the same sense as, for example, he calls a man's body 'human', will be perfectly correct to do so.[11] It is for this reason, I think, that wise Paul said: '*Even if we have known Christ in flesh, nevertheless we now know him no more.*' Being, as I have said, God's own body, it transcended all things human, yet earthly body cannot undergo change into the Godhead's nature—it is impossible, since we should be accusing the Godhead of being created and of acquiring in itself something which does not naturally belong to it. Indeed talk of the body's being changed into Godhead's nature is equally as absurd as talk of the Word's being changed into the nature of the flesh. Just as the latter is impossible (for the Word is unchanging and unalterable) so is the former—that a creature could transfer to Godhead's substance or nature does not come within the realm of possibilities, and the flesh is a created thing. Hence we affirm Christ's body to be divine, seeing that it is God's body, adorned with ineffable glory, incorruptible, holy and life-giving; but that he was changed into Godhead's nature none of the holy fathers has said or thought and we have no intention of doing so either.

11. Your Holiness should be aware of the further fact that after the raising of certain questions in his time our father Athanasius of blessed memory, formerly bishop of Alexandria, wrote a letter full of entirely sound teaching to Epictetus bishop of Corinth. Now seeing that Nestorius was rebutted by the letter

[11] Cyril's language here, taken in conjunction with what he has said about sin and corruption, provokes the issues which were to divide Severus of Antioch from Julian of Halicarnassus, the caricature of whose views is 'aphthartodocetism'. If it is God's body, life-giving and sinless, it must from conception (Julian argued) be incorruptible. Its death and suffering are real (there is no 'docetism' involved); they are voluntary. They are the true miracle of incarnation. Severus argued otherwise: sin and corruption are different; corruption is part of the assumed human condition and Christ's body is incorruptible only after the Resurrection. There can be no doubt that it is Severus who is repeating Cyril's teaching here. See R. Draguet, *Julien d'Halicarnasse et sa controverse avec Sévère d'Antioche sur l'incorruptibilité du corps du Christ* (Louvain, 1924).

Νεστόριος καὶ οἱ τῇ ὀρθῇ πίστει συναγορεύοντες ταύτην ἀναγινώσκοντες ἐξεδυσώπουν τοὺς τὰ αὐτὰ φρονεῖν ἐθέλοντας, ἀπειρηκότες πρὸς τοὺς ἐντεῦθεν ἐλέγχους ἐμηχανήσαντό τι πικρὸν καὶ αἱρετικῆς δυσσεβείας ἄξιον. παραφθείραντες γὰρ τὴν ἐπιστολὴν καὶ τὰ μὲν ὑφελόντες, τὰ δὲ προσθέντες ἐκδεδώκασιν, ὡς δοκεῖν καὶ τὸν 5 ἀοίδιμον ἐκεῖνον συνῳδὰ φρονεῖν Νεστορίῳ καὶ τοῖς ἀμφ' αὐτόν. ἦν οὖν ἀναγκαῖον ὑπὲρ τοῦ μὴ κἀκεῖσέ τινας παρεφθαρμένην αὐτὴν ἐπιδεικνύειν ἐκ τῶν παρ' ἡμῖν ἀντιγράφων τὸ ἴσον λαβόντας ἀποστεῖλαι τῇ σῇ θεοσεβείᾳ. καὶ γὰρ ὁ εὐλαβέστατος καὶ θεοσεβέστατος ὁ τῆς Ἐμεσηνῶν ἐπίσκοπος Παῦλος ἐλθὼν ἐν Ἀλεξαν- 10 δρείᾳ κεκίνηκε περὶ τούτου λόγους καὶ εὑρέθη μὲν ἔχων τὸ ἴσον τῆς ἐπιστολῆς, παρεφθαρμένον δὲ καὶ παραποιηθὲν παρὰ τῶν αἱρετικῶν, ὥστε καὶ ἠξίωσεν ἐκ τῶν παρ' ἡμῖν ἀντιγράφων τὸ ἴσον τοῖς κατὰ τὴν Ἀντιόχειαν ἐκπεμφθῆναι· καὶ δὴ πεπόμφαμεν.

12. Ἀκολουθοῦντες δὲ πανταχῇ ταῖς τῶν ἁγίων πατέρων 15 ὀρθοδοξίαις, κατὰ τῶν Νεστορίου δογμάτων συγγαγράφαμεν βιβλίον, καὶ ἕτερον δὲ διαβεβληκότων τινῶν τῶν κεφαλαίων τὴν δύναμιν, καὶ ταῦτα ἀπέστειλα τῇ σῇ θεοσεβείᾳ, ἵν' εἴ τινες εἶεν ἕτεροι τῶν ὁμοπίστων τε καὶ ὁμοψύχων ἡμῶν ἀδελφῶν ταῖς τινων φλυαρίαις συνηρπασμένοι καὶ νομίζοντες ὅτι μετέγνωμεν ἐπὶ τοῖς 20 κατὰ Νεστορίου λεχθεῖσιν, ἐλεγχθεῖεν ἐκ τῆς ἀναγνώσεως καὶ μάθωσιν ὅτι καλῶς καὶ ὀρθῶς ἐπετιμήσαμεν ὡς πεπλανημένῳ καὶ νῦν οὐδὲν ἧττον ἐγκείμεθα πανταχοῦ μαχόμενοι ταῖς αὐτοῦ δυσφημίαις. ἡ δὲ σὴ τελειότης τὰ ἔτι μείζω νοεῖν δυναμένη καὶ ἡμᾶς ὠφελήσει καὶ γράφουσα καὶ προσευχομένη. 25

and that the advocates of orthodox belief read it and were dis-
crediting his sympathizers, these were unable to cope with the
charges it contained and devised a vicious scheme worthy of
their blasphemous heresy. They falsified the letter with omissions
and additions and published it, to give the impression that the
famous Athanasius was in agreement with Nestorius and his
circle.[12] The need arose, therefore, to make a transcript from
one of our copies here and despatch it to your Reverence in case
people present you there with a corrupt version. The most pious
and religious Paul, bishop of Emesa, when he came to Alexandria
raised the matter in discussion and was found to be in possession
of a copy of the letter corrupted and falsified by the heretics,
with the result that he asked for a transcript from our copies here
to be sent off to the Antiochenes; and we have done so.

12. In complete adherence to the sound teachings of the holy
fathers we have composed one book against Nestorius' dogmas
and another against certain hostile critics of the content of the
Chapters.[13] These too I send your Reverence, in order that any
other of those brethren of ours, who share our faith and sympathies and who may get carried away by certain people's vain
chatter into imagining that we have changed our minds on the
subject of our statements against Nestorius, may be proved
wrong by reading these books and may come to know that the
way we rebuked the errant was fair and right and that at this
very moment we are engaged just as widely in combating his
blasphemies. Your Perfection, with your capacity for greater
insights still, will help us by writing and by prayer.

[12] See p. 58 n. 35.
[13] *Contra Nestorium* (*ACO* 1, 1, 6 pp. 13–106) and the defence of the anathematisms either against Theodoret (*ACO* 1, 1, 6 pp. 107–46) or against the
Orientals (*ACO* 1, 1, 7 pp. 33–65).

6

SECOND LETTER TO SUCCENSUS

Ἕτερον ὑπομνηστικὸν ἀντιγραφὲν πρὸς τὰς πεύσεις ἡμῶν
παρὰ τοῦ αὐτοῦ πρὸς τὸν αὐτὸν Σούκενσον[1]

1. Ἐμφανῆ μὲν ἑαυτὴν καθίστησιν ἡ ἀλήθεια τοῖς ἀγαπῶσιν
αὐτήν, κρύπτεται δὲ οἶμαι καὶ πειρᾶται λανθάνειν τὰς τῶν πολυπλόκων ἐννοίας· οὐ γὰρ ἀξίους ἑαυτοὺς ἀποφαίνουσι τοῦ λαμπροῖς 5
ὄμμασι κατιδεῖν αὐτήν. καὶ οἱ μὲν τῆς ἀμωμήτου πίστεως ἐρασταὶ
ζητοῦσι τὸν κύριον ἐν ἁπλότητι καρδίας,[a] καθὰ γέγραπται· οἱ δὲ
καμπύλας τροχιὰς ἐρχόμενοι καὶ καρδίαν ἔχοντες σκαμβὴν[b] κατὰ
τὸ ἐν ψαλμοῖς εἰρημένον διεστραμμένων ἐννοιῶν πολυπλόκους
ἑαυτοῖς συναγείρουσιν ἀφορμάς, ἵνα διαστρέφωσι τὰς ὁδοὺς κυρίου 10
τὰς εὐθείας καὶ τὰς τῶν ἁπλουστέρων παρακομίσωσι ψυχὰς εἰς τὸ
χρῆναι φρονεῖν ἃ μὴ θέμις. καὶ ταῦτά φημι τοῖς παρὰ τῆς σῆς
ὁσιότητος ὑπομνηστικοῖς ἐντυχών, εἶτά τινα εὑρὼν ἐν αὐτοῖς
οὐκ ἀσφαλῶς προτεινόμενα παρὰ τῶν οὐκ οἶδ' ὅπως ἠγαπηκότων
τῆς ψευδωνύμου γνώσεως τὴν διαστροφήν.[c] ἦσαν δὲ ταῦτα. 15

2. Εἰ ἐκ δύο, φησίν, συνηνέχθη φύσεων ὁ Ἐμμανουήλ, μετὰ δὲ
τὴν ἕνωσιν μία φύσις νοεῖται τοῦ λόγου σεσαρκωμένη, ἕψεται
πάντως τὸ χρῆναι λέγειν αὐτὸν παθεῖν εἰς ἰδίαν φύσιν.

Οἱ μακάριοι πατέρες οἱ τὸ σεπτὸν τῆς ὀρθῆς πίστεως ἡμῖν
ὁρισάμενοι σύμβολον αὐτὸν ἔφασαν τὸν ἐκ θεοῦ πατρὸς λόγον τὸν 20
ἐκ τῆς οὐσίας αὐτοῦ τὸν μονογενῆ τὸν δι' οὗ τὰ πάντα, σαρκωθῆναι
καὶ ἐνανθρωπῆσαι καὶ οὐ δήπου φαμὲν ἀγνοῆσαι τοὺς ἁγίους
ἐκείνους ὅτι τὸ ἑνωθὲν τῷ λόγῳ σῶμα ἐψύχωτο ψυχῇ νοερᾷ, ὥστε
εἴ τις σαρκωθῆναι λέγοι τὸν λόγον, οὐ δίχα ψυχῆς νοερᾶς ὁμολογεῖ
τὴν σάρκα τὴν ἐνωθεῖσαν αὐτῷ. οὕτως γάρ, ὥς γε οἶμαι, μᾶλλον 25

---

[a] cf. Wisd. 1 : 1   [b] cf. Ps. 100 (101) : 4   [c] cf. 1 Tim. 6 : 20

Witnesses : As for first letter to Succensus   *ACO* 1, 1, 6 pp. 157–62

[1] The headings vary with mss. This is Schwartz's composite title.

6

SECOND LETTER TO SUCCENSUS

A second note written in reply to our[1] questions by the same to
the same Succensus

1. Truth makes herself plain to her friends but tries, I think,
to hide from the view of tangled minds, for they shew themselves
unworthy of beholding her with limpid gaze. Lovers of the faith
immaculate 'seek the Lord' (as Scripture has it) 'in simplicity
of heart', whereas travellers on winding paths, possessors of a
'warped heart' (as the psalm says), amass intricate pretexts for
their own distorted notions with the aim of twisting the Lord's
straight ways and getting simpler souls to think they ought to
hold wrong views. I say this after reading the notes from your
Holiness and finding there certain unsound claims made by
people with a strange love for the perversity of 'pseudo-science'.

2. The claims were as follows: 'If Emmanuel was composed
out of two natures and after the union one incarnate nature of
the Word[2] is conceived of, it follows that we have to say he
experienced suffering in his own nature.'

The blessed fathers who laid down our august creed of orthodox belief affirmed that the Word from God the Father, the
Word who is from his substance, Only-begotten, through whom
are all things, personally became incarnate and was made man.
Obviously we do not mean that these holy fathers failed to
recognize the fact that the body united to the Word was endowed
with mental life; and so if one says the Word became incarnate
one is not agreeing with the view that the flesh united to him
lacked mental life. This was, I think (no, rather—confidently

---

[1] The letters then were published by Succensus initially. The problems
which Succensus reports were the debating points made by Cilician 'diphysites',
i.e. of the school of Theodore.

[2] See *To Eulogius*, n. 3.

δὲ ὡς ἔστι τεθαρρηκότως εἰπεῖν, καὶ ὁ πάνσοφος εὐαγγελιστὴς
Ἰωάννης τὸν λόγον ἔφη γενέσθαι σάρκα,[d] οὐχ ὡς ἀψύχῳ σαρκὶ
ἑνωθέντα, μὴ γένοιτο, ἀλλ᾽ οὐδὲ ὡς τροπὴν ἢ ἀλλοίωσιν ὑπομείναντα.
μεμένηκε γὰρ ὅπερ ἦν, τουτέστι φύσει θεός, προσλαβὼν δὲ καὶ τὸ
εἶναι ἄνθρωπος ἤτοι γενέσθαι καθ᾽ ἡμᾶς ἐκ γυναικὸς κατὰ σάρκα, 5
πάλιν εἷς μεμένηκεν υἱός, πλὴν οὐκ ἄσαρκος καθὰ καὶ πάλαι ἤτοι
πρὸ τῶν τῆς ἐνανθρωπήσεως καιρῶν, ἀμφιεσάμενος δὲ ὥσπερ καὶ
τὴν ἡμετέραν φύσιν. ἀλλ᾽ εἰ καὶ μή ἐστιν ὁμοούσιον τῷ ἐκ θεοῦ
πατρὸς φύντι λόγῳ τὸ ἑνωθὲν αὐτῷ σῶμα καὶ ψυχῆς ἐνούσης
αὐτῷ νοερᾶς, ἀλλ᾽ οὖν ὁ μὲν νοῦς φαντάζεται τὸ ἑτεροφυὲς τῶν 10
ἑνωθέντων, ἕνα γε μὴν ὁμολογοῦμεν υἱὸν καὶ Χριστὸν καὶ κύριον
ὡς γεγονότος σαρκὸς τοῦ λόγου· τὸ δὲ "σαρκός" ὅταν εἴπωμεν,
ἀνθρώπου φαμέν. ποία τοίνυν ἀνάγκη παθεῖν αὐτὸν εἰς ἰδίαν φύσιν,
εἰ λέγοιτο μετὰ τὴν ἕνωσιν μία φύσις υἱοῦ σεσαρκωμένη; εἰ μὲν
γὰρ οὐκ ἦν ἐν τοῖς λόγοις τῆς οἰκονομίας τὸ πεφυκὸς ὑπομένειν 15
τὸ πάθος, ὀρθῶς ἂν ἔφασαν ὅτι μὴ ὄντος τοῦ πεφυκότος πάσχειν
πᾶσά πως ἀνάγκη τῇ τοῦ λόγου φύσει συμβαίνειν τὸ πάθος· εἰ δὲ
ἐν τῷ σεσαρκωμένην εἰπεῖν σύμπας ὁ λόγος τῆς μετὰ σαρκὸς
οἰκονομίας εἰσφέρεται (ἐσαρκώθη γὰρ οὐχ ἑτέρως, ἀλλὰ σπέρματος Ἀβραὰμ ἐπιλαμβανόμενος καὶ ὁμοιωθεὶς κατὰ πάντα τοῖς 20
ἀδελφοῖς[e] καὶ μορφὴν δούλου λαβών),[f] εἰκῇ πεφλυαρήκασιν οἱ
λέγοντες ἀκολουθεῖν τὸ χρῆναι πάντως αὐτὸν εἰς ἰδίαν ὑπομεῖναι
φύσιν, ὑποκειμένης τῆς σαρκός, περὶ ἣν ἂν εἰκότως συμβῆναι τὸ
παθεῖν νοοῖτο ἀπαθοῦς ὄντος τοῦ λόγου. ἀλλ᾽ οὐκ ἔξω διὰ τοῦτο
τίθεμεν αὐτὸν τοῦ λέγεσθαι παθεῖν· ὥσπερ γὰρ ἴδιον αὐτοῦ γέγονε 25
τὸ σῶμα, οὕτω καὶ πάντα τὰ τοῦ σώματος δίχα μόνης ἁμαρτίας
λέγοιτο ἂν οὐδὲν ἧττον αὐτοῦ κατ᾽ οἰκείωσιν οἰκονομικήν.

3. Εἰ μία φύσις, φησί, τοῦ λόγου σεσαρκωμένη, πᾶσά πως
ἀνάγκη φυρμὸν γενέσθαι καὶ σύγκρασιν, μειουμένης ὥσπερ καὶ
ὑποκλεπτομένης τῆς ἀνθρωπίνης φύσεως ἐν αὐτῷ.   30

Ἠγνόησαν πάλιν οἱ τὰ ὀρθὰ διαστρέφοντες ὅτι κατὰ ἀλήθειάν
ἐστι μία φύσις τοῦ λόγου σεσαρκωμένη. εἰ γὰρ εἷς ἐστιν υἱὸς ὁ
φύσει καὶ ἀληθῶς ὁ ἐκ θεοῦ πατρὸς λόγος ἀπορρήτως γεννηθείς,
εἶτα κατὰ πρόσληψιν σαρκὸς οὐκ ἀψύχου μᾶλλον, ἀλλ᾽ ἐψυχωμένης
νοερῶς προῆλθεν ἄνθρωπος ἐκ γυναικός, οὐκ εἰς δύο μερισθήσεται 35

---

[d] cf. John 1 : 14   [e] cf. Hebr. 2 : 16 f.   [f] cf. Phil. 2 : 7

declare) wise John the evangelist's meaning when he spoke of the Word as being made flesh—not, God forbid!, as if he were united to lifeless flesh nor again as if he underwent change or alteration. He remains what he was, that is God by nature. After taking on human existence, being made as we are in flesh from a woman, he remains one Son, not discarnate as of old, before the epoch of his becoming man, but clad, as it were, with our nature. Though the body united to the Word springing from God the Father, a body containing mental life, is not consubstantial with the Word, but the mind consequently has intuition of a difference in kind between the united elements, we confess *one* Son, Christ and Lord because the Word has been made flesh—and when we say 'flesh' we mean 'man'. What necessity is there, then, for him to have experienced suffering in his own nature, supposing there is an affirmation of one incarnate nature of the Son after the union? Had the conditions of God's plan not included what was capable of suffering they could validly assert that in the absence of what was capable of suffering the Word's nature must somehow incur the suffering; yet if the term 'incarnate' brings in the full range of meaning involved in the incarnate dispensation (the point being that incarnation involved nothing less than laying hold of Abraham's race, total assimilation to his brethren and taking slave's form) it is silly nonsense for people to talk of his undergoing suffering in his own nature as being a necessary consequence, when the flesh should be seen as the basis for the occurrence of the suffering whilst the Word is impassible. Yet we do not therefore exclude him from the attribution of suffering. Just as the body has been made his own possession, so all features of the body (with the sole exception of sin) are to be attributed to him in accordance with God's plan of appropriation.

3. 'If there is one incarnate nature of the Word, there must have been a sort of merger and mixture, with the human nature in him being diminished by its removal.'

Again they twist the facts, failing to recognize that the reality is one incarnate nature of the Word. If the Word who was begotten mysteriously of God the Father and who afterwards issued as man from woman by assumption of flesh (not lifeless flesh but flesh endowed with life and reason) is truly and actually one Son, he cannot be divided into two persons or sons but

διὰ τοῦτο πρόσωπα καὶ υἱούς, ἀλλὰ μεμένηκεν εἷς, πλὴν οὐκ
ἄσαρκος οὐδὲ ἔξω σώματος, ἀλλ' ἴδιον ἔχων αὐτὸ καθ' ἕνωσιν
ἀδιάσπαστον. ὁ δὲ τοῦτο λέγων οὐ φυρμόν, οὐ σύγχυσιν, οὐχ ἕτερόν
τι τῶν τοιούτων πάντη τε καὶ πάντως δηλοῖ οὔτε μὴν ὡς ἐξ
ἀναγκαίου λόγου τοῦτο ἀκολουθήσει, πόθεν; εἰ γὰρ καὶ εἷς λέγοιτο 5
πρὸς ἡμῶν ὁ μονογενὴς υἱὸς τοῦ θεοῦ σεσαρκωμένος καὶ ἐνανθρωπήσας, οὐ πέφυρται διὰ τοῦτο κατὰ τὸ ἐκείνοις δοκοῦν οὔτε μὴν
εἰς τὴν τῆς σαρκὸς φύσιν μεταπεφοίτηκεν ἡ τοῦ λόγου φύσις, ἀλλ'
οὐδὲ ἡ τῆς σαρκὸς εἰς τὴν αὐτοῦ, ἀλλ' ἐν ἰδιότητι τῇ κατὰ φύσιν
ἑκατέρου μένοντός τε καὶ νοουμένου κατά γε τὸν ἀρτίως ἡμῖν 10
ἀποδοθέντα λόγον ἀρρήτως καὶ ἀφράστως ἑνωθεὶς μίαν ἡμῖν ἔδειξεν
υἱοῦ φύσιν, πλήν, ὡς ἔφην, σεσαρκωμένην. οὐ γὰρ ἐπὶ μόνων τῶν
ἁπλῶν κατὰ τὴν φύσιν τὸ ἓν ἀληθῶς λέγεται, ἀλλὰ καὶ ἐπὶ τῶν
κατὰ σύνθεσιν συνηγμένων, ὁποῖόν τι χρῆμά ἐστιν ὁ ἄνθρωπος ὁ
ἐκ ψυχῆς καὶ σώματος. ἑτεροειδῆ μὲν γὰρ τὰ τοιαῦτα καὶ ἀλλήλοις 15
οὐχ ὁμοούσια· ἑνωθέντα γε μὴν μίαν ἀνθρώπου φύσιν ἀπετέλεσαν,
κἂν τοῖς τῆς συνθέσεως λόγοις ἐνυπάρχῃ τὸ διάφορον κατὰ φύσιν
τῶν εἰς ἑνότητα συγκεκομισμένων. περιττολογοῦσι τοίνυν οἱ
λέγοντες ὡς εἴπερ εἴη μία φύσις τοῦ λόγου σεσαρκωμένη, πάντη
τε καὶ πάντως ἕποιτο ἂν τὸ φυρμὸν γενέσθαι καὶ σύγκρασιν, ὡς 20
μειουμένης καὶ ὑποκλεπτομένης τῆς ἀνθρώπου φύσεως. οὔτε γὰρ
μεμείωται οὔτε καθά φασιν, ὑποκλέπτεται· ἀρκεῖ γὰρ πρὸς δήλωσιν
τὴν τελειοτάτην τοῦ ὅτι γέγονεν ἄνθρωπος, τὸ λέγειν ὅτι σεσάρκωται. εἰ μὲν γὰρ τοῦτο σεσίγηται παρ' ἡμῶν, ἔσχεν ἄν τινα χώραν
αὐτοῖς ἡ συκοφαντία· ἐπειδὴ δὲ ἀναγκαίως προσεπενήνεκται τὸ ὅτι 25
σεσάρκωται, ποῦ τῆς μειώσεως ἤτοι κλοπῆς ὁ τρόπος;

4. Εἰ τέλειος, φησί, θεὸς καὶ τέλειος ἄνθρωπος ὁ αὐτὸς νοούμενος καὶ ὁμοούσιος μὲν τῷ πατρὶ κατὰ τὴν θεότητα, κατὰ δὲ τὴν
ἀνθρωπότητα ὁμοούσιος ἡμῖν, ποῦ τὸ τέλειον, εἰ μηκέτι ὑφέστηκεν
ἡ ἀνθρώπου φύσις; ποῦ δὲ καὶ τὸ ὁμοούσιος ἡμῖν, εἰ μηκέτι ἕστηκεν 30
ἡ οὐσία, ὅπερ ἐστὶν ἡ φύσις, ἡμῶν;
Ἀρκεῖ καὶ τούτοις εἰς διασάφησιν ἡ ἐπὶ τῷ προτεταγμένῳ
κεφαλαίῳ λύσις ἢ γοῦν ἀπολογία. εἰ μὲν γὰρ μίαν εἰπόντες τὴν
φύσιν τοῦ λόγου σεσιγήκαμεν οὐκ ἐπενεγκόντες τὸ σεσαρκωμένην,
ἀλλ' οἷον ἔξω θέντες τὴν οἰκονομίαν, ἣν αὐτοῖς τάχα που καὶ οὐκ 35
ἀπίθανος ὁ λόγος προσποιουμένοις ἐρωτᾶν ποῦ τὸ τέλειον ἐν

remains one, though not discarnate or incorporeal but possessing his very own body in inseparable union. To say this could not possibly mean or entail mingling, merger or anything of that kind, how could it? If we call the Only-begotten Son of God become incarnate and made man 'one', that does not mean he has been 'mingled', as they suppose; the Word's nature has not transferred to the nature of the flesh or that of the flesh to that of the Word—no, while each element was seen to persist in its particular natural character for the reason just given, mysteriously and inexpressibly unified he displayed to us one nature (but as I said, *incarnate* nature) of the Son. 'One' is a term applied properly not only to basic single elements but to such composite entities as man compounded of soul and body. Soul and body are different kinds of thing and are not mutually consubstantial; yet united they constitute man's single nature despite the fact that the difference in nature of the elements brought into unity is present in the composite condition.[3] It is therefore idle for them to claim that if there is one incarnate nature of the Word it follows there must have been a mingling and merger, with the human nature being diminished by its removal. It has neither got smaller nor is it being removed (to use their terminology); for to state that he is incarnate gives completely adequate expression to the fact that he has become man. Had we kept silence on that point, their captious criticism might have had some ground; as it is, seeing that the fact that he is incarnate has of course been added, how can there be any suggestion of diminution or illicit removal?

4. 'If the self-same is seen as fully God and fully man, as consubstantial in Godhead with the Father and consubstantial with us in manhood, what about the fulness if the manhood no longer exists? What about the consubstantiality with us, if our substance (nature) no longer exists?'

The answer, or explanation, in the preceding paragraph adequately covers this further point. If we had spoken of the one nature of the Word without making the overt addition 'incarnate', to the exclusion apparently of the divine plan, there might have been some plausibility to their pretended question about the complete humanity or the possibility of our substance's continued

---

[3] This is the closest Cyril comes to the ἐν δύο φύσεσι of the Chalcedonian definition (see *First Letter*, n. 5 above). There can be no doubt that Cyril affirmed here the permanent co-existence of the pair of mentally distinguishable elements in Christ.

ἀνθρωπότητι ἢ πῶς ὑφέστηκεν ἡ καθ' ἡμᾶς οὐσία· ἐπειδὴ δὲ καὶ
ἡ ἐν ἀνθρωπότητι τελειότης καὶ τῆς καθ' ἡμᾶς οὐσίας ἡ δήλωσις
εἰσκεκόμισται διὰ τοῦ λέγειν σεσαρκωμένην, παυσάσθωσαν καλα-
μίνην ῥάβδον ἑαυτοῖς ὑποστήσαντες.ᵍ τοῦ γὰρ ἐκβάλλοντος τὴν
οἰκονομίαν καὶ ἀρνουμένου τὴν σάρκωσιν ἦν τὸ ἐγκαλεῖσθαι 5
δικαίως, ἀφαιρουμένου τὸν υἱὸν τῆς τελείας ἀνθρωπότητος· εἰ
δέ, ὡς ἔφην, ἐν τῷ σεσαρκῶσθαι λέγειν αὐτὸν σαφής ἐστι καὶ
ἀναμφίβολος ὁμολογία τοῦ ὅτι γέγονεν ἄνθρωπος, οὐδὲν ἔτι κωλύει
νοεῖν ὡς εἷς ὑπάρχων καὶ μόνος υἱὸς ὁ Χριστὸς ὁ αὐτὸς θεός ἐστι
καὶ ἄνθρωπος, ὥσπερ ἐν θεότητι τέλειος, οὕτως καὶ ἐν ἀνθρωπότητι. 10
ὀρθότατα δὲ καὶ πάνυ συνετῶς ἡ σὴ τελειότης τὸν περὶ τοῦ σωτηρίου
πάθους ἐκτίθεται λόγον, οὐκ αὐτὸν τὸν μονογενῆ τοῦ θεοῦ υἱόν,
καθὸ νοεῖται καὶ ἔστι θεός, παθεῖν εἰς ἰδίαν φύσιν τὰ σώματος²
ἰσχυριζομένη, παθεῖν δὲ μᾶλλον τῇ χοϊκῇ φύσει. ἔδει γὰρ ἀναγκαίως
ἀμφότερα σώζεσθαι τῷ ἑνὶ καὶ κατὰ ἀλήθειαν υἱῷ, καὶ τὸ μὴ πάσχειν 15
θεϊκῶς καὶ τὸ λέγεσθαι παθεῖν ἀνθρωπίνως· ἡ αὐτοῦ γὰρ πέπονθε
σάρξ. ἀλλ' οἴονται πάλιν ἐκεῖνοι τὴν καλουμένην παρ' αὐτοῖς
θεοπάθειαν ἡμᾶς εἰσφέρειν διὰ τούτου καὶ οὐκ ἐννοοῦσιν τὴν
οἰκονομίαν, κακουργότατα δὲ πειρῶνται μεθιστᾶν εἰς ἄνθρωπον
ἰδικῶς τὸ πάθος, εὐσέβειαν ἐπιζήμιον ἀσυνέτως ἐπιτηδεύοντες, 20
ἵνα μὴ ὁ τοῦ θεοῦ λόγος ὁμολογῆται σωτὴρ ὡς τὸ ἴδιον ὑπὲρ
ἡμῶν αἷμα δούς, ἀλλ' ἵνα μᾶλλον ἄνθρωπος ἰδικῶς καὶ καθ'
ἑαυτὸν νοούμενος Ἰησοῦς τοῦτο λέγηται κατορθῶσαι. κατασείει δὲ
τὸ οὕτω φρονεῖν ἅπαντα τῆς μετὰ σαρκὸς οἰκονομίας τὸν λόγον καὶ
τὸ θεῖον ἡμῶν μυστήριον εἰς δύναμιν ἀνθρωπολατρείας περιίστησιν 25
οὐκ ἀσυμφανῶς καὶ οὐκ ἐννοοῦσιν ὅτι τὸν ἐξ Ἰουδαίων κατὰ σάρκα,
τουτέστι τὸν ἐκ σπέρματος Ἰεσσαὶ καὶ Δαυὶδ Χριστὸν καὶ κύριον
τῆς δόξηςʰ καὶ θεὸν εὐλογητὸν εἰς τοὺς αἰῶνας καὶ ἐπὶ πάνταςⁱ ὁ
μακάριος ἔφη Παῦλος, ἴδιον ἀποφήνας τὸ σῶμα τοῦ λόγου τὸ τῷ
ξύλῳ προσηλωθὲν καὶ αὐτῷ τὸν σταυρὸν διὰ τοῦτο προσνέμων. 30

5. Μανθάνω δὲ ὅτι καὶ ἕτερόν τι πρὸς τούτοις ἐστὶ τὸ ζητούμενον.
ὁ γάρ τοι λέγων σαρκὶ παθεῖν γυμνῇ τὸν κύριον ἄλογον καὶ ἀκούσιον
ποιεῖ τὸ πάθος· ἐὰν δέ τις εἴπῃ μετὰ ψυχῆς νοερᾶς παθεῖν αὐτόν,

---

ᵍ cf. Is. 36: 6   ʰ cf. 1 Cor. 2: 8   ⁱ cf. Rom. 9: 5

² Schwartz brackets τὰ σώματος

existence. In view, though, of the fact that the introduction of the word 'incarnate' expresses completeness in manhood and our nature, they should cease leaning on that broken reed. There would be good grounds for charging anybody who deprives the Son of his complete manhood with casting overboard the divine plan and denying the incarnation; but if, as I said, to speak of his being incarnate contains a clear, unequivocal acknowledgement of his becoming man, there is no problem to seeing that the same Christ, being one and unique Son, is God and man as complete in Godhead as he is in manhood. Your Perfection expounds the rationale of our Saviour's passion very correctly and wisely, when you insist that the Only-begotten Son of God did not personally experience bodily sufferings in his own nature, as he is seen to be and is God, but suffered in his earthly nature. Both points, indeed, must be maintained of the one true Son: the absence of divine suffering and the attribution to him of human suffering because his flesh did suffer. These people, though, imagine that we are hereby introducing what they call 'divine passibility';[4] they fail to bear in mind God's plan and make mischievous attempts to shift the suffering to the man on his own, in foolish pursuit of a false piety. Their aim is that the Word of God should not be acknowledged as the Saviour who gave his own blood for us but instead that Jesus, viewed as a distinct individual man, should be credited with that. Such an idea overthrows the whole principle of God's plan of incarnation and plainly misinterprets our divine mystery as manworship. They take no notice of the fact that blessed Paul, by calling him who is of the Jews 'in flesh', that is of the stock of Jesse and David, 'Christ', 'Lord of glory' and 'God over all blessed for ever', assigned him the cross and pronounced the body nailed to the wood to be the Word's own body.

5. I am given to understand that a further query has been raised. 'Anyone, surely, who states that the Lord suffered exclusively in the flesh renders the suffering irrational and involuntary, but if you say he suffered with his soul and mind, to

---

[4] The term is new, though the charge old. 'Theopaschite' was to be a regular term for abuse of 'monophysites'.

ἵνα ᾖ τὸ πάθος ἑκούσιον, οὐδὲν κωλύει λέγειν τῇ φύσει τῆς ἀνθρωπότητος αὐτὸν παθεῖν. εἰ δὲ τοῦτο ἀληθές, πῶς οὐ τὰς δύο φύσεις
ὑφεστάναι δώσομεν μετὰ τὴν ἕνωσιν ἀδιαιρέτως; ὥστε εἴ τις λέγει
Χριστοῦ οὖν παθόντος ὑπὲρ ἡμῶν σαρκί,[j] οὐδὲν ἕτερον λέγει
πλὴν ὅτι Χριστοῦ παθόντος ὑπὲρ ἡμῶν τῇ ἡμετέρᾳ φύσει.   5

Μάχεται πάλιν οὐδὲν ἧττον τὸ πρόβλημα τοῖς μίαν εἶναι λέγουσι
τὴν τοῦ υἱοῦ φύσιν σεσαρκωμένην, καὶ οἷον εἰκαῖον ἀποφαίνειν
θέλοντες αὐτό, φιλονεικοῦσι πανταχοῦ δύο φύσεις ὑφεστώσας
ἀποφαίνειν. ἀλλ' ἠγνόησαν ὅτι ὅσα μὴ κατὰ μόνην τὴν θεωρίαν
διαιρεῖσθαι φιλεῖ, ταῦτα πάντως καὶ εἰς ἑτερότητα τὴν ἀνὰ μέρος   10
ὁλοτρόπως καὶ ἰδικὴν ἀποφοιτήσειεν ἂν ἀλλήλων. ἔστω δὲ ἡμῖν εἰς
παράδειγμα πάλιν ὁ καθ' ἡμᾶς ἄνθρωπος. δύο μὲν γὰρ καὶ ἐπ'
αὐτοῦ νοοῦμεν τὰς φύσεις, μίαν μὲν τῆς ψυχῆς, ἑτέραν δὲ τοῦ
σώματος· ἀλλ' ἐν ψιλαῖς διελόντες ἐννοίαις καὶ ὡς ἐν ἰσχναῖς
θεωρίαις ἤτοι νοῦ φαντασίαις τὴν διαφορὰν δεξάμενοι οὐκ ἀνὰ   15
μέρος τίθεμεν τὰς φύσεις οὔτε μὴν διαμπὰξ διατομῆς δύναμιν
ἐφίεμεν αὐταῖς, ἀλλ' ἑνὸς εἶναι νοοῦμεν, ὥστε τὰς δύο μηκέτι μὲν
εἶναι δύο, δι' ἀμφοῖν δὲ τὸ ἓν ἀποτελεῖσθαι ζῷον. οὐκοῦν κἂν εἰ
λέγοιεν ἀνθρωπότητος φύσιν καὶ θεότητος ἐπὶ τοῦ Ἐμμανουήλ, ἀλλ'
ἡ ἀνθρωπότης γέγονεν ἰδία τοῦ λόγου καὶ εἷς υἱὸς νοεῖται σὺν αὐτῇ.   20
τῆς γε μὴν θεοπνεύστου γραφῆς σαρκὶ παθεῖν[k] αὐτὸν λεγούσης,
ἄμεινον καὶ ἡμᾶς οὕτως λέγειν ἢ γοῦν τῇ φύσει τῆς ἀνθρωπότητος,
εἰ καὶ ὅτι μάλιστα, εἰ μὴ δυστρόπως λέγοιτο καὶ τοῦτο πρός τινων,
ἀδικήσειεν ἂν οὐδὲν τὸν τοῦ μυστηρίου λόγον. τί γάρ ἐστιν ἀνθρωπότητος φύσις ἕτερον πλὴν ὅτι σὰρξ ἐψυχωμένη νοερῶς; καὶ   25
πεπονθέναι φαμὲν σαρκὶ τὸν κύριον. περιεργότατα τοίνυν φασὶ τὸ
τῇ φύσει τῆς ἀνθρωπότητος αὐτὸν παθεῖν οἷον ἀποδιστάντες αὐτὴν
τοῦ λόγου καὶ ἔξω τιθέντες ἰδικῶς, ἵνα δύο νοῶνται καὶ οὐχ εἷς ἔτι
σεσαρκωμένος καὶ ἐνανθρωπήσας ὁ ἐκ θεοῦ πατρὸς λόγος. τὸ δὲ
ἀδιαιρέτως προστεθὲν δοκεῖ μέν πως παρ' ἡμῖν ὀρθῆς εἶναι δόξης   30
σημαντικόν, αὐτοὶ δὲ οὐχ οὕτως νοοῦσιν. τὸ γὰρ ἀδιαίρετον παρ'
αὐτοῖς κατὰ τὰς Νεστορίου κενοφωνίας καθ' ἕτερον λαμβάνεται
τρόπον· φασὶ γὰρ ὅτι τῇ ἰσοτιμίᾳ, τῇ ταυτοβουλίᾳ, τῇ αὐθεντίᾳ
ἀδιαίρετός ἐστι τοῦ λόγου ὁ ἐν ᾧ κατῴκηκεν ἄνθρωπος, ὥστε οὐχ
ἁπλῶς τὰς λέξεις προφέρουσιν, ἀλλὰ μετά τινος δόλου καὶ   35
κακουργίας.

[j] 1 Peter 4: 1   [k] cf. ibid.

make the suffering voluntary,[5] there is no bar to saying that he suffered in the manhood's nature. If that is true, must we not be conceding that two natures exist inseparably after the union? With the result that if you quote *"Christ therefore having suffered for us in flesh"* your meaning is the same as if you had said "Christ having suffered for us in our nature".'

The objection is just one more attack upon those who affirm one incarnate nature of the Son; apparently aiming to prove the affirmation idle, they obstinately argue always for the existence of two natures. They forgot, though, that all things regularly distinguished at the merely speculative level isolate themselves completely in mutual difference and separate individuality. Take a normal human being. We perceive in him two natures: one that of the soul, a second that of the body. We divide them, though, merely in thought, accepting the difference as simply residing in fine-drawn insight or mental intuition; we do not separate the natures out or attribute a capacity for radical severance to them, but see that they belong to one man so that the two are two no more and the single living being is constituted complete by the pair of them. So though one attributes the nature of manhood and of Godhead to Emmanuel, the manhood has become the Word's own and together with it is seen one Son. Inspired Scripture tells us he suffered in flesh and we should do better to use those terms than to talk of his suffering 'in the nature of the manhood', even if that statement, unless it be made in certain people's perverse sense, does no damage to the principle of the mystery. What, indeed, is manhood's nature except flesh endowed with life and mind? And that the Lord suffered in flesh we affirm. It is futile, then, for them to talk of his suffering in the nature of the manhood separating it, as it were, from the Word and isolating it from him so as to think of him as two and not one Word from God the Father yet incarnate and made man. The extra word 'inseparable' they add may seem to have our orthodox sense, but that is not how they intend it. 'Inseparability', according to Nestorius' empty talk, is used in a different sense. They say that the man in whom the Word has made his home is inseparable from him in equality of honour, identity of will and sovereignty. The result is that they do not use terms in their plain sense but with a certain trickery and mischief.

[5] i.e. human suffering belongs to human nature in its completeness and is not simply a physical, bodily happening.

7

ON THE CREED

Τοῦ αὐτοῦ εἰς τὸ ἅγιον σύμβολον

1. Τοῖς ἀγαπητοῖς καὶ ποθεινοτάτοις Ἀναστασίῳ Ἀλεξάνδρῳ
Μαρτινιανῷ Ἰωάννῃ Παρηγορίῳ πρεσβυτέροις καὶ Μαξίμῳ
διακόνῳ καὶ λοιποῖς ὀρθοδόξοις πατράσι μοναχῶν καὶ τοῖς σὺν ὑμῖν
τὸν μονήρη βίον ἀσκοῦσι καὶ ἐν πίστει θεοῦ ἱδρυμένοις Κύριλλος ἐν 5
κυρίῳ χαίρειν.

Τὸ φιλομαθὲς καὶ φιλόπονον τῆς ὑμετέρας ἀγάπης καὶ νῦν οὐ
μετρίως ἐπαινέσας ἔχω καὶ ἄξιον εἶναί φημι τοῦ παντὸς λόγου.
τὸ γάρ τοι θείων ἐφίεσθαι μαθημάτων καὶ τῆς τῶν ἱερῶν δογμάτων
ὀρθότητος μεταποιεῖσθαι φιλεῖν πῶς οὐκ ἂν ὑπεραγάσαιτό τις; καὶ 10
γάρ ἐστι ζωῆς τῆς ἀπεράντου καὶ μακαρίας τὸ χρῆμα πρόξενον καὶ
οὐκ ἄμισθος ἡ ἔν γε τούτοις σπουδή· φησὶ γάρ που πρὸς τὸν ἐν
τοῖς οὐρανοῖς πατέρα καὶ θεὸν ὁ κύριος ἡμῶν Ἰησοῦς ὁ Χριστός·
αὕτη δέ ἐστιν ἡ αἰώνιος ζωὴ ἵνα γινώσκωσι σὲ τὸν μόνον
ἀληθινὸν θεὸν καὶ ὃν ἀπέστειλας Ἰησοῦν Χριστόν.[a] 15

2. Ὀρθὴ γὰρ πίστις καὶ ἀκατάσκωπτος, σύνδρομον ἔχουσα τὴν
ἐξ ἔργων ἀγαθῶν φαιδρότητα, παντὸς ἡμᾶς ἐμπίπλησιν ἀγαθοῦ καὶ
διαπρεπῆ λαχόντας τὴν δόξαν ἀποφαίνει· πράξεων δὲ λαμπρότης εἰ
ἀμοιροῦσα φαίνοιτο δογμάτων ὀρθῶν καὶ ἀδιαβλήτου πίστεως,
ὀνήσειεν ἄν, ὥς γε οἶμαι, κατ᾽ οὐδένα τρόπον τὴν τοῦ ἀνθρώπου 20
ψυχήν. ὥσπερ γὰρ ἡ πίστις χωρὶς τῶν ἔργων νεκρά ἐστιν,[b]
οὕτως εἶναί φαμεν ἀληθὲς καὶ τὸ ἔμπαλιν. οὐκοῦν συναναλαμπέτω
τοῖς τῆς εὐζωίας αὐχήμασι καὶ τὸ ἀμώμητον ἐν πίστει· ἄρτιοι γὰρ
οὕτως ἐσόμεθα κατὰ τὸν τοῦ πανσόφου Μωυσέος νόμον. τέλειος
γάρ φησιν ἔσῃ ἐναντίον κυρίου τοῦ θεοῦ σου.[c] οἱ δὲ τοῦ 25
πίστιν ἔχειν ὀρθὴν ἐξ ἀμαθίας ὀλιγωρήσαντες, εἶτα ταῖς ἐπιεικείαις
τὸν ἑαυτῶν κατασεμνύνοντες βίον ἐοίκασί πως ἀνδράσιν εὐφυᾶ μὲν

---

[a] John 17: 3   [b] James 2: 20   [c] Deut. 18: 13

Witnesses: V A R + Latin version, Σ, and citations   *ACO* 1, 1, 4 pp. 49–61

7

ON THE CREED

By the same, On the holy Creed

1. Greetings in the Lord from Cyril to the dear and well-beloved priests Anastasius, Alexander, Martinian, John and Paregorius; to the deacon Maximus;[1] to the rest of the orthodox abbots; and to your colleagues in the monastic life with their firm faith in God.

I must use superlatives to praise your charities' eagerness for hard study and here and now declare it deserves every commendation. How can one fail to admire a yearning for theology and a desire to follow orthodoxy in sacred doctrine? They win endless life and happiness, and the serious attention involved here is well worthwhile. Our Lord Jesus Christ addresses God the heavenly Father at one point: *'This is eternal life that they should know thee the sole, true God and Jesus Christ whom thou didst send.'*

2. An unimpeachably sound faith, with the splendour good deeds produce to go with it, fills us with all goodness and endows us with more than ordinary glory. Excellency in actions, on the other hand, without the evidence of sound doctrines and irreproachable faith can, I believe, in no way benefit man's soul. *'Faith without works is dead'*, and by the same token we assert the truth of the converse. Purity in faith, then, and nobility of life must shine together, for this is how we can completely accord with the law of Moses so utterly wise. *'Thou shalt be perfect'*, he says, *'before the Lord thy God.'* Ignorant despisers, though, of sound faith, who yet bedeck their lives with virtues, resemble men of

---

[1] Only Maximus is otherwise important. He was a zealous opponent of Nestorianism, active in rousing opposition to John his bishop. He had at first refused to accept the reunion of 433 and Cyril wrote two short letters to him (*Epp.* 57 f.) which preach the need for οἰκονομία, 'accommodation', in the matter. The breach was healed, but only temporarily. Five years later Maximus was touring the East campaigning against Theodore. See p. xxvii.

λαχοῦσι τοῦ προσώπου τὸν χαρακτῆρα, πεπλανημένην δὲ καὶ
διάστροφον τῶν ὀμμάτων τὴν βολήν, ὥστε καὶ πρέπειν αὐτοῖς τὸ
διὰ φωνῆς Ἱερεμίου πρὸς τὴν τῶν Ἰουδαίων μητέρα, φημὶ δὴ τὴν
Ἱερουσαλὴμ εἰρημένον παρὰ θεοῦ· ἰδοὺ οὔκ εἰσιν οἱ ὀφθαλμοί
σου οὐδὲ ἡ καρδία σου καλή.[d]   5

3. Χρὴ τοίνυν ὑμᾶς ὑγιᾶ καὶ πρό γε τῶν ἄλλων ἔχειν ἐν ἑαυτοῖς
τὸν νοῦν καὶ διαμεμνῆσθαι γράμματος ἱεροῦ προσφωνοῦντός τε καὶ
λέγοντος· οἱ ὀφθαλμοί σου ὀρθὰ βλεπέτωσαν.[e] ὀρθὴ δὲ βλέψις
ὀμμάτων τῶν ἔσω κεκρυμμένων τὸ ἰσχνῶς καὶ ἀπεξεσμένως
περιαθρεῖν δύνασθαι κατά γε τὸ ἐγχωροῦν τοὺς οἵπερ ἂν γένοιντο   10
περὶ θεοῦ λόγους. βλέπομεν γὰρ ἐν ἐσόπτρῳ καὶ αἰνίγματι καὶ
γινώσκομεν ἐκ μέρους·[f] ὅ γε μὴν ἐκ σκότους ἀποκαλύπτων
βαθέα[g] τὸ τῆς ἀληθείας ἐνίησι φῶς τοῖς ἐθέλουσιν ὀρθῶς τὴν περὶ
αὐτοῦ γνῶσιν ἑλεῖν. χρὴ τοιγαροῦν ἡμᾶς θεῷ προσπίπτειν λέγοντας·
φώτισον τοὺς ὀφθαλμούς μου, μήποτε ὑπνώσω εἰς   15
θάνατον.[h] τὸ γὰρ τῆς ὀρθότητος τῶν ἱερῶν δογμάτων ἀπολισθεῖν
εἴη ἂν ἕτερον οὐδὲν πλὴν ὅτι σαφῶς τὸ ὑπνοῦν εἰς θάνατον· ἐκπίπτο-
μεν δὲ τῆς ὀρθότητος, ὅτε μὴ ταῖς θεοπνεύστοις ἑπόμεθα γραφαῖς,
ἀλλ' ἢ προλήψεσιν οὐκ ἐπαινουμέναις ἢ κατὰ πρόσκλισιν τὴν πρός
γέ τινας οὐκ ὀρθοποδοῦντας περὶ τὴν πίστιν τὰς τῆς ἑαυτῶν   20
διανοίας ἀπονέμοντες ῥοπὰς καὶ πρό γε τῶν ἄλλων τὰς ἑαυτῶν
ψυχὰς ἀδικοῦντες ἁλισκόμεθα.

4. Πειστέον δὴ οὖν τοῖς τῆς ὀρθότητος ἐπιμεληταῖς πρὸς τὸ τοῖς
ἱεροῖς κηρύγμασι δοκοῦν, ἃ καὶ διὰ πνεύματος ἁγίου παρέδοσαν
ἡμῖν οἱ ἀπ' ἀρχῆς αὐτόπται καὶ ὑπηρέται γενόμενοι τοῦ   25
λόγου,[i] ὧν τοῖς ἴχνεσιν ἀκολουθεῖν ἐσπούδασαν καὶ οἱ πανεύφημοι
πατέρες ἡμῶν οἱ τὸ σεπτόν τε καὶ οἰκουμενικὸν τῆς πίστεως
ὁρισάμενοι σύμβολον ἐν τῇ Νικαέων συναγηγερμένοι κατὰ καιρούς.
οἷς δὴ καὶ αὐτὸς σύνεδρος ἦν ὁ Χριστός· ἔφη γὰρ ὅτι ὅπου ἐὰν
ὦσι δύο ἢ τρεῖς συνηγμένοι εἰς τὸ ἐμὸν ὄνομα, ἐκεῖ εἰμὶ   30
ἐν μέσῳ αὐτῶν.[j] ὅτι γὰρ πρόεδρος ἦν ἀοράτως τῆς ἁγίας καὶ
μεγάλης ἐκείνης συνόδου Χριστός, πῶς ἔστιν ἀμφιβάλλειν; κρηπὶς

[d] Jer. 22: 17   [e] Prov. 4: 25   [f] cf. 1 Cor. 13: 12, 9   [g] Job 12: 22
[h] Ps. 12(13): 3   [i] Luke 1: 2   [j] Matt. 18: 20

a handsome cast of countenance but endowed with a squint, so that God's words through the voice of Jeremiah to the Mother of the Jews (Jerusalem, I mean) are apposite to them: '*Behold thine eyes are not and thine heart is not sound.*'

3. Before anything else, then, you should possess within you a sound understanding and recall holy Scripture's address: '*Let your eyes see straight!*' The unseen inner eyes' 'straight' vision is the capacity for taking a rounded look, as clear and precise as possible, at any statements about God which may be produced. We see, in fact, in a glass darkly and know in part, nevertheless he who '*discloses deep things out of darkness*' infuses truth's light into those intent on acquiring a sound knowledge of him. We ought, then, to fall down before God and say: '*Lighten my eyes lest I sleep unto death.*' It is plain, indeed, that 'sleeping unto death' means lapsing from sound and sacred doctrine; and we fall away from soundness when we fail to follow inspired Scripture, and instead let our minds be swayed by prejudices or incline towards parties who do not tread straight the paths of faith and by so doing stand convicted in the first instance of harming ourselves.

4. Custodians of orthodoxy, then, must betake themselves to the judgement of the sacred message which '*those made eye-witnesses and stewards of the Word transmitted to us from the beginning*' by the Holy Ghost, those eyewitnesses whose footsteps our utterly praiseworthy fathers endeavoured to follow when they met in time past at Nicaea and laid down the august and universal symbol of the faith. They had, moreover, Christ in session along with them; for he had said, '*Wherever two or three are gathered together in my name there am I in their midst.*' Is it possible, indeed, to doubt that Christ invisibly presided over that holy and grand

οἷά τις καὶ θεμέλιος ἀρραγὴς καὶ ἀκράδαντος τοῖς ἀνὰ πᾶσαν τὴν
γῆν κατεβάλλετο τῆς ἀκραιφνοῦς τε καὶ ἀμωμήτου πίστεως ἡ
ὁμολογία· εἶτα πῶς ἀπῆν ὁ Χριστός, εἴπερ ἐστὶν αὐτὸς ὁ θεμέλιος
κατὰ τὴν τοῦ σοφωτάτου Παύλου φωνήν; θεμέλιον γὰρ ἄλλον,
φησίν, οὐδεὶς δύναται θεῖναι παρὰ τὸν κείμενον, ὅς ἐστιν 5
Ἰησοῦς Χριστός.ᵏ τὴν τοίνυν ἐκτεθεῖσαν παρ' ἐκείνων καὶ
ὁρισθεῖσαν πίστιν τετηρήκασιν ἀδιαβλήτως καὶ οἱ μετ' αὐτοὺς
γεγονότες ἅγιοι πατέρες καὶ ποιμένες λαῶν καὶ φωστῆρες ἐκκλησιῶν
καὶ εὐτεχνέστατοι μυσταγωγοί. ἐλλελοιπὸς δὲ ὅλως οὐδὲν ἢ γοῦν
παρεωραμένον τῶν ἀναγκαίων εἰς ὄνησιν κατίδοι τις ἂν ἐν ταῖς 10
τῶν πατέρων ὁμολογίαις ἢ γοῦν ἐκθέσεσιν ἃς πεποίηνται περὶ τῆς
ὀρθῆς καὶ ἀκαπηλεύτου πίστεως εἰς ἔλεγχον μὲν καὶ ἀνατροπὴν
αἱρέσεως ἁπάσης καὶ δυσσεβοῦς ἀθυροστομίας, εἰς βεβαίωσιν δὲ
καὶ ἀσφάλειαν τοῖς ὀρθοποδοῦσι περὶ τὴν πίστιν, οἷς ὁ λαμπρὸς
ἀνέτειλεν ἑωσφόρος καὶ διηύγασεν ἡ ἡμέραˡ κατὰ τὰς γραφὰς καὶ 15
τὸ τῆς ἀληθείας ἐνίησι φῶς ἡ διὰ τοῦ ἁγίου πνεύματος χάρις.

5. Ἐπειδὴ δὲ γέγραφεν ὑμῶν ἡ εὐλάβεια ὡς παροχετεύουσί
τινες ἐφ' ἃ μὴ προσῆκε, τὰ ἐν τῷ συμβόλῳ, τῶν ἐν αὐτῷ
ῥημάτων τὴν δύναμιν ἢ οὐ συνιέντες ὀρθῶς ἢ καὶ ἐκ τοῦ προσ-
κεκλίσθαι ταῖς τινων συγγραφαῖς εἰς ἀδόκιμον ἀποφερόμενοι νοῦν, 20
εἶτα χρῆναι κἀμὲ τοὺς περὶ τούτων αὐτῶν πρὸς ὑμᾶς ποιήσασθαι
λόγους καὶ διερμηνεῦσαι σαφῶς τὴν τῆς ἐκθέσεως δύναμιν, δεῖν
ᾠήθην ἅπερ εἰς νοῦν ἥκει τὸν ἐμόν, ἐπιδρομάδην εἰπεῖν. ἑψόμεθα
δὲ πανταχοῦ ταῖς τῶν ἁγίων πατέρων ὁμολογίαις τε καὶ δόξαις,
ὀρθῶς καὶ ἀπροσκλινῶς βασανίζοντες τὰ παρ' αὐτῶν εἰρημένα. ἤδη 25
μὲν γὰρ καὶ ἡ ἁγία σύνοδος, ἡ κατά γε φημὶ τὴν Ἐφεσίων συνειλεγμένη κατὰ βούλησιν θεοῦ, τῆς Νεστορίου κακοδοξίας ὁσίαν καὶ
ἀκριβῆ κατενεγκοῦσα τὴν ψῆφον καὶ τὰς τῶν ἑτέρων κενοφωνίας,
οἵπερ ἂν ἢ γένοιντο μετ' αὐτὸν ἢ καὶ πρὸ αὐτοῦ γεγόνασι, τὰ ἴσα
φρονοῦντες αὐτῷ καὶ εἰπεῖν ἢ συγγράψαι τολμήσαντες, συγκατέ- 30
κρινεν ἐκείνῳ, τὴν ἴσην αὐτοῖς ἐπιθεῖσα δίκην. καὶ γὰρ ἦν ἀκόλουθον,
ἑνὸς ἅπαξ ἐπὶ ταῖς οὕτω βεβήλοις κενοφωνίαις κατεγνωσμένου, μὴ
καθ' ἑνὸς μᾶλλον ἐλθεῖν, ἀλλ', ἵν' οὕτως εἴπω, κατὰ πάσης αὐτῶν

ᵏ 1 Cor. 3: 11   ˡ cf. 2 Peter 1: 19

² ACO 1, 1, 7 pp. 105 f. (in the report of the session of 22 July widely
circularized by Cyril). A deposition from Charisius, a priest, was read reporting

council? The confession of a faith pure and spotless was in process of being laid down, an infrangible basis, an unshakeable foundation, as it were, for men throughout the world—could Christ in that case have been absent if he is, as Paul so wise declares, personally the foundation stone? *'No other foundation'*, he says, *'can anyone lay than that which is laid, namely Jesus Christ.'* Accordingly their successors the holy fathers, pastors of congregations, luminaries of Churches, skilled masters of spirituality as they were, have kept the faith they set forth in a definition with a vigilance that cannot be faulted. One sees no essential omitted, nothing worthwhile overlooked, in the confessional statements the fathers produced dealing with correct and unadulterated faith. Their aim was the refutation and rebuttal of all heresy and blasphemous nonsense on the one hand, and on the other the confirmation and security of those who tread straight the path of faith, people on whom the morning star has arisen and day dawned (as the Bible says) and in whom the grace which comes through the Holy Ghost is infusing truth's light.

5. Now seeing that your reverences write that certain persons are interpreting the contents of the Creed in false directions, either through incorrect understanding of the meaning of the words in it or through being carried off into a depraved interpretation as a result of their attachment to the writings of certain people, and that consequently I ought to address to you on this very theme a clear exegesis of the meaning of the statement, I believe I have an obligation to give a brief review of my understanding of the matter. We shall follow the holy fathers' confessed views at all points making correct and impartial examination of their affirmations. Indeed the holy synod too (I refer to the one assembled by God's will at Ephesus) gave a hallowed and precise judgement against Nestorius' evil dogmas; along with its condemnation of Nestorius it also imposed exactly the same sentence on the empty verbiage of any precursors or successors of his holding the equivalent views and with the impudence to express them orally or in writing.[2] For they followed up their single condemnation of one man for such profane nonsense with an attack not just on an individual but on the whole heretical

the use of a creed, other than the Nicene, as a test of orthodoxy amongst the Philadelphians. Theodore was its alleged author (Cyril *Ep*. 72) though unnamed in the record. The practice was forbidden (the 'Ephesine Decree'), and a blanket condemnation of Nestorius' supporters, scarcely applicable to the dead, followed. Cf. also *Ep*. 33 (to Acacius of Aleppo, another recipient of the Acta), *ACO* 1, 1, 7 p. 148, lines 40 ff.

τῆς αἱρέσεως ἤτοι τῆς συκοφαντίας, ἧς πεποίηνται κατὰ τῶν
εὐσεβῶν τῆς ἐκκλησίας δογμάτων, δύο πρεσβεύοντες υἱοὺς καὶ
διατέμνοντες τὸν ἀμέριστον καὶ ἀνθρωπολατρείας ἔγκλημα κατα-
γράφοντες οὐρανοῦ τε καὶ γῆς· προσκυνεῖ γὰρ μεθ᾽ ἡμῶν ἡ τῶν
ἄνω πνευμάτων ἁγία πληθὺς τὸν ἕνα κύριον Ἰησοῦν Χριστόν. 5

6. Ὑπὲρ δὲ τοῦ μὴ ἀγνοεῖσθαι παρά τισι τοῦ συμβόλου τὴν
δύναμιν, ὃ καὶ ἐν ἁπάσαις ταῖς ἁγίαις τοῦ θεοῦ ἐκκλησίαις καὶ
κρατεῖ καὶ κεκήρυκται, πατέρων ἁγίων δόξας ἢ γοῦν ἐκθέσεις
ἐνέταξα τοῖς αὐτόθι πεπραγμένοις ὑπομνήμασιν, ἵν᾽ εἰδεῖεν οἱ
ἐντυγχάνοντες αὐταῖς τίνα προσήκει νοεῖσθαι τρόπον τῶν ἁγίων 10
πατέρων τὴν ἔκθεσιν ἤτοι τὸ ἀκραιφνὲς τῆς ὀρθῆς πίστεως σύμβολον. οἶμαι δὲ τὴν ἀγάπην ὑμῶν καὶ ἐντυχεῖν τῷ βιβλίῳ ὃ περὶ
τούτων αὐτῶν συγγεγράφαμεν. αὐτὸ δὲ καὶ νῦν, ὡς ἔφην, ἐπὶ
λέξεως αὐτῆς παραθεὶς τὸ σύμβολον, τετράψομαι σὺν θεῷ πρός γε
τὸ δεῖν ἕκαστα τῶν ἐν αὐτῷ κειμένων διερμηνεῦσαι σαφῶς. 15
γεγραφότα γὰρ οἶδα τὸν παναοίδιμον Πέτρον· ἕτοιμοι ἀεὶ πρὸς
ἀπολογίαν παντὶ τῷ αἰτοῦντι ὑμᾶς λόγον περὶ τῆς ἐν
ὑμῖν ἐλπίδος.[m]

7. Πιστεύομεν εἰς ἕνα θεὸν πατέρα παντοκράτορα, πάντων
ὁρατῶν τε καὶ ἀοράτων ποιητήν· καὶ εἰς ἕνα κύριον Ἰησοῦν Χριστὸν 20
τὸν υἱὸν τοῦ θεοῦ, γεννηθέντα ἐκ τοῦ πατρὸς[1] μονογενῆ, τουτέστιν[2]
ἐκ τῆς οὐσίας αὐτοῦ,[3] θεὸν ἐκ θεοῦ, φῶς ἐκ φωτός, θεὸν ἀληθινὸν
ἐκ θεοῦ ἀληθινοῦ, γεννηθέντα, οὐ ποιηθέντα, ὁμοούσιον τῷ πατρί,
δι᾽ οὗ τὰ πάντα ἐγένετο τά τε ἐν τῷ οὐρανῷ καὶ τὰ ἐν τῇ γῇ, τὸν
δι᾽ ἡμᾶς τοὺς ἀνθρώπους καὶ διὰ[3] τὴν ἡμετέραν σωτηρίαν κατ- 25
ελθόντα καὶ σαρκωθέντα καὶ ἐνανθρωπήσαντα, παθόντα καὶ ἀναστάντα τῇ τρίτῃ ἡμέρᾳ, ἀνελθόντα εἰς[3] οὐρανούς, ἐρχόμενον κρῖναι
ζῶντας καὶ νεκρούς· καὶ εἰς τὸ πνεῦμα τὸ ἅγιον.[3]

Τοὺς δὲ λέγοντας "ἦν ποτε ὅτε οὐκ ἦν" καὶ "πρὶν γεννηθῆναι
οὐκ ἦν" καὶ ὅτι ἐξ οὐκ ὄντων ἐγένετο, ἢ ἐξ ἑτέρας ὑποστάσεως ἢ 30
οὐσίας φάσκοντας εἶναι ἢ τρεπτὸν ἢ ἀλλοιωτὸν τὸν υἱὸν τοῦ θεοῦ,
τούτους ἀναθεματίζει ἡ ἀποστολικὴ καὶ καθολικὴ[4] ἐκκλησία.

---

[m] 1 Peter 3: 15

[1] γεννηθέντα—πατρὸς] τὸν V   [2] τουτέστιν—ἅγιον] καὶ τὰ ἑξῆς V
[3] sic, cf. p. 16   [4] sic VARΣ: Latin version trsp. ἀποστολικὴ, καθολικὴ;
cf. p. 16

chicanery (if I may so express it) which they have manufactured against the Church's truly religious doctrines by maintaining two Sons, by sundering the indivisible and indicting heaven and earth on a charge of man-worship—heaven *and* earth, for the holy multitude of higher spirits joins us in worship of the one Lord Jesus Christ.

6. To remove ignorance on anybody's part as to the significance of the Creed which has been published as authoritative in all God's holy Churches I included opinions, or 'statements', by holy fathers in the record of what was enacted at Ephesus,[3] to ensure that readers of these might know how to interpret properly the holy fathers' statement, the pure creed of orthodox faith. Your charities did, I believe, read the book we wrote on this very subject. Even so, as I said, I shall set out the Creed verbatim and then turn with God's help to the task of giving a clear exegesis of each point it contains.

7. 'We believe in one God, Father almighty, maker of all things visible and invisible; and in one Lord Jesus Christ the Son of God, begotten of the Father, only-begotten, that is from his substance, God from God, light from light, true God from true God, begotten not made, consubstantial with the Father, and through him were made all things both in heaven and earth, who for us men and for our salvation came down, was incarnate and made man, suffered and rose again on the third day, ascended into heaven and is coming to judge quick and dead; and in the Holy Ghost.

But as for those who say "there was a time when he did not exist" and "he did not exist before being begotten" and that he was made out of nothing or declare that God's Son comes from a different basis or substance, or that he is mutable or changeable—these the Apostolic and Catholic Church anathematizes.'

---

[3] *ACO* 1, 1, 7 pp. 89–95. These proof-texts are repeated (like the list of signatories) from the session of 22 June. Cyril appears to be saying here, as in *Ep.* 33 (see preceding note), that he was responsible for inserting them in the record as published, i.e. admitting the artificial character of the Acta. Cf. *To Eulogius*, n. 10.

8. Πιστεύειν ἔφασαν εἰς ἕνα θεόν, ἐκ βάθρων ὥσπερ αὐτῶν
κατασείοντες τὰς Ἑλλήνων δόξας, οἳ φάσκοντες εἶναι σοφοὶ
ἐμωράνθησαν καὶ ἤλλαξαν τὴν δόξαν τοῦ ἀφθάρτου
θεοῦ ἐν ὁμοιώματι εἰκόνος φθαρτοῦ ἀνθρώπου καὶ
πετεινῶν καὶ τετραπόδων καὶ ἑρπετῶν,[n] προσεκύνησαν δὲ 5
καὶ τῇ κτίσει παρὰ τὸν κτίσαντα[o] καὶ τοῖς τοῦ κόσμου στοι-
χείοις δεδουλεύκασι,[p] πολλοὺς καὶ ἀναριθμήτους ὑποτοπήσαντες
εἶναι τοὺς θεούς. οὐκοῦν εἰς ἀναίρεσιν τῆς πολυθέου πλάνης ἕνα
θεὸν ὀνομάζουσιν, ἑπόμενοι πανταχοῦ τοῖς ἱεροῖς γράμμασι καὶ τῆς
ἀληθείας τὸ κάλλος τοῖς ἀνὰ πᾶσαν τὴν ὑφ᾽ ἥλιον κατασημαίνοντες. 10
τοῦτο καὶ ὁ πάνσοφος ἔδρα Μωυσῆς, σαφέστατα λέγων· ἄκουε
Ἰσραήλ· κύριος ὁ θεός σου κύριος εἷς ἐστιν.[q] καὶ αὐτὸς δέ
πού φησιν ὁ τῶν ὅλων γενεσιουργὸς καὶ δεσπότης· οὐκ ἔσονταί
σοι θεοὶ ἕτεροι πλὴν ἐμοῦ·[r] ναὶ μὴν καὶ διὰ φωνῆς τῶν ἁγίων
προφητῶν· ἐγὼ θεὸς πρῶτος καὶ ἐγὼ μετὰ ταῦτα καὶ οὐκ 15
ἔστι πάρεξ ἐμοῦ.[s] ἄριστα δὴ οὖν οἱ πανεύφημοι πατέρες
κρηπῖδα τῇ πίστει καταβαλλόμενοι τὸ χρῆναι φρονεῖν καὶ λέγειν
ὡς εἷς καὶ μόνος ἐστὶ φύσει τε καὶ ἀληθείᾳ θεός, πιστεύειν ἔφασαν
εἰς ἕνα θεόν.

9. Προσονομάζουσι δὲ αὐτὸν καὶ πατέρα παντοκράτορα, ἵνα συν- 20
εισφέρηται τῷ πατρὶ δήλωσις υἱοῦ, δι᾽ ὅν ἐστι πατήρ, συνυφεστῶ-
τός τε καὶ συνυπάρχοντος ἀεί. οὐδὲ γὰρ γέγονεν ἐν χρόνῳ πατήρ,
ἀλλ᾽ ἦν ὅ ἐστιν, ἀεί, τουτέστι πατήρ, παντὸς ὑπάρχων ἐπέκεινα
γενητοῦ καὶ ἐν ὑπερτάτοις ὑψώμασι. τὸ γάρ τοι κρατεῖν καὶ
κυριεύειν τῶν ὅλων λαμπρὰν οὕτω καὶ ἀπαράβλητον αὐτῷ προσνέμει 25
τὴν δόξαν.

10. Παρ᾽ αὐτοῦ δέ φασι δεδημιουργῆσθαι τὰ πάντα τά τε ἐν
τοῖς οὐρανοῖς καὶ τὰ ἐπὶ τῆς γῆς, ἵνα κἀντεῦθεν τὸ ἀσυμφυὲς
αὐτοῦ πρὸς πᾶσαν κτίσιν νοοῖτο· ἀσύγκριτος γὰρ ἡ διαφορὰ
ποιητοῦ καὶ ποιήματος, ἀγενήτου καὶ γενητοῦ φύσεώς τε τῆς ὑπὸ 30
ζυγὸν καὶ δουλείαν καὶ τῆς τοῖς δεσποτικοῖς ἀξιώμασιν ἐξωραϊσμέ-
νης θεοπρεπῆ τε καὶ ὑπερκόσμιον λαχούσης τὴν δόξαν.

11. Υἱοῦ γε μὴν διαμνημονεύσαντες, ἵνα μὴ δοκοῖεν ὄνομα
κοινὸν προσνέμειν αὐτῷ, ὅπερ ἂν ἴσως τάττοιτο καὶ ἐφ᾽ ἡμῶν

[n] Rom. 1: 22 f.   [o] Rom. 1: 25   [p] cf. Gal. 4: 3   [q] Deut. 6: 4
[r] Ex. 20: 3   [s] Is. 44: 6

8. They affirmed that they believed in one God, so shaking the opinions of pagans from their very foundations, as it were, pagans who *'claiming to be wise, became fools and changed the glory of the incorruptible God into the likeness of the image of mortal man, of birds, quadrupeds and reptiles'*; who *'worshipped the creature instead of the Creator'*; who are slaves to the elements of the world with their imagination of a countless plurality of gods. To get rid, therefore, of the error of polytheism they use the words 'one God' in full conformity with the sacred writings and indicate to all men under the sun the beauty of Truth. Moses, so complete in wisdom, did the same too when he affirmed with superlative clarity: *'Hear, O Israel, the Lord thy God is one Lord.'* The universe's creator and master too, personally says in one passage: *'Thou shalt have no other gods but me.'* Moreover, he says by the voice of the holy prophets: *'I God am first and I am after these and apart from me there are none.'* The fathers, so utterly praiseworthy, laid down, therefore, the noblest foundation for faith, the obligation to hold and affirm that God is one and unique both in nature and in truth, when they declared their belief in one God.

9. They proceed to name him 'Father Almighty' with the aim of indicating along with the Father the Son, by virtue of whom he is 'Father', the Son who ever exists and has being along with him. He has not come to be Father in time but was ever what he is, Father, transcending in supernal heights every created thing. His domination and lordship over the universe thus allots him glory of incomparable splendour.

10. They affirm that all things both in heaven and on earth have been constructed by him so that thereby he should be recognized as having no natural affinity at all with creation; for the difference between Creator and created is incomparable, between a nature uncreated, adorned with the distinctions of empire, possessed of divine and supramundane glory and a nature under the yoke of bondage.

11. On mentioning the Son, to avoid the suspicion of allotting him an ordinary designation which could also be applied equally

αὐτῶν (κεκλήμεθα γὰρ καὶ ἡμεῖς υἱοί), νουνεχέστατα προσεπάγουσι
τὰ δι' ὧν ἔστιν ἰδεῖν τῆς ἐνούσης αὐτῷ φαιδρότητος φυσικῆς τὸ
ὑπὲρ κτίσιν ἀξίωμα. γεγεννῆσθαι γὰρ καὶ οὐ πεποιῆσθαί φασιν,
ἀσύντακτον μὲν οὐσιωδῶς τῇ κτίσει διὰ τοῦ μὴ πεποιῆσθαι νοοῦντες
αὐτόν, ἐκφῦναι δὲ μᾶλλον διισχυριζόμενοι τῆς οὐσίας τοῦ θεοῦ καὶ 5
πατρὸς ἀχρόνως τε καὶ ἀπερινοήτως· ἦν γὰρ ὁ λόγος ἐν ἀρχῇ.ᵗ
εἶτα τῆς ὠδῖνος τὸ γνήσιον (ἀνθρωπίνως δὲ καὶ τοῦτο εἰρήσθω διὰ
τὸ χρήσιμον) εὖ μάλα κατασημαίνοντες, θεὸν ἔφασαν ἐκ θεοῦ
γεγεννῆσθαι τὸν υἱόν· ἔνθα γὰρ ὅλως γέννησις ἀληθής, ἐκεῖ που
πάντως ἕποιτο ἂν τὸ χρῆναι νοεῖν καὶ λέγειν οὐκ ἀλλότριον τῆς 10
οὐσίας τοῦ τεκόντος τὸ τεχθέν, ἀλλ' ἴδιον αὐτῆς, ὅτι καὶ ἐξ αὐτῆς
κατὰ τὸν αὐτῇ πρέποντά τε καὶ ἐοικότα λόγον. οὐ γὰρ κατὰ σῶμα
τέξεται τὸ ἀσώματον, οὕτω δὲ μᾶλλον ὡς φῶς ἐκ φωτός, ἵν' ἐν
τῷ ἀπαστράψαντι φωτὶ τὸ ἀπαυγασθὲν νοοῖτο φῶς, καὶ ἐξ αὐτοῦ
κατὰ πρόοδον ἀπόρρητόν τε καὶ ἄφραστον καὶ ἐν αὐτῷ καθ' ἕνωσιν 15
καὶ ταυτότητα φυσικήν. οὕτω γὰρ εἶναί φαμεν ἐν μὲν τῷ πατρὶ τὸν
υἱόν, ἐν δὲ τῷ υἱῷ τὸν πατέρα· ὑπογράφει γὰρ ὁ υἱὸς ἐν ἰδίᾳ φύσει
τε καὶ δόξῃ τὸν ἑαυτοῦ γεννήτορα. καὶ γοῦν ἔφη σαφῶς πρὸς ἕνα
τῶν ἁγίων μαθητῶν· Φίλιππος δὲ οὗτος ἦν· οὐ πιστεύεις ὅτι
ἐγὼ ἐν τῷ πατρὶ καὶ ὁ πατὴρ ἐν ἐμοί ἐστιν; ὁ ἑωρακὼς 20
ἐμὲ ἑώρακε τὸν πατέρα·ᵘ ἐγὼ καὶ ὁ πατὴρ ἕν ἐσμεν.ᵛ
οὐκοῦν ὁμοούσιος ὁ υἱὸς τῷ πατρί. ταύτῃ τοι καὶ θεὸς ἀληθινὸς ἐκ
θεοῦ ἀληθινοῦ γεγεννῆσθαι πιστεύεται. καὶ τὸ μὲν τῆς γεννήσεως
ὄνομα τεθὲν εὑρήσομεν καὶ ἐπὶ τῶν κτισμάτων, κατά γε φημὶ τὸ
υἱοὺς ἐγέννησα καὶ ὕψωσαʷ περὶ τῶν ἐξ αἵματος Ἰσραὴλ 25
εἰρημένον παρὰ θεοῦ· ἀλλ' ἐν χάριτος τάξει τὴν τοιάνδε κλῆσιν
ἀποκερδαίνει τὸ ποιηθέν, ἐπὶ δέ γε τοῦ κατὰ φύσιν υἱοῦ κατα-
χρηστικῶς μὲν τῶν τοιούτων οὐδέν, ἀληθῆ δὲ πάντα, καὶ διὰ τοῦτο
μόνος ἐκ πάντων ἐγώ εἰμι, φησίν, ἡ ἀλήθειαˣ ὥστε κἂν γέννησιν
κἂν υἱότητά τις ἐπ' αὐτοῦ λέγῃ, ψευδοεπήσειεν ἂν οὐδαμῶς· αὐτὸς 30
γάρ ἐστιν ἡ ἀλήθεια. ἀσφαλίζονται τοίνυν τὰς ἡμετέρας ψυχὰς οἱ
πανεύφημοι μυσταγωγοί, πατέρα καὶ υἱὸν πανταχοῦ καὶ γέννησιν
ὀνομάζοντες καὶ θεὸν ἀληθινὸν ἐκ θεοῦ ἀληθινοῦ καὶ φῶς ἐκ φωτὸς
ἀπαστράψαι λέγοντες, ἵνα καὶ τὸ ἀσώματον καὶ τὸ ἁπλοῦν ἡ
γέννησις ἔχοι καὶ τὸ ἐξ αὐτοῦ γε καὶ ἐν αὐτῷ καὶ ἑκάτερος ὑπάρχων 35

ᵗ cf. John 1 : 1   ᵘ John 14 : 10, 9   ᵛ John 10 : 30   ʷ Is. 1 : 2
ˣ John 14 : 6

to ourselves (for we too are styled 'sons of God') they most carefully add the means of perceiving the dignity of his inherent
natural splendour, a dignity transcending creation. For they
affirm he has been begotten not made, recognizing that because
of his not being made he does not belong at the level of substance
in the same class as creation; instead they maintain that he
sprang in some incomprehensible, non-temporal way from God
the Father's substance—the Word was 'in the beginning'. Next
they finely indicated the genuineness of the birth (the fact must
be stated in the available human terms) by declaring the Son
to have been begotten, 'God from God'; for where birth is
completely real it necessarily follows that we must think and
speak of what is born as proper to, not alien from, its parent's
substance because it derives from it in accordance with the substance's suitably appropriate condition. The incorporeal will not
give birth corporeally but like light from light so that the light
emitted is perceived in the light which radiated it, both *from* it
by way of inexpressibly mysterious procession and *in* it by way
of union and natural identity. This is what it means to talk of
the Son being in the Father and the Father in the Son—the Son
in his own nature and glory delineates his sire. Indeed he plainly
told one of the holy disciples (Philip it was): '*Do you not believe
that I am in the Father and the Father in me? He who has seen me has
seen the Father. I and the Father are one.*' Therefore the Son is
consubstantial with the Father and by that token too he is believed to have been begotten, true God of true God. We can
find the word 'begetting' applied to creatures, I refer to the words
'*I begat and reared sons*' used by God of Israel's descendants. Yet
a creature enjoys a title like this in the order of grace whereas
with the real Son no such title is metaphorical, all are true.
Therefore he, as absolutely unique, says: '*I am the truth.*' So anyone
predicating birth or sonship of him speaks without shadow of
falsehood, for he is personally the Truth. These utterly praiseworthy spiritual guides safeguard our souls by their constant use
of the terms 'Father', 'Son' and 'birth', and by their declaration
that 'true God' shone out 'of true God' and 'light out of light'.
They mean the birth to possess incorporeal simplicity and that
the fact of being from him yet *in* him should be recognized along
with the individuality of both persons. The Father, indeed, is

ἰδιοπροσώπως νοῆται. πατὴρ γάρ ἐστιν ὁ πατὴρ καὶ οὐχ υἱός, καὶ
υἱὸς ὁ τεχθεὶς καὶ οὐ πατήρ, καὶ ἐν ταυτότητι φύσεως ἴδιον ἑκατέρου
τὸ εἶναι ὅ ἐστιν.

12. Ἁπάντων δὲ ποιητὴν ὁρατῶν τε καὶ ἀοράτων ἀποφήναντες
τὸν πατέρα, δι᾽ υἱοῦ τὰ πάντα δεδημιουργῆσθαί φασιν, οὐ τὸ μεῖον 5
ἐν δόξῃ καθάπερ τινὰ κλῆρον αὐτῷ πρέποντα προσνενεμηκότες,
πολλοῦ γε καὶ δεῖ· ποῦ γὰρ ὅλως ἐστὶ τὸ ἔλαττον ἢ γοῦν τὸ μεῖζον
ὁρᾶν ἐν ταυτότητι τῆς οὐσίας; ἀλλ᾽ ὡς τοῦ θεοῦ καὶ πατρὸς οὐ
πεφυκότος ἑτέρως ἐργάζεσθαί τι καὶ εἰς τὸ εἶναι καλεῖν πλὴν ὅτι
δι᾽ υἱοῦ ἐν πνεύματι ὡς διὰ δυνάμεως καὶ σοφίας τῆς ἑαυτοῦ. 10
γέγραπται γὰρ ὅτι τῷ λόγῳ τοῦ κυρίου οἱ οὐρανοὶ ἐστερε-
ώθησαν καὶ τῷ πνεύματι τοῦ στόματος αὐτοῦ πᾶσα ἡ
δύναμις αὐτῶν.[y] ναὶ μὴν καὶ ὁ πάνσοφος Ἰωάννης ἐν ἀρχῇ
ἦν ὁ λόγος εἰπὼν καὶ ὁ λόγος ἦν πρὸς τὸν θεὸν καὶ θεὸς
ἦν ὁ λόγος, προσεπήνεγκεν ἀναγκαίως ὅτι πάντα δι᾽ αὐτοῦ 15
ἐγένετο καὶ χωρὶς αὐτοῦ ἐγένετο οὐδὲ ἕν.[z]

13. Ὁμοούσιον τοίνυν ἰσοκλεᾶ τε καὶ ἰσουργὸν τῷ πατρὶ τὸν
υἱὸν ἀποδεδειχότες, διαμέμνηνται χρησίμως τῆς ἐνανθρωπήσεως
αὐτοῦ καὶ τῆς μετὰ σαρκὸς οἰκονομίας διατρανοῦσι τὸ μυστήριον,
τελεωτάτην ἔσεσθαι καὶ ἀπροσδεᾶ διὰ τούτου τῆς πίστεως τὴν 20
παράδοσιν εὖ μάλα διεγνωκότες. οὐ γάρ τοι μόνον ἀπόχρη τοῖς
πιστεύουσιν εἰς αὐτὸν τὸ διακεῖσθαι καὶ φρονεῖν ὡς θεὸς ἐκ θεοῦ
γεγέννηται τοῦ πατρὸς ὁμοούσιός τε αὐτῷ καὶ χαρακτὴρ ὑπάρχων
τῆς ὑποστάσεως αὐτοῦ,[a] ἀλλ᾽ ἦν ἀναγκαῖον εἰδέναι πρὸς τούτοις
ὡς τῆς ἁπάντων ἕνεκα σωτηρίας καὶ ζωῆς καθεὶς ἑαυτὸν εἰς 25
κένωσιν ἔλαβε δούλου μορφὴν[b] καὶ προῆλθεν ἄνθρωπος, γεννηθεὶς
κατὰ σάρκα ἐκ γυναικός. διὰ τοῦτό φασι τὸν δι᾽ ἡμᾶς τοὺς ἀνθρώπους
καὶ διὰ τὴν ἡμετέραν σωτηρίαν κατελθόντα σαρκωθέντα ἐνανθρωπήσαντα. ἄθρει δὲ ὅπως ἐν κόσμῳ τῷ δέοντι καὶ ἐν τάξει τῇ
πρεπωδεστάτῃ πρόεισιν ὁ λόγος αὐτοῖς. κατελθεῖν γὰρ ἔφασαν, ἵνα 30
διὰ τούτου τὸν ἐπάνω πάντων ἐννοῶμεν φύσει τε καὶ δόξῃ καὶ
τοῦτον καταφοιτήσαντα δι᾽ ἡμᾶς, εἰς τὸ θελῆσαί φημι τὴν πρὸς
ἡμᾶς ὁμοίωσιν ὑπελθεῖν καὶ ἐπιλάμψαι τῷ κόσμῳ μετὰ σαρκός.
γέγραπται γὰρ ἐν βίβλῳ ψαλμῶν· ὁ θεὸς ἐμφανῶς ἥξει, ὁ θεὸς

---

[y] Ps. 32(33): 6　　[z] John 1: 1, 3　　[a] Heb. 1: 3　　[b] cf. Phil. 2: 7

Father and not Son; the one born is Son and not Father; and within the selfsame nature each has the property of being what he is.

12. Having set forth the Father as 'maker of all things visible and invisible' they declare that all things were constructed through the Son. They have not assigned him an inferiority in glory as if that were his due portion—far from it! Where, indeed, can one see inferiority or superiority in the selfsame substance? No, the fact is that God the Father effectively summons things into existence exclusively through the Son, through his own Wisdom and power, in the Spirit. The Bible says: '*By the Word of the Lord were the heavens made firm and all their power by the Spirit of his mouth.*' Yes, and John, so utterly wise, after declaring '*in the beginning was the Word*' put the vital rider that '*all things were made through him and without him was not anything made*'.

13. Accordingly, having shown us the Son, consubstantial, equal in renown, equal in operation to the Father, they give a valuable reminder of his being made man and put the mystery of his incarnate dispensation in plain terms fully recognizing that the tradition of the faith would thus omit nothing in its total completeness. A mere disposition to regard him as God begotten of God the Father, consubstantial with him by being the '*express image of his person*' is not enough for believers, they must realize as well that he humbled himself to the point of self-emptying for the salvation and life of all, took slave's form and issued as man in fleshly birth from woman. That is why they say: 'Who for us men and for our salvation came down, was incarnate, was made man'. Notice how their statement proceeds in the requisite order and with the most apposite sequence! The point of their saying 'he came down' is that we should see that it was he, he who transcends all in nature and glory, who descended for us— meaning that he voluntarily took on our likeness and dawned with flesh upon the world. It stands written in the book of Psalms: '*God shall clearly come, our God, and shall not keep silence.*'

ἡμῶν, καὶ οὐ παρασιωπήσεται.ᶜ νοηθείη δ᾽ ἄν, εἴπερ ἕλοιτό
τις, καὶ καθ᾽ ἕτερον τρόπον ἡ κάθοδος, οἷον ἐξ οὐρανοῦ καὶ ἄνωθεν
ἢ καὶ ἀπ᾽ αὐτοῦ τοῦ πατρός. φωναῖς γὰρ ταῖς καθ᾽ ἡμᾶς καὶ τὰ
ὑπὲρ νοῦν καταδηλοῦν ἔθος τοῖς ἱεροῖς γράμμασι. καὶ γοῦν ἔφη
τοῖς ἁγίοις προσδιαλεγόμενος μαθηταῖς· ἐξῆλθον ἐκ τοῦ πατρὸς 5
καὶ ἐλήλυθα εἰς τὸν κόσμον· πάλιν ἀφίημι τὸν κόσμον
καὶ πορεύομαι πρὸς τὸν πατέρα.ᵈ καὶ πάλιν· ὑμεῖς ἐκ τῶν
κάτω ἐστέ, ἐγὼ ἐκ τῶν ἄνω εἰμί.ᵉ ἔτι τε πρὸς τούτοις· ἐγὼ
ἐκ τοῦ πατρὸς ἐξῆλθον καὶ ἥκω.ᶠ γράφει δὲ καὶ ὁ θεσπέσιος
Ἰωάννης· ὁ ἄνωθεν ἐρχόμενος ἐπάνω πάντων ἐστίν.ᵍ 10
καίτοι γὰρ ὑπάρχων ἐν ὑπερτάταις ὑπεροχαῖς καὶ ἐπάνω πάντων
οὐσιωδῶς μετὰ τοῦ ἰδίου πατρός, ἅτε δὴ καὶ ταυτότητι φύσεως
τῆς πρὸς αὐτὸν στεφανούμενος, οὐχ ἁρπαγμὸν ἡγήσατο τὸ
εἶναι ἴσα θεῷ, ἀλλ᾽ ἑαυτὸν ἐκένωσε μορφὴν δούλου
λαβὼν ἐν ὁμοιώματι ἀνθρώπων γενόμενος καὶ σχήματι 15
εὑρεθεὶς ὡς ἄνθρωπος ἐταπείνωσεν ἑαυτόν.ʰ ἐπειδὴ γὰρ
θεὸς ὢν ὁ λόγος τὴν ἡμῶν ἠμπέσχετο σάρκα, μεμένηκε δὲ καὶ
οὕτω θεός, ταύτῃ τοι θεὸν ὁ ἱερώτατος Παῦλος ἐν ὁμοιώματι
ἀνθρώπων γενέσθαι φησὶν εὑρεθῆναί τε ὡς ἄνθρωπον σχήματι.
θεὸς γὰρ ἦν, ὡς ἔφην, ἐν εἴδει τῷ καθ᾽ ἡμᾶς καὶ οὐκ ἄψυχόν γε 20
τὴν σάρκα λαβών, καθὰ φρονεῖν ἔδοξέ τισι τῶν αἱρετικῶν, ἐψυχωμένην δὲ μᾶλλον ψυχῇ νοερᾷ. αὐτὸν οὖν ἄρα τὸν ἐκ τῆς οὐσίας τοῦ
πατρὸς προελθόντα λόγον καὶ υἱὸν μονογενῆ, τὸν θεὸν ἀληθινὸν
ἐκ θεοῦ ἀληθινοῦ, τὸ φῶς τὸ ἐκ τοῦ φωτός, τὸν δι᾽ οὗ τὰ πάντα
ἐγένετο, κατελθεῖν ἔφασαν οἱ πατέρες σαρκωθῆναί τε καὶ ἐν- 25
ανθρωπῆσαι, τουτέστιν ὑπομεῖναι γέννησιν τὴν κατὰ σάρκα ἐκ
γυναικὸς καὶ προελθεῖν ἐν εἴδει τῷ καθ᾽ ἡμᾶς· τοῦτο γὰρ τὸ ἐν-
ανθρωπῆσαί ἐστιν.

14. Εἷς οὖν ἄρα κύριος Ἰησοῦς Χριστός, αὐτὸς ὁ μονογενὴς τοῦ
πατρὸς λόγος γενόμενος ἄνθρωπος, οὐκ ἀποφοιτήσας δὲ τοῦ εἶναι 30
ὃ ἦν· ἀπομεμένηκε γὰρ καὶ ἐν ἀνθρωπότητι θεὸς καὶ ἐν δούλου
μορφῇ δεσπότης καὶ ἐν κενώσει τῇ καθ᾽ ἡμᾶς τὸ πλῆρες ἔχων
θεϊκῶς καὶ ἐν ἀσθενείᾳ σαρκὸς τῶν δυνάμεων κύριος καὶ ἐν τοῖς
τῆς ἀνθρωπότητος μέτροις ἴδιον ἔχων τὸ ὑπὲρ πᾶσαν τὴν κτίσιν.

ᶜ Ps. 49(50): 3   ᵈ John 16: 28   ᵉ John 8: 23   ᶠ John 8: 42
ᵍ John 3: 31   ʰ Phil. 2: 6 ff.

One can, though, interpret the descent differently as some sort of descent from heaven above or the Father himself[4]—the point being that holy Scripture habitually uses human terms to reveal what surpasses comprehension. Certainly in conversation with the holy disciples he said: '*I came from the Father and am come into the world; again I leave the world and go to the Father.*' And again: '*You are from below, I am from above.*' And in addition: '*I came forth from the Father and am come.*' Holy John writes also: '*He who comes from above is above all.*' Though he exists in supernal heights along with his Father, transcending all in substance because crowned with the selfsame nature as his Father '*he did not think equality with God a prize to be grasped but emptied himself, taking a slave's form, being made in man's likeness; and being found in fashion as man he humbled himself*'. For the very reason that it was the Word who is God that wore our flesh yet that even so has continued to be God, most holy Paul affirms that it was God who was 'made in man's likeness' and 'was found in fashion as man'. He was, as I said, God in human shape, by taking not inanimate flesh (as some heretics have seen fit to imagine) but flesh endowed with mental life. It is, then, this very Word and only-begotten Son, proceeding from the Father's substance, true God of true God, light of light, through whom all things were made, it is he that the Fathers affirmed 'came down, was incarnate and made man' —that is to say, underwent fleshly birth of woman and issued in human shape—which is what 'being made man' amounts to.

14. There is therefore one Lord Jesus Christ, personally the only-begotten Word of God, become man without departure from being what he was; for even in manhood he has remained God, even in slave's form master, even in human self-emptying possessor of full deity, even in fleshly weakness lord of spiritual powers and even within the compass of manhood owner of transcendence over the whole creation. What he was before incarnation (he

---

[4] That is, as a quasi-physical, rather than as a moral, descent to a lower level of being.

ἃ μὲν γὰρ ἦν πρὸ σαρκός, ἀναποβλήτως ἔχει, θεὸς γὰρ ἦν καὶ υἱὸς
ἀληθινὸς μονογενής τε καὶ φῶς, ζωὴ καὶ δύναμις· ἃ δέ γε οὐκ ἦν,
ταῦτα προσειληφὼς ὁρᾶται διὰ τὴν οἰκονομίαν. ἴδια γὰρ ἐποιήσατο
τὰ τῆς σαρκός· οὐ γὰρ ἦν ἑτέρου τινός, αὐτοῦ δὲ μᾶλλον ἡ ἀφράστως
αὐτῷ καὶ ἀπορρήτως ἑνωθεῖσα σάρξ. οὕτω καὶ ὁ σοφὸς Ἰωάννης 5
σάρκα φησὶ γενέσθαι τὸν λόγον.ⁱ γέγονε δὲ σὰρξ οὐ κατὰ μετάστασιν
ἢ τροπὴν ἢ ἀλλοίωσιν εἰς τὴν τῆς σαρκὸς φύσιν μεταβαλὼν οὔτε
μὴν φυρμὸν ἢ σύγκρασιν ἢ τὴν θρυλουμένην παρά τισι συνουσίωσιν
ὑπομείνας (ἀμήχανον γάρ, ἐπείπερ ἐστὶ κατὰ φύσιν ἀτρέπτως τε
καὶ ἀναλλοιώτως ἔχων), σάρκα δὲ μᾶλλον, ὡς ἔφην, ἐψυχωμένην 10
ψυχῇ νοερᾷ ἐκ παρθενικοῦ καὶ ἀχράντου σώματος λαβὼν καὶ ἰδίαν
αὐτὴν ποιησάμενος. ἔθος δὲ τῇ θεοπνεύστῳ γραφῇ καὶ ἀπὸ μόνης
ἔσθ᾽ ὅτε τῆς σαρκὸς ὅλον ἄνθρωπον ὑποδηλοῦν. ἐκχεῶ γάρ φησιν
ἀπὸ τοῦ πνεύματός μου ἐπὶ πᾶσαν σάρκα.ʲ οὐ γάρ τοι σαρξὶν
οὐκ ἐψυχωμέναις ψυχῇ νοερᾷ τὴν τοῦ πνεύματος χάριν ἐνήσειν 15
θεὸς ἐπηγγέλλετο, ἀνθρώποις δὲ μᾶλλον τοῖς συνεστῶσιν ἐκ ψυχῆς
καὶ σώματος.

15. Οὐκοῦν οὐκ ἀποδραμὼν ὁ λόγος τοῦ εἶναι ὃ ἦν, γέγονεν
ἄνθρωπος, ἀλλὰ καὶ ἐν εἴδει τῷ καθ᾽ ἡμᾶς πεφηνὼς ἀπομεμένηκε
λόγος καὶ οὐ πρότερον ἄνθρωπος νοεῖται Χριστός, εἶθ᾽ οὕτως 20
προελθὼν εἰς τὸ εἶναι θεός, ἀλλὰ θεὸς ὢν ὁ λόγος γέγονεν ἄνθρωπος,
ἵν᾽ ἐν ταὐτῷ νοῆται θεὸς ὑπάρχων ὁμοῦ καὶ ἄνθρωπος ὁ αὐτός.
οἵ γε μὴν αὐτὸν εἰς υἱοὺς μερίζοντες δύο καὶ τολμῶντες λέγειν ὅτι
τὸν ἐκ σπέρματος τοῦ Δαυὶδ ἄνθρωπον ἑαυτῷ συνῆψεν ὁ θεὸς λόγος
καὶ μετέδωκεν αὐτῷ τῆς ἀξίας καὶ τῆς τιμῆς καὶ τοῦ τῆς υἱότητος 25
ἀξιώματος καὶ παρεσκεύασεν αὐτὸν ὑπομεῖναι σταυρόν, ἀποθανεῖν
καὶ ἀναβιῶναι καὶ ἀνελθεῖν εἰς τὸν οὐρανὸν καὶ ἐν δεξιᾷ καθίσαι τοῦ
πατρός, ἵνα προσκυνῆται παρὰ πάσης τῆς κτίσεως, ἀναφορᾷ θεοῦ
δεχόμενος τὰς τιμάς, πρῶτον μὲν υἱοὺς πρεσβεύουσι δύο, εἶτα τοῦ

ⁱ cf. John 1:14   ʲ Joel 2:28

5 συνουσιόω and its cognates were used by Apollinarius and his followers to
designate the unity of human flesh and divine Word, e.g. frag. 116 (ed.
Lietzmann, p. 235): 'His flesh gives us life because of the Godhead essentially
connected (συνουσιωμένην) with it. What gives life is divine, so the flesh is
divine because it is joined with God.' The term was repugnant to Antiochene
theologians. Diodore had written a book against 'synousiasts', and it was
evidently a charge against Eusebius, a presbyter of Antioch and indiscreetly

was God, true only-begotten Son, light, life and power) he maintains without loss; what he was not, he is seen to have assumed for the sake of the divine plan. He made the properties of the flesh his own, for the flesh united in expressibly mysterious fashion with him was his and no other's. This is what wise John means when he says 'the Word was made flesh': he has become flesh not by changing into the nature of flesh by way of trans-ference, variation or alteration, nor by undergoing mingling, mixture or the 'consubstantiation'[5] some people prate about (an impossibility, seeing that he exists unvarying and unalterable!) but, as I said, by taking flesh endowed with mental life from a spotless virginal body and making it his own. Now it is on occasions the practice of divinely-inspired Scripture to use simply 'flesh' to mean the entire man. It says: '*I will pour out my spirit upon all flesh.*' God was not promising to infuse the grace of the Spirit into flesh devoid of animation by intelligent souls but into human beings consisting of soul and body.[6]

15. So the Word has become man without ceasing to be what he was; he has remained God when manifest in our shape. More-over, Christ is not to be thought of as a man who later proceeded to become God; the Word who is God has become man, so that we recognize him as being at once God and man. Yet those who divide him into two sons, who venture to assert that God the Word joined the man of David's stock to himself, gave him a share of his dignity, honour and rank of sonship, made him undergo the cross, die, come to life again, ascend to heaven and sit at the Father's right hand so that he is worshipped by all creation as the recipient of metaphorical divine honours—these start by propounding two sons and proceed to an ignorant

---

fervent supporter, to whom Cyril wrote soon after the peace, telling him to cool down, that he had implied or used it. At that time Cyril could write (*Ep.* 54, *ACO* I, I, 7 p. 165): 'But as for the term "consubstantiation" (συνουσίωσις) we have no idea what it could mean.' He was to find out later, for 17 fragments (Pusey 3, 476–91) survive from his work *Against the Synousiasts* (date unknown but about 438) directed against Apollinarian altera-tion in the Word or negation of his abiding humanity in incarnation but taking a side-swipe evidently at Diodore and Theodore also. Cf. frag. 16 : it is pardon-able for them (unspecified, but Cyril almost certainly refers to respected fathers, like the Cappadocians, who employed the dubious terminology of 'mixture', 'merger', etc.) to have made the odd mistake in apologetic writing, 'but if in such extensive accounts, and in all their books almost, they assault the truth by confessing two sons, what satisfactory explanation can *they* give?' (Pusey 3, 490). See below *Answers to Tiberius* 6, p. 157.

[6] Cf. *Answers to Tiberius* 7, below p. 159.

μυστηρίου τὴν δύναμιν ἀντιστρέφουσιν ἀμαθῶς. οὐ γὰρ ἐξ ἀνθρώπου
θεὸς γέγονεν ὁ Χριστός, ὡς ἔφην, ἀλλὰ θεὸς ὢν ὁ λόγος γέγονε
σάρξ, τουτέστιν ἄνθρωπος· κεκενῶσθαι δὲ λέγεται ὡς πρὸ τῆς
κενώσεως τὸ πλῆρες ἔχων ἐν ἰδίᾳ φύσει καθ᾽ ὃ νοεῖται θεός. οὐ
γὰρ ἐκ τοῦ κενὸς εἶναί τις εἰς τὸ πλῆρες ἀνέβη, ἐταπείνωσε δὲ 5
μᾶλλον ἑαυτὸν ἐξ ὑψωμάτων θεϊκῶν καὶ ἀρρήτου δόξης· οὐ ταπεινὸς
ὢν ἄνθρωπος ὑψώθη δεδοξασμένος, ἔλαβε δὲ δούλου μορφὴν ὡς
ἐλεύθερος· οὐχὶ δοῦλος ὢν εἰς τὴν τῆς ἐλευθερίας ἀνεπήδησε δόξαν·
ἐν ὁμοιώματι ἀνθρώπων γέγονεν ὁ ἐν μορφῇ καὶ ἰσότητι τοῦ πατρός,
οὐκ ἄνθρωπος ὢν τὸ ἐν ὁμοιώματι γενέσθαι θεοῦ πεπλούτηκε 10
μεθεκτῶς.

16. Τί τοίνυν ἀντιστρέφουσι τῆς οἰκονομίας τοὺς λόγους καὶ
παρασημαίνουσι τὴν ἀλήθειαν, ἁπάσαις ἀντανιστάμενοι ταῖς
θεοπνεύστοις γραφαῖς, αἳ θεὸν ὄντα γινώσκουσι καὶ ἐνανθρωπήσαντα
τὸν υἱὸν ἕνα τε αὐτὸν ὀνομάζουσι πανταχοῦ; καὶ γοῦν ἐν τῷ τῆς 15
κοσμοποιΐας βιβλίῳ γέγραφεν ὁ Μωυσῆς ὡς διεβίβασε μὲν ὁ
θεσπέσιος Ἰακὼβ τὸν χειμάρρουν Ἰαβὼκ τὰ παιδία αὐτοῦ καὶ
ἀπέμεινε μόνος, ἐπάλαιε δὲ ἄνθρωπος μετ᾽ αὐτοῦ ἕως πρωὶ
καὶ ἐκάλεσεν Ἰακὼβ τὸ ὄνομα τοῦ τόπου ἐκείνου εἶδος
θεοῦ· εἶδον γάρ, φησί, θεὸν πρόσωπον πρὸς πρόσωπον 20
καὶ ἐσώθη μου ἡ ψυχή. ἀνέτειλε δὲ αὐτῷ ὁ ἥλιος, ἡνίκα
παρῆλθε τὸ εἶδος τοῦ θεοῦ· Ἰακὼβ δὲ ἐπέσκαζε τῷ
μηρῷ αὐτοῦ.[k] προανεδείκνυ γὰρ τῷ πατριάρχῃ θεὸς ὅτι καὶ
ἐνανθρωπήσει κατὰ καιροὺς ὁ μονογενὴς αὐτοῦ λόγος καὶ ἀντίπαλον
ἕξει τὸν Ἰσραὴλ καὶ ὅτι περὶ αὐτὸν οὐκ ὀρθοποδήσουσι, χωλανοῦσι 25
δὲ ὥσπερ, καθά φησιν αὐτὸς διὰ τῆς τοῦ ψάλλοντος λύρας· υἱοὶ
ἀλλότριοι ἐψεύσαντό μοι, υἱοὶ ἀλλότριοι ἐπαλαιώθησαν
καὶ ἐχώλαναν ἐκ τῶν τρίβων αὐτῶν.[l] τουτὶ γὰρ οἶμαι καταδηλοῦν τὸ ἐπισκάσαι τὸν Ἰακὼβ τῷ μηρῷ αὐτοῦ. πλὴν ἐκεῖνο
ἄθρει· ἀνθρώπου παλαίοντος πρὸς αὐτόν, ἑωρακέναι φησὶ θεὸν 30
πρόσωπον πρὸς πρόσωπον καὶ εἶδος αὐτὸν ὀνομάζει θεοῦ. ἀπομεμένηκε γὰρ ὁ τοῦ θεοῦ λόγος, καὶ ἄνθρωπος γεγονώς, ἐν μορφῇ
τοῦ πατρός, κατά γε φημὶ τὴν νοητὴν εἰκόνα καὶ τὸ κατὰ πᾶν
ὁτιοῦν ἀπαραλλάκτως ἔχον. καὶ γοῦν ἔφη πρὸς Φίλιππον, χαρακτῆρα

---

[k] Gen. 32 : 22 ff., 30 f.   [l] Ps. 17(18) : 45

distortion of the meaning of the mystery. Christ, as I said, has not been made God after being man, but the Word who is God has been made flesh, that is to say man; it is affirmed that he has been 'emptied' because before the 'emptying' he had in his own nature the fullness whereby he is recognized as God. He is not someone who attained fullness after being empty; instead he abased himself from his divine heights and unspeakable glory. He is not a lowly man who was exalted in glory, but free, he took slave's form. He is not a slave who made a leap up to the glory of freedom; he who is in the Father's form, in equality with him, has been made in the likeness of men—he is not a man who has come to share the riches of God's likeness.

16. Why then do they twist the principles of the divine plan and misrepresent the truth in opposition to all the divinely inspired Scriptures which recognize him as being God and designate him throughout as the one Son made man? Moses even has written in the book of Genesis that inspired Jacob sent his children across the river Jabbok and stayed on his own '*and a man wrestled with him until dawn and Jacob called the name of that place "God's shape"*'; "for", he said, "I saw God face to face and my life was preserved". And the sun rose when he passed "God's shape", and Jacob limped with his thigh.' God was revealing to the patriarch beforehand that his only-begotten Word would be made man in due time and would have Israel for his opponent because they would not keep to a straight course about him but would 'limp', as he himself said using the psalmist's poetic tones: '*Foreign sons lied to me, foreign sons grew old and limped out of their paths.*' That I believe is what Jacob's limping with his thigh signifies. But consider this point: though it was a man who was wrestling with him, he says he saw God face to face and calls him 'God's shape'. God's Word, indeed, remained in the Father's form even on his being made man, so far, I mean, as the spiritual image and total invariability are concerned. Moreover he said to Philip in revelation of himself as the stamp of the Father's

τῆς ὑποστάσεως τοῦ πατρὸς[m] ἑαυτὸν ἀποφαίνων καὶ μετὰ σαρκός·
ὁ ἑωρακὼς ἐμὲ ἑώρακε τὸν πατέρα.[n]

17. Ἐπειδὴ δέ τινα τῶν ἐκ γενετῆς τεθεράπευκε τυφλόν, εὑρὼν
αὐτὸν ἐν τῷ ἱερῷ, σὺ πιστεύεις, ἔφασκεν, εἰς τὸν υἱὸν τοῦ
θεοῦ; ἐκείνου γε μὴν πρὸς τοῦτο λέγοντος τίς ἐστιν, κύριε, 5
ἵνα πιστεύσω εἰς αὐτόν; ἀπεκρίνατο λέγων· καὶ ἑώρακας
αὐτὸν καὶ ὁ λαλῶν μετὰ σοῦ ἐκεῖνός ἐστιν.[o] τεθέαται δὲ ὁ
τυφλὸς οὐ γυμνὸν ἢ ἄσαρκον αὐτόν, ἀλλ' ἐν εἴδει μᾶλλον τῷ καθ'
ἡμᾶς, καὶ πεπίστευκεν εἰς τὸν ἑωραμένον οὐχ ὡς εἰς υἱὸν υἱῷ
συνημμένον ἑτέρῳ, ἀλλ' ὡς εἰς ἕνα τὸν φύσει τε καὶ ἀληθῶς οὐ 10
δίχα σαρκὸς ἐπιλάμψαντα τοῖς ἐπὶ τῆς γῆς.

18. Μωϋσῆς γε μὴν ὁ θεσπέσιος ἐν εὐλογίαις φησί· δότε Λευὶ
τὴν δήλωσιν αὐτοῦ καὶ τὴν ἀλήθειαν αὐτοῦ τῷ ἀνδρὶ τῷ
ὁσίῳ, ὃν ἐξεπείρασαν αὐτὸν ἐν πείρᾳ· ἐλοιδόρησαν
αὐτὸν ἐφ' ὕδατος ἀντιλογίας. ὁ λέγων τῷ πατρὶ καὶ τῇ 15
μητρὶ οὐχ ἑώρακά σε, καὶ τοὺς ἀδελφοὺς αὐτοῦ οὐκ
ἐπέγνω.[p] προστέταχε μὲν γὰρ ὁ τῶν ὅλων θεὸς τὸν ποδήρη
γενέσθαι τῷ Ἀαρὼν ποικίλως ἐξυφασμένον· φόρημα δὲ τοῦτο μόνῃ
τῇ ἀρχιερωσύνῃ πρέπον καὶ ἐκνεμηθὲν αὐτῇ. πρὸς δέ γε τῷ στήθει
τοῦ ἀρχιερέως λίθοι τινὲς ἦσαν ἀπηρτημένοι, τὸν ἀριθμὸν δυο- 20
καίδεκα, ὧν ἐν μέσῳ τετάχατο δήλωσίς τε καὶ ἀλήθεια, δύο πάλιν
ἕτεροι λίθοι.[q] αἰνιγματωδῶς δὲ διὰ τούτων ὁ τῶν ἁγίων ἀποστόλων
ἐδείκνυτο χορὸς οἷον ἐν κύκλῳ περιέχων τὸν Ἐμμανουήλ, ὅς ἐστι
δήλωσις καὶ ἀλήθεια· δεδήλωκε γὰρ ἡμῖν τὴν ἀλήθειαν, τὴν ἐν
σκιαῖς καὶ τύποις ἀποστήσας λατρείαν.   25

19. Ὅτι δὲ γέγονεν ἡμῶν ἀρχιερεὺς ὁ μονογενὴς τοῦ θεοῦ
λόγος, ὅτε καὶ ἄνθρωπος γέγονε, πῶς ἔστιν ἀμφιβάλλειν, γεγραφότος
ὡδὶ τοῦ θεσπεσίου Παύλου· κατανοήσατε τὸν ἀπόστολον καὶ
ἀρχιερέα τῆς ὁμολογίας ἡμῶν Ἰησοῦν, πιστὸν ὄντα τῷ
ποιήσαντι αὐτόν;[r] τὸ γάρ τοι τῆς ἱερωσύνης ἀξίωμα τοῖς τῆς 30
ἀνθρωπότητος μέτροις οὐκ ἀπεοικὸς νοοῖτ' ἂν εἰκότως καὶ μεῖον
μὲν ἢ κατὰ τὴν τοῦ θεοῦ λόγου φύσιν τε καὶ δόξαν, οὐκ ἀνάρμοστον
δὲ τῇ μετὰ σαρκὸς οἰκονομίᾳ· γεγόνασι γὰρ αὐτοῦ τὰ ἀνθρώπινα.

[m] cf. Hebr. 1 : 3   [n] John 14 : 9   [o] John 9 : 35 ff.   [p] Deut.
33 : 8 f.   [q] cf. Ex. 28   [r] Heb. 3 : 1 f.

person even when incarnate: '*He who has seen me has seen the Father.*'

17. When he had cured someone blind from birth, on finding him in the Temple he said: '*Do you believe in God's Son?*' The man answered this with the words: '*Who, Lord, is he that I may believe in him?*' He replied: '*You have seen him and the one who converses with you is he.*' The blind man has not seen him unclothed with flesh but in our shape; he has believed in him whom he has seen, not in some son conjoined with another son but in one really, actually single Son dawned incarnate on the world of men.

18. In the blessings, moreover, inspired Moses says: '*Give to Levi his manifestation and his truth to the holy man whom they tempted in the temptation; they reviled him at the water of strife. Who says to his father and mother "I have not seen thee", and he knew not his brethren.*' The God of the universe ordained that Aaron should have a tunic wrought of varying design; this garment was the unique prerogative of the high priesthood. To the high priest's breast were attached certain stones, twelve in number and in the middle of these were set two additional stones 'manifestation' and 'truth'. A mysterious allusion was being made here to the band of the twelve holy apostles encircling, as it were, Emmanuel who is Manifestation and Truth; for he has manifested the truth and abolished worship in shadows and types.

19. How can there be any doubt that God's only-begotten Word has been made our high priest even when he has become man if saint Paul writes: '*Consider Jesus the apostle and high priest of our confession, who is faithful to the one who made him*'? The rank of priesthood, though inferior to God the Word's nature and glory, is rightly to be seen as appropriate to the limitations of manhood and consonant with the incarnate dispensation; for what is human has become his own. '*Give then*', he says, '*to Levi*'

δότε τοίνυν, φησί, τῷ Λευί, τουτέστι τῷ ἱερεῖ τὴν δήλωσιν
καὶ τὴν ἀλήθειαν. ποίῳ δέ φησιν ἄρα Λευὶ ἢ γοῦν ἱερεῖ διε-
σάφησεν εἰπὼν τῷ ἀνδρὶ τῷ ὁσίῳ;ˢ οὐ γὰρ ἐποίησεν ἁμαρτίαν
ὁ κύριος ἡμῶν Ἰησοῦς ὁ Χριστός.ᵗ γράφει γοῦν ὁ Παῦλος περὶ
αὐτοῦ· τοιοῦτος ἡμῖν ἔπρεπεν ἀρχιερεύς, ὅσιος ἄκακος 5
ἀμίαντος κεχωρισμένος ἀπὸ τῶν ἁμαρτωλῶν καὶ ὑψηλό-
τερος τῶν οὐρανῶν γενόμενος.ᵘ τοῦτον ἐξεπείρασαν ἐν
πείρᾳ· ἐλοιδόρησαν αὐτὸν ἐφ' ὕδατος ἀντιλογίας.ᵛ ὦ
παραδόξου πράγματος. ἄνδρα λέγων αὐτὸν θεὸν ἀπέφηνεν εὐθύς,
ὃν δὴ παρώξυνέ τε καὶ ἐξεπείρασεν ὁ Ἰσραὴλ ἔν τε τῇ ἐρήμῳ καὶ 10
ἐπὶ τοῦ ὕδατος τῆς ἀντιλογίας. καὶ πιστώσεται λέγων ὁ ψαλμῳδός·
διέρρηξε πέτραν ἐν ἐρήμῳ καὶ ἐπότισεν αὐτοὺς ὡς ἐν
ἀβύσσῳ πολλῇ καὶ ἐξήγαγεν ὕδωρ ἐκ πέτρας καὶ κατ-
ήγαγεν ὡς ποταμοὺς ὕδατα. καὶ τί μετὰ τοῦτο; καὶ ἐξεπείρασαν, φησίν, ἐν τῇ καρδίᾳ αὐτῶν καὶ κατελάλησαν τοῦ 15
θεοῦ καὶ εἶπον· μὴ δυνήσεται ὁ θεὸς ἑτοιμάσαι τράπεζαν
ἐν ἐρήμῳ, ὅτι ἐπάταξε πέτραν καὶ ἐρρύησαν ὕδατα καὶ
χείμαρροι κατεκλύσθησαν; μὴ καὶ ἄρτον δυνήσεται
δοῦναι ἢ ἑτοιμάσαι τράπεζαν τῷ λαῷ αὐτοῦ;ʷ σύνες οὖν
ὅπως διαλελοιδόρηνται θαυματουργοῦντι τῷ θεῷ, ὃν δὴ καὶ ἄνδρα 20
φησὶν ὁ Μωυσῆς. συνεὶς γὰρ οὕτως καὶ ὁ θεσπέσιος Παῦλος
γράφει· ἔπινον γὰρ ἐκ πνευματικῆς ἀκολουθούσης πέτρας·
ἡ δὲ πέτρα ἦν ὁ Χριστός.ˣ οὐκοῦν ὁ λοιδορηθεὶς ἀνὴρ αὐτὸς
ἦν ἐκεῖνος ὃς οὔπω σεσαρκωμένος ἐπειράζετο παρὰ τῶν ἐξ Ἰσραήλ.

20. Ὅτι γὰρ οὐχ ἕτερος ἦν υἱὸς ὁ πρὸ σαρκός, ἕτερος δὲ παρ' 25
αὐτὸν ὁ ἐκ σπέρματος τοῦ Δαυίδ, καθὰ φάναι τολμῶσί τινες, ἀλλ'
εἷς τε καὶ ὁ αὐτὸς πρὸ μὲν τῆς σαρκώσεως γυμνὸς ἔτι λόγος, μετὰ
δέ γε τὴν ἀπότεξιν τὴν ἐκ τῆς ἁγίας παρθένου σεσαρκωμένος καὶ
ἐνανθρωπήσας, καθὰ γεγράφασιν οἱ θεσπέσιοι πατέρες, σημείῳ
πάλιν ἑτέρῳ πεπληροφόρηκεν ὁ Μωυσῆς. ὥσπερ γὰρ ἐρομένου 30
τινὸς καὶ ἀναμαθεῖν ἐθέλοντος περὶ ποίου γέγονεν ἀνδρὸς ὁ λόγος
αὐτῷ, ὃν δὴ καὶ ἐκπεπειρᾶσθαι καὶ λελοιδορῆσθαί φησι παρὰ τῶν
ἐξ Ἰσραήλ, μόνον οὐχὶ καὶ χεῖρα προτείνων καταδείκνυσι τὸν
Ἰησοῦν καί φησιν· ὁ λέγων τῷ πατρὶ καὶ τῇ μητρὶ οὐχ

ˢ Deut. 33: 8   ᵗ cf. 1 Pet. 2: 22   ᵘ Heb. 7: 26   ᵛ Deut. 33: 8
ʷ Ps. 77(78): 15 ff.   ˣ 1 Cor. 10: 4

(the priest, that is) *'manifestation and truth.'* He explained the kind
of Levi (priest) he meant by saying *'the holy man'*, for Our Lord
Jesus Christ committed no sin. Paul writes of him: *'It was fitting
we should have such a high priest, holy, blameless, unstained, separated
from sinners and exalted above the heavens.'* Him, it was, *'they tempted
in the temptation; they reviled him at the water of strife'.* The marvel
of it! 'Man' he said but immediately showed him to be the very
God Israel had goaded to anger in the desert and tempted at
the water of strife. The psalmist will confirm the point: *'He clave
the rock in the wilderness and made them drink as in a great deep. And
he brought water out of the rock and brought waters down like rivers.'*
What follows the passage? *'And they tempted'* him, it says, *'in their
hearts and spoke against God and said: "Will God be able to prepare
a table in the desert, because he smote the rock and the waters flowed
and torrents ran abundantly? Surely he will not be able to give bread
or prepare a table for his people?"'* See how they have abused the
God who works miracles, the God whom Moses calls 'man' as
well! Saint Paul sees this point and writes: *'For they drank from the
spiritual rock which followed them; and the rock was Christ.'* The reviled
'man' who was being tempted by the Israelites was, therefore,
the pre-incarnate Christ.

20. Moses has, indeed, assured us by yet a further token that
there was not one son prior to the flesh and another of David's
stock different from him, as some have the temerity to assert,
but one and the selfsame Word, unclothed as yet before the
incarnation but after his birth from the holy Virgin incarnate
and made man, as the holy fathers have written. It is as if he
had a questioner wanting to find out the sort of man he was
talking about who he says has been tempted and reviled by
Israelites, and so he all but stretches out a hand to point to
Jesus with the words: *'Who says to his father and mother "I have*

ἑώρακά σε, καὶ τοὺς ἀδελφοὺς αὐτοῦ οὐκ ἐπέγνω.ʸ μεμνήμεθα δὲ γεγραφότος ἑνὸς τῶν ἁγίων εὐαγγελιστῶν ὡς διδάσκοντός
ποτε τοῦ Χριστοῦ καὶ μυσταγωγοῦντός τινας ἐπέστησαν ἡ μήτηρ
αὐτοῦ καὶ οἱ ἀδελφοί, εἶτα προσδραμόντος τινὸς τῶν μαθητῶν καὶ
λέγοντος ἰδοὺ ἡ μήτηρ σου καὶ οἱ ἀδελφοί σου ἑστήκασιν 5
ἔξω ἰδεῖν σε θέλοντες, ἐκτείνας τὴν χεῖρα αὐτοῦ ἐπὶ
τοὺς μαθητὰς αὐτοῦ, εἶπεν· μήτηρ μου καὶ ἀδελφοί μου
οὗτοί εἰσιν οἱ ἀκούοντες τὸν λόγον τοῦ θεοῦ καὶ ποιοῦντες.
ὃς γὰρ ἂν ποιήσῃ τὸ θέλημα τοῦ πατρός μου τοῦ ἐν τοῖς
οὐρανοῖς, οὗτος ἀδελφός μου καὶ ἀδελφὴ καὶ μήτηρ 10
ἐστί.ᶻ τοῦτο, οἶμαι, ἔστιν ὅπερ ἔφη Μωυσῆς· ὁ λέγων τῷ
πατρὶ καὶ τῇ μητρὶ οὐχ ἑώρακά σε, καὶ τοὺς ἀδελφοὺς
αὐτοῦ οὐκ ἐπέγνω.ᵃ

21. Ναὶ μὴν καὶ ὁ πάνσοφος Δανιὴλ ἐν εἴδει τῷ καθ' ἡμᾶς
τεθεᾶσθαί φησι τὸν μονογενῆ τοῦ θεοῦ λόγον. ἰδεῖν μὲν γὰρ ἔφη 15
παλαιὸν ἡμερῶν καθήμενον ἐπὶ θρόνου μυρίας τε μυριάδας τῶν
παραστατῶν καὶ χιλίας χιλιάδας τῶν λειτουργῶν, καὶ διὰ μέσου
τινὰ παρενθεὶς ἕτερα, τούτοις ἐπάγει· ἐθεώρουν ἐν ὁράματι
τῆς νυκτός, καὶ ἰδοὺ μετὰ τῶν νεφελῶν τοῦ οὐρανοῦ ὡς
υἱὸς ἀνθρώπου ἐρχόμενος καὶ ἕως τοῦ παλαιοῦ τῶν 20
ἡμερῶν ἔφθασε καὶ ἐνώπιον αὐτοῦ προσηνέχθη καὶ
αὐτῷ ἐδόθη ἡ τιμὴ καὶ ἡ βασιλεία καὶ πᾶσαι αἱ φυλαὶ
καὶ γλῶσσαι αὐτῷ δουλεύσουσιν.ᵇ ἰδοὺ δὴ πάλιν σαφῶς τε
καὶ ἐναργῶς ἀναβαίνοντα πρὸς τὸν ἐν τοῖς οὐρανοῖς πατέρα καὶ
θεὸν τεθέαται τὸν Ἐμμανουήλ. νεφέλη γὰρ ὑπέλαβεν αὐτόν,ᶜ ὃν 25
δὴ καὶ οὐκ ἄνθρωπον ἁπλῶς, ἀλλ' ὡς υἱὸν ἀνθρώπου φησί· θεὸς
γὰρ ἦν ἐν ὁμοιώσει τῇ πρὸς ἡμᾶς γεγονὼς ὁ λόγος. οὕτω συνεὶς
καὶ ὁ πάνσοφος Παῦλος ἐν ὁμοιώματι ἀνθρώπων γενέσθαι φησὶν
αὐτόν, εὑρεθῆναι δὲ καὶ ὡς ἄνθρωπον σχήματι καὶ ἐν ὁμοιώματι
σαρκὸς ἁμαρτίας ὦφθαι τοῖς ἐπὶ τῆς γῆς.ᵈ εἰ δὲ ἄνθρωπος ἦν συν- 30
αφείᾳ τῇ πρὸς θεὸν ὡς θεὸς τιμώμενος, ἔφη γ' ἂν ὁ προφήτης ὡς
θεὸν ἢ ὡς υἱὸν θεοῦ τεθεᾶσθαι τὸν μετὰ τῶν νεφελῶν ἐρχόμενον·
ἀλλ' οὐ τοῦτό φησιν, ἐκεῖνο δὲ μᾶλλον τὸ ὡς υἱὸν ἀνθρώπου. οἶδεν
ἄρα θεὸν ὄντα καὶ ἐνανθρωπήσαντα τὸν υἱὸν ἢ γοῦν ἐν ὁμοιώματι

ʸ Deut. 33: 9   ᶻ Matt. 12: 46 ff., Luke 8: 21   ᵃ Deut. 33: 9
ᵇ Daniel 7: 13 f.   ᶜ cf. Acts 1: 9   ᵈ cf. Phil. 2: 7, Rom. 8: 3

not seen thee", *and he knew not his brethren.*' We call to mind one of the holy evangelists describing how on one occasion Christ was teaching and giving spiritual guidance to some people when his mother and brothers appeared. A disciple ran up and said: '*Behold your mother and your brothers are at this very moment standing outside desirous of seeing you.*' *He stretched out his hand to his disciples and said:* '*My mother and my brothers are those who hear the word and do it. For anyone who does the will of my father in heaven is my brother, sister and mother.*' This, I believe, is what Moses referred to when he said: '*Who says to his father and mother "I have not seen thee" and he knew not his brethren.*'

21. Yes, and Daniel, so utterly wise, declares he saw God's only-begotten Word in our shape. He said he saw an ancient of days seated on a throne with ten thousand times ten thousands of attendants and a thousand thousands of ministers and adds (I omit the intervening passages): '*I beheld in a night-vision and lo with the clouds of heaven one coming like a son of man and he came on to the ancient of days and was presented before him and to him was given honour and kingdom and all tribes and languages will serve him.*' Notice again that it is Emmanuel he saw clearly and plainly ascending to God the Father in heaven. A cloud received the one Daniel calls not simply 'man' but 'son of man'; he was God the Word made in our likeness. Paul, so utterly wise, sees this point and declares he was made in men's likeness, was found in fashion as a man and appeared to men on earth in the likeness of sinful flesh. Had he been a man honoured as God by conjunction with God, the prophet would have said that he saw one coming with the clouds of heaven like God or a son of God. He does not say this; he says 'like a son of man'. He certainly recognizes the Son as being God and as having become man, that is

ἀνθρώπων γενόμενον κατὰ τὴν τοῦ Παύλου φωνήν. πλὴν καὶ ἐν
σαρκὶ πεφηνὼς ἕως τοῦ παλαιοῦ τῶν ἡμερῶν ἔφθασε,
τουτέστιν εἰς τὸν τοῦ ἀιδίου πατρὸς ἀναπεφοίτηκε θρόνον, καὶ
αὐτῷ ἐδόθη ἡ τιμὴ καὶ ἡ βασιλεία καὶ πᾶσαι αἱ φυλαὶ
καὶ γλῶσσαι αὐτῷ δουλεύσουσιν. καὶ τοῦτο ἦν ἄρα τὸ   5
εἰρημένον παρ' αὐτοῦ· πάτερ, δόξασόν με τῇ δόξῃ ᾗ εἶχον
πρὸ τοῦ τὸν κόσμον εἶναι παρὰ σοί.[e]

22. Ὅτι δὲ σαρκωθεὶς ὁ τοῦ θεοῦ λόγος σύνεδρός ἐστι καὶ
ἰσοκλεὴς τῷ θεῷ καὶ πατρὶ καὶ μετὰ σαρκός, ὡς εἷς ὑπάρχων υἱὸς
καὶ ὅτε γέγονεν ἄνθρωπος, σαφηνιεῖ γράφων ὁ πάνσοφος Παῦλος·   10
τοιοῦτον ἔχομεν ἀρχιερέα, ὃς ἐκάθισεν ἐν δεξιᾷ τοῦ
θρόνου τῆς μεγαλωσύνης ἐν ὑψηλοῖς.[f] ναὶ μὴν καὶ αὐτὸς ὁ
κύριος ἡμῶν Ἰησοῦς ὁ Χριστὸς ἐρομένων αὐτὸν τῶν Ἰουδαίων
εἴπερ ἐστὶν αὐτὸς ἀληθῶς ὁ Χριστός, ἐὰν εἴπω, φησίν, οὐ μὴ
πιστεύσητε· καὶ ἐὰν ἐπερωτήσω, οὐ μὴ ἀποκριθῆτε. ἀπὸ   15
τοῦ νῦν δὲ ἔσται ὁ υἱὸς τοῦ ἀνθρώπου καθήμενος ἐκ
δεξιῶν τῆς δυνάμεως τοῦ θεοῦ.[g] οὐκοῦν ἐν τοῖς τῆς θεότητος
θώκοις καὶ ἐνανθρωπήσαντα τὸν υἱὸν ὁ τῶν ἁγίων προφητῶν
ἐθεᾶτο χορός.

23. Ἴδωμεν δὲ καὶ τοὺς τῆς νέας διαθήκης κήρυκας τοὺς τῆς   20
ὑφ' ἥλιον μυσταγωγούς, οἷς αὐτὸς ἔφη Χριστός· οὐχ ὑμεῖς ἐστε
οἱ λαλοῦντες, ἀλλὰ τὸ πνεῦμα τοῦ πατρὸς ὑμῶν τὸ λαλοῦν
ἐν ὑμῖν.[h] εὑρήσομεν τοίνυν λέγοντα τὸν θεσπέσιον βαπτιστήν·
ὀπίσω μου ἔρχεται ἀνήρ, ὃς ἔμπροσθέν μου γέγονεν, ὅτι
πρῶτός μου ἦν.[i] εἶτα πῶς ὁ μετ' αὐτὸν ἰὼν πρῶτος ἦν αὐτοῦ;   25
ὅτι γὰρ ὑστερίζει κατὰ τὸν τῆς σαρκὸς χρόνον Ἰωάννου Χριστός,
πῶς οὐχ ἅπασιν ἐναργές; τί οὖν πρὸς ταῦτα φαίη τις ἄν; ἔλυσεν
ἡμῖν αὐτὸς ὁ σωτὴρ τὸ ζητούμενον. ἔφη γὰρ Ἰουδαίοις προσλαλῶν·
ἀμὴν λέγω ὑμῖν, πρὶν Ἀβραὰμ γενέσθαι, ἐγώ εἰμι.[j] ἦν
μὲν γὰρ καὶ πρὸ Ἀβραὰμ θεϊκῶς, νοεῖται δὲ μετ' αὐτὸν καθὸ   30
πέφηνεν ἄνθρωπος. εἶτα τοῦ θεοῦ καὶ πατρὸς βοῶντος ἀναφανδὸν
τὴν δόξαν μου ἑτέρῳ οὐ δώσω[k] (θεὸς γὰρ ἕτερος παρ' αὐτὸν
οὐδείς), ἔφη πρὸς ἡμᾶς ὁ Χριστός· ὅταν δὲ ἔλθῃ ὁ υἱὸς τοῦ

[e] John 17: 5   [f] Heb. 8: 1   [g] Luke 22: 67 ff.   [h] Matt.
10: 20   [i] John 1: 30   [j] John 8: 58   [k] Is. 42: 8

to say as having been made (as Paul says) in the likeness of men. However, even when manifest in flesh '*he came on to the ancient of days*' (meaning he returned to his eternal Father's throne) '*and to him was given honour and kingdom and all tribes and languages will serve him*'. This is surely what was meant by his words: '*Father, glorify me with the glory I had with thee before the world existed.*'

22. Paul, so utterly wise, will make it plain that God's Word after incarnation has an equal honour and a throne with God the Father along with his flesh because he is one Son even when he has become man. He writes: '*We have such a high priest, who has taken his seat at the right hand of the throne of majesty on high.*' Yes, and our Lord Jesus Christ, in answer to the Jews who asked if he was really the Christ, himself says: '*If I say so, you will not believe; and if I ask you, you will not answer. But henceforth the Son of man will be seated at the right hand of God's power.*' So the band of the holy prophets saw the Son on the throne of Godhead even after he was made man.

23. Let us also take a look at the heralds of the new testament, earth's spiritual guides, to whom Christ himself said: '*It is not you who speak but your Father's Spirit speaking in you.*' We shall find the inspired Baptist saying: '*After me comes a man who has been made prior to me because he was before me.*' How could his successor have been before him? Is it not plain to everybody that Christ is later in point of fleshly time to John? What answer does one give here? The Saviour personally solved the problem. He addressed the Jews in these words: '*Verily I say to you, before Abraham was created, I am.*' Though he was before Abraham, divinely, yet so far as his manifestation as man is concerned, he is seen to be his successor. God the Father expressly proclaims: '*I will not give my glory to any other*' (for there is no other God but him), and so Christ said to us: '*When*' the son of man '*comes in*

ἀνθρώπου ἐν τῇ δόξῃ τοῦ πατρὸς αὐτοῦ μετὰ τῶν ἁγίων
ἀγγέλων.^l υἱοῦ δὲ ἀνθρώπου καταβαίνειν προσδοκωμένου ἐξ
οὐρανῶν, γράφει πάλιν ὁ πάνσοφος Παῦλος· ἐπεφάνη γὰρ ἡ
χάρις τοῦ θεοῦ ἡ σωτήριος πᾶσιν ἀνθρώποις, ἵνα ἀρνη-
σάμενοι τὴν ἀσέβειαν καὶ τὰς κοσμικὰς ἐπιθυμίας 5
σωφρόνως καὶ δικαίως καὶ εὐσεβῶς καὶ ἐπιεικῶς ζήσωμεν
ἐν τῷ νῦν αἰῶνι, προσδεχόμενοι τὴν μακαρίαν ἐλπίδα
καὶ ἐπιφάνειαν τῆς δόξης τοῦ μεγάλου θεοῦ καὶ σωτῆρος
ἡμῶν Ἰησοῦ Χριστοῦ.^m ἔφη δὲ καὶ ἑτέρωθι περὶ τῶν ἐξ αἵματος
Ἰσραὴλ τοὺς λόγους ποιούμενος ὅτι αὐτῶν εἰσιν αἱ ἐπαγγελίαι καὶ 10
ἡ νομοθεσία καὶ ἡ διαθήκη καὶ ἐξ αὐτῶν τὸ κατὰ σάρκα Χριστὸς
ὁ ὢν ἐπὶ πάντων θεὸς εὐλογητὸς εἰς τοὺς αἰῶνας. ἀμήν.ⁿ

24. Οὐκοῦν κατ' ἴχνος ἰόντες ἀποσκλινῶς τῆς τῶν πατέρων
ὁμολογίας αὐτόν φαμεν τὸν ἐκ τοῦ θεοῦ πατρὸς γεννηθέντα υἱὸν
μονογενῆ σαρκωθῆναί τε καὶ ἐνανθρωπῆσαι, παθεῖν, ἀποθανεῖν, τῇ 15
τρίτῃ ἡμέρᾳ ἀναστῆναι ἐκ νεκρῶν. ἀπαθὴς μὲν γὰρ ὁμολογουμένως
τό γε ἧκον εἰς ἰδίαν φύσιν ὁ τοῦ θεοῦ λόγος καὶ οὐδεὶς οὕτως
ἐμβρόντητος, ὡς νομίσαι δύνασθαι πάθους εἶναι δεκτικὴν τὴν ὑπὲρ
πάντα φύσιν· ἐπειδὴ δὲ γέγονεν ἄνθρωπος ἰδίαν ποιησάμενος σάρκα
τὴν ἐκ τῆς ἁγίας παρθένου, ταύτῃ τοι τοῖς τῆς οἰκονομίας ἑπόμενοι 20
λόγοις σαρκὶ τῇ ἰδίᾳ παθεῖν ἀνθρωπίνως διαβεβαιούμεθα τὸν
ἐπέκεινα τοῦ παθεῖν ὡς θεόν. εἰ γὰρ θεὸς ὑπάρχων γέγονεν ἄνθρωπος,
ἀποπεφοίτηκε δὲ οὐδαμῶς τοῦ εἶναι θεός, εἰ γέγονε κτίσεως μέρος
καὶ μεμένηκεν ὑπὲρ κτίσιν, εἰ νομοθέτης ὢν ὡς θεὸς γέγονεν ὑπὸ
νόμον^o καὶ νομοθέτης ἦν ἔτι καὶ δεσπότης ὢν θεϊκῶς δούλου μορφὴν^p 25
ὑπέδυ καὶ ἀναπόβλητον ἔχει τὸ τῆς δεσποτείας ἀξίωμα, εἰ μονο-
γενὴς ὑπάρχων γέγονε πρωτότοκος ἐν πολλοῖς ἀδελφοῖς^q καί ἐστι
μονογενής, τί τὸ παράδοξον, εἰ σαρκὶ παθὼν ἀνθρωπίνως ἀπαθὴς
καὶ οὕτως νοεῖται θεϊκῶς;

25. Καὶ γοῦν ὁ πάνσοφος Παῦλος τὸν ἐν μορφῇ καὶ ἐν ἰσότητι 30
τοῦ θεοῦ καὶ πατρὸς ὑπάρχοντα λόγον τὸν αὐτὸν ὑπήκοον γενέσθαι
φησὶ καὶ μέχρι θανάτου, θανάτου δὲ σταυροῦ.^r ἐν ἑτέρᾳ δὲ
τῶν ἰδίων ἐπιστολῶν περὶ αὐτοῦ φησιν· ὅς ἐστιν εἰκὼν τοῦ

---

^l Mark 8: 38   ^m Titus 2: 11 ff.   ⁿ Rom. 9: 4 f.   ^o cf. Gal. 4: 4
^p cf. Phil. 2: 7   ^q cf. Rom. 8: 29   ^r Phil. 2: 8

his Father's glory with the holy angels'. Because of the expectation of the son of man's descent from heaven, Paul, so utterly wise, writes again: '*For God's saving grace appeared to all men, so that we might renounce irreligion and worldly lusts and live temperate, righteous, devout, and virtuous lives in the present age, awaiting our blessed hope, our great God and Saviour Jesus Christ's manifestation of glory.*' In another passage too he spoke of Israel's blood-descendants saying that theirs were the promises, the law-giving, the covenant and of them '*is Christ so far as flesh is concerned, Christ who is God over all blessed for ever, Amen'.*

24. Consequently we follow the fathers' confession without deviation and affirm that the Father's only-begotten Son, begotten of God the Father, was personally incarnate and made man, that he suffered, died and rose again from the dead on the third day. God's Word is, of course, undoubtedly impassible in his own nature and nobody is so mad as to imagine the all-transcending nature capable of suffering; but by very reason of the fact that he has become man making flesh from the holy Virgin his own, we adhere to the principles of the divine plan and maintain that he, who as God transcends suffering, suffered humanly in his own flesh. If whilst being God he has become man yet has not departed from any aspect of his being God; if he has been made part of creation and yet abides above creation; if whilst being as God the giver of law he has been made under law and yet was still giver of law, and whilst being, divinely, master he put on slave's form, and yet retains unimpaired the dignity of mastership; if whilst being only-begotten he has been made the first-born among many brethren and yet is still only-begotten, does it tax credibility if by the same token he suffered humanly and yet is seen as divinely impassible?

25. Paul, so utterly wise, affirms that the very Word who exists in the form of, and in equality with, God the Father was made obedient '*unto death, the death of the cross'*. In another of his epistles he says of him: '*Who is the image of the invisible God,*

θεοῦ τοῦ ἀοράτου, πρωτότοκος πάσης κτίσεως, ὅτι ἐν
αὐτῷ ἐκτίσθη τὰ πάντα τά τε ἐν τῷ οὐρανῷ καὶ τὰ ἐπὶ
τῆς γῆς καὶ αὐτός ἐστι πρὸ πάντων καὶ τὰ πάντα ἐν αὐτῷ
συνέστηκε,ˢ καὶ αὐτὸν δεδόσθαι φησὶ κεφαλὴν τῇ ἐκκλησίᾳ,ᵗ
γενέσθαι δὲ καὶ ἀπαρχὴν τῶν κεκοιμημένων καὶ πρωτότοκον ἐκ 5
νεκρῶν.ᵘ καίτοι ζωὴ καὶ ζωοποιὸς ὁ ἐκ θεοῦ πατρός ἐστι λόγος ἅτε
δὴ καὶ ἐκ ζωῆς ἀναφὺς τοῦ τεκόντος αὐτόν· εἶτα πῶς γέγονε
πρωτότοκος ἐκ νεκρῶν καὶ ἀπαρχὴ τῶν κεκοιμημένων; ἐπειδὴ γὰρ
τὴν τοῦ θανάτου δεκτικὴν ἰδίαν ἐποιήσατο σάρκα, χάριτι θεοῦ,
καθά φησιν ὁ πάνσοφος Παῦλος, ὑπὲρ παντὸς ἐγεύσατο θανάτουᵛ 10
τῇ παθεῖν αὐτὸν δυναμένῃ σαρκί, οὐκ ἀποβαλὼν αὐτὸς τὸ εἶναι
ζωή. οὐκοῦν κἂν εἰ λέγοιτο σαρκὶ παθεῖν, οὐ φύσει θεότητος
εἰσδέξεται τὸ παθεῖν, ἀλλ᾽ ὡς ἔφην ἀρτίως, ἰδίᾳ σαρκὶ τῇ τοῦ
πάθους δεκτικῇ.

26. Καὶ γοῦν ὁ μακάριος προφήτης Ἡσαίας ἐνανθρωπήσαντα 15
θεὸν τὸν σαρκὶ παθόντα γινώσκων ἔφη που περὶ αὐτοῦ· ὡς πρόβατον ἐπὶ σφαγὴν ἤχθη καὶ ὡς ἀμνὸς ἐναντίον τοῦ κείρον-
τος αὐτὸν ἄφωνος, οὕτως οὐκ ἀνοίγει τὸ στόμα αὐτοῦ.
ἐν τῇ ταπεινώσει αὐτοῦ ἡ κρίσις αὐτοῦ ἤρθη· τὴν γενεὰν
αὐτοῦ τίς διηγήσεται; ὅτι αἴρεται ἀπὸ τῆς γῆς ἡ ζωὴ 20
αὐτοῦ.ʷ καίτοι εἴπερ τις ἦν ἄνθρωπος καὶ ἰδικῶς νοούμενος υἱός,
συνημμένος δὲ θεῷ, καθά φασιν οἱ τῶν ἀνοσίων δογμάτων εἰσηγηταί,
πῶς ἔτι δυσεύρετος ὁ τὴν γενεὰν αὐτοῦ διηγεῖσθαι δυνάμενος;
γέγονεν οὖν ἐκ σπέρματος Ἰεσσαὶ καὶ Δαυίδ, τὴν δέ γε τοῦ θεοῦ
λόγου γέννησιν ἤτοι τὸν τῆς γεννήσεως τρόπον τίς ὁ φάναι δυνά- 25
μενος; αἴρεται γὰρ ἀπὸ τῆς γῆς ἡ ζωὴ αὐτοῦ, τουτέστιν ἡ
ὕπαρξις (τέθεικε γὰρ ἀντὶ τῆς ὑπάρξεως τὴν ζωήν), ὑψοῦ δὲ
διάττει καὶ ὑπερνήχεται τοὺς ἐπὶ τῆς γῆς· ἀπερινόητος γὰρ καὶ
ἀπρόσβλητος παντελῶς ταῖς ἀνθρώπων διανοίαις ὁ περὶ τῆς
ἀρρήτου φύσεως λόγος. 30

27. Προσεποίσω δὲ τοῖς εἰρημένοις καὶ τόδε. εἷς κύριος, μία
πίστις, ἓν βάπτισμα,ˣ καθά φησιν ὁ ἱερώτατος Παῦλος. ἑνὸς
οὖν ὄντος κυρίου πίστεώς τε μιᾶς καὶ ἑνὸς βαπτίσματος, τίς ὁ

ˢ Col. 1: 15 ff.   ᵗ cf. Eph. 1: 22   ᵘ cf. 1 Cor. 15: 20
ᵛ cf. Heb. 2: 9   ʷ Is. 53: 7 f.   ˣ Eph. 4: 5

the first-born of all creation, because all things in heaven and on earth were created in him and he is himself before all things and all things hold together in him'; Paul says too that he has been given to the Church as its head, been made the first-fruits of those asleep and first-born from the dead. The Word of God the Father is Life and life-giving, springing as he does from the life of his parent; how then can he have become the first-born from the dead and first-fruits of those asleep? The answer is that after he had made flesh capable of death his own, he did by God's grace, as Paul so utterly wise affirms, 'taste' death for every man in flesh able to experience it, without ceasing personally to be life. Consequently although it is affirmed that he suffered in flesh there is no question of his suffering in the Godhead's nature but, as I just said, in his flesh which is capable of suffering.

26. The blessed prophet Isaiah, aware that he who suffered in flesh was God made man, declared of him in one passage: '*He was led to slaughter like a sheep, like a lamb dumb in the presence of its shearer, so he does not open his mouth. In his humiliation his judgement was removed; who will tell out his generation? Because his life is being removed from the earth.*' Were he some man, seen as a son on his own but joined with God, as the proponents of unhallowed doctrines assert, it would not still be hard to find somebody capable of telling out his generation, would it? He is, after all, descended from Jesse's and David's stock. But can anyone speak of the generation or mode of generation of God the Word? For '*his life is being removed from the earth*'—meaning his existence ('life' stands for 'existence') flies aloft and transcends earthly men in its sweep; for human minds have no way of understanding, no way of approaching, the condition of his inexpressible nature.

27. I will add this further point to what I have said. As Paul most holy says: '*One Lord, one faith, one baptism*'. Since, then, there is one Lord, one faith and one baptism, who is the Lord, whom

κύριος καὶ εἰς τίνα πεπιστεύκαμέν τε καὶ βεβαπτίσμεθα; ἀλλ'
ἴσως πρέπειν ὅτι μάλιστα φαίη τις ἂν τῷ ἐκ θεοῦ πατρὸς ὄντι
λόγῳ τήν τε κυριότητα καὶ τὴν πίστιν τὴν πρὸς ἡμῶν, ἐπ' αὐτῷ
δὲ τελεῖσθαι καὶ τὸ σωτήριον βάπτισμα. οὕτω γάρ που τοῖς ἁγίοις
ἀποστόλοις ἐνετείλατο λέγων· πορευθέντες μαθητεύσατε 5
πάντα τὰ ἔθνη, βαπτίζοντες αὐτοὺς εἰς τὸ ὄνομα τοῦ
πατρὸς καὶ τοῦ υἱοῦ καὶ τοῦ ἁγίου πνεύματος.ʸ ὅ γε μὴν
θεσπέσιος Παῦλος τὴν τῆς κυριότητος δόξαν καὶ τῆς πίστεως τὴν
ὁμολογίαν καὶ τὴν τοῦ ἁγίου βαπτίσματος δύναμιν ἐμφανῆ καθίστησι, λέγων· μὴ εἴπῃς ἐν τῇ καρδίᾳ σου· τίς ἀναβήσεται 10
εἰς τὸν οὐρανόν; τοῦτ' ἔστι Χριστὸν καταγαγεῖν· ἢ τίς
καταβήσεται εἰς τὴν ἄβυσσον; τοῦτ' ἔστι Χριστὸν ἐκ
νεκρῶν ἀναγαγεῖν. ἀλλὰ τί λέγει ἡ γραφή; ἐγγύς σου τὸ
ῥῆμά ἐστιν ἐν τῷ στόματί σου καὶ ἐν τῇ καρδίᾳ σου,
ὅτι ἐὰν εἴπῃς· κύριος Ἰησοῦς, καὶ πιστεύσῃς ἐν τῇ 15
καρδίᾳ σου ὅτι ὁ θεὸς αὐτὸν ἤγειρεν ἐκ νεκρῶν, σωθήσῃ.ᶻ
γράφει δὲ πάλιν· οὐκ οἴδατε ὅτι ὅσοι ἐβαπτίσθημεν εἰς
Χριστὸν Ἰησοῦν, εἰς τὸν θάνατον αὐτοῦ ἐβαπτίσθημεν;ᵃ
ἰδοὺ δὴ σαφῶς περίστησιν εὐτεχνῶς τῆς τε κυριότητος καὶ τῆς
πίστεως τὴν ὁμολογίαν, καὶ αὐτὴν δὲ τὴν τοῦ ἁγίου βαπτίσματος 20
χάριν εἰς τὸν παθόντα νὸν θάνατον καὶ ἐγηγερμένον ἐκ νεκρῶν.

28. Ἆρ' οὖν εἰς υἱοὺς πιστεύομεν δύο; ἆρα τὸν ἐκ θεοῦ πατρὸς
ἀπαστράψαντα παραδραμόντες λόγον ὡς υἱῷ παρ' αὐτὸν ἑτέρῳ τῷ
παθόντι προσάψομεν τὴν τῆς κυριότητος δόξαν, καὶ αὐτὴν δὲ τῆς
πίστεως τὴν ὁμολογίαν καὶ τὸ οὐράνιον βάπτισμα; εἶτα πῶς οὐκ 25
εὔηθες, μᾶλλον δὲ ἀναμφιλόγως δυσσεβὲς τὸ οὕτω φρονεῖν ἢ λέγειν;
τί οὖν ἐροῦμεν; εἷς κύριος ἀληθῶς μία τε πίστις καὶ ἓν βάπτισμα.ᵇ
καὶ γάρ ἐστιν εἷς υἱὸς καὶ κύριος οὐκ ἄνθρωπον κατὰ συνάφειαν
λαβὼν ὁ λόγος καὶ μέτοχον αὐτὸν ἀποφήνας τῶν ἰδίων ἀξιωμάτων
καὶ μεταδοὺς υἱότητός τε καὶ κυριότητος αὐτῷ, καθά φασι καὶ 30
γεγράφασι ληροῦντές τινες, ἀλλ' αὐτὸς ἐνανθρωπήσας καὶ σαρκωθεὶς
ὁ ἐκ θεοῦ θεὸς λόγος, τὸ φῶς τὸ ἐκ τοῦ φωτός. εἰς τὸν τούτου
θάνατον βεβαπτίσμεθα, παθόντος μὲν ἀνθρωπίνως αὐτοῦ ἰδίᾳ σαρκί,
μεμενηκότος δὲ ἀπαθοῦς θεϊκῶς καὶ ζῶντος ἀεί· ζωὴ γάρ ἐστιν
ἐκ ζωῆς τοῦ θεοῦ καὶ πατρός. οὕτω νενίκηται θάνατος, ἐπιπηδῆσαι 35

ʸ Matt. 28: 19   ᶻ Rom. 10: 6 ff.   ᵃ Rom. 6: 3   ᵇ cf. Eph. 4: 5

have we believed in and been baptized into? You would doubt-less answer that lordship over us and faith on our part attach to the Word who is of God the Father, and that the performance of saving baptism has him in view. That is why he charged the holy apostles at one point in these words: '*Go out, make disciples of all the nations, baptizing them in the name of the Father and of the Son and of the Holy Ghost.*' Inspired Paul makes clear the glory of lordship, the acknowledgement of faith and holy baptism's power when he says: '*Do not say in your heart, "Who will ascend into heaven?" (that is to bring Christ down) or "Who will descend into the abyss?" (that is to raise Christ from the dead). But what does Scrip-ture say? "The word is near you in your mouth and in your heart"— because if you say "Jesus is Lord" and believe in your heart that God raised him from the dead you will be saved.*' He writes again: '*Do you not know that all of us who were baptized into Christ Jesus were baptized into his death?*' Note how clearly and skilfully he attaches the acknowledgement of lordship and faith, and the very grace of holy baptism, to him who suffered death and has been raised from the dead.

28. Do we believe, then, in two sons? Shall we by-pass the Word shone forth from God the Father and annex the glory of lordship, the acknowledgement of the faith and heavenly baptism to a son different from him, a son who suffered? To think or talk like this must surely be stupidity—no, more, indis-putable blasphemy? What are we to say then? There really is one Lord, one faith and one baptism. He is one Son and Lord—not, as some fools have asserted in writing, as being the Word who assumed man by way of conjunction, made him a partner in his dignities and shared his sonship and lordship with him, but as being the Word personally, God of God, light of light, who was made man and incarnate. Into his death we have been baptized, his who suffered humanly in his own flesh yet has remained divinely impassible and always alive, because he is Life from God the Father's Life. This is the way Death has been vanquished, which had made bold to attack the body of Life;

τολμήσας τῷ σώματι τῆς ζωῆς· καταργεῖται δὲ οὕτω καὶ ἐν ἡμῖν
ἡ φθορὰ καὶ τὸ αὐτοῦ τοῦ θανάτου κράτος ἀσθενεῖ. καὶ γοῦν ἔφη
Χριστός· ἀμὴν λέγω ὑμῖν· ἐὰν μὴ φάγητε τὴν σάρκα τοῦ
υἱοῦ τοῦ ἀνθρώπου καὶ πίητε αὐτοῦ τὸ αἷμα, οὐκ ἔχετε
ζωὴν ἐν ἑαυτοῖς.ᶜ ζωοποιὸν οὖν ἄρα τὸ ἅγιον σῶμα καὶ αἷμα 5
Χριστοῦ. σῶμα γάρ, ὡς ἔφην, ἔστιν οὐκ ἀνθρώπου τινὸς μετόχου
ζωῆς, ἴδιον δὲ μᾶλλον τῆς κατὰ φύσιν ζωῆς, δῆλον δὲ ὅτι τοῦ
μονογενοῦς.

29. Ταῦτα φρονεῖ μεθ' ἡμῶν ὁ φιλόχριστος τῶν ἁγίων πατέρων
χορός, καὶ αὐτὸς δὲ ὁ νυνὶ τὸν τῆς ἁγίας Κωνσταντινουπολιτῶν 10
ἐκκλησίας κατακοσμήσας θρόνον ὁ ὁσιώτατος καὶ θεοσεβέστατος
ἀδελφὸς καὶ συνεπίσκοπος Πρόκλος. γέγραφε γὰρ καὶ αὐτὸς πρὸς
τοὺς τῆς Ἑῴας θεοσεβεστάτους ἐπισκόπους αὐταῖς λέξεσιν ὧδε·
"καὶ σαρκοῦται μὲν ἀτρέπτως ὁ ἀνείδεος, τίκτεται δὲ κατὰ σάρκα ὁ
ἄναρχος· προκόπτει δὲ τῇ κατὰ σῶμα ἡλικίᾳ ὁ φύσει παντέλειος 15
καὶ παθῶν ἀνέχεται ὁ παθῶν ἀνώτερος, οὐχ ᾧ ἦν, ὑπομείνας τὰς
ὕβρεις, ἀλλ' ᾧ γέγονε, καταδεξάμενος τὰ τοῦ σώματος πάθη."
ἐλέγχεται τοίνυν τῶν ἕτερα παρὰ ταῦτα φρονούντων ἢ γεγραφότων
ἡ κακοπιστία πανταχοῦ νοσοῦσα τὸ βέβηλον καὶ τὸ τοῖς τῆς
ἀληθείας ἀπᾷδον δόγμασι. 20

30. Διαπεράναντες δὲ τὸν περὶ Χριστοῦ λόγον οἱ τρισμακάριοι
πατέρες τοῦ ἁγίου πνεύματος διαμνημονεύουσι· πιστεύειν γὰρ
ἔφασαν εἰς αὐτὸ καθάπερ ἀμέλει εἰς τὸν πατέρα καὶ τὸν υἱόν.
ὁμοούσιον γάρ ἐστιν αὐτοῖς καὶ προχεῖται μὲν ἢ γοῦν ἐκπορεύεται
καθάπερ ἀπὸ πηγῆς τοῦ θεοῦ καὶ πατρός, χορηγεῖται δὲ τῇ κτίσει 25
διὰ τοῦ υἱοῦ· ἐνεφύσησε γοῦν τοῖς ἁγίοις ἀποστόλοις λέγων·
λάβετε πνεῦμα ἅγιον.ᵈ οὐκοῦν ἐκ θεοῦ καὶ θεὸς τὸ πνεῦμά ἐστι
καὶ οὐκ ἀλλότριον τῆς ἀνωτάτω πασῶν οὐσίας, ἀλλ' ἐξ αὐτῆς τε
καὶ ἐν αὐτῇ καὶ ἴδιον αὐτῆς.

31. Αὕτη μὲν οὖν τῶν ἁγίων πατέρων ἡ εὐθυτενὴς καὶ ἀπλανε- 30
στάτη πίστις ἤτοι τῆς πίστεως ἡ ὁμολογία· ἀλλ' ὡς ὁ Παῦλός φησιν,
ὁ θεὸς τοῦ αἰῶνος τούτου ἐτύφλωσε τὰ νοήματα τῶν
ἀπίστων εἰς τὸ μὴ αὐγάσαι τὸν φωτισμὸν τοῦ εὐαγγελίου
τῆς δόξης Χριστοῦ.ᵉ ἀφέντες γοῦν τὸ εὐθὺ τῆς ἀληθείας ἰέναι
τινὲς ᾄττουσι κατὰ πετρῶν, μὴ νοοῦντες μήτε ἃ λέγουσι, 35

ᶜ John 6: 53   ᵈ John 20: 22   ᵉ 2 Cor. 4: 4

this is the way corruption in us too is being annihilated and Death's power enfeebled. Hence Christ declared: *'Verily I say to you, unless you eat the flesh of the son of man and drink his blood you have no life in yourselves.'* Surely then Christ's holy body and blood are life-giving. For the body, as I said, does not belong to some human participant in Life but is personally owned by Life himself, that is the Only-begotten.

29. This view we share with the loyal band of holy Christian fathers and with that Proclus, our most holy and religious brother and fellow bishop, who but recently came to grace the throne of Constantinople's holy Church. Proclus has written to the most religious bishops of the East in these very terms: 'The formless becomes incarnate without changing, the unbeginning is born in flesh. The utterly complete in nature progresses in bodily age, the transcender of suffering endures suffering, undergoing insult not in what he was, but in what he has been made accepting the body's sufferings.'[7] The mischievous belief of those who think or write differently from this is, then, exposed as altogether rotten with profanity and incompatibility with the doctrines of truth.

30. After completing their account of Christ the thrice-blessed fathers call to mind the Holy Ghost, declaring their belief in him just as in the case of the Father and the Son. He is consubstantial with them; he pours out (or proceeds) from, as it were, the fount of God the Father and is bestowed on creation through the Son—he breathed, remember, on the holy apostles saying: *'Receive the Holy Ghost.'* The Spirit, therefore, is God and from God, not alien to the substance transcending all substances but from it, in it and belonging to it.

31. This, then, is the holy fathers' straight, unswerving faith or confession of faith. However, as Paul says: *'The god of this world blinded the minds of disbelievers to prevent the light of the gospel of Christ's glory shining on them.'* Certain people, you know, have ceased going the straight way of truth and rush over boulders

---

[7] The rest of the letter is lost. It must have belonged to the correspondence between John of Antioch and Proclus connected with the reception of Proclus' *Tomus ad Armenios* (435) by the Easterns. See Introduction, p. xxvii.

μήτε περὶ τίνων διαβεβαιοῦνται.ᶠ περιστάντες γὰρ τὴν τῆς
υἱότητος δόξαν εἰς μόνον τὸν ἐκ θεοῦ πατρὸς φύντα λόγον, ὡς
υἱὸν ἕτερον τὸν ἐκ σπέρματος Ἰεσσαὶ καὶ Δαυὶδ συνῆφθαί φασιν
αὐτῷ καὶ μετέχειν υἱότητος καὶ τιμῆς θεοπρεποῦς καὶ τῆς ἐν-
οικήσεως αὐτοῦ τοῦ λόγου καὶ πάντα μᾶλλον ἐσχηκέναι παρ' αὐτοῦ, 5
ἴδιον δὲ παντελῶς οὐδέν. περὶ τῶν τοιούτων, ὥς γε οἶμαι, γεγράφασι
τοῦ σωτῆρος οἱ μαθηταί· παρεισέδυσαν γάρ τινες ἄνθρωποι
οἱ καὶ πάλαι προγεγραμμένοι εἰς τοῦτο τὸ κρίμα ἀσεβεῖς,
τὴν τοῦ θεοῦ χάριν μετατιθέντες εἰς ἀσέλγειαν καὶ τὸν
μόνον δεσπότην καὶ κύριον ἡμῶν Ἰησοῦν Χριστὸν ἀρνού- 10
μενοι.ᵍ Ἰησοῦς δὲ Χριστὸς ὀνομάζοιτο ἂν εἰκότως ἐν ἀνθρωπείᾳ
μορφῇ πεφηνὼς ὁ λόγος. ἐπεὶ φραζέτωσαν ἐρομένοις οἱ δι' ἐναντίας
οἱ τὰ Νεστορίου τε καὶ Θεοδώρου φρονεῖν καὶ λαλεῖν ἐκ πολλῆς
ἄγαν ἀσυνεσίας οὐ παραιτούμενοι· ἐκβάλλετε τοῦ εἶναι θεὸν καὶ
υἱὸν ἀληθινὸν τοῦ θεοῦ καὶ πατρὸς τὸν ἐκ τῆς ἁγίας παρθένου, τὸ 15
παθεῖν αὐτῷ προσνέμοντες μόνῳ καὶ ἀποσοβοῦντες αὐτὸ τοῦ
θεοῦ λόγου, ἵνα μὴ θεὸς λέγοιτο παθητός; ταῦτα γὰρ τῆς ἐκείνων
ἐθελακριβείας τὰ εὑρήματα καὶ ἡ τῶν ἐννοιῶν χυδαιότης. οὐκοῦν
μὴ ὀνομαζέσθω Χριστὸς ἰδικῶς καὶ κατὰ μόνας ὁ ἐκ θεοῦ πατρὸς
λόγος· ὥσπερ γάρ ἐστιν ἀπεοικὸς αὐτῷ τὸ παθεῖν, ὅταν ἔξω νοῆται 20
σαρκός, οὕτω καὶ ἡ χρίσις ἀνάρμοστόν τι χρῆμα καὶ ἀλλότριον
αὐτοῦ. Ἰησοῦν γὰρ τὸν ἀπὸ Ναζαρὲτ ἔχρισεν ὁ θεὸς πνεύματι
ἁγίῳ,ʰ αὐτοτελὴς δὲ πάντως ὁ ἐκ θεοῦ λόγος καὶ οὐκ ἂν ἐδεήθη
χρίσεως τῆς διὰ τοῦ ἁγίου πνεύματος. οὐκοῦν ἀρνήσασθε τὴν
οἰκονομίαν, ἀποστήσατε τὸν μονογενῆ τῆς εἰς τὸν κόσμον ἀγάπης· 25
μὴ ὀνομαζέσθω Χριστὸς παρ' ὑμῶν. ἢ οὐ σμικρὸν αὐτῷ τὸ ἐν τοῖς
καθ' ἡμᾶς γενέσθαι μέτροις; οὐκοῦν ἐπειδήπερ καὶ τοῦτό ἐστιν
ἀπεοικὸς αὐτῷ, ὁμολογείτω μηδεὶς ὅτι γέγονεν ἄνθρωπος, ἵνα καὶ
αὐτοῖς εἴπῃ Χριστός· πλανᾶσθε μὴ εἰδότες τὰς γραφὰς μηδὲ
τὴν δύναμιν τοῦ θεοῦ.ⁱ οὐκοῦν ὡς τῆς ἀληθείας ἐχθροὺς τοὺς 30
ὧδε φρονεῖν ᾑρημένους ἡγούμενοι φεύγωμεν αὐτῶν τὰς ὀλεθρίους
κενοφωνίας, ἐπώμεθα δὲ μᾶλλον ταῖς δόξαις τῶν ἁγίων πατέρων
καὶ τῇ παραδόσει τῶν ἁγίων ἀποστόλων καὶ εὐαγγελιστῶν. αὐτὸς
γὰρ ἦν ὁ λαλῶν ἐν αὐτοῖς ὁ ἐνανθρωπήσας λόγος, δι' οὗ καὶ μεθ'
οὗ τῷ θεῷ καὶ πατρὶ τιμὴ δόξα κράτος σὺν ἁγίῳ πνεύματι εἰς 35
τοὺς αἰῶνας τῶν αἰώνων. ἀμήν.

ᶠ 1 Tim. 1 : 7   ᵍ Jude 4   ʰ cf. Acts 10 : 38   ⁱ Matt. 22 : 29

'*not knowing what they are saying or what they are making claims about*'.
They attribute the glory of sonship solely to the Word sprung
from God the Father, declaring that another son, of Jesse and
David's stock, has been joined with him, partakes in the Word's
sonship, divine honour and indwelling, and has everything from
him with nothing of his own at all. It is of such people, I believe,
that the Saviour's disciples have written: '*For some men, who long
ago were designated for this condemnation, secretly entered, godless people,
perverters of God's grace into impiety and deniers of our only master
and Lord, Jesus Christ.*' The Word manifest in human form is
rightly named 'Jesus Christ.' Why, then, our opponents, who
in their extreme folly do not forbear to hold or express the views
of Nestorius and Theodore,[8] must answer our question: 'Do you
refuse to allow him who is of the holy Virgin his being God and
true Son of God the Father? Do you allot the suffering to him
alone, fending it off from God the Word to avoid God's being
declared passible?' This is the point of their pedantic, muddle-
headed fictions. In that case, the Word of God the Father on
his own and by himself should not be called 'Christ'; for just
as suffering is out of character with him when he is considered
in isolation from the flesh, so is anointing an inconsistent feature
alien to him. For God anointed Jesus of Nazareth with the Holy
Ghost, but the Word of God is utterly complete in himself and
required no anointing through the Holy Ghost. In which case,
deny God's plan, banish the Only-begotten from any love towards
the world! 'Christ' you must not call him. Was not his created
existence within human limitations a lowly thing? In which case,
seeing that *that* is out of character with him, nobody must acknowledge that he has become man, with the result that Christ
can tell them: '*You err, knowing neither the scriptures nor God's
power.*' Let us, then, deem the holders of opinions like this
Truth's enemies and shun their baleful vanities; let us instead
follow the views of the holy fathers and the tradition of the holy
apostles and evangelists. The Word made man was, indeed, he
who spoke in them, and through him and with him be honour,
glory and power to God the Father with the Holy Ghost for
ever and ever. Amen.

[8] The name of ill omen is reserved to the very end, though all the piece has
it in mind.

8

ANSWERS TO TIBERIUS AND HIS COMPANIONS

The letter to blessed Cyril, archbishop of Alexandria, by the brethren who came from Palestine

When . . .[1] we expel the odious winter of the generation below and bring vision and the day of peace in the winter season by seeing the calm of your countenance. Of this we had hoped never to be deprived but having suffered the involuntary removal . . . God . . . we are delighting in . . . and we pray that from this we may never fall and pray to God that no hint of grief may happen again to this present joy, since we have one who fights on our behalf with your prayers, both with love and understanding. Behold, therefore, we are yours, bound with the bands of love.[2] Leaving all, we follow led by the word and love. But we do not doubt that the things pertaining to your fatherly love in Christ have become for us a copy of these things, what has happened being a pledge to us. I believe that being a sort of beloved son, towards the father . . . love. The matters involved in the petition will be received for the help of our souls, and the works against the heretical questions, which are set out below in the petition, will redound to the glory of your Beatitude.

God the Son, even God the Word, desiring to call and restore the race of men to its initial state, willed to live in humility with us and exalt us with him through his superiority, by God the Father's will. He accomplished the mystery on our behalf and perfected his Church, fixing to it godly discretion as its immovable wall. Against Satan's external assaults, against the tares which sprout up by the agency of

[1] The Syriac text contains a number of lacunae in the first paragraph which were evidently present in the manuscript copied by the scribe, who indicated them by dots. The general sense is plain: the sight of Cyril is a breath of Spring.

[2] As the following sentences make plain, Tiberius' approach to Cyril is prompted by respect for his status as an expositor of the faith gained particularly in his contest with Nestorius, and not by his having ecclesiastical jurisdiction over him. Palestine at this period belonged to the diocese of the East, with Antioch as its metropolis. Juvenal, bishop of Jerusalem, was busy intriguing to establish his see as metropolitical by splitting Palestine, Phoenicia and Arabia from Antioch. Cyril, though glad of Juvenal's support at Ephesus (431), thwarted these attempts. But Juvenal outlasted him and supported the majority at Ephesus (449)—the Latrocinium—and Chalcedon (451) gaining as his prize the three provinces of Palestine (*ACO* 2, 1 p. 364).

the evil-minded emerging from our midst,[a] he has personally established in all generations his helpers of true religion, in order that they might burn up the tares at enmity with the wheat by the apostles' tongue of spiritual fire[b] and conquer the tempter by the confession of truth. Because, therefore, God, who knows all things before they exist,[c] brought out your fathers of old against the enemy and latterly you, in your ability to grasp and comprehend the fullness of true religion, you rose up, confessed and proclaimed a noble confession,[d] witnessed before angels and men and guided Christ's flock to good pasturage. And now, released from the dangers endured for it (or rather sheltered by God's providence for our sake) lead the faithful in due season in order that a double victory of the faith may be bestowed upon you. For in your undeserved suffering you suffered nobly out of generosity even wicked Nestorius' hirelings in order that all this grace should come to you. They plaited for you, by your degradation, a richly-flowered crown adorned with all the glory of martyrdom.[3] For they did not know that the very means they expected to cause you much suffering were preparing you a heavenly victory. Since indeed Christ has said to you, as to Paul, 'Speak always and do not keep silence, have no fear, for I am with you and will save you from everything',[e] he has kept us, that is, the fullness of his one Church.

Therefore rightly thanking God for this as we do and in the full and complete knowledge that to this end you are ordained and consecrated, namely to be prepared for the defence of the divine mysteries, we have become your summoners to further contests and crowns for Christ's sake and offer to the jealous God who enters into battle for religion's sake your writing and bring him our master's learning on the heresies of evil-minded people, a learning which has just made itself known to the Empire.[4] We pray, therefore, that you may stand up in the Spirit and stir up Christ who speaks in you, sharpening the word which defines sound teaching. To the items of their errors which are set out below in this letter may you oppose in strength the power of truth, so that we, who, when fit, feed on the shoots of Holy Church may the fitter feed on the flowers of spiritual herbage and that they, who hitherto have been children in their ideas and learners with respect to God, may receive

---

[a] cf. Matt. 13 : 24 ff. [b] cf. Acts 2 : 3 [c] cf. Hist. Sus. 42
[d] cf. 1 Tim. 6 : 12 [e] cf. Acts 18 : 9 f.

---

[3] Fulsome praise, since the nearest Cyril got to more than *mental* anguish during the evidently recent events of 431–433 was a period of house arrest at Ephesus (see p. xxiv). He complained of the soldiers sleeping in front of the bedroom (*Ep.* 27, *ACO* 1, 1, 3 p. 45, 36 ff.), and everybody became worn out with the heat of Ephesus and with waiting upon the Emperor to close the assembly (*ACO* 1, 3 p. 178, 27 ff.).

[4] Literally: (learning) which has (just) now sprung up amongst the Romans.

plain guidance and those very persons who have spewed forth error may discover that, having roused themselves by some evil spirit, they have found a new destruction or, perhaps, may be converted by your work through Christ the God and saviour of all who wills that every man should come to a knowledge of the truth.*f*

But as for you, having completed this contest and demonstrated the faith to the world, you will lay up a crown of righteousness*g* and will receive, in due season, your wages from God, since not only do you always offer acceptable prayers to God for us, but embracing us in your hands, us who by your teaching are disciplined and saved, you will bring in, saying, 'Behold, I and the children whom thou hast given me, O Lord'.*h*5 As for our poor selves, we will be exceedingly grateful for not falling away from what we believe by your prayers and for being aided by the mystic wisdom granted you by God along with all these things. And now we do not rest from offering prayers to God for your peace and long life, and as we journey towards him we freely display the character of your piety impressed on our souls.

Questions addressed to the celebrated Cyril, archbishop of Alexandria, by Tiberius the deacon and eight brethren

New and perverse heresies have again sprung up. Novel statements of twisted teachings have again appeared. Again folk from somewhere or other have come to our area[6] and are attempting to sow the tares of their teachings amongst our pure wheat of piety. The members of the body are again becoming disordered, and, planning a rebuttal, we need at once your knowledge of healing.

For the past year blasphemy has been spoken and evil doctrines have been secretly given out which had formerly been suppressed. But because they had not been removed from the roots of the tree of evil, a shoot has sprung up which will quickly fill the neighbourhood of Palestine with its fruits, and though these have been removed hitherto the cancer has continued to occur. We had a simple love of silence, only mourning the death of the diseased members or admonishing them with prayers to return to their former health. But because the enemy was not satisfied with his previous spoils, he is adding the destruction

f cf. 1 Tim. 2 : 4   *g* cf. 2 Tim. 4 : 8   *h* Is. 8 : 18

[5] The same Biblical text and the same sentiment appear in the (possibly) original ending of Tiberius' letter, below p. 182 n. 3.

[6] We are not told where in Palestine Tiberius' monastery was, except that it was 'far from the world', p. 181. For a lively and detailed picture of the development of the religious life see Derwas Chitty, *The Desert a City, an introduction to the study of Egyptian and Palestinian monasticism under the Christian Empire* (Oxford, 1966). He does not consider our texts. For the background to these intruders see below n. 12.

of the healthy body. Indeed he is now attempting to put stumbling
blocks in the way of outsiders to the Church's body who want to come
to the truth. Rightly speaking the urgent problem for us, the main evil,
is that the inventors of evils, to deceive the simple, assume the garb[7]
of the priesthood, live in the monasteries and desire to be called 'master'
by the majority. They outdo the rest in age, beard, priestly honour and
hospitality for God's sake.[8] They want to be deemed worthy of extra[9]
honour and praise by those who live in the same place. Dressed as sheep
they conceal the wickedness and savagery of wolves[a] and are really
clouds without water.[b] Instead of a fragrant breeze and dewy drops of
rain they drop coals of fire on those with very child-like ideas the whole
season, drowning them in eternal fire.

That is why we come, trusting that when your piety shall at last rise
up and you are fervent in the Holy Spirit, you will give us a true
and clear explanation of all the points mooted hitherto. For Christ
has made you the light and eye of his heavenly body,[c] so that you may
enlighten the souls of the sons of light and truth by the light of true
religion; the right hand of his Church, so that you may establish and
strengthen their minds by right faith; and he has fixed you for the
defence of spotless faith in him, to stop the mouth of those who wickedly
blaspheme against God. Because we are confident that it will not be
very irksome to give an answer, do not conceal the truth supposing us
to be dull of hearing, since you are aware that our petitions will be
rendered in person for you in front of Christ's judgement seat on the
day of resurrection whereas for us your Holiness' teaching on these
points will be our confirmation, a support for the wavering and a
rebuttal or a cause of conversion to the truth for those evil-doers. For
we seek no verbal contention but seek to avoid being dragged into error
in our mind. For if[10] the spiritual gift of the kingdom on high is directed
aright with piety and justice by someone perfect towards God and if
those who are being perfected in Christ are being adorned by both these
qualities which have two-fold trophies, with an unfading crown of glory,
then those dear disciples of Christ, who have fought nobly, will rejoice
in the victories of the divine spiritual gift. In the absence of one of them
the destitute is necessarily lame and being lame does not enter God's
house;[d] and being deprived of one of these two graces, it is clear that

[a] cf. Matt. 7: 15   [b] cf. Jude 12   [c] cf. Matt. 6: 22   [d] cf. 2 Sam. 5: 8

[7] Or 'appearance'/'guise'—the underlying Greek is σχῆμα.
[8] i.e. they plead God's will as grounds for special food and veneration.
[9] Or 'more honour and praise than those . . .'.
[10] Tiberius' Sunday-best language defeats clarity. He means: we need both
devotion and right faith to get to heaven (cf. On the Creed, § 2), and the function
of the ministry ('the spiritual gift of the kingdom on high') is to ensure that
both exist in us.

G

he does not enter into that rest. Hence, released from all blame, indeed rather made worthy of all praise, we have confidence to seek and enquire about right faith, in the hope that thereby being justly found worthy as a result of these two (piety, I mean, and persistence in the virtues which they contain) by means of the presence of that divine understanding bestowed on you from above, we may obtain some small grace, however slender, to aid us at the time when the righteous judge gives to each man according to his works. We trust your piety, therefore, that we shall get an exact solution of these matters from you, we who, learning to fear God, through you, take to ourselves the fortification of right faith. Fervent again in righteousness of nature through your holiness and receiving from the Spirit the good portion of heavenly ways we shall frankly avow before Christ Our Lord's judgement seat that this spiritual gift has been granted us by God through Cyril the high priest. The evil statements they are making which have just now come to light and on which we seek your answer are set out below.[11]

Copy of Cyril, archbishop of Alexandria's letter written to Tiberius the Deacon and the rest of the brethren

I

To those who assert that deity is human in form and dealing with the written queries[12]

[11] In its original form, the questions, which are only summarized in the headings to the *Answers*, will have followed in sequence as in the subsequent petition, see below p. 182 n 3.

[12] Apart from the Ps.-Clementine *Homilies* and Melito (see nn. 15 f. below) the most famous representatives of anthropomorphism were: (1) the Audians, followers of the Mesopotamian ascetic Audius, who lived in the first half of the fourth century. They rejected the Easter rule of Nicaea (325) but were orthodox in the doctrine of the Trinity. The sect seems to have outlasted its founder only briefly, with followers deserting to the Catholic church or being mingled with more dubious groups. Epiphanius, the authority for them, who treats them as schismatics rather than heretics, tells us they had by 376/7 abandoned their monasteries in Taurus, Palestine, and Arabia, but some survived around Chalcis and in Mesopotamia (*Ancor.* 14, 3; *Panar.* 70 and *Anac.* in *PG* 42, 870B). See *RAC* s.v. Audianer. There is no connection between Audians and (2) the monastic opponents of Origen (from upper Egypt) in the time of Theophilus (see Socrates *Hist. Eccles.* 6, 7 ff.) who were called 'anthropomorphians' by 'Origenists' (from Nitria, in lower Egypt). An incident in the controversy features in the Coptic text edited by E. Drioton ('La Discussion d'un moine anthropomorphite Audien avec le patriarche Théophile d'Alexandrie en l'année 399', *Revue de l'Orient Chrétien* 10, 1915–17); 'Audien', though, does not figure in the text and is Drioton's (false) supposition. For the development of the controversy in Palestine, see Chitty op. cit. (n. 6), pp. 58 ff. Both (1) and (2) form a background for Tiberius' troubles

Answer

I hear divine Scripture saying '*Stick to your superiors and obey them, for they are watchmen on behalf of your souls as rendering an account for them.*'[a] For the flocks of sheep should stick to the pastors' mind and go without hesitation where they take them, for they feed them on good pasture and in a fertile spot,[b] as it is written. For the good sort of pastor should not expose them to wolves or willingly await marauding beasts, else those who are wont to do so will discover that they must answer to God for their lives.

I write this on learning that certain people are disturbing you not with accurate or scriptural matters but rather are spewing out of their hearts unhealthy and untrue arguments. For they have lapsed into this utterly wicked way of thinking, so that they somehow suppose and think the all-transcending divine nature to be human in appearance or form. For my part I do not believe it, for to want to think this is a manifest proof of extreme folly. Indeed, I am amazed that those who dispute and talk this way or can suppose the thing should be ignorant of the fact that divine Scripture proclaims that idolaters thought this. Therefore Paul says of them '*Claiming to be wise, they have become fools and changed the glory of the incorruptible God into the form of corruptible man.*'[c] Therefore those who think God is human in form are fools along with idolaters and, caught in the same wickedness, are clearly convicted of it. One learns from other considerations that they are straying from the truth and are remote from a properly holy understanding. For all-wise Paul writes again with reference to the Word of God the Father, '*Let each of you have this mind in you which was also in Christ Jesus, who being in the form of God did not think equality with God a prize to be grasped but emptied himself, taking a slave's form, being made in man's likeness.*'[d] Seeing that 'emptying' (that is, becoming man) rendered the Son a slave's form (that is, a human one), but he was in God's form, God's form must be separate from ours. For were the divine nature human in appearance, he would not have assumed our different one whilst being God the Word.

This careful steward of the mysteries of our salvation, indeed, has another reason for calling people who think like this 'fools'

[a] Heb. 13: 17   [b] cf. Ez. 34: 14   [c] Rom. 1: 22 f.   [d] Phil. 2: 5 ff.

but from Epiphanius it is clear the intruders are not Audians, and the reasons for their anthropomorphism seem different from (2) 30-odd years before. See p. xxix and cf. *Answer* 10, *Doctrinal Questions and Answers* 1 and *Letter to Calosirius*, ad init. See further G. Florowsky, 'The anthropomorphites in the Egyptian Desert' in *Aspects of Church History* (= Florowsky's collected papers), vol. 4, pp. 89–129 (Belmont, Mass., 1975).

and 'ignorant'. All-wise Paul writes again in a passage from the epistle to the Galatians *'My children with whom I am again in travail until Christ be formed in you'*[e] though men's form belonged to them (since obviously this is why he is writing to them). But if Christ's form is being created in us in a different way, perceptible to the mind and spiritually,[13] the appearance of the divine nature cannot be like our visible appearance. For it does not consist of parts and limbs as we do but as incorporeal without quantitative and limiting shape. That is why, therefore, our Saviour addressing the crowds of Jews about God the Father said *'Verily I say unto you, you have never heard his voice or seen his shape.'*[f] Yet if God had our form and appearance, how could people have failed to see the Father when they looked at one another? How can the Son be his unique image and his person's splendour and stamp if, as they assert, he has exactly the same appearance as men? Do they not perceive that they are infected with a diseased imagination? Do they not see the ridiculous absurdity of their opinions and fancies? Do they not recollect blessed Paul addressing the Athenians and saying, *'For we ought not to suppose that the Godhead is like gold or silver or engraving made by human artifice and imagination'*,[g] despite the fact that the makers of idols and craftsmen of this sort of thing stamp a human appearance on their falsely-named gods? But if it is wrong to suppose that the Godhead is like their engraving, how can any people announce that he exists in human appearance? Do they therefore feel no shame at their intemperate descriptions?

For they should have recollected reading the sacred Scriptures and that blessed Paul writes again, *'For those whom he knew he predestined to share his Son's form and these he called* etc.'[h] Why do all men not share the form and appearance of God's Son, if he is human in form? Or why, in that case, are some called by election to be sharers in his Son's form and image rather than everybody being said to be a sharer in the form? No, it is clear that deity is without appearance and does not exist in shape, configuration or image inasmuch as he is incorporeal whereas we are quantitative both in appearance and configuration.

But perhaps they will ask why divinely inspired Scripture mentions God as having a face and affirms that he has hands, feet, ears, eyes and a mouth? To which we answer that God's Spirit employs human expressions and speaks to us in terms we can comprehend.[14] But if we suppose that these are grounds for

---

[e] Gal. 4: 19   [f] John 5: 37   [g] Acts 17: 29   [h] Rom. 8: 29 f.

[13] The underlying Greek is νοητῶς καὶ πνευματικῶς.
[14] Cf. *Doctrinal Questions and Answers* 1 and n. 3.

thinking the Godhead has a human form what are we to make of the other cases when we hear divine Scripture saying, '*These are the seven eyes of God which keep watch over the whole earth*',[i] and again, '*He spread his wings and bore them*'?[j] Will they tell us how we can have seven eyes in our faces or outspread wings and after that how he can have a human form? For we do not have seven eyes, nor does man sprout wings.[15]

So thinkers and talkers in this senseless fashion must desist. For, as I have said, God being incorporeal has no bodily form or appearance at all but is beyond all thought and language. He is, indeed, viewed intellectually by the reality of the heart as one possessing supra-mundane glory and he transcends all visible and invisible reality, for as creator of all he is in nature apart from all. Man on the other hand, we say, was created on earth in God's image[16] because he is capable of being righteous, holy, good and wise. He attained authority over all on earth for, as it is written, '*He put all things in subjection under his feet*',[k] and this, along with the rest, is implied in the gracious gift of the form.[17]

Restrain, therefore, those who want to teach otherwise and quiet such people exhorting them to silence. Let them seek, rather, to attain in Christ the world above by leading lives appropriate to religious and by special amendment of conduct in various ways.

[i] Zech. 4: 10   [j] Deut. 32: 11   [k] 1 Cor. 15: 27

---

[15] The same answer, including the quotation from Zech., was given by Origen, quoted by Theodoret *Quaest. in Gen.* 20 (*PG* 80, 113A ff.), controverting Melito who had written a book on the embodied existence of God.

[16] The Alexandrian tradition from Philo onwards, with which the Cappadocian fathers concur, places the 'image of God' in the soul or mind of man (cf. Philo *De op. mundi* 69(23), Clement *Strom.* 2, 19, Origen *In Gen. Hom.* 1, 13, Athanasius *C.G.* 34, Basil *Ep.* 233, 1, Gregory Naz. *Poemata Dog.* 8, 74 f. and Gregory Nyss. *De hom. op.* 16). The heterodox (or simply primitive) *Clementine Homilies* 10, 6 ff. and 11, 4 ff. locate the image in man's body, cf. 17: 7 and 10. For Theodoret (loc. cit., n. 15) the image is found in man's function as ruler, though there is an imitation of the divine in the rational faculty. See the places collected by W. J. Burghardt, *The Image of God in Man according to Cyril of Alexandria* (Washington, 1957), chapter 2, who concludes that the non-Alexandrine Greek tradition places the 'image' in man's soul but some writers attempt to include the body without anthropomorphism. The Latin tradition with few exceptions refers the 'image' to the soul.

[17] God's image in man, for Cyril, consists in certain innate capacities dependent for their exercise upon divine grace given through the Incarnation, together with the special relationship of 'sonship', a gift of God not present in man's nature. Burghardt (see n. 16) summarizes the features of the image: reason, freedom, dominion, holiness, incorruptibility, and sonship.

Β' ι

Πρὸς τοὺς λέγοντας ὅτι ὁ υἱὸς κατὰ μὲν τὴν τῆς θεότητος ἀξίαν συνῆν τῷ πατρί, καὶ² ὅτε γέγονεν ἄνθρωπος καὶ ἦν ἐπὶ γῆς, καθ' ὑπόστασιν δέ, οὐκ ἔτι.

Ἐπίλυσις

Μανθάνω³ τινὰς εἰκῇ καὶ ἀπερισκέπτως καὶ ἐπὶ τοῖς οὕτω 5 μεγάλοις καὶ ἀναγκαίοις πράγμασιν φλυαρεῖν εἰωθότας φάναι τι τοιοῦτον, ὡς ὁ μονογενὴς τοῦ θεοῦ υἱὸς κατὰ μὲν τὴν τῆς θεότητος καὶ οὐσίας⁴ ἀξίαν συνῆν τῷ θεῷ καὶ πατρί, ἡνίκα ἐπὶ τῆς γῆς ἐχρημάτιζε καὶ τοῖς ἀνθρώποις συνανεστρέφετο,ᵃ ὡς ὁμοούσιος ὢν αὐτῷ· κατὰ δὲ τὸν τῆς ὑποστάσεως λόγον οὐκ ἔτι. κεκένωτοᵇ γὰρ 10 πᾶσα, ὡς αὐτοί φασιν,⁵ ἡ υἱοτικὴ⁶ ὑπόστασις ἔκ τε τῶν οὐρανῶν καὶ αὐτῶν τῶν πατρικῶν κόλπων. οὐ γὰρ συναπτέον ὑπόστασιν ὑποστάσει, οὔτε τὰς ἐν μιᾷ οὐσίᾳ ὑπαρχούσας. ἐγὼ δὲ τὸ προπετὲς τῆς ἀμαθίας τῶν ταῦτα πεφρονηκότων θαυμάσας, δεῖν ᾠήθην ἀναγκαίως ἐκεῖνο εἰπεῖν, ὅτι πεπόσωται παρ' αὐτοῖς ἡ οὐσία τοῦ 15 θεοῦ, καὶ καταληπτὴν αὐτὴν εἶναί φασι καὶ πεπερατωμένην, καὶ οὐκ ἔτι μὲν ἀπεριόριστον οὐδὲ ἀκατάληπτον, ἀλλ' ἤδη καὶ τόποις χωρητὴν καὶ διαστήμασι περιληπτήν, ἁρμόζει δὲ ταῦτα τοῖς τῶν σωμάτων⁷ λόγοις. οὐκοῦν καὶ σῶμα, πάντως δέ που καὶ ἐν εἴδει, καὶ οὐ δίχα σώματος· ἕπεται γὰρ τὰ τοιάδε τοῖς σώμασιν. εἶτα 20 πῶς ὁ σωτὴρ πνεῦμά φησιν ὁ θεός;ᶜ⁸ πνεῦμα γὰρ εἶναί φησιν αὐτὸν ἵν' ἔξω σωματικῆς φαντασίας ἀγάγῃ τὴν ὑπερφυᾶ καὶ ἀπόρρητον φύσιν. ἆρ' οὐκ ἄν τις εἴποι δικαίως τοῖς τὰ τοιάδε τεθρυληκόσιν, ἢ καὶ τολμῶσι φρονεῖν ἐδικαιώθη Σόδομα ἐκ σοῦ;ᵈ εὐσεβέστερον γὰρ οἱ παρ' Ἕλλησι σοφοὶ δοξάζουσι⁹ τὸ θεῖον 25 ἀσώματον καὶ ἀνείδεον, ἄποσόν τε καὶ ἀμερές, καὶ ἀσχημάτιστον εἶναι διαβεβαιούμενοι, καὶ πανταχῇ μὲν ὑπάρχειν, ἀπολιμπάνεσθαι δὲ οὐδενός.

2. ᵃ cf. Baruch 3: 37   ᵇ cf. Phil. 2: 7   ᶜ John 4: 24   ᵈ cf. Ezek. 16: 52

Witnesses : ll. 1–4 G Syr   l. 5–p. 148, l. 32 C G Syr

Heading in G: πεύσεις δογματικαὶ προτεθεῖσαι παρὰ Τιβερίου διακόνου καὶ τῶν ἀδελφῶν τῷ ἁγίῳ Κυρίλλῳ ἀρχιεπισκόπῳ Ἀλεξανδρείας
2. ¹ ἆ G   ² καὶ om. Syr   ³ δὲ add. Syr   ⁴ καὶ οὐσίας om. Syr
⁵ φμσιν C   ⁶ ὔιτικὴ C   ⁷ ἀσωμάτων C   ⁸ ὁ θεός φησι G
¹ δοξάζουσι σοφοὶ C

2

Against those who say that the Son was with the Father in the rank[18] of the Godhead when he became man and was on earth, but was no longer with him in his hypostasis[19]

Answer

I have been given to understand that some habitual proponents of idle and ill-considered nonsense on very weighty and essential issues are asserting something to this effect: that God's only-begotten Son was with God the Father in respect of the rank of Godhead and substance when he had dealings on earth and converse with men, as being consubstantial[20] with him, but was no longer with him in the category of hypostasis. Because his entire filial hypostasis was, they say, emptied out of heaven and the paternal bosom itself. For hypostases cannot be joined together or exist in one substance.[21] I am astonished at the ignorance and recklessness of people who think this and feel myself obliged to point out that they have made God's substance a quantity and are talking of it as confined, bounded and no longer unlimited and unconfined but as spatially finite and contained within dimensions. But these attributes conform with the defining principles of bodies. So God's substance must be a body, must exist in a shape and not be separate from body, for attributes like these belong to bodies. In which case why does the Saviour say, '*God is Spirit*'? He calls him Spirit, indeed, to debar the supra-natural and ineffable nature from any corporeal imagining. One would be justified in saying to people who babble or dare to think such thoughts 'Sodom is more in the right than you.' For pagan philosophers[22] take a more religious view when they insist that the Godhead is incorporeal, without shape, quantity, parts or configuration, that it exists everywhere and is remote from nothing.

[18] i.e. rank or status with its outward signs.

[19] i.e. individual being.

[20] i.e. of the same physical stuff, cf. *PGL* s.v. ὁμοούσιος I.

[21] The same phrase p. 144. Perhaps translate: 'nor can the (hypostases) existing in one substance (be joined together)', i.e. 'existing in one substance' = 'being consubstantial'; see n. 20. In either case the implication is that the individual beings of the Trinity, though of the same physical stuff, cannot be united physically, and, if one of them descends to earth, heaven loses the individual, but the common stuff, the form of God of which the Son divested himself, remains behind.

[22] Cf. the texts collected by Clement *Protrepticus* 5 ff., *Strom.* 5, 12 ff. and Cyril *Contra Jul.* 1 (*PG* 76, 548 ff.).

Πῶς δὲ κἀκεῖνο διέλαθεν αὐτούς; εἰ γὰρ ὁμοούσιος ὢν ὁ υἱὸς
τῷ πατρί, κεκένωκε τῆς αὐτοῦ παρουσίας τὸν οὐρανόν, ὅτε γέγονεν
ἄνθρωπος, καὶ συνανεστρέφετο τοῖς ἐπὶ[10] γῆς, ἄραρεν ὅτι κενὴ καὶ ἡ
γῆ τῆς τοῦ πατρὸς ὑποστάσεως ἦν, ὅτι μὴ αὐτὸς γέγονεν ἄνθρωπος,
μήτε μὴν ἀνθρώποις συνανεστρέφετο, ἀλλ᾽ ἵνα τι κατὰ τὴν αὐτῶν 5
ἀσυνεσίαν εἴπω, μεμένηκεν ἐν τοῖς οὐρανοῖς. πῶς οὖν ἔφασκεν ὁ
σωτήρ, ὅτι ὁ πατὴρ[11] ἐν ἐμοὶ μένων ποιεῖ[12] τὰ ἔργα αὐτός;[e]
πῶς δὲ διὰ τοῦ προφήτου φησί μὴ οὐχὶ τὸν οὐρανὸν καὶ τὴν
γῆν ἐγὼ πληρῶ, λέγει κύριος; καὶ πάλιν θεὸς ἐγγίζων ἐγὼ
εἰμί, λέγει κύριος, καὶ οὐχὶ θεὸς πόρρωθεν;[f] πάντα γὰρ 10
ἐγγὺς ἔχει, τὰ πάντα πληρῶν ὁμοῦ τῷ πατρὶ ὁ ἐξ αὐτοῦ κατὰ
φύσιν γεγεννημένος Χριστός.[13] καὶ γοῦν ὁ προφήτης Δαυίδ, ποῦ
πορευθῶ, φησίν, ἀπὸ τοῦ πνεύματός σου, καὶ ἀπὸ τοῦ
προσώπου σου ποῦ φύγω;[g] οὐ γὰρ ἔστιν, οὐκ ἔστιν οὐρανοὺς ἢ
γῆν εὑρεῖν δύνασθαί ποτε κενοὺς τῆς ἀρρήτου θεότητος. πληροῖ γὰρ 15
ὡς ἔφην τὰ πάντα ἡ θεία τε καὶ ὁμοούσιος τριάς. μεμνήμεθα δὲ
ὅτι καὶ ὁ τῶν ὅλων σωτὴρ καὶ κύριος τοῖς ἁγίοις ἀποστόλοις
ἔφασκε συμφέρει ὑμῖν ἵνα ἐγὼ ἀπέλθω, ἐὰν γὰρ μὴ ἀπέλθω,
ὁ παράκλητος οὐκ ἐλεύσεται πρὸς ὑμᾶς· ἐὰν δὲ πορευθῶ,
πέμψω αὐτὸν πρὸς ὑμᾶς.[h14] ἐπειδὴ δὲ πεπόρευται, τὴν ἰδίαν 20
ὑπόσχεσιν ἀποπληρῶν, ἔπεμψεν ἡμῖν ἐξ οὐρανοῦ τὸν παράκλητον,
τουτέστι τὸ πνεῦμα. ἔστι δὲ ὁμοούσιον τῷ πατρὶ καὶ υἱῷ. ἆρ᾽ οὖν
ὅτε καταπεφοίτηκεν εἰς γῆν ὁ παράκλητος ἵνα ἡμᾶς ἁγιάσῃ, τὸ
πνεῦμα οὐκ ἦν ἐν τοῖς οὐρανοῖς; ἀλλ᾽ ἐκεῖνο φάναι πρέποι ἄν, ὅτι
ἁγιάσαν ἡμᾶς ἀνέβη πάλιν εἰς τὸν οὐρανόν, καὶ οὐκ ἔστι μεθ᾽ ἡμῶν, 25
καίτοι γέγραπται ὅτι[15] πνεῦμα κυρίου πεπλήρωκε τὴν οἰκουμένην.[i] ἀλλὰ καὶ αὐτὸς ἔφη Χριστὸς μέλλων ἀναβαίνειν πρὸς τὸν
πατέρα ἰδοὺ ἐγὼ μεθ᾽ ὑμῶν εἰμι πάσας τὰς ἡμέρας καὶ[16]
ἕως τῆς συντελείας τοῦ αἰῶνος.[j] εἰ δὲ μεθ᾽ ἡμῶν ἐστι, κενοί
που πάντως καὶ νῦν εἰσι τῆς, ὡς αὐτοί φασιν, υἱοτικῆς[17] ὑπο- 30
στάσεως οἱ οὐρανοί, καὶ τὸν τοῦ πατρὸς κόλπον ἀφεὶς[18] τοῖς ἐπὶ γῆς
ἥδιον μᾶλλον συνδιαιτᾶται.

---

[e] John 14: 10   [f] Jer. 23: 24, 23   [g] Ps. 138(139): 7
[h] John 16: 7   [i] Wisdom 1: 7   [j] Matt. 28: 20

[10] τῆς add. C   [11] ὁ add. G   [12] ποιεῖ after αὐτός G   [13] υἱός Syr
[14] ἐὰν δὲ—ὑμᾶς om. C   [15] ὅτι om. G   [16] καὶ om. G   [17] ὑϊτικῆς C
[18] ἀφιεὶς C

Why have they missed this fact too, that if the Son, who is consubstantial with the Father, emptied heaven of his presence when he became man and had converse on earth, it follows that the earth must have been void of the Father's hypostasis as well, because the Father did not become man or have converse with men but (to continue their witless train of argument) remained in heaven? So why did the Saviour say *'The Father abides in me and personally does the works'*? Why does he say through the prophet *' "Do not I fill heaven and earth?", says the Lord'*, and again *' "I am a God who is nigh and not a God who is far off", says the Lord'*? For Christ, begotten of the Father by nature, fills all things together with him and is nigh to all. Moreover the prophet David says *'Where shall I go from thy spirit and where shall I flee from thy face?'* No, it is impossible to be able to find heaven or earth ever void of the ineffable Godhead, for, as I said, the divine and consubstantial Trinity fills all things. Indeed we recollect that the Lord and Saviour of all said to the holy apostles *'It is good for you that I should depart, for unless I depart the Comforter will not come to you, but if I go I shall send him to you.'* When he had gone he fulfilled his promise by sending us the Paraclete, the Spirit, from heaven. The Spirit is consubstantial with Father and Son. Was the Spirit, then, not in heaven when the Paraclete descended to earth to hallow us? Would it be proper to say that after hallowing us he returned to heaven and is not with us despite the fact that Scripture has it that *'the Lord's Spirit has filled the world'*? But Christ himself said just before his ascension to the Father *'Behold I am with you, always, even to the end of the world.'* If he is with us, then heaven must now (in their words) be empty of his filial hypostasis; he must have abandoned the Father's bosom and be dwelling with men on earth.

Ταῦτα γὰρ ἐκεῖνοι ψυχρολογοῦσιν, ὡς ἔφην. εἶτα τίς τῆς ἐκείνων
ἀβελτερίας[19] ἀνέξεται; ἢ τίς τῶν νουνεχεστέρων οὐκ ἂν αὐτοῖς
ἀμφιλαφὲς ἐπιστάξει[20] δάκρυον, οἵ γε τὰς ἱερὰς καὶ θείας ἠγνοη-
κότες γραφὰς τὸ εἰς νοῦν ἧκον ἀβασανίστως ἐρεύγονται, καὶ τῶν
ὀρθῶν τῆς ἐκκλησίας δογμάτων ἐκπίπτουσι; τί τῷ Φιλίππῳ περὶ 5
τοῦ πατρὸς λέγοντι προσπεφώνηκεν ὁ υἱός; οὐ πιστεύεις ὅτι
ἐγὼ ἐν τῷ πατρὶ καὶ ὁ πατὴρ ἐν ἐμοί ἐστιν;[k] οὐκοῦν ἀμήχανον
εἶναί ποτε δίχα τοῦ ἑτέρου τὸ ἕτερον· ἀλλ' ἔνθαπερ ὁ πατὴρ εἶναι
νοοῖτο[21] (ἔστι δὲ πανταχοῦ) ἐκεῖ που πάντως καὶ ὁ υἱός,[22] καὶ
ἔνθαπερ ἂν ὁ υἱός, ἐκεῖ καὶ ὁ πατήρ. εἰ γάρ ἐστιν ἀπαύγασμα τοῦ 10
πατρὸς ὁ υἱός, καὶ λόγος αὐτοῦ καὶ σοφία καὶ δύναμις, πῶς ἐνδέχεται δίχα λόγου καὶ σοφίας καὶ δυνάμεως νοεῖσθαί ποτε τὸν
πατέρα; πῶς δὲ ἡ[23] σοφία τοῦ θεοῦ καὶ λόγος αὐτοῦ καὶ ἡ δύναμις
αὐτοῦ νοοῖτ' ἄν ποτε δίχα τοῦ πατρός; ἢ πῶς οὐκ ἐνυπάρξει ποτὲ
αὐτῷ ὁ χαρακτὴρ αὐτοῦ; πῶς δὲ καὶ ὁ χαρακτὴρ δίχα τοῦ πατρὸς 15
οὗ ἐστι χαρακτήρ;
Ἀλλά φασιν ὅτι οὐ συναπτέον ὑπόστασιν ὑποστάσει, οὔτε τὰς ἐν
μιᾷ οὐσίᾳ ὑπαρχούσας, καὶ τάχα που τὰ καθ' ἡμᾶς παρακομίζουσιν
εἰς ἀπόδειξιν τῶν αὐτοῖς πεφλυαρημένων.
Εἶτα πῶς οὐκ ἔδει νοεῖν αὐτούς, ὅτι τὰ τῆς θείας φύσεως ἴδια 20
καὶ ἐξαίρετα οὐ διὰ τῶν καθ' ἡμᾶς κανονίζεται μᾶλλον, ἀλλ' ἐν
ἰδίοις εἰσὶ λόγοις, καὶ πίστει λαμβάνεται, περιεργοτέρων δὲ
λογισμῶν οὐκ ἀνέχεται; μία γὰρ φύσις ἐστὶ τῆς ἀρρήτου θεότητος
ἐν ὑποστάσεσι τρισί τε καὶ ἰδικαῖς, ἔξω δὲ τῶν καθ' ἡμᾶς ἐστι
λόγων, καὶ τοῖς τῶν κτισμάτων ἔθεσιν οὐκ ἀκολουθεῖ. καὶ τοῦτο 25
ἐκ πολλῶν ἔστιν ἰδεῖν. ἡμεῖς μὲν γὰρ πατέρες ἐσμὲν τῶν ἰδίων
τέκνων κατὰ ἀπόρροιαν καὶ μερισμόν. ἀναχωρεῖ γὰρ τὸ γεννώμενον
εἰς ἰδικὴν ἑτερότητα τὴν εἰς ἅπαν καὶ ὁλοσχερῶς. ἀλλ' οὐχ οὕτως
ἐκ τοῦ θεοῦ καὶ πατρὸς γεννηθῆναί φαμεν τὸν υἱόν· ἐξέλαμψε μὲν
γὰρ τῆς οὐσίας αὐτοῦ, καὶ ἐξηυγάσθη φωτὸς δίκην, ἀλλ' οὐκ ἔξω 30
γέγονεν αὐτοῦ, ἀλλ' ἐξ αὐτοῦ τέ ἐστι καὶ ἐν αὐτῷ· καὶ πρεσβύτεροι
μὲν οἱ παρ' ἡμῖν πατέρες τῶν ἰδίων τέκνων· ἥκιστα δὲ[24] τοῦτο
ἀληθὲς ἐπὶ θεοῦ. συνυφέστηκε γὰρ ἀεὶ τῷ πατρί, καὶ συνάναρχον

[k] John 14: 10

---

[19] ἀβελτηρίας G   [20] Read ἐπιστάξειε or ἐπιστάξαι?   [21] νοοῖτο εἶναι G
[22] υἱός] κύριος G   [23] ἡ om. G   [24] δὲ καὶ G

These, as I said, are their vapid arguments. Who is going to tolerate their futility? What sensible man will not shed copious tears over people who ignore the divine Scriptures, belch out unexamined notions and lapse from the Church's correct teachings? Why did the Son address Philip when he spoke to him about the Father the words '*Do you not believe that I am in the Father and the Father in me?*' So one cannot exist without the other; wherever the Father is (and he is everywhere) there the Son is, and wherever the Son is, there the Father is too. If the Son is the Father's effulgence, his Word, Wisdom and Power, how can the Father be conceived of as ever without word, wisdom, or power? How can God's Wisdom, his Word and his Power be conceived of without the Father? How can his stamp ever fail to exist in him? How can the stamp exist without the Father whose stamp he is?

But they are asserting that hypostases cannot be joined together or exist in one substance, and are somehow maybe misusing our human condition to prove their own nonsense.

In that case, ought they not to have noticed that the distinctive properties of the divine nature are not regulated by our condition but exist by their own principles, are apprehended by faith and are not susceptible to inquisitive reasonings? For the ineffable Godhead's one nature exists in three distinct hypostases outside the principles involved in our condition and does not follow the ways of created beings. There are many evidences of this. We are fathers of our children by way of an outflow and division, because what is born attains to a complete and absolutely distinct individuality. But this is not what we mean when we say that the Son was begotten of God the Father. He shone forth from his substance and radiated from him like light; he is not outside him but is of him and in him. Human fathers are older than their children but this is not at all the case with God. He ever co-exists with the Father and possesses unoriginate

ἔχει τὴν ὕπαρξιν τῷ ἰδίῳ γεννήτορι, ἵνα καὶ ἀεὶ φαίνηται πατήρ.
οὐ γὰρ ἦν ὅτε τοῦτο οὐκ ἦν. ἔστι τοίνυν ταὐτὸν μὲν τῷ πατρὶ τῇ
φύσει τὸ θεῖόν τε καὶ ὑπερκόσμιον γέννημα, ἐν ἑτερότητι δὲ τῇ
κατὰ υἱότητα μόνην. οὐ γάρ ἐστι πατήρ, ὅτι μηδὲ ἐκεῖνος υἱός.
πάντα τοίνυν πληρούσης, ὡς ἔφην, τῆς ἀνωτάτω πασῶν οὐσίας, 5
ὅτι καὶ ὑπὲρ κτίσιν ἐστὶ καὶ νοῦν καὶ λόγον, μὴ βατταριζέτωσάν
τινες, τὰ ἀπὸ καρδίας αὐτῶν λαλοῦντες, καὶ οὐκ ἀπὸ στόματος κυρίου,[l25] καθὰ γέγραπται, ἵνα μὴ παραλύοντες τὴν
ἀλήθειαν ταῖς ἑαυτῶν ψυχαῖς τὴν τοῖς τοῦτο δρᾶν εἰωθόσι πρέπουσαν
ἐπαντλήσωσι[26] δίκην. 10

Γ′[1]

Πρὸς τοὺς λέγοντας ὅτι γενόμενος ἄνθρωπος ὁ μονογενὴς κενοὺς
ἀφῆκε[2] τῆς ἑαυτοῦ θεότητος τοὺς οὐρανούς.

᾿Επίλυσις

Ἄπιστά τινες, ὡς ἔμαθον, καὶ γελοιότητος τῆς ἐσχάτης ἐπίμεστα
ῥημάτια περικομίζουσι, τὰ ἀπὸ καρδίας αὐτῶν λαλοῦντες, 15
καὶ οὐκ ἀπὸ στόματος κυρίου,[a] κατὰ τὸ γεγραμμένον. ὅπου
γὰρ τὸ τῆς ἀληθείας οὐ διαφαίνεται κάλλος, ἐκεῖ πάντως ὁ τοῦ
ψεύδους πατὴρ ἐκχεῖ τῆς ἐνούσης αὐτῷ σκαιότητος τὸν ἀνδρο-
κτόνον ἰόν. μανθάνω τοίνυν τινὰς ἐκ πολλῆς ἄγαν ἀσυνεσίας
διακεῖσθαι καὶ λέγειν, ὅτι γενόμενος ἄνθρωπος ὁ μονογενὴς τοῦ 20
θεοῦ λόγος, καὶ μετὰ σαρκὸς συναναστραφεὶς[3] τοῖς ἐπὶ[4] γῆς, κενοὺς
ἀφῆκε τῆς ἑαυτοῦ[5] θεότητος τοὺς οὐρανούς. τοῦτο δέ ἐστιν ἕτερον
οὐδὲν ἢ ἐκεῖνο φάναι, ὅτι ποσότητι μετρητός ἐστι, καὶ περιληπτὴν[6]
ἔχει τὴν φύσιν, καὶ ἐν τόπῳ μένει καθὰ καὶ τὰ σώματα, ἤγουν τὰ
ἕτερα τῶν κτισμάτων. ἠγνόησαν δὲ ἴσως ὅτι τὸ θεῖον ἀσώματόν 25
ἐστιν, ἀσχημάτιστον, ἀμερές, οὐ ποσότητι μετρητόν,[7] οὐ τόπῳ
περιγραφόμενον, ἀλλὰ πληροῦν μὲν τὰ πάντα καὶ ἐν πᾶσιν ὄν,

---

[l] Jer. 23: 16   3. [a] ibid.

[25] θεοῦ G   [26] ἐπαντλήσουσι CG   3. [1] β̄ CG   [2] ἐφῆκε C
[3] συναναστρεφεὶς C   [4] τῆς add. C   [5] αὐτοῦ G   [6] περιληπτικὴν G
[7] ἐστιν—μετρητὸν om. G

existence along with his parent so that the Father too is always
being revealed, because there was no time when this was not so.
The divine and supra-mundane offspring, then, is identical in
nature with the Father, differing from him only in his sonship;
for he is not the Father, nor is the Father the Son. So seeing, as
I have said, that the substance, which transcends all substances
because it is beyond creation and rational understanding, fills
all things, the persons in question are not to babble away *'speaking
what comes from their own hearts and not God's mouth'*, as Scripture
has it, lest they undermine the truth and flood their souls with the
punishment befitting such behaviour.

3

To those who say that on becoming man the Only-begotten left
heaven empty of his Godhead[23]

Answer

Some people, I am given to understand, are going the rounds
with incredible phrases chock full of absurdity in the extreme,
'speaking' (as Scripture has it) *'what comes from their own hearts and
not God's mouth'*. For the father of falsehood always pours out the
poisonous venom of his malice wherever the beauty of truth
fails to show itself. I am given to understand, then, that some are
prompted by utter stupidity to take the line that the only-
begotten Word of God on becoming man and having dealings
in the flesh with men on earth, left heaven empty of his Godhead.
This amounts to saying that he is quantitatively measurable,
has a limited nature and occupies a position like bodies or the
rest of created things. Perhaps they did not know that the Godhead is incorporeal, without configuration or parts, not quantitatively measurable, or limited by position but that it fills all

---

[23] Both issue and answer look like an alternative version of the previous.
The arguments and Biblical quotations overlap. A different point, though, is
being made. Here it is whether the Son took his Godhead with him when he
descended; previously whether he left it behind. Perhaps the original question
was obscure and Cyril gave Tiberius alternative answers.

ἀχώρητον ὂν⁸ κατ᾿ ἰδίαν φύσιν. γέγραπται γὰρ ὅτι ποῦ πορευθῶ
ἀπὸ τοῦ πνεύματος σοῦ, καὶ ἀπὸ τοῦ προσώπου σου ποῦ
φύγω; ἐὰν ἀναβῶ εἰς τὸν οὐρανόν, σὺ ἐκεῖ εἶ· ἐὰν καταβῶ
εἰς τὸν ᾅδην, πάρει· ἐὰν ἀναλάβοιμι τὰς πτέρυγάς μου
κατ᾿ ὄρθρον καὶ κατασκηνώσω εἰς τὰ ἔσχατα τῆς θαλάσ- 5
σης, καὶ γὰρ ἐκεῖ ἡ χείρ σου ὁδηγήσει με.ᵇ ἔδει τοίνυν
αὐτοὺς οὐκ ἐξ ἀμαθίας προπετεῖς ἐρεύγεσθαι φωνάς, ἀλλ᾿ ἐννοεῖν
οἷά τε καὶ ὅση καὶ ἐν τίσιν ὑπεροχαῖς ἡ θεία⁹ καὶ ὑπερμεγέθης καὶ
ἀπόρρητος τοῦ θεοῦ φύσις ἐστί.¹⁰ πότε γὰρ ὁ θεὸς λόγος ἀπέστη
τοῦ εἶναι μετὰ τοῦ πατρὸς ἢ τοῦ ἐν αὐτῷ μένειν; εἰ γὰρ ἐνδέχεται 10
τοῦ φωτὸς ἐκπεσεῖν καὶ χωρισθῆναι τὸ ἀπαύγασμα τὸ ἀπ᾿ αὐτοῦ,
ἦν ἂν εἰκὸς ἐννοῆσαι ὅτι καὶ τὸν υἱὸν ἐνδέχεται μὴ εἶναι μετὰ
τοῦ πατρός. πῶς δὲ οὐκ ἐνενόησαν ὅτι γενητὸς¹¹ ὢν ὁ ἥλιος
(κτίσμα γάρ ἐστι δι᾿ αὐτοῦ τοῦ λόγου παρενεχθεὶς εἰς γένεσιν)
διέρπει μὲν τὴν¹² ἄνω καὶ αὐτῷ ταχθεῖσαν ὁδόν, καθίησι δὲ τοῖς 15
ἀπανταχόσε φῶς, καὶ πάντα πληρῶν τῆς ἐξ αὐτοῦ προχεομένης
αὐγῆς, ἔχει πάλιν αὐτὴν ἐν ἑαυτῷ; πότε¹³ τοίνυν οὐκ ἦν ἐν πατρὶ τὸ
ἀπαύγασμα τῆς δόξης αὐτοῦ;¹³ πότε κεχώρισται τῆς ὑποστάσεως
αὐτοῦ ὁ χαρακτὴρ αὐτοῦ; καὶ εἰ τὰ πάντα πληροῦντος τοῦ πατρὸς
οὐκ ἔχει τοῦτο κατὰ φύσιν ἰδίαν ὁ υἱός, τὸ πάντα φημὶ πληροῦν 20
καὶ εἶναι πανταχοῦ καὶ οὐδενὸς ἀπολιμπάνεσθαι, ἑτεροφυὴς ἄρα
παρ᾿ αὐτόν ἐστιν. ἐκπίπτουσι τοίνυν εἰς τὴν Ἀρειανῶν πεπλανημένην δόξαν οἱ ταῦτα περὶ αὐτοῦ τολμῶντες λέγειν. εἰ μὲν γὰρ
πεπιστεύκασιν ἀληθῶς ὅτι καὶ θεὸς καὶ ἐκ θεοῦ πατρὸς κατὰ φύσιν
πέφηνεν ὁ¹⁴ υἱός, τί μὴ νέμουσιν αὐτῷ τὰ τῇ θείᾳ πρέποντα φύσει; 25
εἰ δὲ ὄνομα μὲν αὐτῷ τὸ τοῦ θεοῦ περιπλάττουσιν, ἀποστεροῦσι
δὲ τῶν τῆς θεότητος ἀξιωμάτων, ἠγνοήκασιν ὅτι καταφέρουσιν ἐν
κτίσμασι τὸν ποιητήν, καὶ τῇ τῶν γεγονότων μοίρᾳ τάττουσι τὸν
τῶν ὅλων γενεσιουργὸν καὶ κύριον· οὐκοῦν ἦν μὲν ἐπὶ γῆς
ὁρώμενος κατὰ σάρκα ἄνθρωπος, πλήρεις δὲ ἦσαν καὶ οὕτω τῆς 30
θεότητος αὐτοῦ οἱ οὐρανοί. πληροῖ γὰρ ὡς ἔφην τὰ πάντα θεὸς ὢν
ὁ λόγος.

ᵇ Ps. 138(139): 7 ff.

---

⁸ ὂν om. G   ⁹ τε add. G   ¹⁰ ἐστι before τοῦ C   ¹¹ γεννητὸς G
¹² τῶν C   ¹³ πότε—αὐτοῦ om. G   ¹⁴ ὁ om. G

and exists in all, being infinite by its very nature. Scripture has it *'Where shall I go from thy Spirit and where shall I flee from thy face? If I ascend to heaven thou art there. If I descend to Hades, thou art present. If I take up my wings in the morning and pitch my tent in the extremities of the ocean, thou art there and thy hand will lead me.'* They ought not, then, to give vent to rash and ignorant utterances but should realize the quality, the greatness and the majestic attributes of God's divine, supernal and ineffable nature. When did God the Word stop being with the Father or cease abiding in him? If the radiance can fall away and be cut off from its light, it would be possible to imagine that the Son might not exist with the Father. Have they not noticed that the sun, a created being (a created thing, brought into existence by the Word himself) glides upon its high appointed course yet sends down its light on all sides; though the radiance it sheds forth from itself fills all things it maintains it within itself? When, therefore, did the radiance of his glory not exist in the Father? When was his stamp parted from his hypostasis? If the Father fills all things but the Son does not possess this property by right of his own nature (the property, I mean, of filling all things, being omnipresent and remote from nothing) then the Son must be of a different stock from him. So people who venture to say this about him are lapsing into the aberrant doctrine of the Arians.[24] If they really believe that the Son is God and issues naturally from God the Father, why do they not ascribe to him the attributes appropriate to divine nature? If, on the other hand, the name 'God' they give him is a fiction and they rob him of divine attributes, they are ignorant of the fact that they are reducing the creator to the level of creatures and are putting the author and Lord of all into the same class as his products. It follows that even when he was visible as man on earth in the flesh, heaven was full of his Godhead, for, as I said, as God the Word he fills all.

---

[24] A parting shot, since the intruders are clearly not Arians, but accept the consubstantiality and the natural issue of the Son from the Father (next sentence). Cyril was, no doubt, glad to find a point that might strike home: a created God (the Arian view) and a God who leaves heaven can only be called 'God' by a misuse of terms.

Δ'[1]

Πρὸς τοὺς λέγοντας ὅτι ἠγνόησεν ὁ υἱὸς τὴν ἐσχάτην ἡμέραν.[2]

Ἐπίλυσις

Φασί γε μὴν καὶ ἑτέρους ἀκούσαντας λέγοντος τοῦ Χριστοῦ
περὶ δὲ[3] τῆς ἡμέρας ἢ τῆς ὥρας ἐκείνης οὐδεὶς οἶδεν,
οὐδὲ οἱ ἄγγελοι τῶν οὐρανῶν, οὐδὲ[4] ὁ υἱός, εἰ μὴ ὁ πατὴρ   5
μόνος,[a] ἀσυνετώτατα λέγειν, μὴ εἰδέναι κατὰ ἀλήθειαν τὸν ἐκ τῆς
οὐσίας τοῦ θεοῦ καὶ πατρὸς πεφηνότα λόγον, μήτε τὴν ὥραν μήτε
τὴν ἡμέραν ἐκείνην, ἵνα τοῖς ἀγγέλοις συντάττηται, καὶ κατὰ
μηδένα τρόπον διαφέρειν δοκῇ τῶν δι' αὐτοῦ γεγονότων. εἶτα πῶς
ἐν ἴσῃ τάξει τε καὶ φύσει ποίημα καὶ ποιητής; πῶς δὲ οὐκ ἄπορον[5]   10
τὸ μεσολαβοῦν; ὁ μὲν γάρ ἐστι πάντων ἐπέκεινα τὸ δὲ ἐν τοῖς
πᾶσιν. εἰ δὲ οἴονται κατὰ ἀλήθειαν ἠγνοηκέναι τι[6] Χριστόν, καθ'
ὃ νοεῖται θεός, ἔξω φέρονται σκοποῦ, καὶ τρέχουσι κατὰ πετρῶν,
καὶ τὸ κέρας ἐγείρουσι κατὰ τῆς δόξης αὐτοῦ.[7] εὑρεθήσεται γάρ,
ἂν οὕτως ἔχῃ καθά φασιν αὐτοί,[8] οὐδὲ[9] ὁμοούσιος ἔτι τῷ θεῷ καὶ   15
πατρί. εἰ γὰρ οἶδε μὲν ὁ πατήρ, ἀγνοεῖ δὲ ὁ υἱός, πῶς ἴσος ἔσται
αὐτῷ, ἤγουν ὁμοούσιος; δεῖ γὰρ πάντως ἐν μείοσιν εἶναι τοῦ
εἰδότος τὸ μὴ εἰδός. καὶ τὸ ἐπὶ τούτων παραλογώτερον, βουλὴ καὶ
σοφία τοῦ θεοῦ καὶ πατρὸς ὁ υἱὸς ὠνόμασται. Παῦλος μὲν γὰρ ἔφη
περὶ αὐτοῦ ὃς ἐγενήθη ἡμῖν σοφία[10] ἀπὸ θεοῦ,[b] καὶ πάλιν ἐν   20
ᾧ εἰσι πάντες οἱ θησαυροὶ τῆς σοφίας καὶ γνώσεως
ἀπόκρυφοι·[c] ψάλλει δὲ καὶ ὁ θεσπέσιος Δαυὶδ πρὸς τὸν ἐν
οὐρανοῖς πατέρα καὶ θεὸν ἐν τῇ βουλῇ σου ὡδήγησάς με,[d]
βουλὴν αὐτοῦ λέγων τὸν ἐξ αὐτοῦ φύντα υἱόν.[11] εἶτα πῶς οὐ γελοῖον
ἀγνοεῖν οἴεσθαί τι τῶν ἐν τῷ πατρὶ τὴν σοφίαν αὐτοῦ καὶ τὴν   25
βουλὴν αὐτοῦ; καὶ ὁ μόνος εἰδὼς τὸν πατέρα, πῶς ἀγνοεῖ τὴν τῆς

---

4. [a] Mark 13: 32, cf. Matt. 24: 36   [b] 1 Cor. 1: 30   [c] Col. 2: 3
[d] Ps. 72(73): 24

Witnesses: l. 1–p. 152, l. 22 C G Syr + Flor. Cyr. to p. 152, line 18

---

4. [1] Γ' C: om. G+Syr   [2] τὴν ἡ. τὴν ἐσχ. G   [3] δὲ om. Flor. Cyr.
[4] οὔτε C: οὐτὲ (sic) G   [5] ἄτοπον Flor. Cyr.   [6] τι] τὸν G   [7] καθ'
ὅ—αὐτοῦ om. G   [8] ἂν—αὐτοί] κατὰ τὴν αὐτῶν ἀπόφασιν G   [9] οὔτε
Flor. Cyr.   [10] ἐγεννήθη ὑμῖν G: ἐγεννήθη σοφία ἡμῖν Flor. Cyr.   [11] υἱόν
λόγον Syr

4

To those who assert that the Son did not know the final day

Answer

They state that others,[25] on hearing Christ saying '*No one knows about that day or hour, not even the angels of heaven or the Son but the Father alone*' are most foolishly asserting that the Word, issuing from God the Father's substance, actually does not know either that hour or day, in order that he may be ranked alongside the angels and may be deemed to differ in no respect from his creatures.[26] How can creature and creator belong in the same rank and nature? Must there not surely be an impassable gulf between them? The Creator transcends the universe, the creature belongs in the universe. If they suppose that Christ, in so far as he is viewed as God, was actually ignorant of something, they are going off course, careering over boulders and raising their horn against his glory. For, if it be as they say, then he will no longer be found to be consubstantial with God the Father.[27] For if the Father knows but the Son does not know, how can he be equal or consubstantial with him? Ignorance must be inferior to knowledge. Even more anomalously for them, the Son is called God the Father's Wisdom and Counsel. For Paul said of him '*Who was made Wisdom for us by God*' and again '*In whom are hidden all the treasures of Wisdom and Knowledge*'. Inspired David hymns the heavenly God and Father in the words '*Thou hast guided me with thy counsel*', meaning by God's 'counsel' the Son springing from him. In that case must it not be absurd to suppose that the Father's Wisdom and Counsel could be ignorant of any feature of him? How could the only knower of the Father be ignorant of the day of consummation? Which is the superior

---

[25] The intruders again?

[26] Cf. the anonymous confession of faith presented to Jerome in Palestine (*ACO* 1, 5 pp. 4 f.) by someone accused of Origenist errors and now recanting them, item 4: 'As for those who interpret the text . . . (Mark 13 : 32) . . . in the blasphemous sense of the Arians and not in accordance with the incarnate dispensation, let them be anathema.' The Origenist context and milieu make this the nearest parallel I can find to the present. On this confession see J. N. D. Kelly, *Jerome, his life, writings and controversies* (London, 1975), p. 259 with n. 2.

[27] A regular Arian objection to the Son's consubstantiality. Cyril reverses the argument here : since you admit the consubstantiality you must allow his full knowledge.

συντελείας ἡμέραν; ποῖον ἄρα τὸ προὔχον ἐν[12] γνώσει, τὸ εἰδέναι
τί ἐστιν ὁ πατήρ, ἤγουν τὴν ἐσχάτην ἡμέραν; γέγραπται δὲ πάλιν
ὅτι τὸ πνεῦμα πάντα ἐρευνᾷ καὶ τὰ βάθη τοῦ θεοῦ.[e] ὅτε
τοίνυν τὸ πνεῦμα τὸ εἰδὸς τὰ βάθη τοῦ θεοῦ καὶ πάντα τὰ ἐν αὐτῷ,
πνεῦμά ἐστι καὶ αὐτοῦ τοῦ υἱοῦ,[13] πῶς οὐκ οἶδε τὰ ἐν τῷ ἰδίῳ πατρί;[14] 5

Πολλῶν τοιγαροῦν εἰς ἀτοπίαν ἐννοιῶν συνωθουσῶν τὸν ἀμαθῆ
καὶ κίβδηλον[15] ἐκείνων λόγον, ἀναγκαῖον ἐλθεῖν ἐπὶ τὴν οἰκονομίαν, φάναι τε,[16] ὅτι πεφόρηκε μὲν[17] ὁ μονογενὴς τοῦ θεοῦ
λόγος μετὰ τῆς ἀνθρωπότητος καὶ πάντα τὰ αὐτῆς, δίχα μόνης[18]
ἁμαρτίας.[f] ἀνθρωπότητος δὲ μέτροις πρέποι ἂν εἰκότως καὶ τὸ 10
ἀγνοεῖν τὰ ἐσόμενα· οὐκοῦν καθ' ὃ μὲν νοεῖται θεός, οἶδε πάντα
ὅσα καὶ ὁ πατήρ· καθά[19] γε μὴν ἄνθρωπος ὁ αὐτός[20] οὐκ[21] ἀπο-
σείεται τὸ καὶ ἀγνοῆσαι δοκεῖν, διὰ τὸ τῇ ἀνθρωπότητι πρέπον.
ὥσπερ δὲ αὐτὸς ὢν ἡ πάντων ζωὴ καὶ δύναμις τροφὴν ἐδέχετο
σωματικήν, οὐκ ἀτιμάζων τὸ τῆς κενώσεως μέτρον, ἀναγέγραπται 15
δὲ καὶ ὑπνῶν καὶ κοπιάσας, οὕτω καὶ πάντα εἰδὼς τὴν τῇ ἀνθρωπότητι πρέπουσαν ἄγνοιαν οὐκ ἐρυθριᾷ προσνέμων ἑαυτῷ· γέγονε
γὰρ αὐτοῦ[22] πάντα τὰ τῆς ἀνθρωπότητος, δίχα μόνης ἁμαρτίας.
ἐπειδὴ δὲ τὰ ὑπὲρ ἑαυτοὺς ἤθελον οἱ μαθηταὶ μανθάνειν, σκήπτεται
χρησίμως τὸ μὴ εἰδέναι καθὸ ἄνθρωπος, καί φησι, μηδὲ αὐτοὺς 20
εἰδέναι τοὺς κατὰ τὸν οὐρανὸν ὄντας ἁγίους ἀγγέλους, ἵνα μὴ
λυπῶνται ὡς μὴ θαρρηθέντες τὸ μυστήριον.

[e] 1 Cor. 2: 10   [f] cf. Heb. 4: 15

---

[12] τῇ add. Flor. Cyr.   [13] Χριστοῦ Syr   [14] τὰ—πατρί] τὰ δι' αὐτοῦ
Syr?: ὁ υἱός add. Flor. Cyr.   [15] ἀκίβδηλον G   [16] φαίνεται Flor. Cyr.
[17] μὲν om. Flor. Cyr.   [18] τῆς add. Flor. Cyr.   [19] καθ' ὃ Flor. Cyr. Syr?
[20] ὁ αὐτὸς ἄνθρωπος G   [21] οὐκ om. G   [22] ἑαυτοῦ Flor. Cyr.

---

28 Cf. *Third Letter to Nestorius* § 10 and *Anathematism* 9, pp. 26 and 30 above.
Cyril's most connected discussions of the mode of being of the Spirit are
Thesaurus, cc. 33 f. (*PG* 75, 565 ff.) and *Dialogues on the Trinity* 7 (ibid. Aubert
631 ff.). The Spirit, for Cyril, belongs equally to the Son and Father. He
indwells Christ and is bestowed by Christ (see p. 27) but his being is derived
from the Father. Cyril certainly did not hold to the double procession of the

kind of knowledge, knowledge of what the Father is or knowledge of the final day? Scripture again has it that '*The Spirit searches out all things, even the depths of God*'. So when the Spirit, which knows the depths of God and all that is in him, is the Spirit of the Son himself,[28] must he not know what belongs to his Father?

There are many considerations which reduce this ignorant and shoddy argument of theirs to absurdity, but we ought to touch on the divine plan and remark that God's only-begotten Word took on along with his humanity all its attributes save sin alone. Ignorance of future events properly belongs to the limitations of humanity and so, in so far as he is viewed as God, he knows all the Father knows; in so far, though, as the same Son is man, he does not repudiate the appearance of ignorance because it is an attribute of humanity.[29] Just as he who is personally the Life and Power of all took bodily nourishment out of respect for the measure of his self-emptying and is recorded as having slept and been weary, so, though knowing all things, he is not ashamed to allot himself the ignorance which belongs to humanity; because his were all the attributes of humanity save sin alone. But seeing that the disciples wanted to learn things beyond them, he helped them by claiming not to know as man, and tells them that not even the angels in heaven know, in order that they might not be disappointed at not being entrusted with the mystery.

Spirit, though his authority has been claimed for it. All the texts of Cyril asserting the derivation of the Spirit from the Son apply to the 'economy', i.e. God's saving action in the world, not to his mode of being.

[29] Cf. the parallel passages *Thesaurus*, c. 22 (*PG* 75, 368 ff.) and *Dialogues on the Trinity* 6 (ibid. Aubert 623). Cyril's solution derives directly from Athanasius' *Third Oration against the Arians*, cc. 42 ff., owing nothing to the important discussions by Basil *Ep.* 236 or Gregory Naz. *Or.* 30, 15 f. All refer the ignorance to the conditions of the Incarnation, but the Cappadocians are subtler. For a discussion of Cyril's view and survey of the literature on it, see J. Liébaert *La Doctrine christologique etc.*, pp. 87–100; he concludes that, for Cyril, 'Christ's ignorance was simply an educational process bearing no relation to any actual ignorance'. This needs qualification, for clearly the ignorance is as real as the hunger and thirst (see next sentence). Cyril's view is, rather, that Christ does not feign ignorance, any more than he feigns hunger. It belongs with the human condition he has taken on, and therefore when asked about a mystery beyond human comprehension, he gives the only possible human answer. Cf. also Cyril's slightly different solution in a frag. *In Matt.* 24: 36 (*PG* 72, 441C, cf. ibid. 444C); both passages are included in *Doctrina Patrum*, c. 16 (a section of the florilegium directed against Agnoetes and Aphthartodocetists). For a Latin debate see the case of Leporius and his *Libellus Emendationis* (*PL* 31, 1221 ff.), para. 10, ibid. 1229.

Ε΄¹

Πρὸς τοὺς λέγοντας ὅτι ἰδικῶς ὁ λόγος ἐνεργεῖ τὰς θεοσημίας,
οὐδὲν πρὸς τοῦτο ἐχούσης τῆς ἁγίας αὐτοῦ σαρκός.

Ἐπίλυσις²

Τοὺς δὲ λέγοντας, ὅτι οὐ χρὴ κοινοποιεῖν τὴν σάρκα τῇ θεότητι
τοῦ μονογενοῦς, οὐδὲ τὴν θεότητα τῇ σαρκὶ ἐν ταῖς θαυματουργίαις·   5
ἢ καὶ ὅτι τὸν Λάζαρον ἤγειρεν ἐκ τοῦ μνημείου φωνήσαςᵃ ὁ θεὸς
λόγος καὶ οὐχ ὁ ἄνθρωπος, καὶ ὅτι οὐχ ὁ θεὸς ἐκοπίασεν ἐν τῇ
ὁδοιπορίᾳ,ᵇ ἀλλ᾽ ὁ ἀναληφθεὶς³ ἄνθρωπος, καὶ αὐτὸς ἐπείνασε καὶ
ἐδίψησε καὶ ἐσταυρώθη καὶ ἀπέθανεν· ὁλοτρόπως τῆς ἀληθείας
διημαρτηκέναι φαμέν, καὶ τῆς μετὰ σαρκὸς οἰκονομίας ἀγνοῆσαι τὸ   10
μυστήριον. οὐ γὰρ εἶναί φαμεν υἱοὺς δύο, οὐδὲ δύο χριστούς, ἀλλ᾽
ἕνα Χριστὸν καὶ υἱόν, τόν ἐκ θεοῦ μὲν πατρὸς πρὸ παντὸς αἰῶνος
καὶ χρόνου γεννηθέντα θεὸν μονογενῆ καὶ ἐνυπόστατον αὐτοῦ
λόγον, ἐν ἐσχάτοις δὲ τοῦ αἰῶνος καιροῖς τὸν αὐτὸν κατὰ σάρκα ἐκ
γυναικός. μὴ τοίνυν ἀποδιοριζέτωσαν ὡς δίψυχοι, μηδὲ δύο ἡμῖν   15
εἰσκομιζέτωσαν υἱούς, ἀλλ᾽ ἕνα καὶ τὸν αὐτὸν ὁμολογείτωσαν, ὡς
ἐνανθρωπήσαντα θεοῦ λόγον, καὶ αὐτοῦ πάντα καὶ φωνὰς καὶ
ἐνεργείας. ἐπειδὴ γὰρ ἦν ὁ αὐτὸς θεός τε ὁμοῦ καὶ ἄνθρωπος, λαλεῖ
καὶ θεοπρεπῶς καὶ ἀνθρωπίνως· ἐνεργεῖ δὲ ὁμοίως καὶ τὰ ἀνθρώπινα καὶ τὰ⁴ θεοπρεπῆ. ὅταν τοίνυν ὁμολογῶσιν ἕνα υἱὸν καὶ   20
Χριστὸν καὶ κύριον, πεπαύσονται διαιροῦντες ἀμαθῶς καὶ διιστάντες
εἰς δύο, ὡς ἕνα μὲν ἰδικῶς καὶ ἀνὰ μέρος υἱὸν νοεῖσθαι τὸν ἐκ θεοῦ
πατρὸς λόγον, ἕτερον δὲ πάλιν ἰδικῶς καὶ ἀνὰ μέρος υἱὸν τόν, ὡς
αὐτοί φασιν, ἀναληφθέντα ἄνθρωπον. ἡμεῖς γὰρ οὐχ οὕτως φαμέν,
οὐδὲ οὕτως πιστεύομεν, ἀλλ᾽ ὅτι θεὸς ὢν ὁ⁵ λόγος γέγονε σὰρξ   25
τουτέστιν ἄνθρωπος, οὐκ ἀποβαλὼν τὸ εἶναι θεός, ἀλλὰ καὶ
μεμενηκὼς ὅπερ ἦν ἀτρέπτως καὶ ἀναλλοιώτως, καὶ μετεσχηκὼςᶜ
σαρκὸς καὶ αἵματος κατὰ τὰς γραφάς· τὴν δέ γε ἐνωθεῖσαν αὐτῷ
καὶ ἰδίαν αὐτοῦ γενομένην σάρκα ἐψυχῶσθαί φαμεν ψυχῇ νοερᾷ.

5. ᵃ cf. John 11:43   ᵇ cf. ibid. 4:6   ᶜ cf. Heb. 2:14

Witnesses: l. 1–p. 160, l. 28 C G Syr

5. ¹ Δ΄ CG   ² om. CG   ³ ὁ add. G   ⁴ καὶ τὰ om. G
⁵ ὁ om. G

5

To those who say that the Word effects the miracles on his own whilst his holy flesh contributes nothing[30]

Answer

As for those who assert that we ought not to regard the Only-begotten's flesh as sharing with his Godhead, or his Godhead with his flesh, in the performance of miracles, or that it was God the Word, and not the man, who raised Lazarus from the tomb and that it was not God who was weary in his journeying but the assumed man and he it was who was hungry and thirsty, who was crucified and who died—these we say utterly miss the truth and ignore the mystery of the incarnate dispensation. For we declare not that there are two Sons or two Christs, but that there is one Christ and Son, the only-begotten God, his personally existing Word, who was begotten of God the Father before any world and time and that this very one was born in flesh of a woman in the final period of the world's history.[31] So they must not waver[32] and divide or fetch us in two Sons, but must acknowledge one and the same as God's Word made man and confess that to him all belongs both of words and actions. For since the same is both God and man, he speaks both in human and divine terms and effects human and divine things alike. When they acknowledge one Son, Christ and Lord they will desist from this ignorant division and separation into two, asserting as they do that God the Word is viewed as one distinct separate Son and the assumed man as another distinct, separate Son. That is not what we say or believe. No, our affirmation and belief is that the Word who is God became flesh (that is, man) without abandoning his being God but remaining unalterably and unchangeably what he was, whilst 'sharing our flesh and blood', as Scripture has it; as for the flesh united with him which became his own, we declare it was endowed with mental life.[33]

[30] The Christological dualism here rebutted is similar to that of Nestorius and the answer proceeds accordingly (cf. no. 9 below which takes up the theme again). It is too crude to derive directly from Nestorius.

[31] Cf. the *Formula of Reunion*, p. 222, lines 7 f.

[32] δίψυχος is alleged, *PGL* s.v. 2, to mean 'believing in two souls' on the strength of this passage alone. But clearly the word has here its ordinary sense of 'being in two minds' over something. The reading δίψυχον has no authority.

[33] Cyril's habitual disclaimer of Apollinarianism, cf. pp. 4 and 10.

ς΄ι

Πρὸς τοὺς λέγοντας ὅτι οὐκ ἀνελήφθη μετὰ τῆς ἐνωθείσης αὐτῷ
σαρκός, ἐν ᾧ πρὸς τοὺς λέγοντας ὅτι τὸ ἀναληφθὲν σῶμα τῇ ἁγίᾳ
τριάδι συγκέκραται.

Ἐπίλυσις²

Ὅτι δὲ καὶ ἀνελήφθη μετὰ τῆς ἐνωθείσης αὐτῷ σαρκὸς πῶς ἂν   5
ἐνδοιάσειέ τις; τὸν γὰρ ἐκ νεκρῶν ἐγηγερμένον, αὐτὸν δηλονότι
καθὸ νοεῖται καὶ πέφηνεν ἄνθρωπος, κεκάθικεν ὁ πατὴρ ἐν δεξιᾷ
τοῦ θρόνου τῆς μεγαλωσύνης ἐν τοῖς ὑψηλοῖς, ὑπεράνω
πάσης ἀρχῆς καὶ ἐξουσίας καὶ δυνάμεως³ καὶ κυριότητος
καὶ παντὸς ὀνόματος ὀνομαζομένου·ᵃ ἥξει δὲ οὕτω κατὰ   10
καιρούς. καὶ ἀρκέσει πρὸς τοῦτο τῶν ἁγίων ἀγγέλων ἡ φωνὴ τοῖς
θεωμένοις αὐτὸν ἀναβαίνοντα μετὰ τὴν ἐκ νεκρῶν ἀναβίωσιν,
ἀναφανδὸν εἰρηκότων οὗτος ὁ Ἰησοῦς ὁ ἀναληφθεὶς ἀφ'
ὑμῶν⁴ οὕτως ἐλεύσεται ὃν τρόπον ἐθεάσασθε⁵ πορευόμενον αὐτὸν⁶ εἰς τὸν οὐρανόν.ᵇ εἰ μὲν οὖν οἱ τῆς ἀναλήψεως   15
αὐτοῦ γεγονότες θεωροί, γυμνὸν τῆς σαρκὸς τὸν λόγον τεθέανται,
οὕτως αὐτὸν καὶ ἥξειν ὑπονοείτωσάν τινες· εἰ δὲ πεπληροφόρηκε
τοὺς ἁγίους ἀποστόλους, τὸ ψηλαφητὸν αὐτοῖς δείξας σῶμα, καὶ
οὕτως ἀνελήφθη, οὕτω πάλιν ἐλεύσεται, καὶ οὐκ ἂν διαψεύσαιτο
τῶν ἁγίων πνευμάτων⁷ ὁ ἐπ' αὐτῷ λόγος.   20

Ἀλλὰ μηδὲ ἐκεῖνό τινες φαντάζέσθωσαν κακῶς, μήτε μὴν
ὑπονοείτωσαν, ὅτι τὸ ἑνωθὲν τῷ λόγῳ σῶμα τῇ τῆς ἁγίας τριάδος
συγκέκραται φύσει. ἀμήχανον γὰρ τὴν ἀπόρρητον⁸ ἐκείνην καὶ
ὑπερφυᾶ καὶ παντὸς ἐπέκεινα καὶ νοῦ καὶ λόγου νοουμένην οὐσίαν,
προσθήκην τινὰ καὶ μάλιστα τὴν ἔξωθεν καὶ ἑτέρας φύσεως   25
δύνασθαι λαβεῖν. ἔστι γὰρ ἐν τοῖς καθ' ἑαυτὴν παντελεία, καὶ οὔτε
μείωσιν ἐπιδέχεταί τινα, διὰ τὸ ἀτρέπτως καὶ ἀναλλοιώτως ἔχειν
ἀεί, οὔτε μὴν ὡς ἔφην προσθήκης ἂν δέοιτό τινος. περιττολογοῦσι
τοίνυν οἱ ἐκ πολλῆς ἀμαθίας κατὰ σύγκρασιν⁹ ἤγουν συνουσίωσιν ἐν

---

6. ᵃ Heb. 8: 1 and 1: 3, Eph. 1: 21   ᵇ Acts 1: 11

6. ¹ ἐ CG: om. Syr   ² λύσις G   ³ δυνάμεως καὶ ἐξουσίας G
⁴ ἡμῶν G   ⁵ ἐθεάσασθαι C   ⁶ πορευόμενον αὐτόν] αὐτὸν ἀναβαίνοντα
G   ⁷ τοῦ ἁγίου πνεύματος Syr perh. rightly   ⁸ ἀμήχανον (again) G
⁹ σύγκρισιν C

6

To those who say that he was not taken up along with the flesh united with him, including also an answer to those who declare that the assumed body was merged with the Holy Trinity[34]

Answer

How can anyone doubt that he was taken up along with the flesh united with him? For the Father set '*at the right hand of the throne of majesty in the heights*' '*above all rule, authority, power, lordship and every name that is named*' him who was raised from the dead, him, that is, as he is viewed and manifest as man. This is how he will come in due time. The words of the angels to those who beheld him ascending after his coming to life again from the dead, will suffice on the point. They clearly said '*This Jesus who has been taken up from you will come again in the same way that you saw him going into heaven.*' If the observers of his assumption, then, had seen the word denuded of flesh, then the people in question should take it that that is how he will come; but if he assured the holy apostles by showing them a palpable body and that is how he was assumed, then that is how he will come again and the holy spirits' statement will not belie him.

The people in question must not entertain the evil fancy of supposing that the body united with the Word was merged with the nature of the Trinity. It is impossible for that ineffable and supra-natural substance which is viewed as beyond all understanding and speech to be able to acquire any addition and especially not the addition of another nature from outside. It is utterly complete in its attributes and undergoes no diminution because it is ever unchangeable and unalterable, nor, as I said, does it need any addition. Those who ignorantly assert that the body merged or became consubstantiated[35] with the nature of

---

[34] Kindred notions are refuted by Athanasius *Letter to Epictetus*, para. 2 (*PG* 26, 1052c) and Gregory Naz. *Ep*. 101 (first to Cledonius) (*PG* 37, 181A). Cf. also p. 75.

[35] Cf. p. 111 n. 5.

τῇ φύσει τῆς ἁγίας τριάδος χωρῆσαι τὸ σῶμα λέγοντες. διακείμεθα
γὰρ οὐχ οὕτως ἡμεῖς, ἀλλ' ὀρθὴν ἔχομεν[10] περὶ τοῦ πάντων ἡμῶν
σωτῆρος Χριστοῦ τὴν δόξαν. ἐνανθρωπῆσαι γάρ φαμεν αὐτὸν τὸν
μονογενῆ τοῦ θεοῦ λόγον, οὐκ εἰς σάρκα τὴν ἰδίαν μεταποιήσαντα
φύσιν, ἀλλ' ἐκ τῆς ἁγίας παρθένου λαβόντα αὐτήν, ἥξοντά τε σὺν   5
αὐτῇ, πλὴν ἐν τῇ δόξῃ τοῦ πατρὸς μετὰ τῶν ἁγίων ἀγγέλων.

Z΄[1]

Πῶς χρὴ νοεῖσθαι τό ὁ λόγος σὰρξ ἐγένετο.[a]

Ἐπίλυσις

Ἐπειδὴ δέ, ὡς μανθάνω, προσποιοῦνταί τινες ἐρωτᾶν τό τί ἂν
εἴη ἢ κατὰ τίνα νοεῖται τρόπον τό ὁ λόγος σὰρξ ἐγένετο,[b]   10
πάλιν ἀναγκαίως ἐκεῖνό φαμεν ἔθος τῇ θεοπνεύστῳ γραφῇ καὶ ἀπὸ
μόνης σαρκὸς ὀνομάζειν ἔσθ' ὅτε τὸν ἄνθρωπον. καὶ γοῦν ἐν
προφήταις ἐπηγγέλλετο[2] θεὸς ἐκχεῖν τὸ ἑαυτοῦ πνεῦμα ἐπὶ
πᾶσαν σάρκα,[c] εἴρηται δὲ πάλιν ὅτι ὄψεται πᾶσα σὰρξ τὸ
σωτήριον τοῦ θεοῦ.[d] καὶ οὐ δήπου φαμὲν ὡς ἐπὶ μόνην τὴν   15
σάρκα τὸ θεῖον ἐκχεῖται πνεῦμα, ἀλλ' οὐδὲ ὅτι μόνη ἡ σὰρξ[3] τὴν
σωτηρίαν τεθέαται τὴν διὰ Χριστοῦ· ἀλλ' ἐπ' ἀνθρώπους ἐξεχύθη
τὸ πνεῦμα, καὶ αὐτοὶ τεθέανται τὴν σωτηρίαν. ὅταν τοίνυν ὁ
εὐαγγελιστὴς λέγῃ καὶ ὁ λόγος σὰρξ ἐγένετο,[e] οὐκ εἰς σάρκα
μεταπεποιῆσθαι διδάσκει τὸν τοῦ θεοῦ λόγον· ἄτρεπτος γάρ ἐστιν   20
ὡς ἐξ ἀτρέπτου πατρός· ἀλλ' ὅτι σάρκα ἐψυχωμένην νοερῶς ἰδίαν
ποιησάμενος, παραδόξως προῆλθεν ἄνθρωπος παρὰ τῆς ἁγίας
παρθένου, ἐπειδὴ δὲ οὐκ ἄνθρωπος ὢν πρότερον τεθεοποίηται
μᾶλλον, ἀλλὰ θεὸς ὢν φύσει, πέφηνεν ἄνθρωπος.

---

7. [a] John 1: 14   [b] ibid.   [c] Joel 2: 28   [d] Is. 40: 5
[e] John 1: 14

[10] ὀρθὴν ἔχομεν] ὀρθῶς ἔχοντες ἐσμὲν G   7. [1] ϛ΄ CG   [2] ἐπηγγείλετο
C: ἐπηγγέλετο G: corr.   [3] ἡ σὰρξ μόνη G

the holy Trinity are talking nonsense. That is not the view we take; we maintain orthodoxy concerning Christ the Saviour of us all. We assert that the only-begotten Word of God himself became man, not by changing his own nature into flesh but by taking it from the holy Virgin, and with it he will come again but in the Father's glory in company with the holy angels.

7

How the phrase 'the Word became flesh' ought to be interpreted

Answer

Seeing that some (as I am given to understand) make a pretence of asking the meaning and interpretation of the phrase '*The Word became flesh*' we are bound to say that inspired Scripture is sometimes wont to designate man simply by the term 'flesh'.[36] God promised by prophets that he would pour out his Spirit '*on all flesh*' and it says again that '*All flesh shall see God's salvation.*' We do not mean that the divine Spirit has only been poured out on flesh or that flesh alone has seen salvation through Christ—no, the Spirit was poured out on men and men have seen the salvation. So when the evangelist says '*And the Word became flesh*' he is not teaching us that God's word was turned into flesh (he is changeless, coming from a changeless Father) but making flesh animate with mind his own, in miraculous fashion he issued as man from the holy Virgin, and since he was not an existing man who was deified, but rather God by nature, he was manifest as man.

[36] Cf. *In Jo.* 1, 9 (Pusey 1 p. 138) and *On the Creed*, p. 111.

Η΄[1]

Πρὸς τοὺς ζητοῦντας εἰ προσέθηκέ τι τῇ τοῦ ἀνθρώπου φύσει παραγενόμενος ὁ Χριστὸς ἐν σαρκί· καὶ πῶς κατ᾽ εἰκόνα θεοῦ ὁ ἄνθρωπος.

Ἐπίλυσις

῞Οτι δὲ παντὸς ἀγαθοῦ πρόξενος τῇ τοῦ ἀνθρώπου γέγονε φύσει γενόμενος ἄνθρωπος ὁ μονογενὴς τοῦ θεοῦ λόγος,[2] τίς ὁ μὴ φάναι 5
τολμῶν; ἢ τίς καταρνήσεται, καὶ ἀνόνητον ἡμῖν γενέσθαι φήσει τὴν εἰς τόνδε τὸν κόσμον ἀποστολὴν αὐτοῦ; γέγονε μὲν γὰρ κατ᾽ εἰκόνα τὴν πρὸς αὐτὸν ὁ ἄνθρωπος ἐν ἀρχαῖς, καὶ ἦν ἡ φύσις ἐπιτηδείως ἔχουσα πρὸς ἀνάληψιν παντὸς ἀγαθοῦ καὶ εἰς κατόρθωσιν ἀρετῆς. ἔκτισε γὰρ ἡμᾶς ἐπὶ ἔργοις ἀγαθοῖς,[a] ὡς γοῦν[3] 10
ὁ πάνσοφος γράφει Παῦλος. ἀλλ᾽ ἠφάνισε τῆς θεοειδοῦς εἰκόνος τὸ κάλλος ἡ ἁμαρτία, καὶ ῥυποῦ μεστὸν ἀπέφηνεν ὁ σατανᾶς τὸ λαμπρὸν τῆς ἀνθρωπότητος πρόσωπον· ἀλλ᾽ ἐπέφανεν ὁ ἀνακαινιστής, ὁ ἀναμορφῶν εἰς τὸ ἐν ἀρχαῖς τὸ ἠδικημένον καὶ πάλιν ἡμᾶς εἰς τὴν ἑαυτοῦ μεταπλάττων εἰκόνα, ὥστε τῆς θείας αὐτοῦ φύσεως 15
ἐμπρέπειν ἡμῖν τοὺς χαρακτῆρας δι᾽ ἁγιασμοῦ καὶ δικαιοσύνης καὶ τῆς κατ᾽ ἀρετὴν εὐζωΐας. αὐτὸς γάρ ἐστιν ἡ θύρα καὶ ἡ ὁδός, δι᾽ ἧς πρὸς πᾶν ὁτιοῦν τῶν ἀρίστων εἰσελάσαι δεδυνήμεθα, καὶ ὀρθὰς ποιήσασθαι[4] τροχιάς· ὥστε ἐν ἡμῖν μὲν τοῖς ἐν Χριστῷ τὸ τῆς ἀρίστης εἰκόνος ἐκφαίνεται κάλλος, οἳ δι᾽ αὐτῶν τῶν ἔργων 20
ἠνδραγαθήσαμεν. ἐν δέ γε τῷ πρωτοπλάστῳ πᾶσα μὲν ἐπιτηδειότης ἦν, ἀποφέρουσα δύναμιν πρὸς ἀνάληψιν ἀρετῆς, οὐ πάντως δὲ καὶ ἐνεργείᾳ. τοιγαροῦν καὶ αὐτὸς ἔφη Χριστὸς περὶ ἡμῶν, ἤτοι τῶν ἰδίων προβάτων ἐγὼ ἦλθον ἵνα ζωὴν[5] ἔχωσι, καὶ περιττὸν[6] ἔχωσιν.[b] ἀποδέδοται μὲν γὰρ τῇ ἀνθρώπου φύσει τὸ ἐν Ἀδὰμ ἐν 25
ἀρχῇ, τουτέστιν ὁ[7] ἁγιασμός· τὸ δὲ περιττόν, ὥστε οἶμαι, φησί, τὸ κατ᾽ ἐνέργειαν ὁρᾶσθαι σεπτούς, καὶ δι᾽ αὐτῶν τῶν κατορθωμάτων καταφαιδρύνεσθαι.

---

8. [a] Eph. 2: 10   [b] John 10: 10

8. [1] Ζ΄ C: om. G   [2] ὁ μονογενὴς τοῦ θεοῦ λόγος γενόμενος ἄνθρωπος G
[3] γοῦν om. G   [4] ποιῆσαι G   [5] ζωὴν αἰώνιον Syr   [6] περιστὸν
(sic) G   [7] ὁ om. G

[37] i.e. did it give human nature any new constituent properties? Cyril's answer is that it did not, but that it restored the image distorted by sin but

8

To those who ask if Christ's coming in the flesh added anything[37] to human nature, and how man is in God's image

Answer

Who will dare deny that God's only-begotten Word has been productive of all good for human nature by his becoming man? Who can gainsay it and assert that his mission to this world has been of no benefit to us? Man was made in his image[38] to begin with and his nature was made capable of acquiring everything good and of accomplishing virtue. For he created us 'for good works' as all-wise Paul writes. But sin marred the beauty of the image and Satan befouled the bright visage of humanity; the restorer appeared, refashioning into its initial state what had been damaged and re-moulding[39] us into his own image, so that the marks of his divine nature shine in us through holiness,[40] righteousness and virtuous living. For he is the door and the way, whereby we have been enabled to enter upon all that is noblest and beat a straight path towards it; and so the beauty of the noblest image shines out in us who are in Christ and who have acquitted ourselves bravely in our deeds. In the first-formed man the aptitude, carrying with it a potentiality to acquire virtue, was present but not the actuality. So Christ himself said of us, his sheep, '*I came that they might have life and have it in abundance.*' What was in Adam at the beginning, holiness that is, has been restored to human nature; by 'abundance' he means, I think, actually being seen to be worthy of reverence and being resplendent by the very achievements.

---

not lost (cf. *Answer* 10, p. 167, lines 7ff.) and made it possible for man actually to be what he was intended to be.

[38] Cf. *Doctrinal Questions and Answers* 4.

[39] Cyril's 'image' is a relief or a statue (cf. Plotinus *Enn.* 1, 6, 9, where the soul is compared with a statue which has to be made beautiful; the whole treatise *On Beauty* much influenced Christian writers, so that no direct borrowing on Cyril's part is implied) rather than Athanasius' painting (see *De Inc.* c. 14). For Gregory Nyss. it is like the imprint on a coin which has been hidden by dirt (*De Virg.* 12, 3—see the edition of M. Aubineau, *SC* 119 (Paris, 1966), with his note *ad loc.*).

[40] Various senses of sanctification are distinguished by Cyril *In Jo.* 7 frag. (Pusey 2 pp. 259 f.) and *Dialogues on the Trinity* 6 (*PG* 75 Aubert 589). Holiness, in the present sense, means participation in the Holy Ghost and so in the divine nature, and for Cyril the divine nature is life itself. The divine image restored in man is man revitalized in body and soul for the life of faith.

Θ´1

Ὅτι[2] διὰ τῆς ἰδίας σαρκὸς ἐνεργεῖ τὰς θεοσημίας[3] θεὸς ὢν ὅ[4] λόγος.

Ἐπίλυσις[5]

Ἄνθρωπον δὲ γενέσθαι φαμὲν τὸν μονογενῆ τοῦ θεοῦ λόγον, οὐχ
ἵνα τὸ εἶναι θεὸς ἀποβάλῃ,[6] ἀλλ´[7] οὐδ᾽ ἵνα γυμνὸς νοῆται[8] λόγος,
ἐνανθρωπήσας δὲ μᾶλλον, καὶ ἴδιον ποιησάμενος σῶμα τὸ ἐκ τῆς 5
ἁγίας καὶ θεοτόκου παρθένου.[9] οὐκοῦν ὁ Χριστὸν ὀνομάζων, οὔτε
λόγον σημαίνει γυμνόν, οὔτε ἄνθρωπον κοινόν, ἢ[10] ὡς ἕνα τῶν καθ᾽
ἡμᾶς· ἐνανθρωπήσαντα δὲ ὡς ἔφην τὸν ἐκ θεοῦ πατρὸς λόγον, καὶ
κεχρισμένον εἰς ἀποστολήν. οὐ γὰρ ἄνθρωπος ἐθεοποιήθη, καθά
φασί[11] τινες, ἑνωθεὶς τῷ λόγῳ, ἀλλ᾽ αὐτὸς ὁ λόγος σάρκα λαβὼν 10
καὶ γενόμενος ἄνθρωπος μεμένηκε καὶ[12] οὕτω θεός.

Ὅταν οὖν[13] ἐργάζηται[14] τὰς[15] θεοσημίας,[16] μὴ διορίσας[17] ἀνὰ
μέρος τῆς ἁγίας αὐτοῦ σαρκὸς[18] τὸν ἐκ θεοῦ λόγον αὐτῷ[19] κατὰ
μόνας τὴν ἐπὶ τοῖς τελουμένοις ἀνάψῃς δύναμιν· νόει δὲ μᾶλλον
εὐσεβῶς ὅτι γενόμενος ἄνθρωπος ὁ μονογενὴς τοῦ θεοῦ λόγος, καὶ 15
διὰ τῆς ἰδίας ἑαυτοῦ[20] σαρκὸς ἐνήργει πολλάκις, ὡς ἰδίαν ἔχων
αὐτήν, οὐ κατὰ σύγχυσιν ἢ φυρμόν. καὶ ὥσπερ ἔστιν[21] ἐπὶ ἀνθρώπου
τεχνίτου νοεῖν[22] τέκτονος τυχὸν[23] ἢ σιδηρέως, ὅτι ποιεῖ τὰ ἔργα
μετὰ τοῦ ἰδίου σώματος ἡ ψυχή· καὶ οὐκ ἄν τις εἴποι ψυχῆς ἔργα
μόνης[24] εἶναι, εἰ καὶ αὐτὴ κινεῖ πρὸς ἔργα τὸ σῶμα, ἀλλὰ τοῦ 20
συναμφοτέρου· οὕτω νόει καὶ ἐπὶ Χριστοῦ. πρὸ μὲν γὰρ τῆς ἐνανθρωπήσεως γυμνὸς[25] ὢν ἔτι καὶ καθ᾽ ἑαυτὸν ὁ λόγος εἰργάζετο τὰ
θεοπρεπῆ, γεγονὼς δὲ ἄνθρωπος, ἐνήργει καὶ διὰ τῆς ἑαυτοῦ σαρκός,
ὡς ἔφην. οὕτως ἥψατο[a] τῶν τυφλῶν,[26] ἤγειρε δὲ[27] καὶ τὸν τῆς χήρας
υἱὸν πάλιν ἐκτείνας τὴν χεῖρα καὶ ἀψάμενος τῆς σοροῦ·[b] οὕτω πτύσας 25
καὶ ποιήσας πηλὸν ἔχρισε τοὺς ὀφθαλμοὺς τοῦ ἐκ γεννητῆς[28] τυφλοῦ.[c]

[a] cf. Matt. 9: 29   [b] cf. Luke 7: 14   [c] cf. John 9: 6

Witnesses: l. 1–p. 170, l. 28 C G O Syr

9. [1] Η´ CG   [2] Ὅτι] πρὸς τοὺς λέγοντας ὅτι Syr   [3] ἐνείργει . . .
θεοσημείας O   [4] ὁ om. G   [5] λύσις G: trsp. before Ὅτι O: om. C
[6] ἀποβάλλει O   [7] ἀλλ᾽ om. G   [8] νοεῖται C   [9] καὶ+παρθένου om. G:
καὶ θεοτόκου om. O   [10] ἢ om. O   [11] φησί O   [12] δὲ καὶ G
[13] οὖν] τοίνυν O   [14] ἐργάζεται O   [15] τὰς om. G   [16] θεοσημείας
O   [17] διορίσῃς O   [18] σαρκὸς αὐτοῦ G   [19] δὲ add. O   [20] αὐτοῦ O
[21] ἔστιν ἰδεῖν G   [22] νοεῖν om. GO   [23] τυχὸν C: om. O   [24] μόνον O
[25] γυμνὸς om. O   [26] καὶ τὸν τυφλὸν O   [27] δὲ om. O   [28] γενητῆς G

9

That the Word who is God effects miracles by means of his flesh[41]

Answer

We declare that the only-begotten Word of God was made man, not that he should abandon his being God or be perceived as pure Word, but rather as being made man by becoming man and making his own the body derived from the holy Virgin and Mother of God. So if one uses the name 'Christ' one does not mean the pure Word or an ordinary man like one of us, but, as I said, the incarnate Word of God the Father anointed for his mission.[42] There was not, as some assert, a deified man united with the Word, but the Word himself took flesh, being made man, and remained, even in this state, God.

When, therefore, he effects miracles, you are not to separate the Word of God from his sacred flesh[43] and attribute the power involved in their accomplishment to the Word on his own, but are to see, rather, with true religion that God's only-begotten Word on being made man often uses his flesh to act by, because he possesses it as his own, without merger or mingling. One can observe in the case of a carpenter, say, or a smith, that the soul performs the acts with the aid of its body, and no one would say that the acts belong just to the soul even though it moves the body into action but would say that they belong to the complex of both; that is how you are to look at Christ. Before his being made man the Word existed pure and effected his divine acts by himself; but after being made man he performed them, as I said, by means of his flesh. That is why he touched the blind and raised the widow's son by stretching out his hand and touching the bier; that is why he spat, made clay and applied it to the eyes of the man blind from birth.

---

[41] Cf. no. 6.

[42] See above p. 19 n. 8. Cf. also *Or. ad Theodosium* 28 (*ACO* 1, 1, 1 p. 60, 17 ff.), *Or. ad Dominas* 20 (*ACO* 1, 1, 5 p. 69, 18 ff.), and *In Ep. ad Hebr.* (Pusey 3, 378 ff.).

[43] i.e. the whole man, body and mind (see above no. 7). The following analogy, though, might suggest that the manhood is inert, mere body, with the Word as the active principle ('Apollinarianism'). The analogy must not be pressed: Cyril is not denying the existence of a human will in Christ, but asserting that the body is the medium through which he acts (the point at issue). The human will is implicitly affirmed in the comment on Christ's miracles, below. For two wills in Christ cf. *Thesaurus*, c. 24 (*PG* 75, 396D–397B) and *In Jo.* 4, 1 (Pusey 1 p. 487, 1–23). For the body as an ὄργανον cf. *Or. ad Theodos.* 21 (*ACO* 1, 1, 1 p. 55, 16 ff.), *Scholion* 24 (*ACO* 1, 5 p. 203, 28 ff.).

Εἰ δὲ καὶ διῆγε πνευματικῶς, ἐννόει πάλιν, ὅτι τὰ²⁹ καθ' ἡμᾶς
ἀναβιβάζων εἰς πνευματικὴν πολιτείαν, αὐτὸς ἤρξατο τοῦ πράγματος ἀνθρωπίνως, ἵν' ὁδὸς καὶ ἀρχὴ γένηται τῇ ἀνθρώπου φύσει
πρὸς τὸ δύνασθαι διαζῆν, οὐκέτι σαρκικῶς καὶ φιληδόνως,³⁰ ἁγίως
δὲ μᾶλλον καὶ πνευματικῶς. ἀρχὴ γὰρ ἡμῖν παντὸς³¹ γέγονεν 5
ἀγαθοῦ, καὶ διὰ τοῦτο πέφηνεν ἄνθρωπος, ἵνα τῆς ἐν Ἀδὰμ
ἀσθενείας ἐλευθερώσας³² τὴν ἡμῶν φύσιν, ὡς ἐν ἑαυτῷ³³ καὶ
πρώτῳ δείξῃ³⁴ πνευματικήν.

Γ'¹

ʿΟμοίως² πῶς κατ' εἰκόνα θεοῦ ὁ ἄνθρωπος.

Ἐπίλυσις³   10

Ἐπειδὴ δέ φασι καὶ ἑτέρους ζητεῖν, πῶς δεῖ⁴ κατ' εἰκόνα θεοῦ
νοεῖσθαι⁵ τὸν ἄνθρωπον, εἶτά τινες ἀσυνέτως κομιδῇ τὴν τοῦ
σώματος εἰκόνα, καὶ τὸ ὁρώμενον εἶδος αὐτό φασιν καὶ οὐχ ἕτερον
εἶναι τὴν πρὸς θεὸν ὁμοίωσιν· δεῖν ᾠήθην⁶ εἰπεῖν, ὅτι πεπλάνηνται,
καὶ τῆς ἀληθείας⁷ ἀφιλοθεάμονα τὴν διάνοιαν ἔχουσι. τοῦ γὰρ 15
σωτῆρος ἐναργῶς λέγοντος πνεῦμα ὁ θεός,ᵃ αὐτοὶ σωματοειδῆ
εἶναί φασιν τὴν θείαν φύσιν, καὶ ἐν χαρακτῆρι τοιούτῳ ἐν ᾧ καὶ
ἡμεῖς ἐσμέν. ἆρ' οὖν σῶμα καὶ αὐτός, καὶ οὐκ ἔτι πνεῦμα νοεῖται;
ἀκολουθεῖ γὰρ πάντως τὰ εἴδη τοῖς σώμασιν. ἐπειδὴ δὲ⁸ πνεῦμά
ἐστιν ὁ θεός, ἀνείδεός⁹ που πάντως ἐστί, καὶ τύπου καὶ σχήματος 20
καὶ περιγραφῆς ἐπέκεινα ἁπάσης.¹⁰ μεμορφώμεθα δὲ πρὸς αὐτὸν
κατὰ πρῶτον μὲν καὶ κυριώτατον¹¹ τρόπον, ὅσον ἂν νοοῖτο, κατ'
ἀρετὴν καὶ¹² ἁγιασμόν. ἅγιον γὰρ τὸ θεῖον, καὶ ἀρετῆς ἁπάσης
πηγὴ καὶ ἀρχὴ καὶ γένεσις. ὅτι δὲ πρέποι ἂν οὕτω νοεῖσθαι μᾶλλον
τὸ κατ' εἰκόνα θεοῦ γενέσθαι¹³ τὸν ἄνθρωπον, διδάξει¹⁴ καὶ ὁ 25
πάνσοφος Παῦλος τοῖς ἐν Γαλατίᾳ¹⁵ λέγων τεκνία οὓς πάλιν
ὠδίνω, ἄχρις οὗ μορφωθῇ Χριστὸς ἐν ὑμῖν.ᵇ μορφοῦται

___

10. ᵃ John 4: 24   ᵇ Gal. 4: 19

²⁹ τὰ om. O   ³⁰ φιληδόνως C   ³¹ παντὸς om. O   ³² ἐλευθερῶσαι O
³³ αὐτῷ G   ³⁴ δείξει C   10. ¹ Θ' CG   ² om. G   ³ om. G
⁴ δὴ C   ⁵ προσήκει νοεῖσθαι C   ⁶ ὀηθεῖν O   ⁷ καὶ add. G
⁸ δὲ om. O   ⁹ ἀνείδεως (sic) O   ¹⁰ πάσης O   ¹¹ κυριότατον O
¹² κατὰ add. O   ¹³ γεγενεῖσθαι (sic) O   ¹⁴ διδάξῃ O   ¹⁵ γαλατείᾳ O

Though his course was spiritual, you must again notice that
he initiated the deed in a human way because he was elevating
our state of life to the level of spiritual citizenship, intending
that he should be a way and a beginning for man's nature to be
able to live a life that is no longer fleshly and sensual but holy
and spiritual. He is the beginning of all our good and he was
manifest as man in order that he might free our nature from its
enfeeblement in Adam and render it, as it is first of all in himself,
spiritual.[44]

10

Likewise, how is man in God's image?

Answer

In view of the fact that they say others are asking how we
are to understand man's being in God's image and furthermore
that the people in question are making the utterly senseless
assertion that the likeness to God consists in the image and
visible shape of the body and in that alone,[45] I feel obliged to
state that they are in error and that they possess minds which
have no desire to contemplate the truth. Despite the clear
declaration of the Saviour *'God is Spirit'* they assert that the divine
nature has a corporeal shape with the same characteristics as
we have. Is he then a body as well and no longer to be thought
of as Spirit? Because shapes belong to bodies. But since God is
Spirit he must be without shape, be beyond outline, configuration and all limitation. We are formed in relation to him in the
most literal sense conceivable, first and foremost by virtue and
holiness. For Godhead is holy and is source, principle and origin
of all virtue. But all-wise Paul shall teach you this better interpretation of man's being made in God's image, when he says
to the Galatians, *'My children with whom I am again in travail until
Christ be formed in you'*. For Christ is being formed[46] in us by

[44] i.e. the miracles are spiritual, divine acts which are mediated by the
human act of touch prompted by a human act of volition. This is the model
for the life of faith—embodied but spiritual—the possibility of which Christ
creates in his own person. Cyril does not bring in the notion of the 'image'
here, but the paragraph is the best illustration of what he meant by it.

[45] The body, as so much quantitative stuff, has no part in the divine image
in man. But the image, for Cyril, is not simply in the soul; it exists in man
as an embodied soul with spiritual capacities.

[46] The process is continuous. Baptism ('the summons to faith in him') begins
it, but the image is constantly being marred by sin and so its regeneration
through the Spirit is continuous, cf. *Doctrinal Questions and Answers* 3.

μὲν[16] γὰρ ἐν ἡμῖν[17] δι᾽ ἁγιασμοῦ τοῦ διὰ Πνεύματος, διὰ κλήσεως τῆς[18] ἐν πίστει τῇ[19] εἰς αὐτόν· ἐν δέ γε τοῖς παραβαίνουσι τὴν πίστιν, οὐκ ἐκλάμπουσιν[20] οἱ χαρακτῆρες ὑγιῶς. διὰ τοῦτο χρή- ζουσιν ἑτέρας ὠδῖνος πνευματικῆς καὶ ἀναγεννήσεως νοητῆς, ἵν᾽ ἐναστράψαντος[21] αὐτοῖς τοῦ ἁγίου πνεύματος δι᾽ ἁγιασμοῦ τὴν 5 θείαν εἰκόνα, πάλιν ἀναμορφωθεῖεν εἰς Χριστόν.

Οὐκ ἀπίθανον[22] δὲ καὶ κατὰ τὸ ἀρχικὸν τὴν ὁμοίωσιν τὴν πρὸς θεὸν ἐνεῖναι[23] λέγειν τῷ ἀνθρώπῳ. δέδοται γὰρ αὐτῷ[24] τὸ ἄρχειν ἁπάντων τῶν ἐπὶ τῆς[25] γῆς. καὶ δεύτερος οὗτος[26] τῆς πρὸς αὐτὸν ὁμοιώσεως λόγος. εἰ δὲ ἐν τῇ[27] τοῦ ἀνθρώπου σώματος 10 φύσει τε καὶ εἴδει κείμενον[28] ἦν τὸ πεπλάσθαι ἢ τὸ πεποιῆσθαι κατ᾽ εἰκόνα τοῦ δημιουργοῦ, πῶς ἦν δύνασθαί τινας ἀπολλύειν[29] αὐτό; ἀποβεβλήκαμεν γὰρ οὐδὲν[30] τῶν ἐνόντων[31] οὐσιωδῶς. ἐπειδὴ δὲ ἡμᾶς ὁ ἁγιασμὸς καὶ ἡ δικαιοσύνη διαμορφοῖ πρὸς θεόν, τοὺς μηκέτι ζήσαντας κατ᾽ ἀρετὴν καὶ ὡς ἐν ἁγιασμῷ, φαμὲν 15 ἀποβαλεῖν τὸ οὕτω σεπτὸν καὶ ἐξαίρετον κάλλος. διὸ καὶ ἀνα- λαμβάνεται πάλιν δι᾽ ἁγιασμοῦ καὶ ἀρετῆς καὶ τῆς κατ᾽ εὐσέβειαν ζωῆς. εἰ δὲ οἴονταί τινες ἐκ πολλῆς ἄγαν ἐλαφρίας ἀνθρωποειδῆ[32] τὴν θείαν εἶναι[33] φύσιν, πῶς Ἰουδαίοις ἔφασκεν[34] ὁ σωτὴρ περὶ τοῦ θεοῦ καὶ πατρός ἀμὴν[35] λέγω ὑμῖν, οὔτε φωνὴν αὐτοῦ ἀκη- 20 κόατε[36] πώποτε, οὔτε εἶδος αὐτοῦ ἑωράκατε;[c] εἰ γὰρ ἦν, ὡς ἔφην, ἀνθρωποειδής, πῶς οὐ τεθέανται[37] οὐκ Ἰουδαῖοι[38] μόνον, ἀλλὰ γὰρ καὶ[39] πάντες οἱ[40] ἄνθρωποι[41] τὸ εἶδος αὐτοῦ;

IA´[1]

Ὅτι τὴν εὐχαριστίαν ἐν μόναις χρὴ ταῖς καθολικαῖς ἐκκλησίαις
ἐκτελεῖσθαι.[2]   25

Ἐπίλυσις[3]

Τὸ δέ γε δῶρον, ἤτοι τὴν προσφορὰν ἣν[4] τελοῦμεν μυστικῶς, ἐν

---

[c] John 5: 37

[16] μὲν om. G   [17] μορφοῦται—ἡμῖν om. O   [18] τοῖς O   [19] τῆς CO
[20] ἐλάμπουσιν (sic) C   [21] ἀναστρέψαντος (sic)   [22] ἀπιθανῶν O
[23] ἐν εἶναι O   [24] αὐτὸ O   [25] τῆς om. O   [26] οὗτος om. G   [27] τῷ C
[28] μένων O   [29] ἀπολύειν GO   [30] οὐδὲν om. O   [31] ἐνωνόντων
(sic) ἡμῖν O   [32] ἀνθρώπῳ εἴδει O   [33] εἶναι om. O   [34] ἔφασκεν
Ἰουδαίοις G   [35] ἀμὴν add. O   [36] ἀκηκόατα (sic) O   [37] τεθέαται O
[38] ἰδίοις O   [39] πᾶσι add. O   [40] οἱ om. GO   [41] ἀνθρώποις O
11. [1] Ι´ CG   [2] ἐπιτελεῖσθαι O   [3] om. G   [4] ἣν C

hallowing through the Spirit, by the summons to faith in him; but in people who transgress the faith the marks give a feeble light. That is why they require a special spiritual travail, an ideal re-birth, in order that the Holy Ghost may light up in them the divine image by his hallowing and they may be re-formed in Christ.

There are good grounds too for saying that the likeness to God existed in man at the beginning, because it has been given to man to rule the inhabitants of the earth. This is a second explanation of the likeness to God. If a fashioning or creation in the Creator's image resided in man's body and shape how could anybody lose it, because we have thrown away none of our essential properties? But seeing that holiness and righteousness bring conformity with God, we declare that those who ceased to live in virtue and holiness threw away that distinctive and august beauty. Which is why it is restored by holiness, virtue and religious living. If the people in question are empty-headed enough to think that the divine nature has a human shape, how is it that the Saviour said to the Jews about God the Father *'Verily I say unto you, you have never heard his voice or seen his shape'*? If, as I said, he has a human shape how is it that the Jews, not to mention all the rest of mankind, have not seen his shape?

11

That the eucharist should only be celebrated in Catholic churches[47]

Answer

The gift, the sacramental oblation we make, must be offered

---

[47] i.e. not in schismatic churches—cf. below, *Letter to Calosirius*. Evidently some of the brethren (perhaps the intruders) are lax in the matter.

ἀγίαις ἐκκλησίαις ταῖς τῶν ὀρθοδόξων χρὴ προσφέρεσθαι μόναις,
καὶ οὐχ ἑτέρωθί που. ἢ οἱ τοῦτο δρῶντες παρανομοῦσιν ἐμφανῶς.
καὶ τοῦτο ἔστιν ἰδεῖν ἐκ τῶν ἱερῶν γραμμάτων. ἐκέλευε γὰρ ὁ νόμος
θύεσθαι τὸ πρόβατον κατὰ τὴν ἡμέραν ἤτοι τὴν ἑορτὴν τοῦ πάσχα,
καὶ ἦν εἰς τύπον⁵ Χριστοῦ· ἀλλ' ἐν οἰκίᾳ μιᾷ βρωθήσεται, 5
φησί, καὶ⁶ οὐκ ἐξοίσετε⁷ τῶν κρεῶν αὐτοῦ ἔξω.ᵃ ἔξω τοίνυν
ἐκφέρουσι τὸ δῶρον, οἳ⁸ μὴ ἐν τῇ μιᾷ καὶ καθολικῇ οἰκίᾳ τοῦ
Χριστοῦ,⁹ τουτέστι τῇ ἐκκλησίᾳ,¹⁰ τελοῦντες αὐτό·¹¹ καὶ δι' ἑτέρου
δὲ νόμου τοιοῦτόν τι¹² σημαίνεται. γέγραπται γὰρ πάλιν καὶ ὃς
ἐὰν θύσῃ μόσχον ἢ πρόβατον ἐν τῇ παρεμβολῇ, καὶ ἐπὶ 10
τὰς θύρας τῆς σκηνῆς μὴ ἐνέγκῃ, ἐξολοθρευθήσεται ἡ
ψυχὴ ἐκείνη ἐκ τοῦ λαοῦ αὐτῆς.ᵇ οὐκοῦν οἱ ἔξω θύοντες τῆς
σκηνῆς, εἶεν¹³ ἂν οὐχ ἕτεροί τινες παρὰ τοὺς αἱρετικούς, καὶ ὄλεθρος
αὐτοῖς ἐπήρτηται¹⁴ τοῖς¹⁵ τοῦτο τολμῶσι δρᾶν. πιστεύομεν τοίνυν
τὰς ἐν ταῖς ἐκκλησίαις δωροφορίας¹⁶ καὶ ἁγιάζεσθαι καὶ εὐλογεῖσθαι 15
καὶ τελειοῦσθαι παρὰ Χριστοῦ.

IB′¹

"Οτι τὰς σαρκικὰς ἡδονὰς εἴτουν φυσικὰς² κολοβῶσαι δυνάμεθα, ἐκκόψαι
δὲ παντελῶς³ οὐκέτι.⁴

'Επίλυσις⁵

Δοκεῖ δέ⁶ τισιν ὁ πάνσοφος Παῦλος δυσχερῆ τινα λέγειν, ἤτοι 20
δυσνόητα, κατὰ τὴν τῶν ἁγίων ἀποστόλων φωνήν.ᵃ ὅτι δὲ σοφίας
τῆς ἄνωθεν⁷ μεμέστωται ταῦτα, οὐκ ἔστιν ἀμφιβαλεῖν·⁸ λαλεῖ γὰρ
ἐν αὐτῷ Χριστός. ἔφη τοίνυν ὅτι συνήδομαι γὰρ τῷ νόμῳ
τοῦ θεοῦ⁹ κατὰ τὸν ἔσω ἄνθρωπον, βλέπω δὲ ἕτερον νόμον
ἀντιστρατευόμενον τῷ νόμῳ τοῦ νοός μου, καὶ αἰχμαλω- 25
τίζοντά με τῷ νόμῳ τῆς ἁμαρτίας,ᵇ καὶ πάλιν ταλαίπωρος

---

11. ᵃ Ex. 12: 46   ᵇ Lev. 17: 3 f.   12. ᵃ cf. 2 Peter 3: 16
ᵇ Rom. 7: 22 f.

---

5 add. τοῦ G   6 καὶ om. O   7 ἐξοίσεται O   8 εἰ O
9 κυρίου Syr   10 τῆς ἐκκλησίας C   11 αὐτῷ O   12 τὸ τοιοῦτον
τί (sic) O   13 εἶ ἂν (sic) O   14 ἐπήρτηται αὐτοῖς G   15 τοῖς om. CG
16 δωρυφορίαις (sic) O   12. ¹ IA′ CG   ² τὰς—φυσικὰς] τὰς φυσικὰς
ἡδονὰς G   εἴτουν] ἤγουν O   ³ παντελῶς om. G   4 οὐ δυνάμεθα C:
οὐ G   5 om. CG   6 δέ om. O   7 ἄνω O   8 ἀμφιβάλλειν O
9 Χριστοῦ Syr

in holy churches belonging to the orthodox and nowhere else. Otherwise the action is plainly contrary to the law. The sacred texts provide evidence on the point. For the law ordered the sheep to be sacrificed on the day, the feast, of Passover, and it typified Christ. '*In one house*', it says, '*it shall be eaten and you are not to bring any of its meat outside.*'[48] Those who do not celebrate it in Christ's one Catholic house (I mean, the Church) bring the gift out. A similar meaning is conveyed by another law. Scripture again has it '*Anyone who sacrifices cattle or sheep in the camp and does not bring them to the door of the tabernacle, that soul shall be made to perish from its people.*'[49] So those who sacrifice outside the tabernacle are nothing less than heretics and destruction hangs over their presumptuous acts. So we believe that the sacramental gifts made in the churches are hallowed, blessed and consecrated by Christ.

12

That we can curtail but not yet totally eradicate our fleshly, natural sensuality[50]

Answer

All-wise Paul is supposed by some people to say hard, that is, intellectually hard, things, according to what the holy apostles say. It is impossible, though, to doubt that these things are crammed with higher wisdom because Christ speaks in him. Paul said '*I delight in the law of Christ in the inner man, but I observe another law which is at war with the law of my mind and makes me a prisoner of sin's law*', and again, '*Wretched man that I am! Who will*

[48] The same interpretation in Cyprian *De Eccles. Cath. Unit.* c. 8, *ad fin.*, Jerome *Ep.* 22 (to Eustochium), 38.

[49] Cf. *Glaph. in Lev.* (*PG* 69, 552BC).

[50] Some (the intruders?) are probably claiming to have reached spiritual perfection, the serene state idealized by Clement (cf. *Strom.* 6, 9) and Evagrius (see the texts and discussion by A. and C. Guillaumont in their edition of Evagrius' *Traité Pratique*, SC 170 f. (Paris 1971), vol. 1, pp. 98 ff., 'L'impassibilité'). Cf. Cassian *Conferences* 12: 6 f., 11 and 15. For Cyril this is an impossibility—final stability lies only in the life beyond, cf. above n. 46 and *Doctrinal Questions and Answers* 5.

ἐγὼ ἄνθρωπος, τίς με ῥύσεται ἐκ τοῦ σώματος τοῦ θανα-
του τούτου; χάρις δὲ τῷ θεῷ διὰ Ἰησοῦ Χριστοῦ τοῦ
κυρίου ἡμῶν.ᶜ καταστρατεύεται μὲν¹⁰ γὰρ τοῦ νοῦ¹¹ βλέποντος
εἰς ἐγκράτειαν διὰ τὸν τοῦ θεοῦ φόβον τὸ κίνημα τῆς σαρκός, καὶ
ταῖς εἰς ἁγνείαν ὁρμαῖς ἀντιτάττεται καὶ ἀντεξάγει δεινῶς. ἀλλ' οἱ   5
νήψει χρώμενοι τῇ πρεπούσῃ τοῖς θεὸν σεβομένοις, ἐπιτιμῶσι τῷ
κινήματι τῆς σαρκός, καὶ τὸ τῆς ἁμαρτίας ἀπαμβλύνουσι κέντρον
ἀσκήσει¹² καὶ πόνοις καὶ ταῖς ἄλλαις ἐπιεικείαις χρώμενοι. ὥστε
ἀποριζῶσαι μὲν τῆς σαρκὸς τὴν ἔμφυτον αὐτῆς ἐπιθυμίαν οὐκ
ἔνεστι· νήψει¹³ δέ, ὡς ἔφην, οὐκ ἐᾶν¹⁴ καταθρασύνεσθαι τοῦ νοῦ¹⁵   10
δυνατόν, μάλισθ' ὅτι γέγονεν ἄνθρωπος ὁ μονογενὴς τοῦ θεοῦ
λόγος, καὶ ἀγριαίνοντα τῆς ἁμαρτίας τὸν νόμον τὸν ἐν τοῖς μέλεσιν
ἡμῶν οὐκ ἔτι νεανιεύεσθαι συγκεχώρηκε καθ' ἡμῶν. καὶ τοῦτο
διδάξει σαφῶς ὁ πανάριστος Παῦλος γράφων τὸ γὰρ ἀδύνατον
τοῦ νόμου, ἐν ᾧ ἠσθένει διὰ τῆς σαρκός, ὁ θεὸς τὸν ἑαυτοῦ   15
υἱὸν πέμψας ἐν ὁμοιώματι σαρκὸς ἁμαρτίας καὶ περὶ
ἁμαρτίας κατέκρινε τὴν ἁμαρτίαν ἐν τῇ σαρκί, ἵνα τὸ
δικαίωμα τοῦ νόμου πληρωθῇ ἐν ἡμῖν τοῖς μὴ κατὰ
σάρκα περιπατοῦσιν, ἀλλὰ κατὰ πνεῦμα.ᵈ περιεσόμεθα¹⁶
τοίνυν τῶν ἐμφύτων κινημάτων οὐκ εἰς ἅπαν, οὐδὲ ὁλοτελῶς·   20
τετήρηται γὰρ τοῦτο τῇ παμμακαρίᾳ¹⁷ ζωῇ τῇ ἔσεσθαι προσδοκω-
μένῃ κατὰ τὸν αἰῶνα τὸν μέλλοντα· δυνάμεθα δὲ κατανδραΐζεσθαι,¹⁸
καὶ ἐπιπλήττειν τοῖς τῆς σαρκὸς κινήμασι, θεοῦ συμπράττοντος,
καὶ τὴν ἐξ ὕψους ἡμῖν χορηγοῦντος δύναμιν. καὶ ἁδροτέρα μέν
ἐστιν ἐν τοῖς ῥαθυμοῦσιν ἡ ἐπιθυμία, καὶ οἷον κατεξουσιάζουσα τῆς   25
αὐτῶν¹⁹ καρδίας· ἀδρανὴς²⁰ δὲ καὶ ῥᾳδίως ἐπιτιμωμένη καὶ ἐκ-
πεμπομένη τοῦ νοῦ ἐν τοῖς τὸν θεῖον ἔχουσι φόβον. γέγραπται γὰρ
ὅτι ὁ φόβος²¹ κυρίου ἁγνός,ᵉ τουτέστιν ἁγνοποιός.

ᶜ Rom. 7: 24 f.   ᵈ Rom. 8: 3 f.   ᵉ Ps. 18(19): 9

¹⁰ μὲν om. O   ¹¹ νόμου Syr   ¹² ἀσκήσεσι O   ¹³ νίψει G   ¹⁴ ἐᾷ O
¹⁵ νόμου O   ¹⁶ περιγενώμεθα O   ¹⁷ μακαρίᾳ G   ¹⁸ κατανδρίζεσθαι O
¹⁹ ἑαυτῶν G   ²⁰ ἀδρανεῖς O   ²¹ νόμος CG

*deliver me from this body of death? But thanks be to God through Jesus
Christ our Lord.'* The excitement of the flesh fights against the
mind bent on continence because of its fear of God, and it puts
up a terrible battle against the impulses towards chastity. Those
who make use of a fasting appropriate to God-fearing people
check the excitement of the flesh, and by employing discipline,
exercise and other suitable aids take the sharpness off sin's spur.
The upshot is that it is impossible to eliminate from the flesh
its innate desire, but, as I said, it is possible by vigilance to
prevent it from dominating over the mind, especially in view of
the fact that God's only-begotten Word was made man and
no longer allows the law of sin to run riot in our members.
All-wise Paul will teach you this plainly because he writes *'For
the Law's impotence wherein it was feeble throughout the flesh [has
ceased, for] God, by sending his own Son in the likeness of sinful flesh
and for sin, condemned sin in the flesh, in order that the requirement of
the Law might be fulfilled in us who do not behave in accord with flesh
but in accord with spirit.'*[51] So we are not victorious over our innate
impulses absolutely all at once; that is reserved for the life of
total bliss we expect in the world to come. But we can play the
man and with God's co-operation providing us with power from
on high, we can curb the excitements of the flesh. Desire is
keener in the slack and dominates their hearts, as it were. In
those who maintain a divine fear it is frail, easily checked and
expelled from the mind. Scripture has it that *'The fear of God
is holy'*, meaning sanctifying.

[51] See p. 77 n. 9.

ΙΓ΄[1]

Πρὸς τοὺς λέγοντας[2] εἰ ἐνεδέχετο ἁμαρτῆσαι Χριστὸν[3] φορέσαντα τὴν
ὁμοίωσιν τοῦ Ἀδὰμ διὰ τὴν σάρκα.

Ἐπίλυσις[4]

Ἀσύνετοι δὲ παντελῶς οἱ καὶ αὐτὸν πλημμελῆσαι τὸν Χριστὸν
δύνασθαι οὐκ οἶδ᾽ ὅπως ὑποτοπήσαντες,[5] διὰ τὸ ἐν εἴδει γενέσθαι   5
τῷ καθ᾽ ἡμᾶς οἰκονομικῶς καὶ μορφὴν δούλου λαβεῖν καὶ συνανα-
στραφῆναι τοῖς ἐπὶ γῆς ἀνθρώποις. εἰ μὲν γὰρ ἀπέστη τοῦ εἶναι
ὃ ἦν, εἰ μεταπεφοίτηκεν ἐκ τοῦ εἶναι θεὸς εἰς τὸ καθ᾽ ἡμᾶς εἶναι
μόνον, ζητήτωσαν ἐν αὐτῷ τῆς ἀνθρωπίνης ἀσθενείας τὰ ἐγκλήματα.
εἰ δὲ πεφόρηκε[6] διὰ τοῦτο τὴν ἀνθρώπου φύσιν, ἵν᾽ ὡς ἐν Ἀδὰμ   10
ἀσθενήσασαν ἐν αὐτῷ δείξῃ δυνατωτάτην καὶ ἁμαρτίας κρείττονα,
τί περιεργάζονται μάτην ὃ εὑρεῖν οὐ δύνανται; πῶς δὲ ἐπελάθοντο[7]
λέγοντος αὐτοῦ ἔρχεται ὁ ἄρχων τοῦ κόσμου τούτου, καὶ
ἐν ἐμοὶ εὑρήσει οὐδέν.[a] κατηγορεῖ μὲν γὰρ[8] ὁ τῆς ἁμαρτίας
εὑρετὴς πάσης σαρκός· ἀλλ᾽ ἦν ἄπρακτος ἐν Χριστῷ τῆς ἐκείνου   15
σκαιότητος ἡ περιεργία, ηὕρηται γὰρ ὅλως οὐδὲν[9] ἐν αὐτῷ. καὶ
γοῦν ἔφη πρὸς Ἰουδαίους τίς ἐξ ὑμῶν ἐλέγχει με περὶ
ἁμαρτίας; εἰ ἀλήθειαν λέγω, διὰ τί ὑμεῖς οὐ πιστεύετέ
μοι;[b] ὥσπερ τοίνυν κατεκρίθημεν ἐν Ἀδὰμ διὰ τὴν παρακοὴν καὶ
τῆς θείας ἐντολῆς τὴν παράβασιν, οὕτως ἐν Χριστῷ δεδικαιώμεθα   20
διὰ τὸ ἀπλημμελὲς ὁλοτρόπως καὶ τὴν εἰς ἅπαν καὶ ἀμώμητον
ὑπακοήν. καὶ τὸ καύχημα τῆς ἀνθρωπείας φύσεως ἐν τούτῳ
γέγονε. πέπαυται[10] γοῦν ἡ ἀρά, καὶ τὸ τῆς ἁμαρτίας ἐμπέφρακται
στόμα, καὶ σὺν αὐτῷ τὸ τοῦ θανάτου κατηργήθη κράτος, ὥσπερ
οἰκείᾳ ῥίζῃ συναπομαρανθέν. εἰ γὰρ πρόξενος ἡμῖν ἁπάντων τῶν   25
κακῶν ἡ ἁμαρτία γέγονεν, ἀναίρεσις ἔσται τῶν συμβεβηκότων ἡ
ἐν Χριστῷ δικαίωσις, δι᾽ ὑπακοῆς εἰσβαίνουσα, καὶ τὸ ἀνυπαίτιον
ἔχουσα παντελῶς. ὥστε καὶ εἰ πεφόρηκεν[11] ὥς φασι τὸν Ἀδάμ,

13. [a] John 14: 30   [b] John 8: 46

Witnesses: l. 1–p. 174, l. 5 C G Syr

13. [1] ΙΒ΄ CG   [2] πρὸς τοὺς λέγοντας om. G   [3] τὸν κύριον ἡμῶν Ἰησοῦν
Χριστὸν G   [4] om. CG   [5] ὑπεπτήσαντες (!) G   [6] πεφόρεκε C
[7] ἐπελάθετο G   [8] γὰρ om. G   [9] οὐδὲν ὅλως G   [10] πέφρακται C
[11] πεφόρεκεν CG

13

To those who ask if Christ could have sinned when he wore Adam's likeness because of the flesh[52]

Answer

It is utterly foolish for people to imagine somehow or other that because Christ came to exist in our shape for the divine plan, took slave's form and had dealings with men on earth, he could have sinned. Had he ceased to be what he was, had he changed from being God to being only what we are, they would have to investigate charges of human frailty in him. But if he wore man's nature in order to render it a most potent master of sin after it had sickened in Adam, why do they make a fruitless search for something they cannot find? Why have they forgotten that he said '*The prince of this world is coming and will find nothing in me*'? For the inventor of sin brings a charge against all flesh; nevertheless his malicious curiosity finds no work to do in Christ's case, because absolutely nothing was to be found in him. Indeed he said to the Jews, '*Which of you convicts me of sin? If I speak truth why do you not believe me?*' As we are condemned in Adam for disobedience and transgression of the divine command, so we have been justified in Christ because of his utter faultlessness and his total, immaculate obedience. Human nature has its boast in him. The curse has been stayed, sin's mouth stopped and with him the force of death has been nullified, withering away, as it were, along with its root. If sin occasioned all our ills, justification in Christ, coming in through his obedience and possessing his utter irreproachability, will mean the removal of all sin's accompaniments. The consequence is that though he clothed himself, as they say, in Adam, he was not, as Adam was,

---

[52] The first recorded discussion (so far as I know) of the question whether the Incarnation involved the possibility of Christ's sinning, though Catholics and Arians had debated whether the pre-incarnate Word, as created, was capable of sin (see Alexander of Alexandria *Ep. Encycl.*, ed. H. G. Opitz, *Athanasiuswerke* 3 p. 8), and Julian of Eclanum accused Augustine of teaching that not even Christ was free from sin (Augustine *Contra duas epp. Pel.* 1, xii, 25, cf. ibid. viii, 13). It would seem here to be a supplementary question to the previous, viz. if tension between flesh and spirit is a condition of human existence, what are we to say of Christ? Cyril's answer is that Christ is unique because he creates the conditions for a righteous life. The hypothetical possibility of Christ's sinning is of no theological interest for him—and rightly. As well ask if standard c^1 is capable of not sounding at 512 vibrations per second.

ἀλλ' οὐ κατ' ἐκεῖνον ἦν, τὸν ἐκ γῆς χοϊκόν, ἀλλ' ὡς ἐπουράνιος
ἀσυγκρίτως ἀμείνων τοῦ χοϊκοῦ. καὶ τοῖς τῆς ἀναμαρτησίας[12]
ἐπαίνοις τὴν ἀνθρώπου φύσιν στεφανουμένην ἐν αὐτῷ θεωρῆσαι τις
ἄν,[13] ἐπιμαρτυρούσης αὐτῷ τῆς θεοπνεύστου γραφῆς, ὅτι ἁμαρτίαν
οὐκ ἐποίησεν οὐδὲ εὑρέθη δόλος ἐν τῷ στόματι αὐτοῦ.[c]   5

IΔ'[1]

Πρὸς τοὺς λέγοντας εἰ καὶ ἄγγελοι[2] κατ' εἰκόνα θεοῦ.

'Eπίλυσις[3]

Τὸ δέ κατ' εἰκόνα θεοῦ διερμηνεύοντες ἐπὶ τοῦ ἀνθρώπου, οὐ
τὴν τοῦ σώματος εἰδέαν[4] μεταμορφοῦσθαι[5] πρὸς αὐτὸν ἐλέγομεν.
ἀσώματον γὰρ ἄϋλόν τε καὶ ἀναφὲς[6] τὸ θεῖον, καὶ ποσότητος   10
ἐπέκεινα καὶ περιγραφῆς, εἴδους τε καὶ σχήματος.[7] ἐφαρμόζοντες
δὲ τῷ ἀνθρώπῳ τὸν θεῖον ἐξεικονισμόν, ἐλέγομεν ὅτι κατὰ τὴν τῶν
ἠθῶν ἤτοι τῶν τρόπων ποιότητα, καὶ κατ' εἶδος τὸ πνευματικόν,
ὃ διὰ τῆς τῶν ἀρετῶν εὐειδίας ἐκφαίνεται, πεποιῆσθαί[8] φαμεν
καθ' ὁμοίωσιν αὐτοῦ τοῦ δημιουργοῦ. ἐν παντὶ γὰρ καλῷ τὸ θεῖον,   15
καὶ ἁπάσης ἀρετῆς αὐτοπηγὴ[9] καὶ ῥίζα καὶ γένεσις, ἤκει δὲ καὶ
εἰς ἡμᾶς ἐκεῖθεν τὰ ἀγαθά. εἰ τοίνυν κατά γε[10] τὴν ἐξ ἀρετῶν
εἰδέαν[11] διαμορφούμεθα πρὸς θεόν, ἔνεστι[12] δὲ τοῦτο καὶ τοῖς
ἁγίοις ἀγγέλοις καὶ ἀσυγκρίτως ὑπὲρ ἡμᾶς· οὐκ ἀμήχανον ἐννοεῖν
ὅτι καὶ πᾶσα κτίσις λογικὴ δι' ἁγιασμοῦ καὶ δικαιοσύνης καὶ διὰ   20
πάσης ἀρετῆς μορφοῦται πρὸς θεόν. εἰ γὰρ ἡμῖν τοῖς ἐπὶ τῆς[13] γῆς
ἐμπρέπει τὸ θεῖόν τε καὶ ὑπερκόσμιον κάλλος, πῶς οὐ μᾶλλον ταῖς
ἄνω δυνάμεσι[14] λογικαῖς, αἷς[15] ἐπαναπαύεται ὁ[16] θεός; διὰ γὰρ τοῦτο
καὶ θρόνον αὐτοῦ τὸν οὐρανὸν ὀνομάζουσιν αἱ θεῖαι γραφαί.

[c] 1 Peter 2: 22

Witnesses: l. 6–end C G O Syr

---

[12] ἀμαρτίας C   [13] θεωρήσειεν ἄν τίς G   14. [1] IΓ' CG   [2] πρὸς
τοὺς λέγοντας and καὶ om. G   [3] om. CG   [4] ἰδέαν G   [5] μετα-
μορφῶσθαι Ο   [6] ἀναφανὲς Ο   [7] πλημμελήματος Ο   [8] πεποιεῖσθαι Ο
[9] αὐτῷ πηγὴ Ο   [10] τε C   [11] ἰδέαν G   [12] ἐνέστη Ο   [13] τῆς
om. Ο   [14] οὐσίαις G   [15] οὐσίαις Ο   [16] ὁ om. CG

of the earth earthy, but was celestial and so incomparably superior to what was earthy. One can see man's nature in him crowned with the praises of sinlessness; inspired Scripture testifies of him that *'he did no sin neither was deceit found in his mouth'*.

14

To those who ask if angels exist in God's image

Answer

When we interpreted the phrase 'in God's image' as applied to man we said it did not mean that the body's appearance was altered into God's form, because deity is incorporeal, immaterial and impalpable, beyond quantity, limitation, shape or con-figuration.[53] In applying the divine imaged-ness to man we said that man was made in the likeness of his Creator in terms of his behaviour, his moral qualities and the spiritual shape which shines out through the noble appearance of virtues. Deity is, indeed, in all that is fine and is the absolute source, root and origin of all virtue and from it comes to us what is good. If we are formed like God in terms of the appearance which virtues produce, so can the holy angels be and incomparably more so than we. It is not impossible to think of the whole of rational creation as being formed like God by holiness, righteousness and all virtue. If divine, supra-mundane beauty can bedeck us earthly men, must it not bedeck even more the rational powers on high upon whom God rests? Which is why the divine Scrip-tures call heaven God's 'throne'.

[53] See above no. 10.

IE'[1]

Πρὸς τοὺς λέγοντας[2] πῶς ἀσώματοι ὄντες οἱ δαίμονες ἐμίχθησαν
γυναιξίν;

Ἐπίλυσις

Ἐπειδὴ δέ φασί τινας λέγειν[3] πῶς ἀσώματοι ὄντες οἱ πονηροὶ
δαίμονες κεκοινωνήκασι γυναιξίν, αἱ δὲ ἐγέννων αὐτοῖς τοὺς
γίγαντας· ἀναγκαῖον καὶ πρὸς τοῦτο ἡμᾶς[4] ἐπιτροχάδην εἰπεῖν, οὐ
τῷ μήκει τῶν διηγημάτων συνεκτεινομένους, ἀλλ' ὡς[5] ἐν ἐπιτομῇ
τὴν τοῦ πράγματος διάνοιαν ἐμφανίζοντας.[6] φασὶ τοίνυν κατὰ τοὺς
ἄνωθεν ἔτι καιροὺς ἤτοι[7] χρόνους διηρῆσθαι,[8] τούς τε ἀπὸ τοῦ
Καῒν γεγονότας φημὶ καὶ τοὺς ἀπὸ τοῦ Ἐνώς,[9] ὃς[10] διὰ τὴν[11]
πολλὴν ἄγαν δικαιοσύνην ὠνόμασται παρὰ τοῖς τηνικάδε θεός·
ἤλπισε γὰρ ἐπικαλεῖσθαι, φησί, τὸ ὄνομα κυρίου τοῦ
θεοῦ αὐτοῦ.[a] ἀλλ' οἱ μὲν ἀπὸ Ἐνὼς γεγονότες, ἐπιμεληταὶ[12]
δικαιοσύνης[13] καὶ ἁπάσης ἀγαθουργίας,[14] ἔθεσιν ἑπόμενοι τοῖς τοῦ
πατρός· οἵ γε μὴν ὑπὸ τοῦ Καῒν θρασεῖς καὶ ἐπάρατοι καὶ πᾶν
εἶδος φαυλότητος ἑτοίμως ἐπιτηδεύοντες, ἦν γὰρ αὐτοῖς τοιοῦτος
καὶ[15] ὁ πατήρ. ἕως μὲν[16] οὖν ἦσαν ἀλλήλοις ἄμικτα τὰ[17] γένη,
διεσώζετο παρὰ τοῖς ἀπὸ Ἐνὼς γεγονόσι[18] τὸ ἐν ἀρίστῃ διαπρέπειν
ζωῇ. ἐπειδὴ δὲ οἱ υἱοί, φησί,[19] τοῦ ἐπικληθέντος θεοῦ, τουτέστι
τοῦ Ἐνώς, τὰς ἐκ τοῦ Καῒν θυγατέρας τεθέανται, ἃς καὶ τῶν
ἀνθρώπων θυγατέρας εἶπεν ἡ γραφή·[b] εἶτα προσεφθάρησαν αὐταῖς,
καὶ ἥττους γεγόνασιν αἰσχρῶν ἐπιθυμιῶν, εἰς τὰ ἐκείνων ἤθη[20]
μετετράπησαν. ὅθεν ἀγανακτήσας ὁ θεὸς παρεσκεύασε τὰς αἱρε-
θείσας[21] παρ' αὐτῶν γυναῖκας δυσειδῆ τίκτειν τέρατα, οὓς καὶ
ἐκάλουν γίγαντας, διὰ τὸ εἰδεχθὲς[22] καὶ ἀπηνὲς τῶν τρόπων καὶ τὸ
ἀνήμερον θράσος.

---

15. [a] Gen. 4: 26   [b] cf. Gen. 6: 2

15. [1] ΙΔ' CG   [2] πρὸς τοὺς λέγοντας om. G   [3] τινες and om.
λέγειν G   [4] ἡμᾶς om. O   [5] ὡς om. O   [6] ἐμφανίζοντος O
[7] ἢ G   [8] διαιρεῖσθαι O   [9] ἑνὸς G   [10] οὓς G: ὡς O   [11] τὴν
om. O   [12] ἐπιμελειταὶ O   [13] ἦσαν add. O   [14] ἀγαθοεργίας G
[15] καὶ om. O   [16] γε μὴν O   [17] τὰ om. O   [18] γεγόνωσι O
[19] φασὶ G   [20] ἔθη G   [21] αἱρεθείσας] ληφθείσας καὶ ἐπιθυμηθείσας O
[22] καὶ τὸ ἐν τῷ ὁρᾶσθαι μεμισημένον γένος γηγάντων καὶ δυσειδὲς ἤγουν διὰ τὸ
εἰδεχθὲς add. O

15

To those who ask how demons which are incorporeal could have had intercourse with women[54]

Answer

Since they say that some people are asking how evil demons, which are incorporeal, could have had relations with women and how these could have borne them giants, we must speak cursorily on this point without extending the length of the discussion but giving a summary clarification of the meaning of the incident. They say, then, that a distinction was made during the still earlier epochs or periods, a distinction that is between Cain's descendants and those of Enosh who was named by his contemporaries 'God' because of his very great righteousness. *'For he hoped to be called'*, it says, *'by the name of the Lord his God.'* Some of Enosh's descendants practised righteousness and complete virtue following their father's ways; Cain's, on the other hand, were fierce, execrable men, ready to undertake every type of wickedness because their father had been like that. Now so long as the races were unmixed, Enosh's descendants preserved their superior excellence of life. But when, it says, the sons of him who was called God (that is, Enosh) saw the daughters descended from Cain (whom Scripture has called 'the daughters of men') then they were corrupted by them, succumbed to ugly desires and were converted to their ways. This angered God and so he arranged for their chosen wives to bear ugly monsters whom they styled 'giants' owing to the odious cruelty of their ways and their brutal fierceness.

[54] This is Cyril's own variant of the interpretation which equates 'sons of God' with 'righteous men'. He discusses the passage elsewhere in the *Glaphyra in Gen.* (*PG* 69, 49 ff.) and the *Contra Julianum* (*PG* 76, 945 ff.). See further my article 'The Sons of God and the daughters of men: Genesis vi 2 in early Christian exegesis', *Oudtestamentische Studien* 19 (1974), 135–47. Cf. also Cassian *Conferences* 8, 20.

Καὶ γοῦν οἱ μετὰ τοὺς ἑβδομήκοντα²³ γεγονότες²⁴ ἑρμηνευταὶ τέσσαρες²⁵ ἐκδιδόντες τὰ περὶ²⁶ τὸν τόπον,²⁷ οὐ γεγράφασιν ὅτι οἱ υἱοὶ τοῦ θεοῦ ἰδόντες τὰς θυγατέρας τῶν ἀνθρώπων· ἀλλ' ὁ μέν,²⁸ οἱ υἱοὶ τῶν δυναστευόντων, ὁ δέ, οἱ²⁹ υἱοὶ τῶν δυναστῶν.³⁰ ἀσύνετον δὲ τὸ οἴεσθαι τοὺς ἀσωμάτους δαίμονας ἐνεργεῖν δύνασθαι τὰ σωμάτων, καὶ τὸ³¹ παρὰ φύσιν ἰδίαν ἐπιτελεῖν. οὐδὲν γὰρ τῶν ὄντων δύναται τὰ³² παρὰ³³ φύσιν δρᾶν, ἀλλ' ἕκαστον ὡς γέγονεν οὕτω μένει, τάξιν ὁρίσαντος ἑκάστῳ³⁴ θεοῦ. αὐτὸς γάρ ἐστιν ὁ πάντων γενεσιουργὸς καὶ τοῖς αὐτοῦ νεύμασιν ἕκαστον τῶν ὄντων ἐστὶν ὅ ἐστιν. ἰστέον δὲ πρὸς τούτοις³⁵ κἀκεῖνο. ἔχει μὲν γάρ τινα τῶν ἀντιγράφων, ὅτι ἰδόντες οἱ ἄγγελοι τοῦ θεοῦ³⁶ τὰς θυγατέρας τῶν ἀνθρώπων. παρεγγραφὴ³⁷ δέ ἐστιν ἔξωθεν τιθεμένη·³⁸ τὸ γὰρ ἀληθές ἐστιν³⁹ ἰδόντες οἱ υἱοὶ τοῦ θεοῦ τὰς θυγατέρας τῶν ἀνθρώπων.

²³ ὃ O   ²⁴ γεγονότας O   ²⁵ τέσσαρες ἑρμηνευταὶ G   ²⁶ τὰ περὶ] τὰς περὶ τούτων O   ²⁷ τρόπον O   ²⁸ ὁ μέν om. O   ²⁹ οἱ om. G   ³⁰ ὁ δέ—δυναστῶν om. O   ³¹ τὸ om. O   ³² τὰ om. O   ³³ τὴν add. O   ³⁴ τοῦ add. O   ³⁵ τοῦτο O   ³⁶ τοῦ θεοῦ om. G   ³⁷ παραγραφὴ O   ³⁸ τιθεμένη] τεθησομένη τοῦτο O   ³⁹ τὸ add. O

The four translators who came after the seventy in their edition of the passage did not write 'the sons of God seeing the daughters of men', but variously: 'the sons of those ruling'[55] and 'the sons of the rulers'. It is foolish to suppose that incorporeal demons can do what bodies do and can act contrary to their nature. No being can act contrary to nature but each thing stays as it was created, God having given each its appointed station. For God is the author of all and at his bidding each being is what it is. This further point is to be noticed: some of the copies have 'The *angels* of God seeing the daughters of men'. But this is an alien interpolation, because the true text is 'The *sons* of God seeing the daughters of men'.[56]

[55] Symmachus' translation, see *Glaphyra*, loc. cit. n. 54.
[56] 'Sons' and 'angels' appear to have equal attestation in the LXX manuscript tradition. Aquila and Symmachus both read 'sons', see *Glaphyra*, loc. cit. n. 54.

9

DOCTRINAL QUESTIONS AND ANSWERS

Ἀξίωσις ἐπιδοθεῖσα τῷ ἁγίῳ Κυρίλλῳ πιστῷ ἀρχιερεῖ, γνησίῳ
θεράποντι θεοῦ, [ἁγίῳ Κυρίλλῳ] ἀρχιεπισκόπῳ Ἀλεξανδρείας παρὰ
τῆς ἀδελφότητος.[1]

Ἦν μὲν εὖ ἔχειν ἡμᾶς ἡσυχάζοντας, εἰ καί τι κατορθοῦντας ἴσως
τῶν σπουδαζομένων, οὐδὲν δὲ ἧττον κἀκεῖθεν ἀποδημοῦντας, ἡμᾶς 5
αὐτοὺς ὠφελεῖσθαι νομίζομεν διὰ τὴν σὴν μόνον θέαν, καὶ μάλιστα
κερδανοῦμεν ἐξ αὐτοῦ τοῦ στόματός σου τὴν εὐσέβειαν διδασκόμενοι.
Τὸ μὲν γὰρ καὶ πόρρω γῆς κατησχημένους ἀναγινώσκειν τὰς βίβλους
καὶ τὰ πονήματα τῆς σῆς ὁσιότητος, καλὸν ἅμα καὶ ὠφέλιμον καὶ
εἰς τὰ πρόσω φέρον τοὺς προσέχοντας· τὸ δ’ ἐξ αὐτῶν τῶν θείαν χάριν 10
καὶ πνευματικὴν γλυκύτητα πηγαζόντων χειλέων τὴν διδασκαλίαν
ἀρδεύεσθαι, βεβαιότερον ἅμα καὶ ζωτικώτερον ὑπάρχει. ἥκομεν τοίνυν
αὖθις διὰ τὴν εἰς σὲ καὶ τὴν εὐσέβειαν ἐπιθυμίαν, προκοπήν θ’ ἡμετέραν
ἅμα καὶ ἑτέρων διόρθωσιν. δεξάμενοι γὰρ πρόσθεν ἐκ τῶν σῶν ἁγίων
χειρῶν τὴν περὶ τῶν καθ’ ἡμᾶς ὀρθῶν δογμάτων ζήτησιν ἐπιλύουσαν 15
βίβλον,[2] οὐκ ὀλίγην τὴν ὄνησιν ἀπηνεγκάμεθα. ἡμῖν μὲν γὰρ γέγονεν
εἰς βεβαίωσιν ὁ λόγος, ἑτέροις δὲ εἰς διόρθωσιν· ὀλίγοι δ’ εἰσὶν οἱ μὴ
προσελθόντες τῇ ὑγιαινούσῃ διδασκαλίᾳ, ὧν ἐνεφράγη τὰ στόματα.
ἀλλ’ οἱ τῆς Ἀβηλινῆς χώρας κακῶς πρὸς ἀλλήλους διατεινόμενοι
δογματικῶν ἔνεκά τινων ζητημάτων εἰς τοσοῦτον μανίας ἤλασαν ὡς 20
καὶ καθαιρέσεις καὶ ἀναθεματισμοὺς κατ’ ἀλλήλων ὁρίζειν καὶ διωγμοὺς
πρὸς ἀλλήλους φέρειν καὶ διαρπαγὰς ὑπομένειν καὶ μητ’ ἐπισκόποις
μήτε πατράσιν εἴκειν τοῖς αὐτόθι, μήτε μὴν τοῖς παρ’ ἡμῖν, μητ’
ἄλλοις τισὶν ἁγίων παραχωρεῖν, τὸ μείζονος μέτρου γνώσεως ἠξιῶσθαι,
οὕτω κατακράτος ἡ σατανικὴ ἀκαταστασία πόρρω τῆς θείας εἰρήνης 25
αὐτοὺς ἐξηχμαλώτισε. πρὸς τούτοις αὖθις καὶ τῶν Αἰγυπτίων τινὲς
οὐκ ὀρθῶς φρονεῖν περὶ θεοῦ δεδιδαγμένοι, τὴν αὐτὴν ἐκείνοις νοσοῦντες
μανίαν, τοῖς ἴσοις τῆς πλεονεξίας σπουδάσμασι κατ’ ἀλλήλων προσ-
φέρονται, ἀλλὰ θειόθεν μέρος ἑκάτερον νυγέντες πρὸς τοὺς ἐν Παλαιστίνῃ
ἁγίους ἥκασι, καὶ τούτοις τὰς ζητουμένας πεύσεις προσήγαγον. 30

Witnesses: 1. 1–p. 182, 1. 27 C Arm

[1] Of Cyril, archbishop of the city of the Alexandrians, solution of the dogmatic
questions of Tiberius the priest Arm. The printed edition heads the following
section Letter of Tiberius   [2] βιβλίον C: Pusey corr.

9

DOCTRINAL QUESTIONS AND ANSWERS

Petition presented to holy Cyril, the faithful high priest, true-born servant of God and archbishop of Alexandria by the brotherhood

It was good for us to be at peace and accomplish perhaps also some part of our aims, but no less good do we reckon it to come away and be helped simply by seeing you, and we shall derive special profit by being taught true religion from your very mouth.

Reading your Holiness's books and works in seclusion far from the world is fine, helpful and productive of progress for those who attend to it, but it is a sounder, more vitalizing thing to be watered by teaching from the very lips which gush forth divine grace and spiritual sweetness So we come again out of longing towards yourself and towards true religion, for the sake of our advancement as well as the correction of others. For we derived no little profit previously from having received at your sainted hands the volume which answered our inquiry concerning sound doctrine. The book has served us as a confirmation and others as a corrective; a few there are who had not had recourse to wholesome teaching and their mouths were stopped. However, the people of Abilene,[1] in evil mutual contention over certain doctrinal issues, have driven on to such a pitch of insanity as to decree mutual depositions and anathematisms, to harass one another, undergo depredations, and not yield to the bishops and fathers there or with us and not concede to any other saints the claim to a larger measure of knowledge, so powerfully has satanic disorder captured and removed them from divine peace. In addition to these again, some Egyptians uninstructed in correct theology have caught the same madness as these and attack one another with each side equally aiming to get the upper hand. However, both parties have been stimulated by God into coming to the saints in Palestine and bringing them the questions at issue.

---

[1] From the reference to coming to the saints in Palestine (below) this is evidently not the present Tel-Abil in Jordan (anciently in Palestina secunda) but present-day Suq-Wadi-Barada in Syria, 14 miles N.W. of Damascus (anciently in Phoenicia secunda, within the jurisdiction of Antioch—so Cyril is fishing in troubled waters); see *DHGE* I s.v. 2. ABILA.

Ἡμεῖς δὲ τὴν ἑαυτῶν μετρήσαντες δύναμιν ἐκρίναμεν μὴ δεῖν ἡμᾶς
αὐτοὺς περὶ τούτων ὁρίζειν, μήτε μὴν ἱκανῶς ἔχειν τὸν περὶ τῶν
τοιούτων ἐξετάσεων ἀποδοῦναι λόγον. μαθόντες τοίνυν οἱ προειρημένοι
παρρησίαν πρὸς τὴν σὴν ἡμᾶς ἔχειν ὁσιότητα, ἐξελιπάρησαν διὰ τῆς
ἡμῶν βραχύτητος πέρας δέξασθαι τῆς πρὸς ἀλλήλους μάχης τὸν τῆς 5
ὑμετέρας διδασκαλίας λόγον. συναινεσάντων οὖν τῶν καθ' ἡμᾶς ἁγίων
πατέρων, αὐθαίρετοι τὴν παράκλησιν ἐδεξάμεθα, ἑαυτοῖς μᾶλλον ἢ
ἐκείνοις χαριζόμενοι τῷ καὶ αὐτῶν τῶν ὄψεων ἀπολαῦσαι καὶ παρόντι
συνευφρανθῆναι καὶ λόγῳ ζῶντι καὶ οὐ γράμματι δι' ἑτέρων πεμπομένῳ
καὶ πλέον τὴν ἐπιθυμίαν ἐξάπτοντι. ἡρπάσαμεν τοίνυν τὴν ἄφιξιν οὐ 10
μετρίως χαίροντες ὅπως καὶ δι' ἡμῶν τῶν ἐλαχίστων, ἣν μὲν πρὸς
ἀλλήλους συγκροτοῦσι καταθῶνται μάχην, διὰ δὲ τῆς ὑγιαινούσης σου
διδασκαλίας ἡ τοῦ Χριστοῦ εἰρήνη αὐτοῖς τε καὶ ἡμῖν ὡς τάχιστα
βραβευθείη· εἴτ' ἀπιόντων ἡμῶν διὰ φίλην ἡσυχίαν, εἴτε μενόντων διὰ
τὴν ἀγάπην καὶ συγκρότησιν καὶ τὴν ἐκ τούτων προκοπὴν καὶ τὰ 15
γραφησόμενα πεμπόντων εὐκαιρότερον.

Ἀλλ' αὐτός, πάτερ ἁγιώτατε, γνησίως ἡμᾶς ὁρᾶν μὴ παραιτοῦ,
πατρὸς σπλάγχνα καὶ εἰς ἡμᾶς διασώζων. οὔτε γὰρ ὡς οἶμαι καὶ
ἀπολογίας δεήσομεν, παρρησίας μετέχοντες μετὰ αἰδοῦς διὰ θεοῦ
χάριν καὶ τὴν σὴν χρηστότητα, ἣν καὶ πλατυνθῆναι ἡμῖν αὐτοῖς 20
ἰσορρόπως τῆς ἡμετέρας γνησιότητος ἀπαιτοῦμεν, καὶ τοῦτο μετὰ
σωφροσύνης. οὕτω γάρ γ' ἂν γένοιτο καὶ ἡμᾶς τῶν ἀμοιβαίων τέως
τυγχάνειν καὶ τὴν σὴν ὁσιότητα καὶ εἰς ἡμᾶς τὰ εἰκότα πράττουσαν
εὐγνωμονεῖν, ἣν πλέον ὁ τῶν ὅλων σωτὴρ ἀποδέξεται καὶ εἰς ἡμᾶς
τοὺς ἐλαχίστους κατὰ τὴν αὐτοῦ μίμησιν καταγομένην οὐ βίας ἀνάγκῃ, 25
ἀλλ' ἀγάπης γνησιότητι καὶ τοῦτο δῶρον αὐτῷ προσφέρουσαν. ἔστι δὲ
τὰ ζητούμενα τὰ ὑποτεταγμένα.[3]

[3] The scribe has added the following note: τὰ μὲν κεφάλαια ἐνέκειντο τῇ
ἀξιώσει, ἀλλ' ἵνα μὴ δὶς ταὐτὰ ἐγγράψωμεν, συνεζεύξαμεν ἕκαστον κεφάλαιον
ἐν τῇ ἑρμηνείᾳ. His practice is here followed. Arm. preserves the original form,
listing here the questions and then adds: *Touching these matters we ask you to
establish in us the same piety of your holiness's teaching, so as to confirm us and those
who accept your word and behave themselves in seemly fashion and practice right actions
and with a view to admonishing or correcting unbelievers, praying as all we poor
creatures do. And so we shall fitly strive after the things in which God is well pleased,
finding mercy in due season to be at your feet and then be bold to say 'Behold, I and
the children whom God has given me'* (Is. 8: 18), *children who have followed your
word, with whom you have bestowed on me the word of your teaching.*

We took the measure of our own capacity and decided we ought not to give our ruling on the matter and indeed that our powers were insufficient to render a statement on questions of this kind. The people we have mentioned have heard that we exercise boldness towards your Holiness and so through our humble selves they begged you to grant a word of your teaching to obtain an ending of their mutual strife. With the approval of our holy fathers we have willingly taken up the role of advocate, doing ourselves rather than them a favour in the enjoyment our very eyes have and the accompanying pleasure of an immediate, living word instead of a letter sent through others still further inflaming our longing. We took our departure, then, with no small measure of joy, so that through our insignificant selves they may settle the battle they wage with one another and Christ's peace may be adjudicated on as quickly as possible, for their benefit and ours, through your wholesome teaching, whether it be given after we have taken our leave for the sake of the calm so dear to us, or as we stay for the sake of the love, the support and the progress they produce, and despatch a letter at leisure.

But you, most holy father, do not disdain the courtesy of seeing us, treasuring as you do a father's love towards us. Nor indeed, I think, shall we lack a defence, having, as we do, a portion of reverent boldness, because of God's grace and your kindness which we ask to be extended to ourselves in measure correspondent with our sincerity, and wisely too. For in this way it will turn out that whilst we obtain our recompense we are repaying your Holiness for acting fittingly towards us. The Saviour of all will welcome you all the more for having imitated him and condescended to our humble selves not by forcible constraint but in sincere love, offering, as you do, this gift to him. The issues in question are set out below.

Πρῶτον κεφάλαιον ἐπιλύσεως δογματικῶν ζητημάτων
προτεθέντων τῷ ἁγιωτάτῳ Κυρίλλῳ.[1]

Α΄

Εἰ ὁ ἐπὶ πάντων θεὸς χεῖρας, πόδας, ὀφθαλμούς, ὦτά τε καὶ πτέρυγας
ἔχειν[2] ὑπὸ τῆς θείας γραφῆς ὀνομαζόμενος, οὕτω παρ' ἡμῶν ὀφείλει
νοεῖσθαι, οὐκ ἀνθρωποειδῶς ὡς ἐπὶ σώματος τῶν μελῶν λαμβανομένων·   5
ἀσώματος γάρ· ἀλλὰ καθώς[3] ἐστιν οὐσία,[4] οὕτω καὶ τὰ λεχθέντα τῆς
οὐσίας ὄντα, μέλη[5] θεῖα καὶ αὐτὰ κατὰ τὴν οὐσίαν ὑπάρχει.

Ἐπίλυσις

Οἱ φρενὸς ὄντες ἐν καλῷ, καὶ τοῖς περὶ τῆς ἀρρήτου θεότητος
λόγοις ἰσχνὸν ἐνιέντες τῆς ἑαυτῶν διανοίας τὸν ὀφθαλμόν,[6] ὁρῶσιν   10
αὐτὴν παντὸς μὲν ὑπάρχουσαν ἐπέκεινα γενητοῦ,[7] ὑπερανίσχουσαν
δὲ καὶ[8] παντὸς ὀξύτητα νοῦ καὶ φαντασίας σωματικῆς πέρα τε
οὖσαν παντελῶς, καὶ καθά φησιν ὁ πάνσοφος Παῦλος φῶς
οἰκοῦσαν ἀπρόσιτον.[a] εἰ δὲ ἀπρόσιτόν ἐστι τὸ περὶ αὐτὴν φῶς,
πῶς ἂν αὐτὴν καταθρήσειέ τις; βλέπομεν γὰρ ἐν ἐσόπτρῳ καὶ[9]   15
αἰνίγματι, καὶ γινώσκομεν ἐκ μέρους.[b] ἔστι τοίνυν ἀσώματον παντελῶς τὸ θεῖον, ἄποσόν τε καὶ ἀμέγεθες,[10] καὶ οὐκ ἐν
εἴδει περιγράπτῳ.[11] τὸ δὲ οὕτως ἔχον ἐν ἰδίᾳ φύσει, πῶς ἂν ἐκ
μορίων νοοῖτο[12] καὶ μελῶν; εἰ γάρ τις δοίη[13] τοῦτο ὑπάρχειν
ἀληθές, ἀσώματον οὐκ ἔτι[14] νοεῖται.[15] τὸ γὰρ ὅλως ἐν σχήματι,   20
πάντως που καὶ ἐν ποσῷ, τὸ δὲ ἐν ποσῷ καὶ ἐν τόπῳ·[16] καὶ τὸ ἐν
τόπῳ νοούμενον, οὐκ ἔξω[17] περιγραφῆς. ταῦτα δὲ σωμάτων μὲν
ἴδια, τῆς δὲ ἀσωμάτου[18] φύσεως ἀλλότρια παντελῶς. οὔτε τοίνυν
ὀφθαλμοὺς ἢ ὦτα, οὔτε μὴν χεῖράς τε καὶ πόδας ἢ πτέρυγας ἐπὶ

---

1. [a] 1 Tim. 6: 16   [b] 1 Cor. 13: 12

Witnesses: ll. 1–16 C G O N (selected readings only, see p. xlix) Arm   l. 16–
p. 186, l. 4 C G O N Arm Flor. Cyr.

    1. [1] Heading as C: τὰ παρὰ τῆς ἀδελφότητος προτεθέντα κεφάλαια τῷ ἁγίῳ
Κυρίλλῳ ἐπισκόπῳ Ἀλεξανδρείας. πρῶτον G: no heading in O: Arm places
heading before Tiberius' letter   [2] ἔχει O   [3] καθὸ O   [4] οὐσίας CGO
[5] μέλη ὄντα G   [6] ταῖς αὐτῶν διανοίαις τῶν ὀφθαλμῶν O   [7] γεννητοῦ G
[8] καὶ om. G   [9] καὶ] δι' O: ἐν add. G   [10] ἀμέγεθον Flor. Cyr.
[11] περιγραπτόν Flor. Cyr.   [12] νοήτῳ O   [13] δοίει O   [14] ἔστι O
[15] νοοῖτο G   [16] τὸ δὲ—τόπῳ om. O: καὶ—τόπῳ om. Arm   [17] ἐξὸν O
[18] ἴδια—ἀσωμάτου om. Flor. Cyr.

First item in the answer to the doctrinal questions propounded to most holy Cyril

I

Whether the all-transcending God named by divine Scripture as having hands, feet, eyes, ears and wings should be thought of by us, not in anthropomorphic terms, with the limbs being taken as belonging to a body, because he is incorporeal; but in this way, that, just as he is substance, so too the entities, spoken of as pertaining to the substance, the divine limbs, themselves have substantial existence?[2]

Answer

Men of good sense who focus their minds' eyes sharply on the attributes of the ineffable Godhead, see it as existing beyond every created thing, transcending all acuity of intellect, being wholly outside bodily appearance and, as all-wise Paul says, '*dwelling in light unapproachable*'. But if the light surrounding it is unapproachable, how can one gaze on it? We see '*in a glass darkly and know in part*'. Deity, then, is wholly incorporeal, without dimensions or size and not bounded by shape. How could one who is like this in his own nature be thought to consist of parts and limbs? Were one to grant the truth of that, he ceases to be thought of as incorporeal. What exists in a figure must have dimensions and what has dimensions must exist in place; and what is thought of as existing in place cannot be unbounded. These are the properties of bodies but they are totally foreign to incorporeal nature. So one must not conceive of eyes or ears, or indeed hands, feet and wings as belonging to God, even though

---

[2] Cf. *Answers to Tiberius* 1. These questioners reject simple anthropomorphism but ask whether there is anything actual, but spiritual, corresponding with the language of e.g. Deut. 32 : 11, Ps. 18 : 8 ff. The idea was dear to Irenaeus that God's 'hands' mean the Word and the Spirit (cf. *Proof of the Apostolic Preaching* c. 11, *Adv. Haer.* 5, 1, 3, etc.)—there may be a hint of that here.

θεοῦ νοητέον, κἂν[19] εἰ μή τις ἔλοιτο τυχὸν ὡς ἐν ἁπτοῖς[20] καὶ παχέσι[21]
σώμασι τὰ τοιάδε[22] νοεῖν, ἀλλ᾽ ὡς ἐν ἰσχνῷ καὶ ἀΰλῳ, καὶ κατά γε
τὴν τοῦ θεοῦ φύσιν· εὔηθες γὰρ παντελῶς τὸ βούλεσθαί τι τοιοῦτον
ἐννοεῖν. πνεῦμα γὰρ ὁ θεός·[c] καὶ τοῦτο ὑπάρχων,[23] πάντων ἔχει τὴν
γνῶσιν, ἐφορᾷ πάντα καὶ κατασκέπτεται, λανθάνει δὲ αὐτὸν τῶν 5
ὄντων οὐδέν. εἰ δὲ μορίων ἤτοι μελῶν ἡ θεία μέμνηται γραφή,
πρὸς ἡμᾶς λαλοῦσα τὰ περὶ αὐτοῦ, ἰστέον ὅτι ἐξ ὧν ἴσμεν τε καὶ
πεφύκαμεν εἶναι πρὸς ἡμᾶς διαλέγεται. οὐ γὰρ ἦν ἑτέρως ἡμᾶς
νοεῖν δύνασθαι[24] τὰ περὶ θεοῦ. αἰτία τοίνυν καὶ πρόφασις ἀληθὴς
τοῦ σωματικῶς περὶ θεοῦ τοὺς πρὸς ἡμᾶς ποιεῖσθαι λόγους τὴν 10
θεόπνευστον γραφήν, καὶ νοῦ[25] καὶ γλώττης ἐν ἡμῖν ἡ[26] πτωχεία.
ἄρρητα γὰρ παντελῶς τὰ περὶ αὐτοῦ· καὶ οὐκ ἦν συνιέναι τι τῶν
ἀναγκαίων δύνασθαι τοὺς ἐν ἁπτοῖς καὶ παχέσιν ὄντας σώμασιν,
εἰ μὴ ἐν τάξει παραδειγμάτων τὰ ἑαυτῶν δεχόμενοι μέλη, μόλις
οὕτως ἄνιμεν εἰς[27] ἐννοίας ἰσχνὰς τὰς[28] περὶ[29] θεοῦ. 15

Βʹ

Ἔκτισεν ὁ θεὸς ἐκ γῆς τὸν ἄνθρωπον καὶ ἐνεφύσησεν εἰς τὸ
πρόσωπον αὐτοῦ πνοὴν ζωῆς καὶ ἐγένετο ὁ ἄνθρωπος εἰς
ψυχὴν ζῶσαν.[a1] καὶ οἱ μὲν ὑπὸ τοῦ ἐμφυσήματος τὴν ψυχὴν λέγουσι
δεδημιουργῆσθαι, ὡς ὑπὸ χειρῶν τὸ σῶμα· οἱ δὲ ὅτι τὸ ἐμφύσημα
ἐκεῖνο ψυχὴ αὐτῷ γέγονεν· οἱ δὲ ἕτεροι πάλιν ὅτι τῷ κτισθέντι ἀνθρώπῳ 20
ὁλοκλήρῳ ζωτικὴν δέδωκε δύναμιν τὸ ἐμφύσημα ἐκεῖνο· ἄλλοι δὲ ὅτι
ὁ νοῦς ἐστι τὸ ἐμφύσημα τοῦτο, καὶ διώρισται τῆς ψυχῆς, καὶ τοῦτό
ἐστι τὸ κατ᾽ εἰκόνα, ὡς ἐκ τριῶν τούτων συνίστασθαι τὸν ἄνθρωπον,
νοῦ καὶ ψυχῆς καὶ σώματος ἰδιαζόντως ἐν ἑνώσει. καὶ ἴδιον[2] τῆς
οὐσίας τοῦ θεοῦ ἢ ἀλλότριον τὸ ἐμφύσημα τοῦτό ἐστιν. 25

Ἐπίλυσις

Τὰ οὕτως ἰσχνὰ καὶ οὐκ εὐτριβῆ τῶν ζητημάτων, οὐκ ἀπο-
φάσεως δεῖται δογματικῆς, ἐπαπορήσεως δὲ μᾶλλον καὶ βασάνου

---

[c] John 4:24   2. [a] Gen. 2:7

Witnesses: ll. 4–15 C G O N Arm   l. 16–p. 196, l. 5 C G N Arm

19 κἂν] οὐκ ἂν Flor. Cyr.: καὶ Ο   20 αὐτοῖς Flor. Cyr.   21 πάθεσι C
22 τοῖα Ο   23 τούτῳ ὑπάρχον Ο   24 δύνασθαι νοεῖν Ο   25 νοῦν C
26 ἡ om. C   27 ἀνειμένης Ο   28 τὰ Ο   29 τοῦ add. G
2. 1 καὶ ἐγένετο—ζῶσαν om. Arm   2 καὶ σώματος—ἴδιον] καὶ ἰδιαζόντως
ἐν αἰνέσει· καὶ εἰ ἴδιον G

one elects to conceive of such things not as they exist in palpable, gross bodies but as existing in fine-drawn immateriality and in correspondence with God's nature; it is utterly silly to entertain such an idea. For *God is spirit*; and being spirit he has knowledge of all things, oversees and looks down over everything and no reality escapes him. If divine Scripture mentions parts or limbs in telling us of his attributes, it is to be interpreted as speaking to us in terms of what we know and are.[3] In no other way was it possible for us to conceive of God's attributes. Our poverty of mind and speech is the real cause and occasion, therefore, of inspired Scripture's addressing us about God in bodily terms. For his attributes are wholly ineffable and it would be impossible for those who exist in palpable and gross bodies to be able to understand any essential fact unless we take our own limbs by way of illustrations and thus with difficulty go on to fine-drawn ideas about God.

2

God created man from the earth '*and he breathed into his face the breath of life and man became a living soul*'. Some assert that the soul was fashioned by the in-breathing as the body was by hands; some that that in-breathing became his soul; others again that the in-breathing gave vital force to the whole created man; others that the in-breathing is the mind, that it is separate from the soul and that this is the meaning of the phrase 'in (God's) image' so that man is constituted of these three, mind, soul and body, having his proper being in their union. This in-breathing either belongs or is alien to God's substance.[4]

Answer

Such subtle and out-of-the-way problems do not require a doctrinal decision so much as a questioning and speculative

[3] Cf. above p. 138 and *In Is.* (*PG* 70, 1084A), *Contra Jul.* 4 (*PG* 76, 713C), and for a detailed discussion of certain anthropomorphic expressions see *In Mich.* (ed. Pusey p. 605, 4 ff.): they describe God, not as he is in himself, but his activity in relation to the world.

[4] The problems here are ancient. Two groups of questions are posed: (1) What is the relation between God's breath and the soul—does the in-breathing of God merely describe a special mode of the soul's creation, does it imply that the soul is God's breath and so divine in substance, or does it indicate the way in which Adam was endowed with life? (2) Is the mind distinct from soul and body and, if so, was it distinctively formed by the divine breath to be in God's image, whether divine in substance or not? For the view that the soul is divine in substance cf. Nilus *Epp.* 2, 82 (*PG* 79, 237B) and for a parallel refutation to Cyril's, see Theodoret *Quaestiones in Gen.* 23 (*PG* 80, 121AB). Cyril does not discuss the point when he comments upon the passage, *Glaph. in Gen.* (*PG* 69, 20BC).

στοχαστικοῦ, μετὰ τοῦ μὴ ἀνέχεσθαι διαπίπτειν τὸν λόγον ἐᾶν³ ἐφ᾽
ἃ μὴ προσῆκεν, ἤγουν ἔξω φέρεσθαι³ τοῦ εἰκότος. γέγραπται γάρ,
ὅτι⁴ ζητῶν ζήτει, καὶ παρ᾽ ἐμοὶ οἴκει.ᵇ ὃ δὲ σαφῶς οὐκ ἔφη τὸ
γράμμα τὸ ἱερόν, πῶς ἄν τις ἐξηγοῖτο σαφῶς; οἷόν τί φημι ἐν
τῷ τῆς κοσμοποιίας βιβλίῳ γέγραπται, ὅτι ἐν ἀρχῇ ἐποίησεν ὁ   5
θεὸς τὸν οὐρανὸν καὶ τὴν γῆν. καὶ ὅτι μὲν πεποίηκεν ἔφη τὸ
γράμμα τὸ ἱερόν, καὶ ἀληθὲς ἐν πίστει τοῦτο δεχόμεθα. τὸ δὲ
ὅπως ἢ πόθεν, ἢ τίνα τρόπον παρήχθη πρὸς ὕπαρξιν⁵ οὐρανός τε καὶ
γῆ καὶ τὰ ἕτερα τῶν κτισμάτων πολυπραγμονεῖν οὐκ ἀζήμιον· οὐ
γὰρ δεῖ τοῖς βαθυτέροις ἐγκαθιέναι τὸν νοῦν. ὅσα τοίνυν μὴ σφόδρα   10
σαφῶς ἡ θεία λέγει γραφή, ταῦτα χρὴ λανθάνειν καὶ ἐν σιωπῇ
παρατρέχειν.

Εἰ δὲ χρὴ κατατεκμαίρεσθαι μετὰ λογισμοῦ βλέποντος εἰς
ὀρθότητα, φαμὲν ὅτι ὁ τῶν ὅλων δημιουργὸς ἔπλασε μὲν ἀπὸ γῆς
τὸν ἄνθρωπον, ἤτοι τὸ σῶμα· ψυχώσας δὲ αὐτὸ ψυχῇ ζώσῃ τε καὶ   15
νοερᾷ, καθ᾽ ὃν οἶδε τρόπον, παντὸς ἀγαθοῦ πράγματος ἔφεσίν⁶ τε
καὶ γνῶσιν ἐγκατεβάλετο φυσικῶς αὐτῷ. τοῦτο γὰρ οἶμαι δηλοῦν
τὸ εἰρημένον διὰ τοῦ μακαρίου εὐαγγελιστοῦ Ἰωάννου ἦν τὸ φῶς
τὸ ἀληθινόν, ὃ φωτίζει πάντα ἄνθρωπον ἐρχόμενον εἰς
τὸν κόσμον.ᶜ τίκτεται γὰρ τὸ ζῷον φυσικὴν ἔχον ἐπιτηδειότητα   20
πρὸς τὸ ἀγαθόν. καὶ τοῦτο διδάξει γράφων ὁ πάνσοφος Παῦλος,
ὅτι αὐτοῦ ἐσμεν ποίημα, κτισθέντες ἐπὶ ἔργοις ἀγαθοῖς,
οἷς προητοίμασεν ὁ θεὸς ἵνα ἐν αὐτοῖς περιπατήσωμεν.ᵈ
διοικεῖται μὲν γὰρ ὁ ἄνθρωπος προαιρετικῶς καὶ τὰς ἡνίας πεπί-
στευται τῆς αὐτοῦ διανοίας, ὥστε ἐφ᾽ ὅπερ ἂν βούλοιτο τρέχειν, εἴτε   25
πρὸς τὸ ἀγαθόν, εἴτε⁷ πρὸς τὸ ἐναντίον. ἔχει δὲ ἡ φύσις ἐγκατα-
βεβλημένην ἑαυτῇ καὶ τὴν εἰς πᾶν ὁτιοῦν τῶν ἀγαθῶν ἔφεσίν τε καὶ
προθυμίαν, καὶ⁸ τὸ ἐπιμελεῖσθαι θέλειν ἀγαθότητος⁹ καὶ δικαιοσύνης.
οὕτω γὰρ τὸν ἄνθρωπον κατ᾽ εἰκόνα¹⁰ καὶ ὁμοίωσιν γενέσθαι φαμέν,
καθὸ καὶ ἀγαθὸν καὶ δίκαιον πέφυκεν εἶναι τὸ ζῷον. ἐπειδὴ δὲ ἐχρῆν   30
οὐ λογικὸν εἶναι μόνον, καὶ ἐπιτηδείως ἔχον¹¹ εἰς ἀγαθουργίαν
καὶ δικαιοσύνην, ἀλλὰ γὰρ καὶ ἁγίου πνεύματος μέτοχον, ἵνα

ᵇ Is. 21: 12   ᶜ John 1: 9   ᵈ Eph. 2: 10

3 ἐᾶν, φέρεσθαι N and apparently Arm: ἐὰν, φέρεται CG   4 ὁ add. G
5 ὁ add. G   6 ἄφεσιν C   7 ἤτουν C   8 καὶ om. G   9 τε
add. C   10 κατ᾽ εἰκόνα τὸν ἄνθρωπον C   11 ἔχοντα G

investigation accompanied by a refusal to let the mind fall into improper views or be carried away from reasonableness. For it is written '*seeking do thou seek and dwell with me*'. How can one clearly explain what holy writ has not stated clearly? For example it is written in the book of Genesis that in the beginning God made heaven and earth. Holy writ declared that he has made it and we accept this truth in faith. But meddlesome inquiry into the means, origin or method whereby heaven, earth and the rest of creation were brought into being has its harmful side, for there is no need to involve the mind in profundities. What divine Scripture does not state very clearly must remain unknown and be passed over in silence.

If we have to make a conjecture with the aid of a reasoning which aims at correctness, we say that the creator of all formed man, man's body, from the ground; and having animated it with living and intelligent soul[5] he instilled into him, by a mode he knows, a natural longing for and knowledge of every good thing. This is what I think the saying of blessed John the evangelist means: '*He was the true light which lightens every man coming into the world.*' For a living being is born with a natural aptitude for goodness. This is what all-wise Paul will teach when he writes that '*we are his work, created for good deeds which God has prepared for us to walk in*'. For man conducts himself as he chooses; he is entrusted with the reins of his understanding and so runs towards whatever he wishes, whether goodness or its opposite.[6] His nature has built into it a longing and desire for every good thing whatsoever and the will to cultivate goodness and righteousness.[7] It is with this meaning that we say man was created in his image and likeness, according as the living being was born to be good and righteous. But seeing that he ought to be not merely rational with an aptitude for doing good and right, but also a participator in the Holy Spirit, he breathed into him, so that he might have

---

[5] Cyril does not distinguish soul and mind. His habitual expression is 'body', σῶμα, and 'reasoning/intelligent soul', ψυχὴ λογική/νοερά. In this he follows Athanasius and opposes Apollinarius who held to the three-fold division: body, soul and mind—a division which determined his Christology. Cf. *In Jo.* 2, 1 (Pusey 1, 219) . . . σύνθετόν τι καὶ οὐχ ἁπλοῦν κατὰ φύσιν ὁ ἄνθρωπος, ἐκ δύο κεκρασμένος, αἰσθητοῦ δηλονότι σώματος καὶ ψυχῆς νοερᾶς ' . . . man is something composite and not simple by nature, a compound of two things, sensible body and intelligent soul'. Cf. *First Letter to Succensus* § 7.

[6] A phrase Cyril liked to use to describe man's freedom of will, cf. e.g. *De Ad.* 1 (*PG* 68, 145D) *Contra Jul.* 8 (*PG* 76, 937C).

[7] Cf. *Answers to Tiberius*, 1 p. 139 and note 17.

λαμπροτέρους ἔχῃ τῆς θείας[12] φύσεως τοὺς χαρακτῆρας ἐν ἑαυτῷ,
καὶ[13] ἐνεφύσησεν αὐτῷ πνοὴν ζωῆς. τοῦτο δέ ἐστι τὸ δι᾽ υἱοῦ τῇ
λογικῇ κτίσει[14] χορηγούμενον πνεῦμα, καὶ διαμορφοῦν αὐτὴν εἰς
εἶδος τὸ ἀνωτάτω, τουτέστι τὸ θεῖον.

Ὅτι γὰρ οὐκ εἰς ψυχὴν[15] ἀνθρώπῳ τὸ ἐμφυσηθὲν αὐτῷ γέγονε 5
πνεῦμα, οὔτε μὴν εἰς νοῦν, ὡς οἴονταί τινες, ἐντεῦθεν ἔστιν ἰδεῖν.[16]
πρῶτον μὲν γὰρ ὁ ἐμφυσήσας νοεῖται ὁ[17] θεός, τὸ δὲ ἐμφυσηθὲν ἐξ
αὐτοῦ πάντως που νοεῖται καὶ ἴδιον αὐτοῦ, ἤτοι τῆς οὐσίας αὐτοῦ.
εἶτα πῶς ἂν τὸ ἐκ θεοῦ πνεῦμα μετέβαλεν εἰς φύσιν ψυχῆς,[18] ἢ
καὶ νοῦς ἐγένετο; ἀμήχανον γάρ ἐστι τοῦ τρέπεσθαι τὸ πνεῦμα.[19] 10
εἰ δὲ δοίη τις εἶναι καὶ κατὰ τροπὴν γενέσθαι ψυχὴν ἢ νοῦν[20] (ὅπερ
ἐστὶ τῶν ἀμηχάνων) ἀλλ᾽ ἐκεῖνό γε εὐθὺς ἔστιν ἰδεῖν. εἰ γὰρ εἰς
ψυχὴν τῷ ἀνθρώπῳ τὸ θεῖον πνεῦμα γέγονεν, ἔμεινεν ἂν ἡ ψυχὴ
καὶ ὁ νοῦς ἀνεπίδεκτος ἁμαρτίας. εἰ δὲ ὑποπέπτωκεν ἁμαρτίαις εἰς
ψυχὴν μεταβεβλημένον τὸ ἐκ θεοῦ πνεῦμα, διττὸν αὐτῷ τὸ ἔγκλημα 15
παρ᾽ ἡμῶν ἐπάγεται. πρῶτον μέν, ὅτι τροπὴν ὑπέμεινε τὴν εἰς
ὅπερ οὐκ ἦν, εἶτα πρὸς τούτῳ[21] καὶ ἁμαρτίας αὐτό φαμεν γενέσθαι
δεκτικόν. οὐκοῦν ἐψυχώθη μὲν τὸ ζῷον ἀρρήτῳ δυνάμει θεοῦ, καὶ
ἐν ὁμοιώσει τῇ πρὸς αὐτὸν[22] γέγονε, καθ᾽ ὃ πέφυκεν εἶναι καὶ
ἀγαθὸν καὶ δίκαιον καὶ ἀρετῆς ἁπάσης δεκτικόν· ἡγιάσθη δὲ 20
μέτοχον ἀποδεδειγμένον τοῦ θείου πνεύματος ὃ καὶ ἀποβέβληκε
διὰ τὴν ἁμαρτίαν. ἔφη γάρ που ὁ θεὸς ὅτι οὐ μὴ καταμείνῃ[23]
τὸ πνεῦμά μου ἐν τοῖς ἀνθρώποις τούτοις διὰ τὸ εἶναι
αὐτοὺς σάρκας,[e] τουτέστι μόνα φρονεῖν τὰ τῆς[24] σαρκός. ἐπειδὴ
δὲ ηὐδόκησεν ὁ θεὸς καὶ[25] πατὴρ ἀνακεφαλαιώσασθαι τὰ 25
πάντα ἐν τῷ Χριστῷ,[f] τουτέστιν εἰς τὸ ἀρχαῖον ἀναγαγεῖν, τὸ
ἀποπτὰν καὶ ἀποφοιτῆσαν ἡμῶν ἅγιον πνεῦμα πάλιν ἡμῖν ἀπο-
καθιστῶν, τοῦτο ἐνεφύσησε τοῖς ἁγίοις ἀποστόλοις, λέγων λάβετε
πνεῦμα ἅγιον.[g] ἀνανέωσις γὰρ τῆς ἀρχαίας ἐκείνης δωρεᾶς, καὶ
τοῦ δοθέντος ἡμῖν ἐμφυσήματος, τὸ διὰ Χριστοῦ γέγονεν, ἀνα- 30
μορφοῦν ἡμᾶς εἰς ἁγιασμὸν τὸν πρῶτον, καὶ ἀνακομίζον[26] τὴν

---

[e] Gen. 6: 3   [f] Eph. 1: 10   [g] John 20: 22

---

[12] θείας om. G   [13] καὶ om. G   [14] φύσει G   [15] τῷ add. G
[16] ἰδεῖν ἔστι G   [17] ὁ om. G   [18] ψυχῆς] ἀνθρωπίνην Arm   [19] ἐστι
after πνεῦμά C   [20] γενέσθαι—νοῦν] ἢ νοῦν γενέσθαι G   [21] τούτῳ N:
τοῦτο CG   [22] θεὸν G   [23] καταμείνει C   [24] τῆς om. C   [25] ὁ add. C
[26] ἀνακομίζον N: ἀνακομίζων CG

brighter marks of the divine nature within him, the breath of life. This is the Spirit furnished through the Son to rational creation and shaping it into the sublimest, that is the divine, form.

Thus we can see that the in-breathed spirit did not become man's soul or his mind, as some imagine. For in the first place the in-breather is understood to be God, and what he breathed out must also belong to him, his substance. How in that case could the Spirit of God have changed into the nature of a soul or become a mind? The Spirit is incapable of change. Were anyone to concede that the Spirit is the soul or mind and has become such by a process of change (which is impossible) he can still see the following point: if the divine Spirit became man's soul, soul and mind would have remained incapable of sin. But if the Spirit of God transformed into soul fell victim to sins, a two-fold charge is preferred against him by us—first that he underwent change into what he had not been and then, besides this, we are declaring him to have been made capable of sin. It follows that the living being was animated by God's ineffable might and was made in likeness to him, and accordingly was born to be good, righteous and capable of all excellence; but he was hallowed by being appointed sharer in the divine Spirit which he lost because of his sin.[8] For God declared in one passage that '*my Spirit shall not abide in these men because they are flesh*', meaning they think only fleshly thoughts. But seeing that God the Father was pleased *to sum up all things in Christ* (meaning bring them back to the primal state by re-establishing in us the Holy Spirit who had taken flight and quitted us) he breathed it into the holy apostles with the words '*Receive the Holy Spirit.*' Christ's act was a renewal of that primal gift and of the in-breathing bestowed on us, bringing us back to the form of initial hallowing and carrying man's nature up, as a kind of first-fruits

---

[8] Man is, for Cyril, naturally good, having an innate inclination to goodness which he is free to follow or to check. This feature of the image man never loses. But the hallowing by the Spirit in-breathed by God and also constituting part of the image was lost as the Spirit left man. Cyril seems to envisage a gradual withdrawal of the Spirit, cf. *In Jo.* 2, 1 (Pusey 1, 183).

ἀνθρώπου φύσιν, ὡς ἐν ἀπαρχῇ τοῖς ἁγίοις ἀποστόλοις, εἰς τὸν ἄνωθεν καὶ ἐν πρώτῃ κατασκευῇ δοθέντα ἡμῖν ἁγιασμόν.

Γ′

Εἰ ἕτερον τὸ "κατ᾽ εἰκόνα" καὶ ἕτερον τὸ "καθ᾽ ὁμοίωσιν" ἢ ταὐτόν· φασὶ γὰρ ὅτι τὸ μὲν "κατ᾽ εἰκόνα" ἐλάβομεν εὐθὺς κτισθέντες, τὸ δὲ "καθ᾽ ὁμοίωσιν" οὔ,[1] τετήρηται γὰρ[2] ἡμῖν εἰς αἰῶνα τὸν μέλλοντα. διό, 5 φησί, γέγραπται ὅταν ὁ Χριστὸς φανερωθῇ, ὅμοιοι αὐτῷ ἐσόμεθα.[a] καὶ πάλιν εἴρηται, φησί, ποιήσωμεν ἄνθρωπον κατ᾽ εἰκόνα καὶ καθ᾽ ὁμοίωσιν ἡμετέραν,[b] καὶ μετὰ τὴν τοῦ ἀνθρώπου δημιουργίαν εἴρηκε καὶ ἐποίησεν ὁ θεὸς τὸν ἄνθρωπον, κατ᾽ εἰκόνα ἑαυτοῦ ἐποίησεν αὐτόν,[c] σιωπήσας ἐνταῦθα τὸ "καθ᾽ 10 ὁμοίωσιν", ἵνα δείξῃ, φησί, μήπω ἡμᾶς τοῦτο δεδέχθαι, τετηρῆσθαι δὲ ἡμῖν ἐν τῇ μακαρίᾳ[3] ἐκείνῃ ζωῇ.

Ἐπίλυσις

Εἰ μὲν ἕτερον καὶ ἕτερον εἶναί φασι τὸ "κατ᾽ εἰκόνα" καὶ "καθ᾽ ὁμοίωσιν", διδασκέτωσαν τὴν διαφοράν. διακείμεθα γὰρ ἡμεῖς, ὡς 15 οὐδὲν ἕτερον τὸ "κατ᾽ εἰκόνα" δηλοῖ, πλὴν ὅτι καθ᾽ ὁμοίωσιν, καὶ ὁμοίως τὸ "καθ᾽ ὁμοίωσιν", τὸ καὶ "κατ᾽ εἰκόνα"· τὴν δέ γε πρὸς θεὸν ὁμοίωσιν ἐλάχομεν ἐν πρώτῃ κατασκευῇ, καί ἐσμεν εἰκόνες θεοῦ. δεκτικὴ γάρ, ὡς ἔφην, ἡ τοῦ ἀνθρώπου φύσις ἐστὶ καὶ ἀγαθότητος καὶ δικαιοσύνης καὶ ἁγιασμοῦ, καὶ τὴν ἐν τούτοις ἔφεσιν ἐγκατα- 20 βεβλημένην ἔχει παρὰ θεοῦ. καὶ τοῦτο ἔστιν ἐντεῦθεν ἰδεῖν. ἡ ἐκτροπὴ γέγονε τῇ ἀνθρώπου διανοίᾳ, οὐκ ἀπό γε τῶν φαύλων εἰς τὸ ἀγαθόν, ἀλλ᾽ ἐκ τοῦ ἀγαθοῦ πρὸς τὸ φαῦλον. πρῶτον οὖν ἐκεῖνο προϋποκεῖσθαι χρή, ὃ δὴ καὶ ἀφέντες ἐκτετράμμεθα. ὅτι γὰρ ἐνεσπάρη τῇ τοῦ ἀνθρώπου ψυχῇ ἐκ πρώτης κατασκευῆς παντὸς 25 ἀγαθοῦ ἔφεσίς τε καὶ προθυμία καὶ γνῶσις, σαφηνιεῖ λέγων ὁ ἀπόστολος Παῦλος ὅταν γὰρ ἔθνη τὰ μὴ νόμον ἔχοντα φύσει τὰ τοῦ νόμου ποιοῦσιν,[4] οὗτοι νόμον μὴ ἔχοντες ἑαυτοῖς εἰσι νόμος, οἵτινες ἐνδείκνυνται τὸ ἔργον τοῦ νόμου γραπτὸν ἐν ταῖς καρδίαις αὐτῶν, συμμαρτυρούσης 30 αὐτῶν τῆς συνειδήσεως.[d] εἰ δὲ καὶ τοῖς ἔθνεσι τοῖς ἔξω

---

3. [a] 1 John 3 : 2   [b] Gen. 1 : 26   [c] ibid. 27   [d] Rom. 2 : 14 f.

3. [1] οὐ om. Arm   [2] γὰρ] παρ᾽ C: om. Arm   [3] παμμακαρίᾳ? Arm
[4] ποιῇ GN

amongst the holy apostles, into the hallowing bestowed on us initially at the first creation.

3

Are 'in (God's) image' and 'in (God's) likeness' different or the same thing? They say that we received the 'image' immediately on creation but not the 'likeness', for it is reserved for us till the world to come. Which is why (it is asserted) it is written '*When Christ appears, we shall be like him*' and again it is said '*Let us make man in our image and likeness*'; and after man's creation it is said '*And God made man and made him in his own image*', making no mention here of the 'likeness', to demonstrate (it is said) that we have not received it but that it is reserved for us in that blessed life.[9]

Answer

If they assert 'in (God's) image' and 'in (God's) likeness' to be different things, they must explain the distinction. Our attitude is that 'image' means nothing other than 'likeness' and similarly 'likeness' nothing other than 'image'. We obtained our likeness to God at the first creation and are images of God. For man's nature is, as I said, capable of goodness, righteousness and hallowing and has an inbuilt desire for these things, given by God. This can be seen from the fact that man's understanding underwent a diversion not from bad to good but from good to bad. What therefore we abandoned when we turned aside must first have been in existence beforehand. The apostle Paul makes it plain that a desire for, a readiness for, and a knowledge of all that is good was sown in man's soul by virtue of the first creation, when he says '*For when the Gentiles, who do not have the law, naturally practise the law's requirements, they, not having law, are a law for themselves; they show the work of the law written on their hearts, their conscience bearing witness along with it.*' Now if the Gentiles outside

---

[9] An ancient problem is involved here. Irenaeus (*Adv. Haer.* 5, 6, 1; 5, 16, 2) apparently distinguished 'image' and 'likeness', the second being lost at the fall and restored by Christ; Clement (*Strom.* 2, 22), Origen (*De Prin.* 3, 6, 1; *Contra Cel.* 4, 30; *In ep. ad Rom.* (*PG* 14, 978); *In Jo.* 20, 22) and Chrysostom (*In cap. I Gen. hom. 9*, 3 (*PG* 53, 78)) distinguish also—cf. esp. the passages in Origen referring the 'likeness' to the consummation. Neither Philo, Athanasius nor the Antiochenes, Theodore and Theodoret, make a distinction. See Burghardt, op. cit. (n. 16 p. 139), chap. 1, *PGL* s.v. εἰκών III c.

νόμου φυσικῶς ἔνεστι τὸ εἰδέναι⁵ νόμον, ἤτοι τοῦ νομοθέτου τὸν
σκοπόν· δῆλον ἔσται παντί τῳ⁶ λοιπόν, ὅτι δικαία καὶ ἀγαθὴ
γέγονεν ἐν ἀρχαῖς ἡ ἀνθρώπου φύσις, καὶ εἰς τοῦτο παρήχθη παρὰ
θεοῦ, τὴν αὐτοῦ φοροῦσα μόρφωσιν καὶ τῆς ἀγαθότητος εἰκόνα.
καὶ γὰρ ἦν ἅγιος ὁ πρῶτος τῆς ἀνθρώπου ζωῆς χρόνος· παρεισ- 5
βαλούσης δὲ τῆς ἁμαρτίας, οἱ τῆς πρὸς θεὸν ὁμοιώσεως χαρακτῆρες
οὐκ ἔτι λαμπροὶ μεμενήκασιν ἐν ἡμῖν. ἐπειδὴ δὲ γέγονεν ἄνθρωπος
ὁ μονογενὴς τοῦ θεοῦ λόγος, ἁγία πάλιν ἡ ἀνθρώπου γέγονε
φύσις, ἀναμορφουμένη πρὸς αὐτὸν δι' ἁγιασμοῦ καὶ δικαιοσύνης.
οὕτω πού φησιν ὁ πάνσοφος Παῦλος ὅτι ἡμεῖς δὲ πάντες 10
ἀνακεκαλυμμένῳ προσώπῳ τὴν δόξαν κυρίου κατοπτρι-
ζόμενοι, τὴν αὐτὴν εἰκόνα μεταμορφούμεθα ἀπὸ δόξης
εἰς δόξαν, καθάπερ ἀπὸ κυρίου πνεύματος. ὁ δὲ κύριος
τὸ πνεῦμά ἐστιν.ᵉ οὐκοῦν ἀνανέωσις καὶ οἷον ἀναπλασμὸς τῇ
ἀνθρώπου φύσει γέγονεν ἐν Χριστῷ, καταρρυθμιζομένης ἡμῶν τῆς 15
σαρκὸς εἰς ἁγίαν ζωὴν ἐν πνεύματι.

Εἰ δὲ ἔφη που τὸ ἱερὸν γράμμα, ὅτι πεποίηκεν ὁ θεὸς τὸν ἄνθρωπον κατ' εἰκόνα ἑαυτοῦ,ᶠ σεσίγηκε δὲ τό καθ' ὁμοίωσιν, ἐννοῆσαι
χρὴ ὅτι ἠρκέσθη τῷ κατ' εἰκόνα εἰπεῖν, ὡς οὐδὲν ἕτερον δηλοῦντος
τοῦ καθ' ὁμοίωσιν. περιττὸν γὰρ τὸ λέγειν ὅτι τοῦτο ἡμῖν τετήρηται 20
εἰς αἰῶνα τὸν μέλλοντα. θεοῦ γὰρ εἰπόντος ὅτι ποιήσωμεν
ἄνθρωπον κατ' εἰκόνα ἡμετέραν καὶ καθ' ὁμοίωσιν,ᵍ τίς
ὁ φάναι τολμῶν ὅτι γέγονε μὲν κατ' εἰκόνα, οὐ μὴν ἔτι⁷ καθ'
ὁμοίωσιν; ὅμοιοι δὲ ἐσόμεθα τῷ Χριστῷ κατά γε τὴν ἀφθαρσίαν,
καὶ τὸ ἐπέκεινα γενέσθαι θανάτου, καὶ μὴν καὶ⁸ κατὰ τὴν δόξαν 25
ἣν ἂν ἡμῖν αὐτὸς χαρίσαιτο. γράφει γὰρ πάλιν ὁ ἀπόστολος Παῦλός
ποτε μὲν ὅτι ἀπεθάνετε γάρ, καὶ ἡ ζωὴ ὑμῶν κέκρυπται
σὺν τῷ Χριστῷ ἐν τῷ θεῷ· ὅταν ὁ Χριστὸς φανερωθῇ ἡ
ζωὴ ὑμῶν, τότε καὶ ὑμεῖς σὺν αὐτῷ⁹ φανερωθήσεσθε ἐν
δόξῃ,ʰ ποτὲ δὲ πάλιν ὃς μετασχηματίσει τὸ σῶμα τῆς 30
ταπεινώσεως ἡμῶν, ὥστε γενέσθαι σύμμορφον τῷ
σώματι τῆς¹⁰ δόξης αὐτοῦ.ⁱ ἐπεὶ καὶ νῦν οὔκ ἐσμεν ἔξω τοῦ
εἶναι καθ' ὁμοίωσιν αὐτοῦ, εἴπερ ἐστὶν ἀληθὲς ὡς ἐν ἡμῖν μορφοῦται

ᵉ 2 Cor. 3: 18, 17   ᶠ cf. Gen. 1 : 27   ᵍ ibid. 26   ʰ Col. 3 : 3 f.
ⁱ Phil. 3: 21

---

⁵ εἰδέναι] δέναι (sic) C   ⁶ τὸ C   ⁷ ἔτι N: ἐστι CG: om. Arm
⁸ καὶ om. G   ⁹ σὺν αὐτῷ om. G   ¹⁰ τῷ σώματι τῆς om. G

law have it in them by nature to know law or the lawgiver's
intentions, everyone must then see that man's nature was made
righteous and good to begin with and that it was brought into
this condition by God, bearing, as it does, his formation and the
image of his goodness. The first epoch of man's life was holy,
but sin intervened and the marks of likeness to God no longer
stay bright within us. When the only-begotten Word of God
became man, man's nature was created again, re-formed by
relation to him through hallowing and righteousness. Thus all-
wise Paul says at one point that *'We all, with unveiled face, gazing
on the Lord's glory are transformed into the same image from glory to
glory, as by the Lord Spirit, and the Lord is the Spirit.'* Man's nature
then underwent a renewal, a re-moulding as it were, in Christ,
with our flesh[10] being realigned with holy life in the Spirit.

If holy writ asserted at some point that God made man in his
own image and did not mention 'likeness' we should appreciate
that it was sufficient to say 'image' because it means the same
thing as 'likeness'. It is out of the question to say that the latter
is reserved for us in the world to come. If God said *'Let us make
man in our image and likeness'* who will rashly assert that man has
been made in God's image but not yet in his likeness? We shall
resemble Christ in his freedom from corruption, his transcendence
of death and moreover in the glory which he will bestow upon
us. The apostle Paul writes again at one point *'For you died and
your life is hidden with Christ in God; when Christ your life appears,
you too will appear with him in glory.'* And again at one point: *'Who
will transform the body of our lowly state so that it will be made in the
form of his body of glory.'* Why even now we are within the compass
of being in his likeness, if it is true that he is being formed in us

---

[10] Though the image of God in man is to be found in man's soul, for Cyril,
it is in the soul as embodied and living the life of faith with the help of the
Spirit, cf. below in text.

διὰ τοῦ ἁγίου πνεύματος. γράφει γὰρ πάλιν Γαλάταις ὁ Παῦλος
τεκνία οὓς πάλιν ὠδίνω, ἄχρις οὗ μορφωθῇ Χριστὸς ἐν
ὑμῖν.[j11] ὅταν γὰρ ἑαυτοὺς πιστοὺς καὶ ἁγίους τηρήσωμεν, τότε
Χριστὸς[12] ἐν ἡμῖν ὁρᾶται μορφούμενος, καὶ ταῖς ἡμετέραις διανοίαις τοὺς ἑαυτοῦ χαρακτῆρας νοητῶς ἐναστράπτων.   5

Δ′

Ὅτι οὔκ ἐσμὲν, φησίν, εἰκὼν[1] θεοῦ, ἀλλ᾽ εἰκὼν εἰκόνος. ὁ μὲν γὰρ
υἱὸς καὶ λόγος τοῦ θεοῦ καὶ πατρὸς εἰκὼν αὐτοῦ ἐστιν· ὁ δὲ ἄνθρωπος
οὐ τοῦ ἀρχετύπου εἰκών, ἀλλὰ τῆς εἰκόνος, τουτέστι τοῦ υἱοῦ, ὡς
εἶναι ἡμᾶς εἰκόνα[2] εἰκόνος. οὐ γὰρ εἴρηται, φησίν, ὅτι εἰκόνα ἑαυτοῦ
ἐποίησεν ὁ θεὸς τὸν ἄνθρωπον, ἀλλὰ κατ᾽ εἰκόνα,[3] ἵνα ᾖ ὁ ἄνθρωπος 10
κατ᾽ εἰκόνα τοῦ θεοῦ καὶ πατρός, τουτέστιν εἰκὼν τοῦ υἱοῦ, ὅπερ ἐστὶν
εἰκὼν εἰκόνος.

Ἐπίλυσις

Εἰδοὺς μὲν ἐπέκεινα παντὸς καὶ φαντασίας σωματικῆς ἡ θεία τέ
ἐστι καὶ ὁμοούσιος τριάς· πιστεύειν δὲ χρὴ ὅτι ὁ πατὴρ ἐν τῷ   15
υἱῷ ἐστι καὶ ὁ υἱὸς ἐν τῷ πατρί, καὶ ὁ τὸν υἱὸν ἑωρακὼς[4] ἑώρακε
τὸν πατέρα.[a] ὁρᾶται[5] δὲ καὶ ὁ υἱὸς ἐν τῷ ὁμοουσίῳ πνεύματι.
γέγραπται γὰρ ὅτι ὁ δὲ κύριος τὸ πνεῦμά ἐστιν.[b] ἔνθα δὲ
ὅλως οὐσίας ταυτότης, ἐκεῖ που πάντως εἴη ἂν[6] τὸ παραλλάττον
οὐδέν. ἀλλ᾽ ὅπερ ἂν εἶναι νοῇς[7] τὸν πατέρα, τοῦτό ἐστι[8] καὶ ὁ υἱός, 20
δίχα μόνου τοῦ εἶναι πατήρ· καὶ ὅπερ ἂν ὑπολάβῃς[9] εἶναι τὸν υἱόν,
τοῦτό ἐστι καὶ τὸ πνεῦμα, δίχα μόνου[10] τοῦ εἶναι[11] υἱός. ὑφέστηκε
μὲν[12] γὰρ τῶν ὠνομασμένων[13] ἕκαστον ἰδιοσυστάτως, καὶ ἔστιν
ἀληθῶς ὅπερ εἶναι λέγεται· ἡ[14] δὲ εἰς πᾶν ὁτιοῦν ὁμοιότης τῆς
ἁγίας τριάδος ἀπαραλλάκτως ἔχει. οὐκοῦν κἂν εἰ γέγονε κατ᾽ 25
εἰκόνα τοῦ υἱοῦ ὁ ἄνθρωπος, καὶ οὕτως[15] ἐστὶ κατ᾽ εἰκόνα[16] θεοῦ.
ὅλης γὰρ αὐτῷ τῆς ὁμοουσίου τριάδος οἱ χαρακτῆρες ἐλλάμπουσιν,[17]

---

[j] Gal. 4: 19   4. [a] cf. John 14: 9   [b] 2 Cor. 3: 17

Witnesses: l. 6–p. 198, l. 13 C G O N Arm

11 ἡμῖν G   12 Χριστὸς om. C (ὁ Χριστὸς N)   4. 1 εἰκόνα O
2 εἰκὼν O   3 ἀλλὰ κατ᾽ εἰκόνα after πατρὸς G   4 ἑωρακὼς before τὸν
υἱὸν G   5 ἑωρᾶται O   6 ἂν om. O   7 νοεῖς O   8 τουτέστι G
9 ὑπολάβοις O   10 μόνου om. CGN   11 ὁ add. G   12 μὲν om. GN
13 ὀνομασμένων O   14 εἰ CO   15 οὗτος O   16 τοῦ add. C
17 ἐκλάμπουσιν O

through the Holy Spirit! For Paul writes again to the Galatians, '*My children with whom I am again in travail until Christ be formed in you*'. When we keep ourselves loyal and holy Christ is seen to be being formed in us, as he irradiates our minds spiritually with his own special marks.

4

It is being said that we are not God's image but an image of an image.[11] For God the Father's Son and Word is his image, but man is not an image of the archetype but of the image (i.e. the Son) and so we are an image of an image. For (it is being said) it is not stated that God made man his own image but *in* his image, so that man should be in God the Father's image (i.e. should be an image of the Son) which means he is an image of an image.

Answer

The divine and consubstantial Trinity is beyond all form and corporeal presentation, but we are to believe that the Father is in the Son and the Son in the Father and one who has seen the Son has seen the Father. Now the Son is seen in the consubstantial Spirit, for it is written that '*The Lord is the Spirit.*' Where there is total identity of substance there can and must be no variation. Whatever you conceive the Father to be, the Son is too, apart only from being Father; and whatever you take the Son to be, the Spirit is too apart only from being Son. Each of those named has his own personal being and truly is what he is said to be, but the utter similarity of the holy Trinity is invariable. Therefore if man was made in the Son's image he is by that token in God's image. For the marks of the whole consubstantial Trinity shine

---

11 Cf. Clement *Protr*. 10: 'For the image of God is his Word . . . and the image of the Word is the true man, the mind which is in man, who is therefore said to have been made " in the image and likeness of God" assimilated to the Divine Word in the affections of the soul, and therefore rational' (trans. W. Wilson, *Ante-Nicene Christian Library*), cf. *Strom*. 5, 14. Clement follows Philo here, cf. *De Op. Mundi* 69–71 (23), *Quis rerum divinarum heres* 230 f. (48). So also Origen *De or*. 22, 4.

ἅτε δὴ καὶ μιᾶς οὔσης τῆς κατὰ φύσιν θεότητος τῆς ἐν πατρὶ καὶ
υἱῷ καὶ ἁγίῳ πνεύματι. γράφει γοῦν[18] ὁ θεσπέσιος Μωυσῆς καὶ
εἶπεν ὁ θεός ποιήσωμεν ἄνθρωπον κατ' εἰκόνα ἡμετέραν
καὶ καθ' ὁμοίωσιν.[c] τὸ δέ ἡμετέραν, οὐχ ἑνὸς δήλωσιν ἔχει
προσώπου, διά τοι τὸ ἐν τρισὶν ὑποστάσεσιν εἶναι τὸ τῆς θείας 5
καὶ ἀρρήτου φύσεως πλήρωμα. περιττὸν οὖν ἄρα τὸ περιεργάζεσθαι
καὶ ἰσχνοεπεῖν[19] καὶ λέγειν ὅτι οὐ τοῦ θεοῦ μᾶλλόν ἐσμεν εἰκόνες,
οὐδὲ[20] τοῦ ἀρχετύπου ἀλλὰ τῆς τοῦ θεοῦ εἰκόνος· ἀρκεῖ δὲ τὸ
πιστεύειν μετὰ ἁπλότητος ὅτι κατὰ θείαν εἰκόνα γεγόναμεν, τὴν
πρὸς θεὸν λαβόντες μόρφωσιν φυσικῶς. εἰ δὲ χρή τι καὶ οὐκ 10
ἀπιθάνως εἰπεῖν, ἀναγκαῖον[21] ἦν ἡμᾶς μέλλοντας υἱοὺς ὀνομάζεσθαι
θεοῦ κατ' εἰκόνα τοῦ υἱοῦ γενέσθαι μᾶλλον, ἵν'[22] ἡμῖν ἐμπρέπῃ[23]
καὶ ὁ τῆς υἱότητος χαρακτήρ.

Ε'

Ὅτι ἐν τῇ μελλούσῃ καταστάσει τὸ[1] λογιστικὸν ἔχουσα ψυχή, καὶ
διὰ τοῦτο γνώσεως οὐκ ἀμοιροῦσα, προκόπτει· οἱ δ' ἕτεροι εἰ προκοπὴν 15
ἕξει, φασίν, ἡ ψυχή, πάντως ὅτι καὶ μείωσιν καὶ πάθος καὶ φθοράν·
ἐκ τούτου καὶ θάνατον καὶ ἀναβίωσιν αὖθις.

Ἐπίλυσις

Οἱ ταῦτα διενθυμούμενοι ἀγνοεῖν ἐοίκασι τὴν δοθησομένην
χάριν τῇ τοῦ ἀνθρώπου φύσει μετὰ τὴν ἐκ νεκρῶν ἀναβίωσιν. εἰ 20
γὰρ δεῖ τὸ φθαρτὸν τοῦτο ἐνδύσασθαι τὴν ἀφθαρσίαν,[a]
καὶ ἀποδύσασθαι τὴν φθορὰν, συναποβαλοῦμεν δηλονότι τῇ φθορᾷ
καὶ τὰ ἐξ αὐτῆς πάθη· ταῦτα δέ ἐστιν ἐπιθυμία πᾶσα σαρκική· καὶ
μεταστησόμεθα λοιπὸν εἰς ἁγίαν καὶ πνευματικὴν ζωήν, νέμοντος
ἡμῖν τὸ ἀραρὸς ἐν τούτοις τοῦ πάντων ἡμῶν σωτῆρος Χριστοῦ. εἰ 25

---

[c] Gen. 1: 26   5. [a] 1 Cor. 15: 53

Witnesses: l. 14–p. 200, l. 12 C G N Arm.

[18] οὖν O   [19] ἰσχνῷ εἰπεῖν O   [20] οὐδὲ om. Arm   [21] ἀναγκαίως G
[22] ἵν'] οὖν O   [23] ἐμπρεπεῖ O   5. [1] λογιστὸν ἤτοι τὸ add. G

[12] Apart from the special case noted in *Answers to Tiberius* 15, 'sons of God'
is, for Cyril, a title and status belonging to Christians alone through their
baptism (cf. esp. *In Ps.* 44: 12 f. (*PG* 69, 1044AB), *Glaph. in Ex.* (*PG* 69, 441A)).
He does not call Adam a 'son of God'. Sonship is the new feature of the image
effected by the Incarnation and gift of the Spirit (see *In Jo.* 1, 9 (Pusey 1,

out in him, inasmuch as there is a single natural Godhead in Father, Son and Holy Ghost. Inspired Moses writes indeed, '*And God said "Let us make man in our image and likeness."* ' The word '*our*', though, does not mean one person, because the fullness of the divine and ineffable nature exists in three hypostases. It is surely useless, therefore, to make the too subtle qualification that we are not images of God or of the archetype, so much as images of the image of God. It is enough to believe with simplicity that we are made in the divine image by receiving a natural formation in relation to God. One might also make the convincing point, that we who were destined to be called sons of God had to be created in the Son's image so that the mark of sonship should be evident in us.[12]

5

That in the future state a soul possessing rationality, and therefore having its share of knowledge, advances; but others assert that if the soul is to have advancement it must also have diminution, passion and corruption, and consequently death and a returning to life again.[13]

Answer

People who draw this conclusion appear ignorant of the grace to be granted to man's nature after its return to life from the dead. For if '*this corruption must put on incorruption*' and put off corruption, we shall obviously jettison corruption along with its consequent passions, which are bodily desire in its entirety; thereafter we shall transfer to a holy and spiritual life, when Christ, the Saviour of us all, has allotted us what befits us in

133 f. and 153) where Cyril carefully distinguishes between Christ's natural, and the Christians' adoptive, sonship). Though the image in man means likeness to the common divine being, there is a sense in which man, as potentially a son of God, has a special relationship with the Son at his creation, but this is of no theological importance for Cyril—a 'convincing point', no more. Cf. also, *Contra Jul.* I (*PG* 76, 537A–540D), *Dial. on the Trin.* 3 (*PG* 75 Aubert 473 ff.).

13 A reference to Origenistic notions of spiritual progress found in Origen himself (*De Princ.* 3, 6, 6), Gregory Nyss. (*De Vita Moysis* paras. 219 ff, cf. *De op. hom.* 21, 2), and Evagrius apparently. For Origen a final stability is attained; for Gregory the progress is infinite toward an infinite God; for Evagrius the cycle of birth and spiritual progress toward ultimate unity for all intellects apparently repeats itself (there is not a single line in Evagrius' surviving writings which conveys this idea clearly, but it was hinted at, esp. in his *Kephalaia Gnostica*, so it would seem, and was certainly *believed* to be his teaching).

I

γὰρ νῦν τὸν ἀρραβῶνα τοῦ πνεύματος ἔχοντες ἁγίως πολιτευόμεθα,
τίνες ἐσόμεθα λαβόντες τὸ πλῆρες; ὅπου δὲ πλήρωσις πνεύματος,
ἐκεῖ που πάντως καὶ ἀσφάλεια νοῦ καὶ καρδίας ἑδραιότης, τῆς
ὁρώσης εἰς τὸ ἀγαθὸν καὶ εἰς ἀκραιφνῆ θεοπτίαν. οὐκοῦν ἐσόμεθα
μὲν ἑαυτῶν ἀμείνους,[2] ἀποδυσάμενοι τὴν φθοράν, καὶ πνευματικὸν 5
ἔχοντες τὸ[3] σῶμα, τουτέστιν εἰς μόνα βλέποντες[4] τὰ τοῦ πνεύματος·
κλόνος δὲ ὁ καταβιβάζων ἡμᾶς εἰς φαυλότητα οὐδεὶς ἔσται τὸ
τηνικάδε, συνέχοντος ἡμᾶς εἰς τὸ ἑαυτοῦ θέλημα τοῦ δημιουργοῦ
διὰ τοῦ ἁγίου πνεύματος, καθάπερ ἀμέλει καὶ τοὺς ἁγίους ἀγγέλους.
τοιοῦτόν τι Χριστὸς ἀπεφήνατο εἰπὼν ἐν τῇ ἀναστάσει οὔτε 10
γαμοῦσιν οὔτε γαμίζονται, ἀλλ᾽ ὡς ἄγγελοι θεοῦ εἰσιν
ἐν τῷ οὐρανῷ.[b]

ϛ′

Διὰ τί ἐν τῷ Ἀδὰμ ἀποθνήσκοντες πατρικὴν εὐθύνομεν[1] δίκην, καὶ
τὴν ἐκείνου παράβασιν ἕκαστος χρεωστεῖ· ἐν δὲ τῷ Χριστῷ ζωοποιηθεὶς
ὁ ἐμὸς πατὴρ καὶ διὰ τοῦ ἁγίου πνεύματος καθαρθεὶς τῆς τε προ- 15
πατορικῆς ὀφλήσεως καὶ τῆς ἰδίας πλημμελείας, οὐ μετέδωκέ μοι τῆς
καθαρότητος τῷ γεννηθέντι, οὔτε ὤνησέ με τῆς εἰς αὐτὸν δικαιοσύνης
ἡ χάρις, καίτοι ὑπερισχύουσα κατὰ τῆς ἁμαρτίας;

Ἐπίλυσις

Ἐξετάσαι χρὴ πῶς εἰς ἡμᾶς ὁ προπάτωρ Ἀδὰμ παρέπεμψε τὴν 20
ἐπενεχθεῖσαν αὐτῷ διὰ τὴν παράβασιν δίκην. ἤκουσεν ὅτι γῆ εἶ
καὶ εἰς γῆν ἀπελεύσῃ,[a] καὶ φθαρτὸς ἐξ ἀφθάρτου γέγονε, καὶ
ὑπηνέχθη[2] τοῖς τοῦ θανάτου δεσμοῖς. ἐπειδὴ δὲ εἰς τοῦτο πεσὼν
ἐπαιδοποίησεν, οἱ ἐξ αὐτοῦ γεγονότες ὡς[3] ἀπὸ φθαρτοῦ φθαρτοὶ

---

[b] Matt. 22: 30　　　　6. [a] Gen. 3: 19

Witnesses: l. 13–p. 204, l. 6 C G O N Arm

---

[2] ἀμείνους ἑαυτῶν G　　　　[3] τὸ om. G　　　　[4] βλέποντα CG: βλέπον
corr. Pusey　　6. [1] εὐθύνωμεν O: ἐκτίνομεν C marg. GN, perh. Arm
[2] καὶ ὑπηνέχθη] ὑπενεχθεὶς G　　　[3] ὡς om. O

---

[14] Cf. Pelagius In ep. ad Rom. (PLS i p. 1137) with Augustine's reply De pecc.
mer. et rem. III (VIII) 16. There is a hint of issues debated in the 20-year-
old Pelagian controversy, predominantly in the Latin West and Palestine
over whether Adam transmitted any defect to his descendants. The questioners are not, of course, Pelagians, for Pelagians held that Adam's trans-

those conditions. If we lead holy lives now that we have the pledge of the Spirit, what shall we be when we receive its fullness? Where there is a filling with the Spirit, there must be a security of mind and a stability of heart which looks towards goodness and the pure vision of God. So when we put off corruption and have a spiritual body (meaning that we look solely at what belongs to the Spirit) we shall excel ourselves. No turmoil driving us down into wickedness will exist then when the Creator will maintain us in his will through the Holy Spirit as indeed he does the holy angels. Christ revealed something of this kind when he said *'In the resurrection they neither marry nor are given in marriage but are as God's angels in heaven.'*

6

Why is it that by dying in Adam we satisfy an ancestor's penalty and each has a debt to pay for Adam's transgression, whereas my father, made alive in Christ and cleansed through the Holy Spirit both of the first forefather's penalty and his own offence, has given me, his offspring, no share in the cleansing, nor did the grace of righteousness in his case, though it prevailed over sin, do me any good?[14]

Answer

We must inquire how Adam, the first forefather, transmitted to us the penalty imposed upon him for his transgression. He had heard *'Earth thou art and to the earth shalt thou return'*, and from being incorruptible he became corruptible[15] and was made subject to the bonds of death. But since he produced children after falling into this state we, his descendants, are corruptible, coming from a corruptible source. Thus it is that we are heirs

gression injured only himself (cf. the first two charges against Celestius at the council in Carthage of 412 of teaching: (1) that Adam was created mortal and would have died even if he had not sinned; (2) that his sin injured himself only, and not the human race—Marius Mercator *Commonitorium*, *ACO* 1, 5 p. 6).

[15] ἀφθαρσία/incorruptibility, φθορά/corruption, and their cognates are important in Cyril's thought, though less so than in Athanasius' (see *De Incarnatione* passim). 'Incorruptibility' for Cyril means 'stable existence', and involves moral as well as physical qualities. It is a feature of the image of God in man (*In Jo.* 9, 1 (Pusey 2, 484)), and being possessed by Adam through divine grace, not natural endowment (cf. *In Jo.* 1, 9 (Pusey 1, 138) οὐκ ἔχων ἐξ οἰκίας φύσεως τό τε ἄφθαρτον καὶ ἀνώλεθρον· μόνῳ γὰρ ταῦτα πρόσεστιν οὐσιωδῶς τῷ θεῷ κ.τ.λ.), was hence capable of forfeit. The soul, of course, for Cyril, is naturally immortal; it is the whole man, a composite of soul and (naturally corruptible) body, which Christ's Incarnation renders incorruptible.

γεγόναμεν. οὕτω καί⁴ ἐσμεν τῆς ἐν Ἀδὰμ κατάρας κληρονόμοι. οὐ
γὰρ πάντως ὡς σὺν ἐκείνῳ παρακούσαντες τῆς θείας ἐντολῆς ἧς⁵
ἐδέξατο τετιμωρήμεθα, ἀλλ' ὅτι, ὡς ἔφην, θνητὸς γεγονώς, εἰς τὸ
ἐξ αὐτοῦ⁶ σπέρμα παρέπεμψε τὴν ἀράν· θνητοὶ γὰρ γεγόναμεν ἐκ
θνητοῦ·⁷ ὁ δέ γε κύριος ἡμῶν Ἰησοῦς⁸ Χριστὸς χρηματίσας   5
δεύτερος Ἀδάμ, καὶ ἀρχὴ τοῦ γένους ἡμῶν δευτέρα μετὰ τὴν
πρώτην, ἀνεμόρφωσεν ἡμᾶς εἰς ἀφθαρσίαν, προσβαλὼν τῷ θανάτῳ,
τῇ ἰδίᾳ σαρκὶ⁹ καταργήσας αὐτόν, καὶ λέλυται τῆς ἀρχαίας ἀρᾶς
ἡ δύναμις ἐν αὐτῷ. διὰ τοῦτό φησιν ὁ πάνσοφος Παῦλος ὅτι
ὥσπερ δι' ἀνθρώπου ὁ θάνατος, οὕτω καὶ δι' ἀνθρώπου   10
ἀνάστασις νεκρῶν,ᵇ¹⁰ καὶ πάλιν ὥσπερ¹¹ ἐν τῷ Ἀδὰμ
πάντες ἀποθνήσκουσιν, οὕτω καὶ ἐν τῷ Χριστῷ πάντες
ζωοποιηθήσονται.ᶜ οὐκοῦν ἡ καθόλου καὶ γενικωτάτη δίκη
διὰ τῆς ἐν Ἀδὰμ παραβάσεως ἡ φθορὰ καὶ ὁ θάνατός ἐστιν· ὁμοίως
ἡ κατὰ πάντων καὶ γενικωτάτη λύτρωσις ἐν¹² Χριστῷ τετέλεσται.   15
ἀπεδύσατο γὰρ ἡ ἀνθρώπου φύσις ἐν αὐτῷ τὸν ἐπιρριφέντα αὐτῇ
θάνατον διὰ τοῦ γενέσθαι φθαρτὸν τὸν πρῶτον ἄνθρωπον. ὁ δὲ
ἑκάστου ἡμῶν πατήρ, κἂν ἁγιασθῇ¹³ διὰ τοῦ ἁγίου πνεύματος καὶ
κομίσηται τῶν πλημμελημάτων τὴν ἄφεσιν, οὐ παραπέμψει¹⁴ καὶ
εἰς ἡμᾶς τὸ δῶρον. εἷς γάρ ἐστιν ὁ πάντας ἁγιάζων καὶ δικαιῶν   20
καὶ ἀνακομίζων εἰς ἀφθαρσίαν ὁ κύριος ἡμῶν Ἰησοῦς¹⁵ Χριστός,
καὶ εἰς πάντας ἐν ἴσῳ¹⁶ δι' αὐτοῦ καὶ παρ' αὐτοῦ τὸ δῶρον ἔρχεται.
ἕτερον δέ ἐστιν ἁμαρτίας ἄφεσις, καὶ ἕτερον θανάτου λύσις. καὶ
ἕκαστος μὲν τῶν ἰδίων πλημμελημάτων κερδαίνει τὴν ἄφεσιν ἐν
Χριστῷ διὰ τοῦ ἁγίου πνεύματος· κοινῇ δὲ ἅπαντες ἀπαλλαττόμεθα   25
τῆς ἐν ἀρχαῖς ἐπενεχθείσης ἡμῖν δίκης, τῆς τοῦ θανάτου φημὶ
δραμούσης εἰς ἅπαντας,¹⁷ καθ' ὁμοιότητα τοῦ πρώτου πεσόντος εἰς
θάνατον. διὰ τοῦτο γὰρ καὶ ὁ πάνσοφος¹⁸ Παῦλός φησιν ὅτι

ᵇ 1 Cor. 15: 21   ᶜ ibid. 22

⁴ οὕτω καί] οὕτως GO   ⁵ ἐκεῖνος add. O   ⁶ ἐξ αὐτοῦ] ἑαυτοῦ O
⁷ θεοῦ O   ⁸ ὁ add. C   ⁹ καὶ add. O   ¹⁰ ζωῆς O Arm
¹¹ γὰρ add. G   ¹² τῷ add. O   ¹³ ἡγιάσθη O   ¹⁴ καὶ οὐ
παραπέμψει O   ¹⁵ ὁ add. C   ¹⁶ ἴδω (sic) C   ¹⁷ ἅπαντα O
¹⁸ πάνσοφος om. O

---

¹⁶ i.e. having inherited his corruptible nature not as a punishment for, but
as a natural consequence of, his sin.

of Adam's curse.[16] That cannot mean at all that we are punished for having disobeyed along with him the divine injunction which he received; it means that he became mortal, as I said, and transmitted the curse to his seed after him (for we are born mortal from a mortal source) whereas our Lord Jesus Christ who bears the title 'second Adam' and is a second beginning of our race after the first, re-formed us into incorruptibility by assaulting death, nullifying it in his own flesh and in him the force of the primal curse has been broken. This is why all-wise Paul says that as *'through man came death, so also through man came the resurrection of the dead'*; and again, *'As in Adam all die, so in Christ will all be made alive.'* So corruption and death are the universal and general penalty involved in Adam's transgression; likewise the general ransom with respect to all men has been accomplished finally in Christ. For man's nature in him put off that death which had been attached to it through the first man's being made mortal. But the father of each of us, though he is hallowed through the Holy Spirit and obtains the forgiveness of his sins, does not hand on the gift to us.[17] For there is one who hallows all, justifies and restores them to incorruption, Jesus Christ our Lord, and through him and from him the gift comes to all alike. Forgiveness of sin and dissolution of death are different things. Each enjoys forgiveness of his own offences in Christ through the holy Spirit. All of us in common are released from the primal penalty imposed upon us, the penalty of death I mean, which reaches all in its course, in resemblance to the first who fell into death.[18] That is why all-wise Paul says that

[17] Because it is a divine gift.

[18] Christ has dissolved death for all men, cf. *In Jo.* 6, 1 (Pusey 2, 220): 'For all will rise again from the dead because of its being granted to the whole race (φύσει) in virtue of the grace of resurrection; and in the one Christ, who was to begin with the first to dissolve death's power and rise to permanent life, the universal category of manhood is being fashioned anew into incorruptibility, in the way that in Adam it was first condemned to death and corruption.' Christ is the beginning of a new race of which he is the fresh root, cf. *In Ep. ad Rom.* (Pusey 3, 182); he has defeated Satan (ibid.) and opened up Hades. All will rise again incorruptible but the righteous to glory, cf. *In Ep. I ad Cor.* (Pusey 3, 309 and 316 f.). Forgiveness of sin, though, is strictly personal and individual. Cyril is thus, like Athanasius, an exponent of a 'physical' theory of salvation, in that death is dissolved because Christ's work affects the whole human race. As to the means whereby this happens, Cyril does not go beyond variations upon the themes mentioned above. To interpret him as prepossessed by the notion of the Platonic universal is as wide of the mark as it is with Gregory Nyss.: see R. Hübner, *Die Einheit des Leibes Christi bei Gregor von Nyssa* (Leiden, 1974)—for one thing, the Platonic universal was not *concrete* (that was *Hegel*'s notion).

ἐβασίλευσεν ὁ θάνατος ἀπὸ Ἀδὰμ καὶ μέχρι Μωυσέος
καὶ ἐπὶ τοὺς μὴ ἁμαρτήσαντας ἐπὶ τῷ ὁμοιώματι τῆς
παραβάσεως Ἀδάμ.ᵈ μέχρι γὰρ¹⁹ νόμου κεκράτηκεν²⁰ ἡ τοῦ
θανάτου δίκη.²¹ Χριστοῦ δὲ λοιπὸν²² ἀναλάμψαντος, εἰσβέβηκεν ἡ
δικαιοσύνη, δικαιοῦσα χάριτι, καὶ ἀποσοβοῦσα τῶν ἡμετέρων 5
σωμάτων τὴν φθοράν.

Ζ'ι

Εἰ γέγονεν ἡ ἀνάστασις ἤδη,² ἣν εἶδεν Ἰεζεκιὴλ ὁ προφήτης· ἡνίκα
προσῆλθεν ὀστοῦν πρὸς ὀστοῦν, καὶ ἁρμονία πρὸς ἁρμονίαν, καὶ σὰρξ
καὶ δέρμα καὶ τρίχες καὶ πνεῦμα, καὶ ὤφθη ἀνάστασις πληθύος³
πολλῆςᵃ ἢ⁴ εἰκόνα τῆς μελλούσης καθολικῆς ἀναστάσεως ἔσεσθαι⁵ 10
ἔδειξεν ἡμῖν ἡ θεία γραφὴ ἐν ὀπτασίᾳ προφητικῇ.

Ἐπίλυσις

Τὰ μεγάλα τῶν πραγμάτων καὶ διὰ τὴν⁶ τοῦ περὶ αὐτὰ θαύματος
ὑπερβολὴν ἐν ὑποψίαις ὄντα τοῦ καὶ ἀπιστηθῆναι πρός τινων, οὐ
διὰ μόνης ἀπαγγελίας⁷ ἐδιδάσκοντο κατὰ καιροὺς οἱ προφῆται, τοῦ 15
ἁγίου πνεύματος ἐναστράπτοντος αὐτοῖς τὴν ἑκάστου γνῶσιν·
ἀλλὰ γὰρ καὶ αὐτοῖς ἑώρων⁸ πράγμασιν, ἵνα πρὸ τῶν ἄλλων αὐτοὶ
πιστεύσαντες, διαθεῖεν οὕτως καὶ τοὺς ἑτέρους.⁹ ἐπαγγειλάμενος
τοίνυν ὁ τῶν ὅλων θεὸς καὶ τοὺς ἤδη τεθνεῶτας¹⁰ ἐπὶ τῆς Βαβυ-
λωνίων ἀνακομίζειν εἰς Ἰερουσαλήμ,ᵇ οὐχὶ¹¹ δήπου πάντως τὴν 20
ἐπὶ γῆς, ἀλλὰ τὴν ἄνω καὶ¹² ἐν τοῖς οὐρανοῖς νοουμένηνᶜ ἔδειξεν
ἐναργῶς τῷ προφήτῃ¹³ τὴν ἀνάστασιν, καὶ τίνα τρόπον ἔσται κατὰ
καιρούς· ἣν δὴ¹⁴ καὶ ὁ θεσπέσιος Δαυὶδ προανεφώνει λέγων περὶ
ἡμῶν, ἤτοι περὶ ἀνθρώπου παντός ἀποστρέψαντός¹⁵ σου τὸ
πρόσωπον ταραχθήσονται, καὶ εἰς τὸν χοῦν αὐτῶν¹⁶ 25

ᵈ Rom. 5: 14   7. ᵃ cf. Ezek. 37: 7 ff.   ᵇ cf. ibid. 12   ᶜ cf.
Gal. 4: 26

Witnesses: l. 7–p. 206, l. 15 G O N Arm

¹⁹ τοῦ add. Arm   ²⁰ κατεκράτησεν G   ²¹ δίκη] βασιλεία O
²² λοιπὸν] πάλιν O   7. ¹ om. G   ² εἶδει O   ³ πλήθους O   ⁴ ἡ O
⁵ ἔσεσθαι after ἡμῖν G   ⁶ τί O   ⁷ ἐπαγγελίας O   ⁸ ἑώρουν
(sic) O   ⁹ τοῖς ἑτέροις ON Arm, perh. rightly   ¹⁰ τεθνηκότας O
¹¹ δὲ add. GN   ¹² καὶ τὴν ἄνω O   ¹³ τῷ προφήτῃ] τοῦ προφήτου τοῖς
ὀφθαλμοῖς G   ¹⁴ ἤδη O   ¹⁵ δὲ add. O   ¹⁶ αὐτὸν GO

'Death ruled from Adam to Moses over those who had sinned in the likeness of Adam's transgression.' For whilst there was law, the penalty of death held sway. But after Christ's dawn, righteousness entered in, justifying by grace and warding off our bodies' corruption.

7

Has the resurrection, which Ezekiel the prophet saw, already occurred, when bone met bone, joint met joint, and flesh, skin, hair and breath met and the resurrection of a great multitude was seen, or has divine scripture revealed to us in prophetic vision an image of the coming general resurrection?[19]

Answer

Mighty events disbelieved and disdained by some because of the miraculous element surrounding them were things prophets learned in bygone days, as the Holy Spirit gave each his flashes of knowledge, not just by means of a message. No, they used in actual fact to see them, in order that having themselves been the first to believe they might dispose others to do the same. The God of all, then, having promised[20] that he would restore those who had died in Babylon to Jerusalem (not by any manner of means the earthly Jerusalem, but the one thought of as being above in the heavens)[21] revealed the resurrection clearly to the prophet and how it would take place in time to come. Inspired David had already proclaimed it before when he said of us, or indeed of every man, *'When thou turnest away thy face they will be troubled and shall return to their dust; thou shalt send forth thy Spirit*

[19] Origen (according to Methodius *De Res.* in Photius *Bibl.* 234, ed. Bekker 300b) interpreted the passage 'allegorically' of the return from exile. Possibly this is the presumption behind the question (cf. no. 9 below), viz. did the vision refer to the return or to the general resurrection? Cyril's own commentary on Ezekiel is lost save for a few fragments (*PG* 70, 1457 f.). See W. H. C. Driessen, 'Un commentaire arménien d'Ezéchiel faussement attribué à saint Cyrille d'Alexandrie', *RB* 68 (1961), 251–61, who disposes of an alleged Cyrillianum.

[20] Cyril reverses the order of the text. Strictly the promise (v. 12) follows the vision of vv. 1 ff.

[21] i.e. the redeemed Church. For Cyril the Biblical Jerusalem, like Judaea, habitually prefigures the Church, usually the Church on earth, but here the Church in heaven. Strictly the prophet refers to the land not the city (vv. 12, 14) but the transition from one figure to another is easy. (The contemporary city Cyril always calls 'Aelia', by the secular name, undermining claims to privilege by Juvenal; see *Answers to Tiberius*, n. 2.) Cyril here unusually rejects a reference to historical events; cf. Theodoret *In Ez.* 15 (*PG* 81, 1189 f.), who finds a subtle promise of hope to the exiles: their restoration is a far easier thing than the general resurrection God will ultimately effect.

ἐπιστρέψουσιν. ἐξαποστελεῖς τὸ πνεῦμά σου καὶ κτι-
σθήσονται, καὶ ἀνακαινιεῖς τὸ πρόσωπον[17] τῆς γῆς.[d]
προσκεκρουκότες μὲν γὰρ ἐν Ἀδὰμ διὰ[18] τὴν παράβασιν, ἐν ἀπο-
στροφῇ γεγόναμεν παρὰ θεῷ. καὶ ταύτης ἕνεκα τῆς αἰτίας εἰς τὸν
ἑαυτῶν[19] χοῦν ὑπεστρέψαμεν, ἐπάρατοι γεγονότες. ἔφη γὰρ ὁ 5
δημιουργὸς ὅτι γῆ εἶ καὶ εἰς γῆν ἀπελεύσῃ.[e] ἀλλ᾿ ἐν ἐσχάτοις
τοῦ αἰῶνος καιροῖς,[20] ἐν δυνάμει τοῦ ζωοποιοῦ πνεύματος, ἐν
Χριστῷ πάντας ἐγερεῖ τοὺς νεκροὺς ὁ θεὸς καὶ πατήρ. ὅτι δὲ
οὔπω γέγονεν ἡ ἀνάστασις τῶν νεκρῶν, ἀλλ᾿ ἔσται κατὰ καιρούς,
πιστώσεται γράφων ὁ πάνσοφος Παῦλος, ὅτι περὶ τὴν πίστιν 10
ἐναυάγησαν Ὑμέναιος καὶ Ἀλέξανδρος,[21] λέγοντες τὴν ἀνάστασιν
ἤδη[22] γεγονέναι.[f] εἰ δὲ ὁ τοῦτο λέγων τὴν ἐπὶ τῇ πίστει ναυαγίαν
ὑπομένει, δῆλον ἂν εἴη λοιπὸν ὅτι τὴν τῆς ἀναστάσεως δύναμιν
ὡς ἐν θεωρίᾳ προφητικῇ τεθέαται χρησίμως ὁ μακάριος προφήτης
Ἰεζεκιήλ. 15

Η´

Ἄνθρωπός τις ἦν πλούσιος, εὐφραινόμενος καθ᾿ ἡμέραν λαμπρῶς·
πτωχὸς δέ τις Λάζαρος ἐπὶ τὸν τούτου πυλῶνα ἐβέβλητο ἡλκωμένος
κατὰ τὴν εὐαγγελικὴν ἱστορίαν.[a] ἐγένετο οὖν ἀμφοτέροις ἀποθανεῖν
καὶ τοῦτον μὲν τὸν πτωχὸν εἰς τὴν ἀνάπαυσιν ἀπελθεῖν, τὸν δὲ εἰς
τὴν κόλασιν. ταῦτα ἤδη γέγονε καὶ ἀνταπόδοσις ἀξία ἐκληρώθη 20
ἑκάστῳ, ἢ τῆς μελλούσης κρίσεως ἀνατυποῖ τὴν εἰκόνα ἐν τούτοις;
ἀλλά, φασίν,[1] ὁπότε ὀνομάζει Λαζάρου προσηγορίαν, ἀληθῶς γέγονε
καὶ ἐπράχθη. διὰ τί γὰρ[2] μὴ εἶπε πτωχὸς δέ τις ἄνθρωπος, ἀλλὰ
Λάζαρος;[b] ἵνα τῇ προσηγορίᾳ δείξῃ πείρᾳ καὶ ἀληθείᾳ ταῦτα
πεπράχθαι.[3] 25

Ἐπίλυσις

Τὴν κρίσιν ἔσεσθαι μετὰ τὴν ἀνάστασιν[4] ἐκ νεκρῶν ἡ θεία
πανταχοῦ[5] λέγει γραφή. ἀνάστασις δὲ οὐκ ἔσται, μὴ αὖθις ἡμῖν

---

[d] Ps. 103(104): 29 f.   [e] Gen. 3: 19   [f] cf. 1 Tim. 1: 19 and
2 Tim. 2: 18   8. [a] cf. Luke 16: 19 ff.   [b] Luke 16: 20

Witnesses: ll. 16–25 G Arm   l. 26–p. 208, l. 22 G N Arm

[17] πρόσωπα (sic) G   [18] διὰ om. O   [19] ἑαυτὸν (sic) O   [20] καιροῖς
τοῦ αἰῶνος G   [21] Ὑ. καὶ Ἀ. before περὶ O   [22] ἤδη before τὴν O
8. [1] φησίν G   [2] φασί add. Arm.   [3] Ἄνθρωπός τις—πεπράχθαι] πρὸς
τοὺς λέγοντας, ὅτι ἑκάστῳ ἀνταπόδοσις ἐκληρώθη ἀξία· οὐ γὰρ εἶπεν ὁ σωτήρ, ὅτι
πτωχός τις ἄνθρωπος, ἀλλὰ Λάζαρος, ἵνα τῇ προσηγορίᾳ δείξῃ πείρᾳ καὶ ἀληθείᾳ
ταύτην πεπράχθαι N   [4] ἀνάστασιν after νεκρῶν N   [5] πανταχοῦ om. N

and they shall be created and thou shalt renew the face of the earth.' For having offended in Adam because of his transgression we are in a state of aversion from God. This is the reason why we turned back to our own dust, having become accursed. For the Creator said, '*Earth thou art and to the earth shalt thou return.*' But in the last times of the world, in the power of the life-giving Spirit, God the Father will awaken all the dead in Christ. All-wise Paul will guarantee that the resurrection of the dead has not yet happened but will take place in time to come, writing, as he does, that Hymenaeus and Alexander had made shipwreck of the faith by asserting that the resurrection had already happened. If someone who says that undergoes shipwreck in the faith, it will be clear from this that the blessed prophet Ezekiel helped us by seeing the mighty work of the resurrection in a prophetic vision.

8

According to the gospel narrative there was a rich man who fared sumptuously every day and a poor man, Lazarus, lay at his gate covered with sores. It came about that both died and the poor man went to his rest but the other to punishment. Have the events already happened and has an appropriate requital been allocated to each or is he delineating here an image of the judgement to come? However (it is said) since he uses Lazarus' name, the events actually occurred and were done. Why did he say '*Lazarus*' and not just '*a certain poor man*'? In order to show by the name that these things took place in actual experience?[22]

Answer

Divine Scripture everywhere teaches that the judgement will take place after the resurrection of the dead. There will be no

[22] Many ancient commentators assume that the events of the parable have actually occurred. For example, Tertullian (*De. An.* 7) and Ambrose (*In. Ev. Luc.* 8, 13) argue that the use of the name implies the actuality of the events; Hilary (*Tract. in Ps. 122*, 11), Jerome (*Ep.* 23, 3, cf. 48, 21 and 77, 6), Cassian (*Conferences* 1, 14 and 6, 3) and Augustine (*In Ps. 6*, 6 and *85*, 18) apparently assume the events are real, as did Origen, according to Methodius (*De Res.* in Photius *Bibl.* 234) and perhaps Basil (*Hom.* 1, 4 (*PG* 31, 168B)). Cyril deals with the parable in *Hom. on Luke* 29 (*CSCO* Scrip. Syri 1/70 pp. 41 ff./ 25 ff.) and 111 f. (R. Payne Smith, *A Commentary upon the Gospel according to S. Luke by S. Cyril Patriarch of Alexandria* (Oxford, 1859), pp. 524–32), explaining the naming of Lazarus but not the rich man by reference to Ps. 16: 4; he does not deal with the question of actuality. For the relation of the parable to an ancient Egyptian tale, see most recently K. Grobel, '. . . whose name was Neves' *NTS* 10 (1963/4), 373–82. Euthymius Zigabenus (12th cent.) on Luke 16: 20 (*PG* 129, 1037C) evidently follows Cyril and gives the rich man the name Νινεύις which corresponds with that in the Egyptian tale.

ἐπιφοιτήσαντος τοῦ Χριστοῦ⁶ ἐξ οὐρανῶν⁷ ἐν τῇ δόξῃ τοῦ πατρὸς
μετὰ τῶν ἁγίων ἀγγέλων.⁸ οὕτω⁹ καὶ ὁ πάνσοφος Παῦλός φησιν
ὅτι αὐτὸς ὁ κύριος ἐν κελεύσματι ἐν φωνῇ ἀρχαγγέλου
καὶ¹⁰ ἐν σάλπιγγι θεοῦ καταβήσεται ἀπ'¹¹ οὐρανοῦ.ᶜ
σαλπίσει γάρ, καὶ οἱ νεκροὶ ἐν Χριστῷ ἐγερθήσονται 5
ἄφθαρτοι.ᵈ οὕπω τοίνυν ἐξ οὐρανῶν¹² καταβεβηκότος τοῦ
πάντων κριτοῦ, οὐδὲ ἡ τῶν νεκρῶν γέγονεν ἀνάστασις.¹³ εἶτα πῶς
οὐκ ἀπίθανον ἐννοεῖν ὅτι γέγονεν ἤδη τισὶν ἀνταπόδοσις¹⁴ ἢ
πονηρῶν ἔργων ἢ ἀγαθῶν; ἔστι τοίνυν παραβολῆς τρόπος ἐσχη-
ματισμένος ἀστείως,¹⁵ τά τε ἐπὶ τῷ πλουσίῳ καὶ τῷ Λαζάρῳ 10
εἰρημένα παρὰ¹⁶ Χριστοῦ. ἔχει δὲ ὁ λόγος, ὡς ἡ Ἑβραίων παράδοσις ἔχει,¹⁷ Λάζαρον εἶναί τινα κατ' ἐκεῖνο καιροῦ ἐν τοῖς Ἱερο-
σολύμοις ἐσχάτῃ νοσοῦντα πτωχείᾳ καὶ ἀρρωστίᾳ,¹⁸ οὗ καὶ
μνημονεῦσαι¹⁹ τὸν κύριον, ὡς εἰς παράδειγμα λαμβάνοντα καὶ αὐτὸν
εἰς ἐμφανεστέραν τοῦ λόγου δήλωσιν. οὕπω τοίνυν ἐξ οὐρανῶν 15
καταφοιτήσαντος τοῦ²⁰ Χριστοῦ, οὔτε ἀνάστασις γέγονεν, οὔτε
πράξεως ἀντίδοσις²¹ ἠκολούθησέ τισιν, ἀλλ' ὡς ἐν εἰκόνι τῇ
παραβολῇ γέγραπται πλούσιος καὶ τρυφῶν καὶ ἀφιλοικτίρμων, καὶ
πένης ἐν ἀρρωστίᾳ· ἵν' εἰδεῖεν οἱ τὸν ἐπὶ γῆς ἔχοντες πλοῦτον,²²
ὡς εἰ μὴ βουληθεῖεν εἶναι χρηστοὶ καὶ εὐμετάδοτοι καὶ κοινωνικοί, 20
καὶ ταῖς τῶν πενήτων ἀνάγκαις ἐπικουρεῖν ἕλοιντο, δεινῇ καὶ
ἀφύκτῳ περιπεσοῦνται δίκῃ.²³

Θ'—Ι'

Θ'. Εἰ ἔλαβεν Ὡσηὲ ὁ προφήτης γυναῖκα πόρνην καὶ ἐτέκνωσεν
ἐξ αὐτῆς πράξει καὶ ἐνεργείᾳ, ἢ προφητικῶς νοούμενα λέγει.

ᶜ 1 Thess. 4: 16   ᵈ 1 Cor. 15: 52

Witnesses: l. 23–p. 210, l. 9 G Arm

⁶ τοῦ Χριστοῦ after οὐρανῶν Arm: τοῦ om. N   ⁷ οὐρανοῦ N   ⁸ τῶν
ἀγγ. τῶν ἁ. N   ⁹ οὕτως G   ¹⁰ καὶ om. G   ¹¹ ἀπὸ τοῦ N   ¹² οὐρανοῦ N
¹³ ἀνάστασις γέγονεν N   ¹⁴ ἀνταπόδοσις om. N   ¹⁵ ἀστείως ἐσχηματι-
σμένος N   ¹⁶ τοῦ add. N   ¹⁷ ἔφη G: ἔχει παράδοσις N   ¹⁸ ἐσχάτη—
ἀρρωστίᾳ] ἐσχάτην πενίας νοσοῦντα N   ¹⁹ μνημονεῦσαι after κύριον N
²⁰ πάντων σωτῆρος add. N   ²¹ ἀνταπόδοσις N   ²² πλοῦτον ἔχοντες N
²³ δίκῃ περιπεσοῦνται N

resurrection without Christ's descending a second time from heaven in the Father's glory with the holy angels. Thus all-wise Paul says that *'The Lord himself will come down from heaven with a shout, an archangel's voice and with God's trumpet'*, *'for the trumpet will sound and the dead in Christ will be raised up incorruptible'*. The judge of all has not yet come down from heaven and so the resurrection of the dead has not occurred. In which case surely the supposition that a requital for deeds bad or good has already taken place for some people is baseless. What Christ says about the rich man and Lazarus is cast in the style of a clever parable. The tale goes (as the Hebrews' tradition has it)[23] that there existed a certain Lazarus at that time in Jerusalem who was at death's door with poverty and weakness, and that the Lord mentioned him, using him as an illustration to make the point clearer still. Christ had not yet descended from heaven, the resurrection had not happened and no requital of action had followed anyone, but the parable picturesquely describes a rich man living in luxury without compassion and a poor man in weakness, with the aim[24] that the owners of wealth on earth may learn that unless they intend to be good men, bountiful and sharing, and choose to help out the necessities of the poor, they will fall under a terrible and inexorable condemnation.

9–10

9. Did Hosea the prophet in actual fact take a harlot as wife and have children by her or is what he says to be interpreted prophetically?[25]

---

[23] Cyril knew Jewish legends and traditions about Old Testament matters (see A. Kerrigan, *St. Cyril of Alexandria, interpreter of the Old Testament* (Rome, 1952), pp. 309 ff.) probably at second hand. The authority for this tradition is unknown.

[24] So most, if not all, ancient commentators on the parable.

[25] i.e. figuratively. The question was hotly debated according to Julian of Eclanum, see *In Os. proph.* 1, 1, ed. L. de Coninck (*CCSL* 88, 1977), p. 119 = *PL* 21, 964 (*PL* 21, 959–1164), ibid. 964A: 'But I am not unaware how much disagreement there has been between scholars over the interpretation of this text, so that entire areas are at variance as to the meaning of it. For Palestine Egypt and all the rest who are specially impressed by Origen's authority deny that this marriage by Hosea the prophet took place in a corporeal sense.' The Syrians, on the other hand, took the opposite view, he adds (ibid. p. 121 = *PL* 21, 965).

Ι'. Εἰ ὁ Μελχισεδὲκ οὐκ ἄνθρωπος[1] ἁπλῶς οὐδὲ πνεῦμα, ἀλλ' ἄνθρωπος ἀρχὴν γενέσεως οὐκ ἐξ ἀνθρώπων ἔχων ἀλλὰ προσφάτως δημιουργηθεὶς ὑπὸ τοῦ θεοῦ.

Ἐπίλυσις

Περὶ τούτων τῶν κεφαλαίων μακρὸς[2] ἡμῖν πεποίηται λόγος, ὅτε 5 ἐγράφομεν εἰς τὸν Ὡσηὲ τὸν προφήτην, καὶ ἐν τῷ βιβλίῳ δὲ τῷ περὶ τῆς Γενέσεως πολλὴ βάσανος εὑρίσκεται περὶ τοῦ Μελχισεδέκ, καὶ ἔξεστι τῇ εὐλαβείᾳ σου ταῖς βίβλοις ἐντυχεῖν κἀκεῖθεν λαβεῖν τῶν εἰρημένων ἐφ' ἑκάστῳ τὸν νοῦν.

IA'

Εἰ ὁ τῶν ὅλων θεὸς τὰ γινόμενα ἤδη καὶ πραχθέντα δύναται 10 ποιῆσαι μὴ γενέσθαι ποτέ, κατὰ τό οὐκ ἀδυνατήσει αὐτῷ[1] πᾶν ῥῆμα.[a] οὐ γὰρ λέγομεν ὡς μὴ γενόμενα,[2] ἀλλὰ μὴ γεγενῆσθαι τὴν ἀρχήν· οἷον, εἰ τὴν πόρνην δύναται παρθένον ποιῆσαι[3] ἐκ κοιλίας μητρός, ἵνα μήτε εἴη ποτὲ πόρνη[4] ἡ πορνεύσασα, ὅτι τ ὰ π α ρ ὰ ἀ ν θ ρ ώ- π ο ι ς ἀ δ ύ ν α τ α δ υ ν α τ ὰ π α ρ ὰ τ ῷ θ ε ῷ.[b] 15

Ἐπίλυσις

Ζητεῖσθαι χρὴ παρ' ἡμῶν τὴν τοῦ θεοῦ δύναμιν, εἰ μεγάλη καὶ ἀξιάγαστος, ὅτε τὸ δρώμενόν ἐστιν οὐκ ἀπεοικὸς τῇ θείᾳ[5] δόξῃ. οὐ γὰρ ὅτι πάντα δύναται, διὰ τοῦτο καὶ τῶν ἀτόπων αὐτὸν ἐργάτην

---

11. [a] Luke 1: 37   [b] Luke 18: 27

Witnesses: l. 10–p. 212, l. 10 G O N Arm

9–10. [1] ἦν add. Arm?   [2] μακρότερος Arm   11. [1] αὐτῷ] παρὰ τῷ θεῷ Arm   [2] γενώμενα O   [3] ποιῆσαι after μητρός O: ποιῆσαι παρθένον N   [4] μήτε—πόρνη] ἵνα μὴ πόρνη ᾖ O   [5] θεοῦ G

[26] Similarly a much debated figure. See for the history of the discussion G. Bardy, 'Melchisedech dans la tradition patristique', RB 35 (1926), 496–509, and 36 (1927), 23–45. An alleged sect of Melchizedekians was detected by Epiphanius, Panar. 55, 1 ff. (ed. Holl, vol. 2, pp. 324 ff.); amongst many other references cited by Bardy, see Mark the Monk, Opusculum X De Melch. (PG 65, 1117 ff.) and Timothy of Constantinople De Rec. Haer. (PG 86, 33).

[27] See In Os. (ed. Pusey pp. 15 ff.). Cyril shared the view of the Syrians (see above n. 25), differing little from Theodore (see In Os. (PG 66, 123–210, esp. 129B)) and Theodoret (see In Os. (PG 81, 1551–1632, esp. 1556c)). He attacks an unnamed man of distinction (probably Didymus, because similar views are propounded by Jerome (PL 25, 816 f.) for whom Didymus composed a commentary on Hosea (ibid. 819 f.)) who rejects the literal sense and allegorizes

10. Is Melchizedek not simply a man or a spirit but a man who does not take his origin of existence from human beings but who was a fresh creation by God?[26]

Answer

We have written a long account of these items when we wrote on Hosea the prophet;[27] and in the volume on Genesis[28] will be found a lengthy investigation of Melchizedek. Your Reverence can read the volumes and thereby get our understanding of each of the points mentioned.

11

Can the God of all make things and events which have already occurred never happen, in accordance with the statement *'With him nothing shall be impossible'*? (We do not mean simply never happen, but never have happened to begin with.) For example, can he make a harlot virgin from her mother's womb, so that she who has committed fornication is not a harlot, because *'things impossible with men are possible with God'*?[29]

Answer

We may ask whether God's power is grand and admirable when the deed is in tune with the divine glory. It is wrong for him to be viewed as the agent of absurdities simply on the grounds that all things are possible for him. We shall observe that it is

the episode as a drama involving the union of the Word (represented by Hosea) with the soul (Gomer).

[28] See *Glaph. in Gen.* 2, 3, where Cyril deals with arguments alleging Melchizedek was the Holy Ghost or an angel (from his being king of Salem = 'peace') and expounds his role as a type of Emmanuel. Cf. *Apoph. Patrum* Daniel 8 (*PG* 65, 160) for a story of how Cyril persuaded a simple monk, who thought Melchizedek to be the Son of God, to pray for an answer; God revealed in a dream all the patriarchs from Adam to Melchizedek, who, he thus saw, was merely human. Cf. also ibid. Copre 3 (ibid. 252D, cf. 1138 n. 24) for the account of a conference of monks on the subject and its abrupt termination by Copre, who told it they had more important things to do. Two sermons on Melchizedek, in Ethiopic translation from Greek, allegedly by Cyril, published by A. Dillmann, *Chrestomathia aethiopica* (Leipzig, 1866), pp. 88–98 and translated into German by S. Euringer 'Übersetzung der Homilien des Cyrillus von Alexandrien . . .', *Orientalia* 12 (1943), 114–27, are certainly not by Cyril.

[29] An unusual question, to be connected with no. 9: could Gomer, or what Gomer represented (viz. the sinful soul), be restored to her original state? Cf. Jerome *Ep.* 22, 5: 'I make bold to say: though God can do all things, he cannot raise up a virgin after her fall' (Audenter loquor: cum omnia Deus possit, suscitare virginem non potest post ruinam).

ὁρᾶσθαι προσήκει. ἐννοῶμεν γὰρ ὅτι ἄτοπόν ἐστι τὸ λέγειν εἰ δύναται⁶ ὁ θεὸς ἑαυτὸν ποιῆσαι⁷ μὴ εἶναι θεόν, εἰ δύναται ἑαυτὸν ποιῆσαι ἁμαρτίας δεκτικόν, εἰ δύναται ἑαυτὸν ποιῆσαι⁸ μὴ εἶναι ἀγαθὸν ἢ ζωὴν ἢ δίκαιον. δεῖ τοίνυν παραιτεῖσθαι παντὶ σθένει τὰς ἀτόπους οὕτω τῶν ἐρωτήσεων. διὰ τί δὲ⁹ ὁ θεὸς οὐ δύναται τὴν 5 πορνεύσασαν ποιῆσαι μὴ¹⁰ γεγενῆσθαί ποτε πόρνην; ὅτι οὐ δύναται τὸ ψεῦδος ἀλήθειαν ποιῆσαι. καὶ οὐκ ἀσθενείας ἔγκλημα τοῦτο, ἀλλὰ φύσεως ἀπόδειξις, οὐκ ἀνεχομένης τι παθεῖν ὃ μὴ αὐτῇ¹¹ πρέπει· ἀλλότριον δὲ θεοῦ τὸ ψεῦδος παντελῶς, ψεῦσμα γάρ ἐστι τὸ τὴν πορνεύσασαν ποιῆσαι μὴ πορνεῦσαί ποτε. 10

Δεῖ δέ, ὡς ἔφην, τὰς οὕτως εὐήθεις τῶν ἐρωτήσεων καὶ πολὺ τὸ ἄτοπον ἐχούσας μηδὲ προσίεσθαι τὴν ἀρχήν· ταῦτα οὐδὲ ἐγγράφως ἐχρῆν γενέσθαι, ὑπὲρ δὲ τοῦ τὴν σὴν¹² εὐλάβειαν καθ᾽ ἑαυτὴν ἐντυχοῦσαν εὖ ἔχουσας τὰς ἑαυτῆς ἐννοίας ἰδεῖν,¹³ τὰ ἐφ᾽ ἑκάστῳ τῶν κεφαλαίων ὡς ἔνι σαφηνίσαι προεθυμήθην.¹⁴ 15

Witnesses: ll. 11–15 G O Arm

---

⁶ ἑαυτὸν add. G   ⁷ ποιῆσαι ἑαυτὸν G   ⁸ μὴ—ποιῆσαι om. G
⁹ δὲ om. G   ¹⁰ μὴ om. G   ¹¹ αὐτῷ G   ¹² ὑμῶν G   ¹³ ἤδειν O
¹⁴ προεθυμήθεμεν G

absurd to ask whether God can make himself not be God, whether he can make himself capable of sin or whether he can make himself not be good or Life or righteous.[30] We shall, then, do our utmost to avoid such absurd questions. Why cannot God make her who has committed fornication never to have been a harlot? Because he cannot make falsehood truth. This is not a charge of weakness but proof that his nature does not admit of experiencing what is inappropriate to it. Falsehood is a total stranger to God and it is, indeed, a fraud to make her who has committed fornication never to have done it.

We ought not, as I said, to entertain silly questions like these, containing a vast deal of absurdity, in the first place. There is no need for these matters to be put into writing, but for the sake of your Reverence's seeing your own good thoughts in your personal reading I readily clarified, as best I could, the relevant points on each item.

[30] The notion that certain things, including altering the past, are impossible to God is a philosophers' commonplace. Pliny (*Natural History* 2, 27) lists five of them. God cannot: commit suicide; make mortals immortal; recall the dead; bring it about that someone who has lived should not have lived, that someone who has enjoyed honours should not have done so; or make twice ten not twenty—see R. M. Grant, *Miracle and Natural Law* (Amsterdam, 1952), pp. 129 ff. For other examples of the *topos* see Gregory Naz. *Or.* 30, 11 (*ad init.*), Augustine *Sermo* 213, 1, cf. 214, 4, and his *De Symb.* 2, *De Civ. Dei* 22, 25 and *Contra Faustum Man.* 26, 5. There is an interesting medieval parallel to this discussion in Peter Damian (*c.* A.D. 1080), *De divina omnipotentia* (PL 145, 595–622)—see esp. c. 3 where his starting-point is the passage from Jerome's letter to Eustochium quoted above n. 29. (I owe the reference to Professor H. Chadwick.)

10

LETTER TO CALOSIRIUS

Ἐπιστολὴ τοῦ ἁγίου
Κυρίλλου
ἐπισκόπου Ἀλεξανδρείας

πρὸς Καλοσίριον ἐπίσκοπον Ἀρσενοΐτην κατὰ τῶν λεγόντων
ἀνθρωπόμορφον εἶναι τὸ θεῖον.   5

Ἀφικόμενοί τινες ἀπὸ τοῦ ὄρους τοῦ Καλαμῶνος ἠρωτῶντο παρ'
ἐμοῦ περὶ τῶν αὐτόθι μοναστῶν,[1] τίνα τρόπον διατελοῦσιν, ἢ καὶ
ὁποίαν ἔχουσι τοῦ βίου τὴν διαγωγήν.[2] οἱ δὲ ἔφασκον εὐδοκιμεῖν
μὲν ἐν ἀσκήσει πολλούς, καὶ σφόδρα βούλεσθαι τὸν μοναχοῖς
πρέποντα κατορθῶσαι βίον· εἶναι δέ τινας τοὺς περιόντας καὶ   10
θορυβοῦντας ἐξ ἀμαθίας τοὺς ἐθέλοντας ἠρεμεῖν, εἶτα λογοποιεῖν
αὐτοὺς διεβεβαιοῦντο[3] τοιαῦτά τινα· ἔφασκον γὰρ ἐπειδὴ κατ'
εἰκόνα θεοῦ γενέσθαι τὸν ἄνθρωπον ἡ θεία λέγει γραφή, χρὴ
πιστεύειν ὅτι[4] ἀνθρωποειδὲς ἤγουν[5] ἀνθρωπόμορφόν ἐστι τὸ θεῖον·
ὅπερ ἐστὶ παντελῶς ἀσύνετον καὶ τοῖς τῆς ἐσχάτης δυσσεβείας   15
ἐγκλήμασιν ὑπενεγκεῖν δυνάμενον τοὺς οὕτω φρονεῖν ἑλομένους.
ἔστι μὲν[6] γὰρ ὁμολογουμένως κατ' εἰκόνα θεοῦ ὁ ἄνθρωπος, ἡ δὲ
ὁμοιότης οὐ σωματική· ὁ γὰρ θεός ἐστιν ἀσώματος. καὶ τοῦτο
διδάξει λέγων αὐτὸς ὁ σωτήρ πνεῦμα ὁ θεός.[a] οὐκοῦν οὐκ
ἐνσώματος, εἰ πνεῦμά ἐστιν, οὐδὲ ἐν εἴδει σωματικῷ. τὸ γὰρ ἔξω   20
σώματος,[7] ἔξω καὶ σχήματος εἴη ἄν. ἄποσον γὰρ καὶ ἀσχημάτιστόν
ἐστι τὸ θεῖον. εἰ δὲ νομίζουσιν ὅτι κατὰ τὴν τοῦ ἀνθρωπίνου
σώματος φύσιν ἐσχηματίσθη καὶ αὐτὸς ὁ ἐπὶ πάντων θεός, λεγέτωσαν

---

[a] John 4: 24

Witnesses: C N (selected readings only, see p. xlix)

[1] μοναχῶν N   [2] ἀγωγήν N   [3] διαβεβαιοῦντας N   [4] ἢ add. C
[5] ἤτοι N   [6] οὖν καὶ add. N   [7] σωματικῷ C

10

LETTER TO CALOSIRIUS

Letter of Saint Cyril, bishop of Alexandria, to Calosirius,[1] bishop of the Arsenoite,[2] against those who assert that the Godhead has a human shape

Some men arrived here from Mount Calamon[3] and were questioned by me about the monks there, the standard of life they achieve and the quality of conduct they are maintaining. They declared that a large number were held in high esteem for their discipline and had a strong desire to practise the life monks ought to practise; but that there are some who go about, prompted by ignorance, disturbing those with a mind to quiet. They went on to maintain that they make out arguments of this kind: since (they say) divine Scripture says that man was created in God's image we ought to believe that the Godhead has a human shape or form. Which is utterly witless and capable of making those who choose to think it incur the charge of most extreme blasphemy. Man is unquestionably in God's image, but the likeness is not a bodily one for God is incorporeal. The Saviour himself will teach you this point, because he says '*God is spirit.*' He cannot therefore be embodied or exist in a bodily form, if he is spirit; because what is outside the category of body is outside configuration—deity is without dimensions or configuration. But if they think that God himself, who is above all, has a configuration like the nature of the human body, they must

---

[1] Known otherwise only from the *Acta* of the Council of Ephesus (449)—the Latrocinium—where he spoke and subscribed in favour of Eutyches through his deacon Julius (or Helias); see *Akten*, ed. Flemming (cf. Introduction p. xxxviii, n. 79), p. 8/9, *ACO* 2, 1 p. 81 and *ACO* 2, 3 p. 188.

[2] The ancient Arse(i)noite nome = present-day Fayyûm.

[3] A hill to the south-west of Fayyûm. The monastery was founded by a certain Samuel about 100 years before Calosirius' time and survived to the 16th century. See Abu Salih, *The Churches and Monasteries of Egypt and some neighbouring countries*, tr. and ed. B. T. A. Evetts, with added notes by A. J. Butler (Oxford, 1895 repr. 1969), pp. 206 ff.

εἰ καὶ αὐτὸς ἔχει πόδας ἵνα περιπατῇ, χεῖρας ἵνα δι' αὐτῶν ἐργάζηται, καὶ ὀφθαλμοὺς ἵνα βλέπῃ δι' αὐτῶν. ποῦ τοίνυν περιπατεῖ;[8] ἢ[9]
ἐκ ποίων τόπων εἰς ποίους ἀπέρχεται[10] ὁ τὰ πάντα πληρῶν; ἔφη
γάρ μὴ οὐχὶ τὸν οὐρανὸν καὶ τὴν γῆν ἐγὼ πληρῶ λέγει
κύριος.[b11] ἢ ποίας χεῖρας εἰς ἔργα κινεῖ ὁ διὰ ζῶντος λόγου 5
δημιουργῶν; καὶ εἰ καθ' ἡμᾶς ἔχει τοὺς ὀφθαλμοὺς ὡς ἐν προσώπῳ
κειμένους, οὐχ ὁρᾷ που πάντως τὰ ὀπίσω· ἀλλ' ὅταν πρὸς ἀνατολὰς
βλέπῃ, οὐκ οἶδε τί πράττουσιν οἱ ἐν δυσμαῖς; κἂν εἰς δυσμὰς ἴδῃ
πάλιν, οὐχ ὁρᾷ τοὺς ἐν ταῖς ἀνατολαῖς;

Ταῦτα καὶ γράφειν αἰσχύνομαι, διὰ δὲ τὴν τινῶν ἀπόνοιαν 10
γέγονα ἄφρων, οὐχ ἑκὼν μᾶλλον, ἀλλὰ παρ' αὐτῶν ἠναγκασμένος.[c]
ἐπιστομιζέσθωσαν τοίνυν οἱ ταῦτα φλυαροῦντες, ὡς ἀμαθεῖς, καὶ
ἠρεμείτωσαν μὴ ἁπτόμενοι τῶν ὑπὲρ δύναμιν, μᾶλλον δὲ μὴ
καταλαλείτωσαν τοῦ θεοῦ. ὁ γὰρ θεὸς ὑπὲρ πᾶσαν κτίσιν ἐστίν,
οὔτε σῶμα νοούμενος, οὔτε ἐν τύποις ἢ σχήμασι σωματικοῖς, ἀλλ' 15
ἔστιν ἁπλοῦς, ἄϋλος, ἀνείδεος,[12] ἀσύνθετος, οὐκ ἐκ μερῶν ἢ μελῶν
ἢ μορίων συγκείμενος καθάπερ ἡμεῖς, πνεῦμα δὲ μᾶλλον, κατὰ τὰς
γραφάς, καὶ τὰ πάντα ἐφορῶν, πανταχοῦ ὢν καὶ τὰ πάντα πληρῶν,
καὶ οὐδενὸς ἀπολιμπανόμενος· πληροῖ γὰρ οὐρανὸν καὶ γῆν. τὸ δὲ
κατ' εἰκόνα θεοῦ πεποιῆσθαι τὸν ἄνθρωπον, ἑτέρας ἐμφάσεις καὶ 20
ὑπονοίας ἔχει. μόνος γὰρ αὐτὸς παρὰ πάντα τὰ ἐπὶ γῆς ζῷα
λογικός ἐστι, φιλοικτίρμων, ἐπιτηδειότητα πρὸς πᾶσαν ἀρετὴν
ἔχων, λαχὼν δὲ[13] καὶ τὸ ἄρχειν ἁπάντων τῶν ἐπὶ γῆς καθ' ὁμοιότητα
καὶ εἰκόνα θεοῦ. οὐκοῦν κατὰ τὸ εἶναι ζῷον λογικὸν καὶ καθὸ
φιλάρετον καὶ ἀρχικὸν τῶν ἐπὶ τῆς γῆς, ἐν εἰκόνι θεοῦ πεποιῆσθαι 25
λέγεται. εἰ δὲ νομίζουσι κατὰ τὸ τοῦ σώματος σχῆμα λέγεσθαι τὴν
εἰκόνα, οὐδὲν λυπεῖ καὶ τοῖς ἀλόγοις τῶν ζῴων σύμμορφον λέγειν
εἶναι τὸν θεόν. ὁρῶμεν[14] γὰρ[15] ὅτι καὶ αὐτὰ ἐκ τῶν αὐτῶν ἡμῖν
εἰσι μορίων, πόδας ἔχοντα καὶ στόμα[16] καὶ ὀφθαλμοὺς καὶ ῥῖνας
καὶ γλῶσσαν καὶ τὰ ἔτερα τῶν τοῦ σώματος μελῶν. παυέτω τοίνυν 30
ἡ σὴ θεοσέβεια τοὺς τοιούτους, μᾶλλον δὲ καὶ ἐπιτιμάτω τοῖς
ταῦτα φλυαρεῖν εἰωθόσιν.

---

[b] Jer. 23: 24   [c] cf. 2 Cor. 12: 11

[8] ἀπέρχεται N   [9] καὶ N   [10] μεταβαίνει N   [11] λέγει κύριος om. N
[12] καὶ add. N   [13] δὲ om. N   [14] ὁρῶ μὲν C   [15] γὰρ om. C
[16] καὶ στόμα om. N

tell us if he also has feet to walk on, hands to work through and eyes to see with. So where does he walk? What places does he travel to and from, he who fills all things? For he said: ' "*Do not I fill heaven and earth?" says the Lord.*' What are the hands he moves into action, he who creates by his living Word? If his eyes are set in his face like ours, he cannot see what is behind him. When he looks toward the East, is he unaware of what people in the West are doing? If he looks towards the West, cannot he see the people in the East?

I feel ashamed of writing this but the folly of some people has made me an unwilling fool under compulsion from them. Ignorant babblers of this rubbish must be silenced and must keep quiet and not handle things beyond their powers—or rather stop blaspheming against God. For God transcends all creation. He is not thought of as a body or as contained in corporeal outlines or configurations, but as simple, immaterial, without shape or composition, not a compound of parts, limbs and portions like we are, but as spirit, as the Bible says, surveying all things, omnipresent, filling all things and absent from nothing; for he fills heaven and earth. Man's being made in God's image has different meanings and implications.[4] Man alone, in distinction from all other living inhabitants of the earth, is rational, compassionate and with an aptitude for all virtue, endowed with sovereignty over all the inhabitants of the earth in the likeness and image of God.[5] In consequence he is said to have been made in God's image, by virtue of his being a rational animal and of his having a love of virtue and a sovereignty over earth's inhabitants. If they think that the image refers to the configuration of the body, there is nothing to stop them saying that God has the same shape as brute beasts. For we see that these too consist of the same parts as we do, possessing feet, mouths, eyes, nostrils, tongues and the other limbs of the body. Your Reverence must put a stop to these people and, more than that, rebuke those who make a habit of spouting this rubbish.

---

[4] 'Meanings' and 'implications' are terms used by writers on rhetoric to designate allusions or the real (as opposed to the apparent) sense of a statement, see *LSJ* s.vv. ἔμφασις III and ὑπόνοια II.

[5] See p. 167, lines 7 ff.

Ἀκούω δὲ ὅτι φασὶν ἀπρακτεῖν εἰς ἁγιασμὸν τὴν μυστικὴν
εὐλογίαν, εἰ ἀπομείνοι λείψανον αὐτῆς εἰς ἑτέραν ἡμέραν. μαίνονται
δὲ ταῦτα λέγοντες· οὐ γὰρ ἀλλοιοῦται Χριστός, οὐδὲ τὸ ἅγιον
αὐτοῦ σῶμα[17] μεταβληθήσεται, ἀλλ᾽ ἡ τῆς εὐλογίας δύναμις, καὶ
ἡ ζωοποιὸς χάρις διηνεκής ἐστιν ἐν αὐτῷ.   5

Περιέρχονται δὲ καὶ ἕτεροί τινες,[18] ὡς φασί, προσποιούμενοι
μόνῃ σχολάζειν τῇ προσευχῇ, καὶ οὐδὲν[19] ἐργαζόμενοι,[20] καὶ ὄκνου
πρόφασιν καὶ πορισμοῦ ποιοῦνται τὴν εὐσέβειαν,[d] οὐκ ὀρθὰ φρονοῦντες. ἐπεὶ λεγέτωσαν ἑαυτοὺς καὶ τῶν ἁγίων ἀποστόλων
κρείττονας,[21] οἳ εἰργάζοντο μὲν ἐνδιδόντος αὐτοῖς τοῦ καιροῦ τὴν   10
εἰς τοῦτο σχολήν,[22] ἔκαμνον δὲ καὶ εἰς τὸν λόγον τοῦ θεοῦ. πῶς δὲ
καὶ[23] ἐπελάθοντο γράφοντος τοῦ μακαρίου Παύλου πρός τινας·
ἀκούω γὰρ περιπατεῖν ἐν ὑμῖν τινας μηδὲν ἐργαζομένους,
ἀλλὰ περιεργαζομένους·[e] οὐκ ἀποδέχεται τοίνυν τοὺς τοῦτο
δρῶντας ἡ ἐκκλησία. δεῖ μὲν γὰρ ὁμολογουμένως εὔχεσθαι συντόνως   15
ἐνηρεμοῦντας τοῖς ἀσκητηρίοις· λυπεῖ δὲ οὐδέν, μᾶλλον δὲ καὶ
ὠφελιμώτατόν ἐστιν ἄγαν τὸ καὶ[24] ἐργάζεσθαι, ἵνα μὴ ἑτέροις
ἐπαχθὴς εὑρεθῇ, τοὺς αὐτῶν ἱδρῶτας εἰς ἰδίαν δεχόμενος χρείαν,
δυνηθῇ δὲ καὶ ἀπὸ τῶν αὐτοῦ πόνων παραμυθήσασθαι χήραν καὶ
ὀρφανὸν καὶ ἀσθενοῦντάς τινας τῶν ἀδελφῶν. εἰ δὲ νομίζουσιν εἶναι[25] 20
καλόν, τὸ ἔργου[26] μὴ ἅπτεσθαι, ὅταν πάντες τὰ αὐτῶν ζηλώσωσι,
τίς ὁ τρέφων αὐτούς; ἀργίας τοίνυν[27] καὶ γαστριμαργίας πρόφασιν[28]
ποιοῦνταί τινες,[29] τὸ δεῖν οἴεσθαι μόνῃ σχολάζειν τῇ προσευχῇ,
ἔργου δὲ ὅλως μὴ ἅπτεσθαι.

[d] cf. 1 Tim. 6: 5   [e] 2 Thess. 3: 11

Witnesses: ll. 6–23+B, headed Κυρίλλου ἐκ τῶν κατ᾽ αὐτῶν, om. πῶς (l. 11)—
ἀδελφῶν (l. 20)

[17] σῶμα om. C   [18] καὶ—τινες om. B   [19] καὶ om., μηδὲν B
[20] ἀλλὰ περιεργαζόμενοι add. B   [21] κρείττους B   [22] τὴν—σχολὴν] καὶ τῆς
εἰς τοῦτο σχολῆς B   [23] καὶ om. C   [24] ἄγαν τὸ καὶ] τὸ N   [25] εἶναι
om. N   [26] ἔργων N   [27] τοίνυν] γὰρ N   [28] πρόφασιν] ἀφορμὴν N
[29] τινες om. B

6 Perhaps arguing from analogy with the manna (Ex. 16: 19 f.) which could
not be reserved.
7 For Cyril's doctrine of the Eucharist cf. above, p. 23, n. 14. The eucharistic

I hear that they say the consecrated sacramental elements lose their hallowing efficacy if a portion remains over to another day.[6] To say this is lunacy—Christ is not altered nor will his sacred body change; no, the power of the sacrament, its life-giving grace, inheres in it constantly.[7]

Some others, they say, gad about claiming to devote their time solely to prayer and doing no work; wrong in their ideas they make religion into a means of livelihood, an excuse for avoiding work.[8] Why, they had better proclaim themselves superior to the holy apostles who worked, when the occasion afforded them leisure for it, and wore themselves out in God's word! How is it they have forgotten that blessed Paul wrote to some *'I hear that some of you are going about doing no work but interfering'*? The Church, then, does not sanction this behaviour. Those who live in disciplined monastic calm must, it goes without saying, pray continuously. But labour does not prevent that; indeed, it is exceedingly beneficial in stopping a man being a burden to others whose toil he benefits from, and in enabling him to offer comfort to widows and orphans and any sick brethren by his own efforts. If they think it a good thing to have nothing to do with work, who is going to provide for them if everybody imitates their behaviour? The people in question, then, are making their alleged duty to devote their time solely to prayer and to do no work at all an excuse for idleness and gluttony.

elements, for Cyril, could no more lose their efficacy than the union of Word and flesh in Christ could be dissolved. The elements are, for Cyril, converted into the body of Christ, the body of Life (see p. 81, lines 5 ff.) which vitalizes the recipients, making them concorporeal (σύσσωμοι) with the incarnate Word. Cyril's eucharistic theology coheres closely with his doctrine of the Incarnation, of which the Eucharist is, in effect, the extension. For a good summary, see Ezra Gebremedhin, *Life-giving Blessing, an inquiry into the Eucharistic Doctrine of Cyril of Alexandria* (Uppsala, 1977).

[8] This is a special ground of complaint against Messalians, or Euchites ('pray-ers'), a widespread pietistic movement of Syrian provenance, condemned at the Council of Ephesus (431), *ACO* I, I, 7 p. 117; see the texts assembled by M. Kmosko, *Patrologia Syriaca* 3, cols. 171–293 and *TRE* 4 s.v. ASKESE 4, p. 221. But there is no other sign of Messalian influence at Calamon, and the charge was no doubt common (cf. Isidore *Epp.* I, 49 (*PG* 78, 212C), Jerome *Ep.* 125, 11, and Cassian *Conferences* 24, 10 ff.). However, in the Berlin codex Phillipicus gr. 1475 the text-fragment is headed 'by Cyril against the same', where 'the same' means Messalians. For Cyril's attitude to the movement, see *Ep.* 82 (ed. Schwartz, *Cod. Vaticanus gr. 1431*, p. 20).

Μὴ συγχώρει δὲ τοῖς ὀρθοδόξοις μετὰ τῶν καλουμένων Μελε-
τιανῶν[30] συνάγεσθαι, ἵνα μὴ γένωνται κοινωνοὶ τῆς ἀποστασίας
αὐτῶν. ἀλλ' εἰ μὲν ἐκεῖνοι μετανοοῦντες ἔρχονται πρὸς τοὺς
ὀρθοδόξους, ἔστωσαν δεκτοί· μηδεὶς δὲ ἀδιαφορείτω, μηδὲ κοινω-
νείτω[31] ἐκείνοις μὴ μεταγινώσκουσιν, ἵνα μή, ὡς ἔφην, κοινωνοὶ 5
γένωνται τῆς ἐνούσης κακοπιστίας αὐτοῖς.[32]

Ταῦτα ἡ σὴ θεοσέβεια ἀναγνωσθῆναι παρασκευασάτω ἐν
ἐκείνοις τοῖς μοναστηρίοις εἰς οἰκοδομὴν τῶν αὐτόθι, καὶ παρ-
αγγελλέτω φυλάττειν αὐτά, ἵνα μήτε οἱ ὀρθόδοξοι κάμνωσι παρα-
λυομένης αὐτῶν τῆς συνειδήσεως, μήτε μὴν οἱ ἀργοτροφεῖν 10
ἐθέλοντες ἔχωσί[33] τινα παρείσδυσιν τοῦ δοκεῖν εἶναι χρηστοί.

Ἐρρῶσθαί σε ἐν κυρίῳ εὔχομαι, ἀγαπητὲ καὶ ποθεινότατε.

---

[30] μελιτιανῶν C   [31] κοινωνήτω C   [32] τῆς—αὐτοῖς] τῆς αὐτῶν
κακοπιστίας N   [33] ἔχουσί C

You are not to allow the orthodox to associate with the so-called Meletians,[9] to prevent their sharing their apostasy. Those who have a change of heart and come over to the orthodox are to be welcomed. Nobody is to treat the matter as a triviality; nobody is to communicate with the unconverted, lest, as I said, they come to share their disloyalty.

Your Reverence is to procure the reading of this letter in those monasteries for the edification of their occupants, and is to urge the safeguarding of its provisions, so that the orthodox may not flag through relaxing their conscientiousness, and lazy bellies may have no way of appearing to be honest men.

I bid you farewell in the Lord, beloved and very dear Calosirius.

9 Followers of Meletius, who originated a schism in Egypt in *c.* 306 during the persecution of Diocletian. Problems with it dominated the early years of Athanasius' career, and it was an important contributory factor in the Arian controversy. The Arsenoite appears to have been a Meletian centre and Meletians are to be found there as late as the 6th century, see *Apoph. Patrum* (*PG* 65, 405).

APPENDIX

A translation of the *Formula of Reunion*
(*Ep.* 39 § 5, *ACO* 1, 1, 4 p. 17, 9 ff.)

Accordingly we acknowledge our Lord Jesus Christ, the only-begotten Son of God, to be perfect God and perfect man made up of soul endowed with reason and of body, begotten of the Father before the ages in respect of his Godhead and the same[1] born in the last days for us and for our salvation of Mary the Virgin in respect of his manhood, consubstantial with the Father in Godhead and consubstantial with us in manhood. A union of two natures has been effected and therefore we confess one Christ, one Son, one Lord. By virtue of this understanding of the union which involves no merging, we acknowledge the holy Virgin to be 'Mother of God' because God the Word was 'made flesh' and 'became man' and united to himself the temple he took from her as a result of her conception. As for the terms used about the Lord in the Gospels and apostolic writings, we recognize that theologians treat some as shared because they refer to one person, some they refer separately to two natures, traditionally teaching the application of the divine terms to Christ's Godhead, the lowly to his manhood.

---

[1] 'the same': this is the sole change of importance made to the Formula between its first appearance in the Easterns' *anaphora* (*ACO* 1, 1, 7 pp. 69 f.) and final ratification. It is surely Cyril's addition.

INDEX OF NON-BIBLICAL PERSONS
MENTIONED IN THE TEXT

INDEX OF BIBLICAL QUOTATIONS
AND ALLUSIONS